THE MEDIA WORLD OF ISIS

INDIANA SERIES IN MIDDLE EAST STUDIES

Mark Tessler, *editor*

THE MEDIA WORLD OF ISIS

Edited by Michael Krona and
Rosemary Pennington

Indiana University Press

This book is a publication of

Indiana University Press
Office of Scholarly Publishing
Herman B Wells Library 350
1320 East 10th Street
Bloomington, Indiana 47405 USA

iupress.indiana.edu

Manufactured in the United States of America

Cataloging information is available from the Library of Congress.

ISBN 978-0-253-04591-1 (cloth)
ISBN 978-0-253-04592-8 (paperback)
ISBN 978-0-253-04594-2 (ebook)

1 2 3 4 5 23 22 21 20 19

Contents

Acknowledgments

THIS BOOK BEGAN as a conversation between colleagues. A passing remark about a paper being presented about the Islamic State at a conference turned into brainstorming about a possible collaboration and then, finally, became this book. What we so seldom discuss in academia is the way in which so much of our scholarship arises from such interactions—conversations between colleagues, quick exchanges of ideas on Twitter, idle chitchat over drinks at a conference that becomes something more later. Though we often write alone, our work relies on our interactions with others—through engagement with literature, yes, but also socially. This book would not exist were it not for those various, often rather small, interactions.

It would also have been impossible without the support of the editors' institutions. Miami University's Department of Media, Journalism, and Film, and in particular former chair Richard Campbell, helped make this work possible, as did the College of Arts and Science. The School of Arts and Communication at Malmö University was also supportive of our work on this book.

The Center for Advanced Research in Global Communication, part of the Annenberg School of Communication at the University of Pennsylvania, also helped midwife this book into being. Through a graduate student research workshop and a symposium on the Islamic State and media, we were able to meet many of the authors included in this volume. This book would not exist were it not for the work and commitment of those contributors. We did not know many of these authors personally before we reached out to them about submitting chapters to the book. We were practically strangers at the interpersonal level, although many of us have read or used each other's work in our own research. That these authors trusted us with their scholarship and that they committed to this project when it was still just the kernel of an idea is the only reason we have been able to bring it to life.

Also important to that process are the individuals at Indiana University Press who helped us push through to the end. Editorial director Dee Mortensen, who has been supportive of so much of this work; acquisitions editor Jennika Baines, who is so patient and thoughtful when answering a deluge of emails; former assistant acquisitions editor Kate Schramm, who loves Nancy Drew but who does not look like her; project manager/editor Rachel Rosolina, and so many other individuals working at the press who saw this project through to its finish. Thank you.

No scholar is an island, and we are only able to produce the work we do because of the support of the friends and colleagues cheering us on. Thank you to Indiana University graduate school colleagues Stacie Meihaus Jankowski, Jessica von Ahsen Birthisel, Lori Henson, Spring Serenity Duvall, and Jason Martin for the continual rah-rahing and the laughter. Thank you too to the Mongeese. Thank you to friends and colleagues at Malmö University and School of Arts and Communication for keeping up with your sometimes pressured and distracted fellow. You know who you are.

Finally, our families. They put up with the bad moods when the writing's not going well, the good moods when everything is clicking, and all the other moods in between. Tim and Sofia Bolda, Rhonda Pennington, as well as close, special, and loved ones in Sweden. Thank you.

Michael Krona
Rosemary Pennington
April 26, 2019

THE MEDIA WORLD OF ISIS

Introduction

Michael Krona
Rosemary Pennington

In August 2014, only weeks after the first rare public appearance by the mythical Abu Bakr al-Baghdadi in the al-Nuri Mosque in Mosul for his initial address to the global Muslim religious community as appointed caliph and leader of ISIS, the now-infamous video showing the beheading of kidnapped US citizen James Foley was released. Titled "A Message to America," it was filmed against a desert background, with Foley in an orange jumpsuit, on his knees. Behind Foley stood his black-dressed executioner, his face covered. In English and with a London accent, the executioner, Mohamed Emwazi (who became known as Jihadi John) spoke directly into the camera, arguing for why Foley needed to die. Foley himself was forced to read a scripted statement blaming the US government for his fate. The video then ended with his beheading.

As a marketing product, the video went viral and reached a global audience.

As propaganda, the video had a clear message and was a wake-up call for many governments.

As a mediation of torture, the video was unfortunately only evidence of what would follow.

Even though such videos have long been produced by other organizations, this particular video clearly illustrated a deliberate strategy of mediation by ISIS—a strategy that aimed to gain global attention through the theatrical beheading of a Westerner and to simultaneously convey the message of the organization as a global phenomenon itself. This was only highlighted by using a man brought up in the UK and speaking English as Foley's executioner.

Mediating Terror

The theater of terror, the desire among terrorist organizations for public exposure and maximum marketing value, is of great importance for ISIS. This does not make them unique in any way; however, their ability and success in communicating what is now one of the most recognized brands in not only the internal jihadosphere but in the entire world separates them from both previous and present groups. Its predecessor, and the organization from which the ISIS of today was born, al-Qaeda, made this strategy of terror through global exposure all too visible with the horrific yet theatrical attacks in New York and Washington on September 11, 2001. Happening in real time in front of a global audience, witnessed in television news coverage and reproduced through various visual media for years to come, the attacks on the World Trade Center and Pentagon were orchestrated with a clear marketing strategy. Since then, the development of new and innovative communication technologies has altered the media pretext and conditions for terrorist organizations. What ISIS has done is to adapt to this new media reality, balancing the need for global exposure with a propaganda strategy implemented to target specific audiences with certain messages, characterized by not only depictions of attacks on enemies but also through communication and positive narratives about the organization itself.

If we were to ask a random person on the street in basically any Western country about what ISIS is and stands for, the answer would most certainly refer to the type of violence, executions, and brutality exemplified by the video of James Foley. As true as that association would be, the media world of ISIS, in particular after the declaration of the caliphate on June 29, 2014, has expanded into a virtual universe with particles that go far beyond this depicted brutality. Producing a plethora of propaganda narratives—including stories about the peaceful and just caliphate, featuring happy children, a functioning state and welfare system as well as the eulogization of martyrs, and discussion of the religious tenets and political history justifying their actions—ISIS's media industry has continuously managed to produce and communicate stories designed to appeal to a global audience. The products of this industry have helped attract tens of thousands of foreign fighters to join the so-called state, helped inspire attacks around the world, produced fear in many communities, and provoked military reactions from adversaries—making the media world of ISIS a highly relevant object of study. This is particularly so as ISIS's media apparatus has seemed to influence other groups who are currently mimicking and learning from the ways ISIS has used its strong propaganda machinery to increase exposure, recruitment, identity building, and territorial expansion. For instance, since the entrance of ISIS on the global stage of terrorism, the group's main rival al-Qaeda's central and regional branches have refined and increased their media propaganda distribution, with a specific focus on international audiences.

The questions at the heart of this volume are: What are the core dimensions of ISIS's use of media and propaganda? What are the characteristics of the group's messaging that have contributed to the unprecedented number of foreigners joining this terrorist organization, and how does its propaganda coincide with other sociocultural and political developments? And maybe above all, how do different media strategies and different media content work to legitimize ISIS's notion of its self-declared caliphate, its state project, which is so heavily amplified in its propaganda?

This book aims to address these and other questions as well as contribute to a holistic and in-depth understanding of the media machinery and virtual universe of one of the most recognized and well-known terrorist organizations in modern history. Taking a holistic approach to this topic could be considered both generalizing and bold at the same time; however, it is motivated by our desire to bring together researchers from diverse backgrounds working on this issue to understand how different perspectives produce different insights.

There is a wealth of material being published about the Islamic State, for obvious reasons. Leaving aside the vast amount of individual journal articles published on the topic, many of the books written about ISIS have been produced by journalists, individuals working within the intelligence sector, academics situated within disciplines such as political science or international relations, as well as practitioners or analysts connected to different private institutions.

ISIS Media in View

As ISIS started to appear in mainstream news media reporting, influencing political debates in the Western world and the Gulf region, several publications dealing with the organization from different perspectives emerged. We can divide this literature into two major sections. The first section is made up of extensive analytical works, mainly aimed at nonspecialist audiences and published in news outlets such as *The Atlantic*[1] or *BuzzFeed*, but also of course academic outlets and academic journals.[2] The second section consists of a rapidly expanding body of more rigorous books and works coming from a variety of both professional practices (journalism, intelligence agencies) and academic disciplines.

One of the first and most ambitious publications on the topic is West Point Military Academy's *The Group That Calls Itself a State: Understanding the Evolution and Challenges of the Islamic State*, in which a large portion of analytical details on ISIS's evolution and political background is combined with an examination of organizational structure.[3] This includes sections on the industrial media operations; however, these sections cannot be considered extensive. There are interesting discussions of how ISIS conducts its information and media operations, but it is placed in a larger political and military framework, not a communication framework. Military and terrorism expert Loretta Napoleoni takes a similar approach in her book *The Islamist Phoenix: The Islamic State and the Redrawing of the Middle East*.[4] She provides a balanced and in-depth description of the geopolitical context from which ISIS arose and highlights how the group has been given a chance to develop in the ashes of prolonged conflicts in Iraq and Syria. Napoleoni chronicles how the group has grown in tune with modernization and currently constitutes a criminal enterprise with deep understanding of not only media technology but Middle East politics and religious affiliations as well.

Benjamin Hall is one of several journalists who has published books on the subject over the last few years. His *Inside ISIS: The Brutal Rise of a Terrorist Army* contains several layers of description concerning ISIS strategic actions and puts a strong focus on the violent and brutal dimensions of the group's emergence as well as its ongoing military and media operations.[5] His journalistic background is evident in the devotion of several chapters focusing on the beheadings of Western journalists and aid workers and the part these acts played in the initial phases of ISIS's information and social media strategies. Michael Weiss and Hassan Hassan's *ISIS: Inside the Army of Terror* looks closely at and engages with the historical evolution of ISIS all the way back to the tidings of al-Zarqawi and AQI but then shifts focus to the current establishment of the caliphate and in particular the information structure and operations of ISIS messaging.[6] Abdel Bari Atwan, in *Islamic State: The Digital Caliphate*, dissects the diverse methods of recruitment used by ISIS, with particular focus on how digital and social media are facilitated in relation to the ideological warfare of the group.[7]

Jessica Stern and J. M. Berger's *ISIS: The State of Terror* almost exclusively focuses on the volume of output from ISIS central media command, with particular focus on the propaganda magazine *Dabiq* and widespread video series.[8] It touches on how the group relies on Twitter and other social networks in their propaganda machinery but also gives developed insights into the political dimensions that are their foundation as well as their continuing efforts to maintain a state. On a similar trajectory, Will McCants in *The ISIS Apocalypse: The History, Strategy, and Doomsday Vision of The Islamic State* uses primary empirical material, for instance ancient Arabic religious texts, to analyze and discuss the apocalyptic vision being promoted in ISIS political, ideological, military, and mediated operations.[9] Finally, worth mentioning is Patrick Cockburn's *The Rise of Islamic State: ISIS and the New Sunni Revolution*.[10] He ties the development of ISIS to failed US foreign policy and emphasizes the political and military backdrops of US-Middle Eastern politics as a pretext for current developments in the region.

There are other publications continuously being released that focus more on the political dimensions of the group or that are designed for a general reading audience. However, there has been a void regarding works dealing specifically and solely with ISIS's highly developed and strategic use of media in recruitment and propaganda operations. In 2018, one of the first books examining this topic was published. The edited volume *ISIS Beyond the Spectacle: Communication Media, Networked Publics, and Terrorism* explores the ways ISIS presents itself and its mission to a broad audience and considers the media world ISIS has helped create.[11] Our book, *The Media World of ISIS*, continues this work and expands it. Media has been a crucial part of ISIS's development and spread; to fully understand this organization, we must examine how it produces, publishes, and uses media in order to support the development and spread of its state project. By bringing together researchers from different backgrounds who are working on the same object of study, we feel this volume approaches a holistic—or whole-view—understanding of the media world of ISIS.

Media Ecology and the Shrinking State

The current political debate about ISIS is, to a large extent, characterized by claims that the organization is losing territory, capabilities, and the means to expand its self-declared caliphate, hinting that its days are numbered as the military coalition fighting it on the ground is advancing. The physical caliphate may well disappear in the near future, at least in the form we have come to know. The geographical loss of territory does cause problems for ISIS, especially as it loses the ability to connect controlled areas but also because of the loss of population and natural resources from which the group can collect taxes and revenue. There is, however, an ideological spread as well as territorial growth in other regions, most recently in Southeast Asia. As ISIS has lost territory in its physical caliphate, the number of terrorist attacks outside the Middle East, coordinated or inspired by the organization or its ideological messaging, has increased. There remains the possibility as well that ISIS will eventually regroup in rural areas of Iraq and Syria, gain strength and support, and come back in a new form.

These current conditions aside, the emergence and growth of ISIS, in particular through the aid of highly developed information operations and media strategies, is of huge importance to critically analyze and reflect on. More than five years have gone by since ISIS announced its caliphate, and for analysts and researchers, this provides an opportunity for a retrospective framework to emerge and offer not only years of empirical material (in terms of media artifacts) but also several trajectories of useful case studies and research publications to apply as focal points for discussion. Significant time has passed for reflection and a corpus of international research to develop, providing a foundation on which to build in-depth and nuanced contributions to this evolving and highly present field.

One aspect to consider when retrospectively approaching the plethora of dimensions concerning ISIS's use of media is the transformative media environment. For the sake of clarity, the work of this volume is informed by the concept of "media ecology," which allows us to consider the media infrastructure and interconnected relationships formed between ISIS's central organization and its global supporter networks as a kind of world of its own. This ecological approach to media refers to "the current rapidly shifting media saturated environment"[12] and, despite oppositional perspectives and nuances within both social sciences and humanities regarding the term, we approach the new media ecology as characterized by "a profound connectivity through which places, events, people, and their actions and inactions, seem increasingly connected."[13] We believe this approach to be sufficiently dynamic in framing both the technical infrastructure and messaging of ISIS communication practices as well as the features of interconnectivity between supporters facilitated by these practices.

Media World Context

A key goal in ISIS's media operations has been to make the communication and content come as close to everyday practices and media consumption as possible. By using widely popular social media platforms, applications, and messaging services, ISIS can ensure a broad audience is both intentionally and unintentionally exposed to its propaganda in the realm of everyday media use. This is not only the result of a strategy to make its media content more accessible, but it is also a deliberate choice by the Islamic State to play on mainly Western notions of how smartphones and social media are technologies contributing to the formation of both collective and individual identities. By embracing and utilizing the massive output on these everyday platforms, the virtual dimensions of ISIS increasingly intersect with media practices common for many.

Considering this in combination with the massive influx of foreign fighters to Iraq and Syria, especially during 2014 and 2015, this propaganda strategy must to a large extent be regarded as successful. But since the military efforts of the coalition against ISIS have increased and gained momentum, the number of propaganda products produced by ISIS has been reduced. This does not mean that the media strategy or operations of ISIS have been reduced in significance. On the contrary, the more population and territory ISIS loses from its caliphate, the more it attempts to reach new populations and supporters in other countries. Much of ISIS's propaganda is published in several languages, and a recent focus on Asia and Africa has resulted in several radical Islamist groups swearing allegiance to ISIS, which would seem to expand the Islamic State's areas of control.

Over the course of 2017, we witnessed the spread of ISIS into North Africa as well as an increase in Europe of attacks directed or inspired by ISIS in cities such as Brussels, Nice, and Paris. All of this helped foment a sense of insecurity and fear, even as the Islamic State lost physical territory. Throughout its entire campaign, but even more intensely since 2016, ISIS has targeted audiences not only to convince them to travel to the caliphate in Iraq and Syria but also to establish networks of ideologically like-minded individuals in countries around the world. By using Western-style visual imagery and sophisticated production techniques, this propaganda is designed to appeal mainly to alienated Muslim youth living on different continents. It is designed to convince them that they can become part of the organization—either by traveling to the Islamic State or serving ISIS abroad—which turns the media into a kind of weapon—one familiar, ubiquitous, and hard to destroy.

And while Western mainstream media tend to emphasize the brutal beheading videos and horrific torture when reporting on ISIS, the vast majority of propaganda messages are about the complete opposite. It is in the nature of propaganda to create alternative views of the world, of politics, of religion, and of other people. Despite their extreme and violent Salafi-jihadist ideology and the enterprise of violence that it has become, ISIS puts much effort into trying to portray itself as something more than simply a brutal regime. Concepts of brotherhood, belonging, significance, equality, and religion are used as key motivational narratives and are all vital to gaining support and recruits from around the world. It is important to realize that in much of ISIS's propaganda, the brutality aspect so widely known to the general public is only a tiny fraction of the entire corpus of ideological messages. The violence itself might appeal to a small number of the ideologically like-minded, but the promise of significance and belonging to something greater is by far more dominant. Images of happy children, caring fathers, a functioning state with education and health care flourish online—produced and spread to create a competitive system of meaning that challenges the Western portrayal of a brutal death cult. That also goes for ISIS's heroic portrayal of their fighters, emphasizing how cool and adventurous it is to go to battle for the caliphate and retaliate against Western governments that they say oppress Muslims (as well as fight Shia Muslims, whom ISIS consider apostates).

Book Organization

Throughout this book, we scrutinize and discuss not only content, techniques, and infrastructure for production and dissemination of propaganda, but the entire media ecology utilized by ISIS. In contrast to security services and agencies, who strategically observe the propaganda with the aim of revealing plots and preventing attacks to keep our societies safe, we consider the media world of ISIS a kind of magnifying lens through which we can enhance our understanding of the organization itself.

The contributions to this volume are divided into three parts. As a contextual introduction to the mediation of legitimacy undertaken for the state project of their caliphate, the section "Media and ISIS's Imaginary Geography" opens the book. Here chapters explore the construction of historical and religious claims of legitimacy in ISIS propaganda and myths around the caliphate, as well as civilizational discourses. As stated above, the media world of ISIS can be considered an extension and amplifier of the now-shrinking physical caliphate in Iraq and Syria, and the contributions in this first section approach this topic through various explanatory models. Combined, they address the existential arguments for the return of the caliphate and, above all, the role of mediation in this argumentation.

The second section, called "Mediating Terror," evolves around more particular ISIS strategies of mediation, propaganda production, and dissemination. This includes an overview of the media infrastructure utilized and aspects of weaponizing social media and users around the world, as well as the different tactics and strategies of integrating supporter networks in the media operations. Dimensions of visual imagery and rhetorical appeals in the messaging, storytelling techniques, and visual strategies for promoting truth claims and justification arguments are also discussed in this section.

Finally, the book moves to the third and final section, "Narratives of the Islamic State," and digs deeper into specific narratives, exploring how ISIS attempts to communicate certain perspectives on, among others, state-building, symbolism, mythology, victimhood, and gender. The magnitude and array of narratives and stories that are part of the media world of ISIS have different functions and target specific audiences. The chapters included in this last section deal with the specificities and narrative structure of these stories.

A Final Note

Our aim with this volume is not only to raise awareness of ISIS as a multidimensional enterprise of violence, but also to contribute to a larger debate on more effective political measures, counter-campaigning, and preventive work against violent extremism. Not only are the chapters of this book written by experts in various fields but they are also deliberately written in order to appeal to a wide audience. While we consider this book an important contribution to such academic disciplines as media and communication studies, peace and conflict studies, political science, history, and religious studies, we believe the book is also of value to the broader public. Our hope is that it not only provides and communicates insights into the goals and strategies of ISIS, but that it will also help us begin to understand how we can collectively work to prevent the spread of violent ideologies.

Notes

1. See, for instance, Graeme Wood, "What ISIS Really Wants," *The Atlantic*, March 2015, http://www.theatlantic.com/magazine/archive/2015/03/what-isis-really-wants/384980/. This article is a good example of a longer in-depth piece about ISIS outside of the academic sphere.

2. Here we could have listed a vast amount of journal articles concerning ISIS and their media operations that have been published over the course of the last years. Many of them are, however, referenced throughout the chapters of this volume, but contributions like James P. Farwell, "The Media Strategy of ISIS," *Survival: Global Politics and Strategy* 56, no. 6

(2014): 49–55, was one of the first very significant contributions within the academic spheres focusing on the overall media and propaganda strategies of ISIS following the declaration of the caliphate in June 2014.

3. Muhammad al-'Ubaydi, Nelly Lahoud, Daniel Milton, Bryan Price, "The Group That Calls Itself a State: Understanding the Evolution and Challenges of the Islamic State," *CTC at Westpoint*, December 2014, https://ctc.usma.edu/app/uploads/2014/12/CTC-The-Group-That-Calls-Itself-A-State-December20141.pdf.

4. Loretta Napoleoni, *The Islamist Phoenix: The Islamic State and The Redrawing of The Middle East* (New York: Seven Stories Press, 2014).

5. Benjamin Hall, *Inside ISIS: The Brutal Rise of a Terrorist Army* (New York: Center Street, 2015).

6. Michael Weiss and Hassan Hassan, *ISIS: Inside the Army of Terror*, 2nd ed. (New York: Regan Arts, 2016).

7. Abdel Bari Atwan, *Islamic State: The Digital Caliphate* (Oakland: University of California Press, 2015).

8. Jessica Stern and J. M Berger, *ISIS: The State of Terror* (London: William Collins, 2015).

9. Will McCants, *The ISIS Apocalypse: The History, Strategy, and Doomsday Vision of the Islamic State* (New York: St. Martin's Press, 2015).

10. Patrick Cockburn, *The Rise of Islamic State: ISIS and the New Sunni Revolution* (London: Verso, 2015).

11. Mehdi Semati, Piotr M. Spuznar, and Robert Alan Brookey, eds., *ISIS Beyond the Spectacle: Communication Media, Networked Publics, and Terrorism* (London: Routledge, 2018).

12. Akil N. Awan, Andrew Hoskins, and Ben O'Loughlin, *Radicalization and Media: Connectivity and Terrorism in the New Media Ecology* (London: Routledge, 2011), 5.

13. Ibid.

Bibliography

al-'Ubaydi, Muhammad, Nelly Lahoud, Daniel Milton, and Bryan Price. "The Group That Calls Itself a State: Understanding the Evolution and Challenges of the Islamic State." *CTC at Westpoint*, December 2014. https://ctc.usma.edu/app/uploads/2014/12/CTC-The-Group-That-Calls-Itself-A-State-December20141.pdf.

Atwan, Abdel Bari. *Islamic State: The Digital Caliphate*. Oakland: University of California Press, 2015.

Awan, Akil N., Andrew Hoskins, and Ben O'Loughlin. *Radicalization and Media: Connectivity and Terrorism in the New Media Ecology*. London: Routledge, 2011.

Cockburn, Patrick. *The Rise of Islamic State: ISIS and the New Sunni Revolution*. London: Verso, 2015.

Farwell, James P. "The Media Strategy of ISIS." *Survival: Global Politics and Strategy* 56, no. 6 (2014): 49–55.

Hall, Benjamin. *Inside ISIS: The Brutal Rise of a Terrorist Army*. New York: Center Street, 2015.

McCants, William. *The ISIS Apocalypse: The History, Strategy, and Doomsday Vision of the Islamic State*. New York: St. Martin's Press, 2015.

Napoleoni, Loretta. *The Islamist Phoenix: The Islamic State and the Redrawing of the Middle East*. New York: Seven Stories Press, 2014.
Semati, Mehdi, Piotr M. Spuznar, and Robert Alan Brookey, eds. *ISIS Beyond the Spectacle: Communication Media, Networked Publics, and Terrorism*. London: Routledge, 2018.
Stern, Jessica, and J. M. Berger. *ISIS: The State of Terror*. London: William Collins, 2015.
Weiss, Michael, and Hassan Hassan. *ISIS: Inside the Army of Terror*, 2nd ed. New York: Regan Arts, 2016.
Wood, Graeme. "What ISIS Really Wants." *The Atlantic*, March 2015. http://www.theatlantic.com/magazine/archive/2015/03/what-isis-really-wants/384980/.

MICHAEL KRONA is Assistant Professor in Media and Communication Studies and Visual Communication at Malmö University, Sweden. He works within a nationally funded research project in Sweden, exploring Salafi-jihadist information operations, with particular focus on ISIS communication practices.

ROSEMARY PENNINGTON is Assistant Professor in Miami University's Department of Media, Journalism, and Film. She is the coeditor, with Hilary Kahn, of *On Islam: Muslims and the Media*.

Part I

Media and ISIS's Imaginary Geography

1 The Myth of the Caliph

Suffering and Redemption in the Rhetoric of ISIS

Jason A. Edwards

Since its founding in 2010, the Islamic State of Iraq and Syria, often called ISIS, has grown in strength.[1] It has filmed high-profile executions for the world to see, recruited thousands of jihadists through sophisticated propaganda techniques, conducted terrorist attacks in more than a dozen countries, and conquered swaths of territory over Iraq and Syria. ISIS controlled so much territory at one time that it declared the formation of a new Islamic caliphate, and ISIS's leader, Abu Bakr al-Baghdadi, anointed himself as Caliph Ibrahim. As later chapters in this volume will show, ISIS is extremely sophisticated in communicating its ideology and propaganda through social media; its magazine, *Dabiq*; and various speeches, sermons, and other public pronouncements setting forth an agenda for the world. ISIS has become one of the international community's most dangerous foes and the focus of a multination military intervention in Iraq and Syria. Understanding the rhetoric ISIS uses to communicate to its supporters, to the Islamic community, and to the world in general offers an opportunity to ultimately combat the group's message.

In his study of extreme Hindu nationalism, Abhik Roy argues it is the job of rhetoricians to explain the rhetoric of extremist groups so their narratives can be understood and confronted and counternarratives can be introduced.[2] Jerry Long and Alex Wilner note in their study of al-Qaeda that it is immersed in a war of narratives among the West, Middle Eastern governments, and its members. Long and Wilner expose the contradictions of al-Qaeda's discourse and offer ways to "delegitimize" it to Muslims and the global community.[3] ISIS has taken its narrative war into extremely sophisticated territory with its recruitment techniques, propaganda, use of social media, and overall rhetoric. Considering the conflict with ISIS is not just a military conflict but a battle of ideas, this chapter argues that it is imperative we gain a better understanding of ISIS's rhetorical strategies. One major strategy is a reliance on mythic narratives.

Robert Rowland and Kirsten Theye claim terrorism is an inherently rhetorical act, and the rhetorical DNA of terrorism is a mythic/symbolic pattern that serves as a persuasive and epistemic device.[4] Anthony Smith asserts the myth of the Golden Age is a narrative that terrorist groups have used to promote national renewal.[5] Similarly, Abhik Roy and Robert Rowland maintain that a myth of return is a fundamental narrative extremists use to promote their belief system.[6] Jason Edwards contends mythic themes of suffering and redemption underwrite the rhetoric of Osama bin Laden.[7] Samuel Perry and Jerry Long explain that ISIS suicide-attack videos construct a mythic account of martyrdom to help recruit members.[8] In this chapter, I argue that a fundamental myth underwriting the rhetoric of ISIS is the myth of the caliph. I suggest ISIS uses this myth to offer a sense of identity to Muslims, make sense of the chaotic modern world, and legitimize their caliphate by chronicling the suffering of Muslims over the past century, emphasizing that ISIS has brought redemption to the Islamic world.

The idea of the caliphate has been an important part of Islamic thought for fourteen hundred years. For some jihadists, the restoration of the caliphate by ISIS and Abu Bakr al-Baghdadi is a vehicle for salvation.[9] If ISIS's followers die in the service of the true caliph, they believe they are guaranteed an exalted place in heaven. Musa Cerantonio, a prominent ISIS defender and spokesperson, asserted that Islam had finally been reestablished with the caliphate.[10] Historically, the caliph is the religious, political, and military leader of all Muslims. Islamic sharia law cannot be truly implemented until a caliphate has been created and a new caliph anointed. Thus, the caliph is extremely important to Islam and to ISIS's cause in general. According to al-Baghdadi's logic, Muslims have long suffered without the strong rule of a supreme leader. Because the caliphate has been reestablished, ISIS argues, Muslims can rise up, cast off their oppressors, and regain the prominence they so richly deserve. Muslims who join, fight, and potentially die for the caliph are working in support of God's anointed leader. By implication, they are part of God's chosen community. Therefore, despite the suffering Muslims have experienced on earth, they are ultimately redeemed in the service of God's chosen leader.

In order to fully explicate this argument, I analyze the rhetoric of ISIS's caliph, Abu Bakr al-Baghdadi. He has made few public statements, but those he did produce, particularly his July 1, 2014, sermon on his new caliphate, offer important insights into the strategies and beliefs of ISIS, while potentially offering a means to counter its message. Thus, I begin with a discussion of the myth of the caliph. Then I unpack al-Baghdadi's rhetorical strategies within the context of this myth. Finally, I offer some suggestions to counter this narrative.

Understanding Myth and the Islamic Caliphate

Myth is a common form of discourse. Rhetoric scholars have analyzed myths in a number of political situations.[11] Myths at their most basic are narratives. However, not all narratives are myths. A narrative of one's day, for example, is not mythic, because myths involve stories that are ingrained into the specific political and cultural discourse of a society. These stories articulate the society's beliefs, dilemmas, and values.[12] Rhetors who use myths offer audiences a way to frame the reality of a situation.

Myths perform a variety of functions for rhetors, three of which are most important to this study. First, myths help us make sense of the world around us. They provide people with a place in the social order of the universe.[13] This function becomes most apparent when some form of disorder has befallen a community. All individuals and communities are struck by some sense of disorder in their lifetimes. This disorder can come in the wake of a natural disaster, an attack by another nation, an illness, a downturn in the economy, or other disturbances to the regularity of life. From this vantage point, the world looks too complicated to grasp—too much information, too many countries, and too many factors to manage all at once. It is here that myths are invoked to offer a sense of stability and structure. They provide a means of coping with all the disturbances around us. Myths, in this sense, work to clarify challenges that are a threat to our universe, opportunities that may pose a threat to our success, and the limitations within which we must work to accomplish an objective.

Second, myths perform an identity function. Myths offer people a worldview that helps them see the world as a whole instead of in pieces.[14] This worldview generates a strong sense of identification. In this sense, myths provide a community with a form of "social glue."[15] Myths work to hold a group together by providing the basis for peoples of diverse backgrounds to find common ground with each other. This common ground defines who *we* were, are, and will be. Often a particular myth can unite a small or larger group around a common ideal, one that can be expanded further if the group accepts a specific casting of the myth. For instance, the myth of divine election holds that a community collectively believes it has an exclusive place within the overall order of communities. This community is special or "chosen" and destined for a unique mission that will demonstrate its exceptional nature to other communities.[16] The sense of closeness within this mythic narrative serves to provide individuals and communities with a sense of identity and place.

Finally, myths work to establish political legitimacy. Obtaining, maintaining, and enhancing legitimacy is one of the key functions of political communication. Rhetors use myths to establish legitimacy by making overtures toward the past and using them in the present for their political purposes. Leaders often discuss important historical events in a way that suggests they are carrying on the legacy of their predecessors. The past is connected to the present to offer seamless continuity. American presidents often discuss their predecessors or historical events in a way that serves to sanction their current policies. For example, George W. Bush often mythologized World War II in his war on terror discourse.[17] Bush discussed the sacrifice and heroism of the "greatest generation" in ways that made them seem larger than life. This is not to say that members of the World War II generation were not heroes. However, the exploits of that generation have become engrained in US social and political culture, exemplifying what it means to sacrifice. Their memory has become almost sacrosanct. For Bush, the mythologizing of World War II became a means to establish legitimacy for the war on terror.

There are a variety of different types of myths and specific themes that animate them. I assert that ISIS's discourse is underwritten by the myth of the caliph, which contains a message of suffering and redemption at its core. George Schopflin asserts that myths that encompass prominent themes of suffering and redemption are used by a nation to explain its "particularly sorrowful history," that it "is undergoing or has undergone a process of expatiating its sins and will be redeemed or, indeed, may itself redeem the world."[18] These themes tell a story of a nation or a people who have suffered but will be compensated for their powerlessness. Ultimately, that group will engage in redemptive acts to stop the suffering, which lays the groundwork to bring that community back to prominence. According to ISIS, true Muslims have long suffered under Western influence and domination, while Middle Eastern governments were not truly dedicated to Islam but maintaining their own power. ISIS is the cure to the ailment of Muslims everywhere. The group's redemptive act has been to restore the Islamic caliphate, which begins the process of restoring Islam to its true roots and its rightful place as God's chosen community.

The position of caliph has been an extremely important aspect of Islamic thought for the past fourteen hundred years. The word *caliph* means *successor*, as in successor to the Prophet Muhammad. The person who declares himself the successor to the Prophet has spiritual, legal, cultural, political, and military authority over Muslims everywhere.[19] The caliph can declare a holy war (jihad) in which all Muslims must participate and can demand all states that identify with the Muslim faith to recognize the caliph as their overlord.[20] Ultimately, the rightful caliph is the leader of Muslims everywhere, and they are compelled to obey his authority.

That said, there is considerable debate among Muslims and Islamic scholars as to who can lawfully claim to be the Prophet's true successor. For the most part, scholars believe that four people—Abu Bakr, Umar ibn Khattab, Uthman Ibn Affan, and Ali ibn Abi Talib—can rightfully claim to be true heirs to the Prophet Muhammad. These four caliphs are often referred to as the righteous or "rightly guided" caliphs.[21] These four men ruled for about thirty years after Muhammad's death in the seventh century. From there, however, there is divergence and disagreement about whether a "true" caliph actually existed after the death of Ali in AD 661. In the centuries that followed, many leaders of the Ummayad, Abbasid, and Ottoman empires declared themselves to be successors to the Prophet Muhammad. However, after the defeat of the Ottoman Empire in World War I, the Turkish National Congress, at the behest of Turkish leader Kemal Ataturk, declared an end to the Ottoman caliphate and sent the last Ottoman sultan into exile. In 1924, Ataturk officially abolished the Ottoman caliphate.[22] It is the abolition of the caliphate after World War I that leaders like Osama bin Laden and Abu Bakr al-Baghdadi mark as a true turning point of Islamic suffering.[23] In the aftermath of the Great War, Britain and France carved up the Middle East to expand their colonial empires. They also aided and helped prop up Middle Eastern states like Saudi Arabia. In turn, those nations became prominent Western allies. The alliance between certain Middle Eastern countries and Western nations demonstrated to some radical Islamists that the leaders of these countries were not "true" Muslims but merely puppets for apostate empires.

In the wake of World War II, America filled the void left by France and Britain. The United States proceeded to support and prop up a number of unpopular dictators who were pro-Western and anticommunist, while also helping overthrow democratically elected leaders (e.g., Mohammad Mossadegh in Iran) who were feared to have communist sympathies.[24] The rise of Western imperial powers in the Middle East and the alliances that these autocrats cultivated with the West only exacerbated Islamic suffering.

To that end, Islamists advocated Muslims' need to return to a time when Islam was an expanding and dominant power in the world, not in perpetual decline. That time could be found during the rule of the caliphs, whether that be the righteous caliphs or the succeeding empires. Those caliphs fought against Western influence, often defeating their enemies on the battlefield. Some Islamists even go so far as to argue that there was no poverty during any of the historical caliphates. For example, Hizb ut Tahrir, a pan-Islamic organization that is active in Western nations, particularly the United Kingdom, asserts that during the various Islamic caliphates, poverty was virtually abolished. Moreover, those caliphates protected women from poverty and enslavement, unlike many Western nations.[25] In other words, the historical caliphate was a golden age when poverty was almost nonexistent, women were protected, and Islam was at the height of its power and influence. Once the caliphate was destroyed and Western nations began collaborating with their Middle Eastern allies, ordinary Muslims were left impoverished and suffering. For ISIS, the return of the caliph through Abu Bakr al-Baghdadi is the way to restore Islam to its true preeminence across the world.

ISIS's Myth of the Caliph

Abu Bakr al-Baghdadi has been the principal leader of ISIS for the past five years. Prior to being raised to the leader of ISI (Islamic State of Iraq), al-Baghdadi was a leader of minor insurgent groups operating in Iraq and, for a time, was a detainee of American forces in Iraq.[26] In 2010, al-Baghdadi was announced as the leader of ISI, following the death of his predecessor. Al-Baghdadi proceeded to expand ISI's efforts with a series of high-profile terrorist attacks in Iraq. In 2013, ISI became involved in the Syrian civil war, where the group quickly won victory after victory, capturing a good deal of territory within Syria and part of northern Iraq. With this new expansion, ISI renamed itself ISIL (Islamic State of Iraq and the Levant), also known as ISIS (Islamic State of Iraq and Syria). ISIS expanded its territorial holdings in 2013 and 2014.[27] In June 2014, as a result of its success, al-Baghdadi declared ISIS had established a worldwide caliphate and renamed himself Caliph Ibrahim. His supporters proceeded to circulate the genealogy of al-Baghdadi's tribe, which they claim has direct ties to the Prophet Muhammad.[28] Therefore, al-Baghdadi can make the argument that he is a true descendant of the Prophet and the next "rightly guided" caliph.

The Suffering of "True" Muslims

In his rhetoric, al-Baghdadi covers several subjects.[29] One of the most prominent is his chronicle of the various wrongs Islam's enemies have carried out against the *ummah*.[30] According to al-Baghdadi, Muslims have suffered for generations. As he noted,

> Indeed the Muslims were defeated after the fall of their khalifah. Then their state ceased to exist, so the disbelievers were able to weaken and humiliate the Muslims, dominate them in every region, plunder their wealth and resources, and rob them of their rights.
>
> They accomplished this by attacking and occupying their lands, placing their treacherous agents in power to rule the Muslims with an iron fist, and spreading dazzling and deceptive slogans such as: civilization, peace, coexistence, freedom, democracy, secularism, baathism, nationalism, patriotism, among other false slogans.[31]

There are a couple of things to note in this passage. First, notice when al-Baghdadi begins the chronicle of suffering for Muslims. For the ISIS leader, Islamic suffering began with the defeat of the previous caliphate. The sultans of the Ottoman Empire often characterized their reign as being the successors to the Prophet Mohammed. However, the Ottoman Empire was defeated after World War I, and its empire subsequently broke into various pieces that were either colonized or became nation-states allied to the West. This has led to Muslims all over the world being humiliated, dominated, occupied, plundered, and robbed of their Islamic heritage. For more than one hundred years, Muslims have been fed a false message that they must coexist with those who practice "democracy" and "secularism." By implication, there is no coexistence with those who espouse such values or a different political belief. They are forever mortal enemies who must be destroyed, because if they are not, they will continue to extend the suffering of true Muslims everywhere.

Second, note the sources of Islamic suffering. They are not only Western nations—the United States, Russia, and Israel—and their "treacherous agents" who embrace "civilization," "Baathism," "nationalism," "democracy," "freedom," and other "slogans." Those treacherous agents run the length of the Middle East. For example, Syria and Iraq, when Saddam Hussein was in power, were both regimes dedicated to the political ideology of Baathism, whereas Saudi Arabia, Jordan, Egypt, and other countries have promoted civilization, peace, nationalism, democracy, or other slogans. For al-Baghdadi, Islam's treacherous agents will ever be governments in the Middle East, past and present. They have strayed from the true path of Islam and the path of the Prophet. Because of this, Muslims everywhere have suffered. The reestablishment of the caliphate can arrest that suffering because true Muslims now have a place and a leader to turn to in their time of suffering—one who will not only listen but will use the resources at his disposal to end it once and for all.

To further demonstrate Islam's suffering since the end of the caliphate, al-Baghdadi chronicles and indicts the West and its allies for scores of crimes against Muslims. These acts of violence include killing Muslims in Burma; dismembering and disemboweling Muslims in the Philippines, Indonesia, and Kashmir; and expelling them from their homes in the Caucasus. Mass graves were created in Bosnia and Herzegovina; homes and sanctuaries were violated, desecrated, and destroyed in Palestine; al-Baghdadi's followers were tortured in the Sinai Peninsula. Muslims, in general, were tortured in East Turkestan and Iran; war was being waged against chastity and the hijab in France and Tunis; and in general, the West was responsible for promoting prostitution and adultery and betraying Islam.[32] Note that this recitation of crimes against the ummah touches three different continents, where most Muslims around the world live. As such, Muslim suffering is everywhere. Almost half of the earth is a battleground for Islam. These crimes provide evidence for al-Baghdadi's claim that Islam is under siege from all sides. It provides a logic and a motive for ISIS's fight against its enemies. Muslims are under attack; they need help, and ISIS is the only group who will stand up to these enemies as the true defenders of the faith. In turn, those who join ISIS and fight against its enemies will be fighting in the service of the "rightly guided" caliph and, by extension, serving God.

One of the more significant aspects of al-Baghdadi's chronicle of Muslim suffering is the lengthy condemnations of those "treacherous agents" of Islam. It is certainly not unusual for terrorist leaders like al-Baghdadi to accuse Muslim nations of colluding with the West. For example, Osama bin Laden often accused leaders in Saudi Arabia and Pakistan of colluding with the United States. However, bin Laden more often than not appeared to focus more on Western culpability for the suffering of Muslims than on those treacherous agents.[33] Al-Baghdadi's rhetoric suggests he emphasizes blaming the governments of Muslim nations more than their Western allies for Islam's suffering. For example, in a May 2015 sermon, the ISIS leader remarked:

> O Muslims, the apostate tyrannical leaders who rule your lands in the lands of the Two Holy Sanctuaries (Mecca and Medina), Yemen, Sham (the Levant), Iraq, Egypt, North Africa, Khorosan, the Caucasus, the Indian Subcontinent, Africa, and elsewhere, are the allies of the Jews and the Crusaders. Rather, they are their slaves, servants, guard dogs, and nothing else. The armies they prepare and arm and which the Jews and Crusaders train are only to crush you, weaken you, enslave you the Jews and the Crusaders, turn away from your religion, and the path of Allah, plunder the goods of your lands, and rob you of your wealth.[34]

For al-Baghdadi, the leaders of Muslim nations are nothing but "guard dogs" for the West—"Jews and Crusaders." They cannot be trusted. They are mere puppets of Western nations, who are out to "enslave" Muslims and turn them away from the true "path of Allah." By continuing to follow, live in these states and on these continents, and let these so-called leaders rule only perpetuates the fate of Islamic suffering. But why does al-Baghdadi focus on these leaders instead of giving more prominent attention to the "Jews and Crusaders"?

First, the suffering caused by the leaders of these states is greater than that of the "Jews and Crusaders." According to al-Baghdadi's logic, it is in the nature of Western apostates to try to conquer Islam, because they are nonbelievers. They do not understand the glory of the Prophet Muhammad. Accordingly, they are natural enemies of Islam. However, when so-called Muslim leaders collaborate with the "Jews and Crusaders," they have proven themselves to be false Muslims. These leaders supposedly operate in the name of the Prophet Muhammad but actually betray the ummah because of their partnership with the West. The betrayal of these Muslim leaders cuts much deeper because they are supposed allies of Muslims but are really apostates and traitors.

Second and perhaps more importantly, the "guard dogs" of the West are the enemies that must be defeated first. They must be ISIS's primary target in order to truly unify all of Islam. In order to get into a house or a community, you must often pass its security—its "guard dog," if you will. The governments of Saudi Arabia, Egypt, North Africa, the Indian subcontinent, and anywhere Muslims are the dominant portion of the population serve as guard dogs. Once that security is bypassed, it opens the doors to ISIS in two ways. First, ISIS will have an expanded base of operations. They will have expanded their caliphate. They can arrest the suffering that Muslims have had at the hands of these apostate governments, create a new Islamic empire, and return Islam to its golden age. Moreover, it gives al-Baghdadi and his supporters greater legitimacy. If al-Baghdadi can defeat these governments, these "guard dogs," "servants," and "slaves," then he must truly be God's anointed leader. He must be true successor to the Prophet Muhammad because God would not give power and leadership to someone who is a nonbeliever. Accordingly, Muslims everywhere will come to truly understand, appreciate, and comply with the new caliphate established by ISIS.

It is not just the governments of Muslim nations in general that al-Baghdadi focuses on. Rather, his harshest criticism is reserved for the Saudi royal family. In a lengthy set of paragraphs in his May 2015 sermon, al-Baghdadi condemns the Saudi royal family and accuses them of betraying Muslims around the world. For example, al-Baghdadi asks a series of rhetorical questions such as, "Where is the support of Al Salul [Saudis] and their allies for a million of the weak Muslims who are without exception being exterminated in Burma?"[35] Another question he asks is, "Where is the jealousy of the Arabian Peninsula's rulers towards the noble women who are raped daily in Sham, Iraq, and the various lands of the Muslims?"[36] The answer is that Saudi Arabia's "treachery has become clear even to the laymen of the Muslims."[37] He then goes on to accuse the Saudi royal family of launching its current war against Yemen as a means to appease their masters in the West: "Their war is nothing but an attempt to prove themselves once again to their masters from amongst the Jews and Crusaders. It is nothing but a desperate attempt to turn the Muslims away from the Islamic State whose voice is high everywhere and whose reality has become clear to all Muslims and therefore the Muslims began to gradually rally around it."[38]

The focus on Saudi Arabia is easy to understand. First, Saudi Arabia is one of the most, if not *the* most, powerful Middle Eastern nations. It buys billions of dollars in American military equipment and is one of America's primary allies in the Middle East. Moreover, it has put down two Muslim uprisings in Bahrain and Yemen in the last four years to cement its control over the Arabian Peninsula. More importantly, Saudi Arabia is home to the two most important holy sites in all of Islam: Mecca and Medina. All Muslims must carry out the five pillars of Islam. One of those pillars is a pilgrimage or *Hajj* to Mecca. Additionally, the Prophet's mosque, known as Masjid Al Nabawi, and the second most holy site in Islam, is located in the Saudi Arabian city of Medina. According to al-Baghdadi's logic, he sees the Saudis for who they truly are. They are apostates. They are traitors. They have corrupted the most holy sites of Islam. Thus, the Saudi royal family are false Muslims. The Saudis are "desperate" to win the hearts and minds of their "masters from among the Jews and Crusaders." The reestablishment of the caliphate threatens to undercut Saudi Arabia's power and influence. Al-Baghdadi's caliphate establishes the "Islamic states" as the "true Muslims," whose voice has finally carried over the din of the Saudi betrayal. As such, thousands of believers are flocking to its banners and to "rally around it." Thus, to follow the Saudi royal family is to perpetuate Muslim suffering, whereas the Islamic State holds the key to redeeming Muslims across the world.

The Islamic State's Redemption

For Abu Bakr al-Baghdadi and ISIS, an earthly redemption for Muslims is at hand. Evidence of this redemption can be found in the recent battles ISIS has fought. For example, al-Baghdadi argues, "Despite the crusade being from the most severe and fiercest of them, it is yet the most failing and disappointing. We see America and its allies stumbling between fear, weakness, inability, and failure. America, Europe, Australia, Canada, their apostate tails and slaves from amongst the rulers of the Muslims lands were terrified by the Islamic State. . . . They fear for their security. They fear the revolt of the Muslim peoples (against their rulers). They fear their defeat. They fear the return of the Khalifah and the return of Muslims to pioneering and leadership."[39]

According to ISIS's propaganda, everywhere the Islamic State has engaged America and its allies, it has found victory. ISIS has the world on the run. Despite a "crusade" that is severe and fierce, America fails at almost every turn. However, the United States and its allies continue to fight because they fear for their "security," for the "revolt of the Muslim peoples," and for the "return of the Khalifah and the return of Muslims to pioneering and leadership." The West fears "true" Muslims because of what they can do for the world. They will expose the West for their lies and their promotion of democracy, freedom, civilization, and the like. True salvation lies in total submission to ISIS's Islamic principles. Everything else is a path to ruin. Because the West and its Muslim allies know this truth, they must hide it from their people, hence their constant "crusade" against Muslims across the world.

Despite this crusade, Abu Bakr al-Baghdadi and ISIS have already begun the process of arresting Islamic suffering. Through their leadership, they will unite the ummah across the world. As al-Baghdadi put it:

> O Muslims everywhere, glad tidings to you and expect good. Raise your head high, for today—by Allah's grace—you have a state and khalifah, which will return your dignity, might, rights, and leadership. It is a state where the Arab and non-Arab, the white man and black man, the easterner and westerner are all brothers. It is a khalifah that gathered the Caucasian, Indian, Shami, Iraqi, Yemeni, Egyptian, Maghribi [North African], American, French, German, and Australian. Allah brought their hearts together and thus, they become brothers by His grace, loving each other for the sake of Allah, standing in a single trench, defending and guarding each other, and sacrificing themselves for one another.[40]

Essentially, al-Baghdadi and ISIS have established paradise on earth. As the new caliph, he has united races, creeds, nations, and regions under the banner of

Islam. There is no racism, no sectionalism, no fight between East and West, but rather brotherhood founded on the tenets of Islam. Ultimately, however, ISIS's power hinges upon the reestablishment of the caliphate. Note that al-Baghdadi states that it was a "khalifah that gathered" all of these races together.

Without the caliph, there is no paradise, no redemption, no harmony in Islam. To reestablish peace on earth, the caliphate must exist. Without it, Islam cannot truly survive and thrive. Muslims will continue to be subjugated without the (re)constitution of the caliph. Al- Baghdadi's rhetoric suggests that he, aside from obeying the five pillars of Islam, is the connection between Muslims and Allah. Without him there is no salvation, no redemption, and no paradise on earth. Islam is incomplete without his rule. As the new caliph, al-Baghdadi completes the identity of what it is to be a "true" Muslim. Through him the "might," "dignity," "rights," and "leadership" have returned to Muslims everywhere. This is why you see consistently in al-Baghdadi's messages and the messages of ISIS for Muslims everywhere to perform *hijrah* (immigration) to the Islamic State. As al-Baghdadi notes, "O Muslims everywhere, whichever is capable of performing hijrah to the Islamic State, then let him do so, because hijrah to the land of Islam is obligatory."[41] For al-Baghdadi it is an obligation of all "true" Muslims to come to the "land of Islam." The land of Islam is not in their current homes, but what the new caliphate established in ISIS-controlled territory.

The ISIS leader encourages hijrah because he needs true Muslims to continue the fight against the West. According to the new caliph, it is the obligatory duty of Muslims everywhere. "There is no deed in this virtuous month or in any other month than jihad in the path of Allah . . . terrify the enemies of Allah and seek death in the places where you expect to find it for the *dunya* [worldly life] will come to an end, and the hereafter will last forever."[42] For al-Baghdadi, Islam is a religion of war. As he explains:

> O Muslims Islam was never for a day the religion of peace. Islam is the religion of war. Your Prophet (peace be upon him) was dispatched with the sword as a mercy to the creation. He was ordered with war until Allah is worshipped alone. He (peace be upon him) said to the polytheists of his people, "I came to you with slaughter." He fought both the Arabs and non-Arabs in all their various in all their various colors. He himself left to fight and took part in dozens of battles. He never for a day grew tired of war.[43]

Al-Baghdadi went so far as to attempt to appropriate the word *terrorism* in a positive way. As he explains, "Terrorism is to disbelieve in those slogans and to believe in Allah. Terrorism is to refer to Allah's law for judgment. Terrorism is to worship Allah as he ordered you. Terrorism is to refuse humiliation, subjugation, and subordination. Terrorism is for the Muslim to live as a Muslim, honorably with might and freedom. Terrorism is to insist upon your rights and not give them up."[44]

These passages provide representative examples of how al-Baghdadi believes redemption can be continued: through constant violence. According to ISIS's version of history, the Prophet Muhammad exemplifies the life all Muslims should lead. Muhammad never stopped fighting. According to al-Baghdadi, he was actually preparing for more battles prior to his death. His companions continued to fight long after his passing.[45] Accordingly, Muslims should fight. They should take up "terrorism." Terrorism is not a tactic for terrifying innocents. Rather it is a way of life. It is the way of life for a true Muslim and follower of Allah. Terrorism is a means to remove the slogans of peace, civilization, democracy, secularism, freedom, and others. Terrorism is a means for Muslims to stand on their feet, instead of being slaves to the cabal of Islam's enemies—the West, Israel, and leaders of Muslim states opposed to ISIS. The reestablishment of the caliphate was the first step to stopping the suffering of the ummah. Now the caliphate must be protected and expanded until "Allah is worshipped alone." By fighting and potentially dying for the new Islamic caliphate, Muslims can fulfill their duty to Allah's "judgment." Committing acts of terrorism is to "worship" as he "ordered" them to, which is to "live as a Muslim, honorably with might and freedom." Through the reconstitution of the caliph, Islam is finally whole again.

Conclusion

Over the past few pages, I have explored rhetorical characteristics of ISIS's discourse by focusing on the rhetoric of their leader, Abu Bakr al-Baghdadi. Similar to other terrorist groups, ISIS's discourse is broadly underwritten by a mythic/symbolic pattern that serves as a persuasive and epistemic device.[46] More specifically, I have argued the myth of the caliph, with its themes of suffering and redemption at its heart, is a primary narrative that Abu Bakr al-Baghdadi uses to foster identification and legitimacy as the supreme leader of ISIS.

The caliphate myth is extremely important to ISIS and must be consistently emphasized to maintain its legitimacy. One aspect of that mythology is the ability of al-Baghdadi and ISIS to control territory in order to speak for all Muslims. Without specific control of different lands, there is no basis for a caliphate. There is no ability for ISIS to demonstrate they can govern. That explains the constant media narrative from ISIS through social media accounts, propaganda videos, and an online magazine (*Dabiq*), which reinforce the rhetorical themes we have discussed here. For example, after the defeat of the Iraqi army for control of Mosul in June 2014, Abu Bakr al-Baghdadi addressed the world for the first time, declaring the return of the Islamic caliphate. Al-Furqan media, ISIS's media arm, produced the video of him giving his sermon and consistently releases statements and messages from al-Baghdadi and his lieutenants.[47] On July 7, 2016, al-Furqan media created a fifteen-minute English-language video that explains the structure of ISIS's caliphate. The video begins with short excerpts from al-Baghdadi's sermons, stating that the Islamic state "will always remain." The next two minutes provide a short explanation of Islamic history. The narrator argues that al-Baghdadi's "caliphate" is a "structure that has become more manifest than the sun in the middle of the sky." He goes on to argue that Muslims had never been without a caliph or imam until the past one hundred years, when the people became "squanderous, neglectful, and chaotic." Furthermore, Muslim lands were "usurped" and "lost." However, Abu Bakr al-Baghdadi is the man who has come to save Islam and its people. Al-Baghdadi will not repeat the "tragedy of Muslims" in the past.

The rest of the video provides details about how it administrates its occupied zones called *wilayats*. According to the narrator, ISIS has nineteen wilayats in the Levant, and the rest are located in "distant" areas.[48] This video, along with other media-related activity (e.g., social media, the online magazine, other propaganda videos), carry forward the mythic narrative outlined by al-Baghdadi. The video chronicles how at the end of World War I, Muslim lands were "usurped" because Western powers carved up what remained of the Ottoman Empire, either by establishing modern nation-states (such as Saudi Arabia) or adding Ottoman territory to their colonial empires. For the next one hundred years, Muslims suffered until the Islamic State returned to counterbalance these forces and restore Muslims to their rightful place in the global order. For ISIS's caliphate to continue to be legitimate, these kinds of videos, along with other forms of propaganda, are consistently needed to reinforce its message that it is the only legitimate voice that Muslims should follow.

So, one of the questions that remains is, Where does that leave us? What can be done with this knowledge? A first step in counteracting any group's discourse is understanding it. Kenneth Burke's famous essay, *The Rhetoric of Hitler's Battle*, provides a model and perhaps the best example of rhetorical scholars making a difference in the fight against extremism, nationalism, and terrorism. Burke's mission was to make apparent Hitler's rhetorical appeals so that American politicians could not get away with the same kind of "swindle."[49] A more contemporary instance of this kind of scholarship come from Samuel Perry and Jerry Long's essay on ISIS. Perry and Long examine suicide-attack narratives to justify their actions and obtain new recruits. This is an excellent example of rhetorical scholars using their scholarly positions to expose one aspect of ISIS's rhetoric to counter it.[50] The purpose of this study has been to make apparent ISIS's discourse, so that it can be exposed and countered.

Another step where rhetoricians and communication scholars can help counter ISIS is to critically discuss the significance of what name we use when referring to it. News media often use the acronym ISIS, ISIL, or IS to reference this terrorist group. Whatever acronym is used by the media, politicians, or the general public, by having the "IS" as part of the acronym that stands for "Islamic

State," it conveys some legitimacy upon this group. It makes it appear that they are a nation-state that has legitimate rights and responsibilities under international law. Former US Secretary of State John Kerry only will refer to ISIS as "Daesh." Daesh is technically an acronym for ISIS's Arabic name, "al-Dawla al-Islamiya fi al-Iraq wa al-Sham." However, Abu Bakr al- Baghdadi eventually rebranded Daesh as ISIS. If Daesh is used in any territory captured by ISIS, the speaker's tongue will be cut out.[51] Daesh in Arabic means "to trample or crush" or "a bigot who imposes his view on others."[52] Considering definition is a fundamental and basic subject that is taught in rhetoric, scholars can and should use Daesh instead of ISIS. Using Daesh undercuts the identity that ISIS has attempted to establish in the Muslim and global community. By using Daesh, we delegitimize their claim to be a true nation-state that speaks for Muslims, while becoming one aspect in a larger counternarrative against ISIS.

Additionally, we should not refer to Abu Bakr al-Baghdadi as Caliph Ibrahim. Not only does he distort his history of being a direct descendant of the "true" caliphs of Islam, but he distorts that important aspect of Islam as well. Rather, Theresa Ford recommends that Baghdadi be referred to as "ad Dajjal." For Muslims, "ad Dajjal" is an evil figure in Islam who appears as a false messenger.[53] In some respects, this is the equivalent of Christianity's Antichrist.

Finally, forums should be held for pundits, politicians, policymakers, media, and the public to discuss the specific strategies and methods ISIS is using to spread its message. Experts can discuss how ISIS misrepresents Islamic history, the Quran, and Muslims in general. These forums can demonstrate the different interpretations of Islam that promote peace, hospitality toward individuals and groups, and solidarity with humanity in general.[54] For example, the Carter Center is promoting a new initiative that seeks to understand ISIS's strategies of recruitment by working with scholarly experts and Muslim leaders to identify flaws in the group's narratives, counter the message to discredit their rhetoric, and discuss the rise of Islamophobia.[55] Rhetoricians/communication scholars are uniquely suited to participate in these forums because we are trained in construction, analysis, and deconstruction of messages. Publicizing these forums and their results can be a small part of the larger counternarrative to disrupt their recruitment techniques and promote a more positive image of Muslims and Islam throughout the world.

Concomitantly, a counter media narrative should be created that uses these different forums. One of the keys to ISIS's success is its media. ISIS is one of the most successful and sophisticated terrorist groups in its use of social media. If the group continues to lose territory in Iraq and Syria, it does not necessarily mean a total defeat, because it has territory that it administers beyond those countries. ISIS can develop a virtual caliphate to go along with its physical control of different pockets of territory throughout the world. In that sense, the group might become even more dangerous in radicalizing and recruiting young men and women to join ISIS and carry out lone wolf attacks, such as have been found in Europe, North America, Asia, and Africa. Brian Moore and Sim Vireak discuss the potential problems with this "virtual caliphate": "Systematic and coordinated responses to the narrative that groups like ISIS are trying to promote through social media is necessary in order to combat radicalization and recruitment efforts. This counternarrative can serve to glorify the successes of anti- extremist military operations, highlight the failures and embarrassments of ISIS, and expose the fallacies of radical ideology."[56]

Ultimately, ISIS will not be defeated by just bombs and bullets. Words can and must make a difference. As Theresa Ford notes, "We must counter words with words."[57] Abhik Roy further argues it is "imperative that rhetorical scholars become more active in exposing narratives that are designed to create national identity by means of tragic scapegoating. Rhetorical scholars have a moral responsibility to deconstruct these messages and advise policy makers concerning the nature of this discourse."[58] Analyzing ISIS's discourse puts more information into the marketplace of ideas for people to examine. In and of itself, that will not win the war against terrorism, but it can contribute to the ongoing battle against extremism.

Notes

1. ISIS is also known as ISIL, the Islamic State, IS, and Daesh.
2. Abhik Roy, "The Construction and Scapegoating of Muslims as 'Other' in Hindu Nationalist Rhetoric," *Southern Communication Journal* 69 (2004): 320–332.
3. Jerry Mark Long and Alex Wilner, "Delegitimizing al-Qaida: Defeating an 'Army Whose Men Love Death,'" *International Security* 39 (2014): 126–164
4. Robert Rowland and Kirsten Theye, "The Symbolic DNA of Terrorism," *Communication Monographs* 75 (2008): 52–85.
5. Anthony Smith, "The Myth of the Golden Age and National Renewal," in *Myths and Nationhood*, ed. Geoffrey Hosking and George Schopflin (New York: Routledge, 1997), 36–59
6. Abhik Roy and Robert Rowland, "The Rhetoric of Hindu Nationalism: A Narrative of Mythic Redefinition," *Western Journal of Communication* 67 (2003): 225–248.
7. Jason A. Edwards, "The Mythology of Suffering and Redemption in Al-Qaeda's Discourse," in *Myth, Ideology, and Culture*, ed. John Perlich and David Whitt (Jefferson, NC: McFarland, 2014), 83–101.
8. Samuel P. Perry and Jerry Mark Long, "Why Would Anyone Sell Paradise? The Islamic State in Iraq and the Making of a Martyr," *Southern Journal of Communication* 81 (2016): 1.
9. Graeme Wood, "What ISIS Really Wants," *The Atlantic*, March 2015, http://www.theatlantic.com/magazine/archive/2015/03/what-isis-really-wants/384980/.
10. Ibid.
11. See A. Abizadeh, "Historical Truth, National Myths and Liberal Democracy: On the Coherence of Liberal Nationalism," *Journal of Political Philosophy* 12 (2004): 291–313;

Hiram Adak, "National Myths and Self-Narrations: Mustafa Kemal's *Nutuk* and Halide Edib's *Memoirs* and *The Turkish Ordeal*," *South Atlantic Quarterly* 12 (2003): 509–527; Leroy G. Dorsey, "The Frontier Myth in Presidential Rhetoric: Theodore Roosevelt's Campaign for Conservation," *Western Journal of Communication* 59 (1995): 1–19; Leroy G. Dorsey and Rachel L. Harlow, "We Want Americans Pure and Simple: Theodore Roosevelt and the Myth of Americanism," *Rhetoric & Public Affairs* 6 (2003): 55–79; Jason A. Edwards, "The Demonic Redeemer Figure in Political Myth: A Case Study of Vladimir Zhirinovsky," *Journal of the Wisconsin Communication Association* 32 (2000): 17–32; Hal W. Fulmer, "Mythic Imagery and Irish Nationalism: Henry Grattan Against Union, 1800," *Western Journal of Speech Communication* 50 (1986): 144–157; Justin J. Gustainis, "John F. Kennedy and the Green Berets: The Rhetorical Use of the Hero Myth," *Communication Studies* 40 (1989): 1–13; Stephanie Kelley-Romano, "Myth-Making in Alien Abduction Narratives," *Communication Quarterly* 83 (2006): 383–406; Mark P. Moore, "Rhetorical Criticism of Political Myth: From Goldwater Legend to Reagan Mystique," *Communication Studies* 41 (1991): 295–308; Kurt W. Ritter, "The Myth-Making Functions of the American Revolution: Frances Hopkinson as a Case Study," *Today's Speech* 23 (1975): 25–30.

12. Janice Hocker Rushing and Thomas S. Frentz, "The Mythic Perspective," in *The Art of Rhetorical Criticism*, ed. Jim A. Kuypers (New York: Allyn and Bacon, 2005), 241–265.

13. Dan Nimmo and James Combs, *Subliminal Politics: Myths and Mythmakers in America* (Englewood Cliffs, NJ: Prentice Hall, 1980), 9.

14. Roy and Rowland, "The Rhetoric of Hindu Nationalism," 225–248.

15. Nimmo and Combs, *Subliminal Politics*, 11.

16. Bruce Cauthen, "The Myth of Divine Election and Afrikaner Ethnogenesis," in *Myths and Nationhood*, ed. Geoffrey Hosking and George Schopflin (New York: Routledge, 1997), 107–131.

17. Denise M. Bostdorff, "George W. Bush's September 11th Rhetoric of Covenant Renewal: Upholding the Faith of the Greatest Generation," *Quarterly Journal of Speech* 89 (2003): 293–319; David Hoogland Noon, "Operation Enduring Analogy: World War II, the War on Terror, and the Uses of Collective Memory," *Rhetoric & Public Affairs* 7 (2004): 339–365.

18. George P. Schopflin, "The Functions and Taxonomy of Myths," in *Myths and Nationhood*, ed. George Schopflin and Geoffrey Hosking (New York: Routledge, 1997), 12.

19. Louay Fatoohi, "The Islamic Caliphate between Past Myths and Present Delusions," *Louay Fatoohi's Blog*, September 5, 2014, http://www.louayfatoohi.com/2014/09/islam/the-islamic-caliphate-between-past-myths-and-present-delusions/.

20. Richard Bulliet, "It's Good to Be the Caliph," *Politico Magazine*, July 7, 2014, http://www.politico.com/magazine/story/2014/07/its-good-to-be-the-caliph-108630.

21. Nick Danforth, "The Myth of the Caliphate," *Foreign Affairs*, November 19, 2014, https://www.foreignaffairs.com/articles/middle-east/2014-11-19/myth-caliphate.

22. Ibid.

23. Edwards, "The Mythology of Suffering and Redemption."

24. Khaled Diab, "The Caliphate Fantasy," *New York Times*, July 2, 2014, http://www.nytimes.com/2014/07/03/opinion/the-caliphate-fantasy.html?_r=0.

25. "ISIS and Myths of History: Did the Caliphate Solve Poverty?" Quilliam Foundation, April 21, 2015, http://www.quilliamfoundation.org/blog/isis-and-myths-of-history-did-the-caliphate-solve-poverty/.

26. Massimo Calabresi, "Abu Bakr al-Baghdadi: The Head of ISIS Exports Extreme Violence and Radical Beliefs Around the Globe," *Time*, December 21, 2015, 100–103.
27. Aryn Baker, "The Nightmare Returns," *Time*, January 20, 2014, 30–36.
28. Theresa Ford, "How Daesh Uses Language in the Domain of Religion," *Military Review* 96, no. 2 (March-April 2016): 19.
29. Al-Baghdadi does not make many public pronouncements. In fact, he has only appeared in public once, when he gave a public sermon in Mosul, Iraq, on July 1, 2014. During that appearance, al-Baghdadi wore all black to evoke memories of caliphs of the past who had ruled from Iraq. Despite the lack of his public speeches, I was able to locate, including his July 1, 2014, sermon, several addresses in which he covers a number of issues for Muslims.
30. *Ummah* means "one Islamic community."
31. Abu Bakr al-Baghdadi, "Islamic State Leader Abu-Bakr al-Baghdadi Encourages Emigration, Worldwide Action," *Insite Blog on Terrorism and Extremism*, July 1, 2014, https://news.siteintelgroup.com/Jihadist-News/islamic-state-leader-abu-bakr-al-baghdadi-encourages-emigration-worldwide-action.html.
32. Ibid.
33. Edwards, "The Mythology of Suffering and Redemption."
34. Abu Bakr al-Baghdadi, "Islamic State leader Al-Baghdadi Issues Call to Arms to All Muslims," *Memri Jihad and Terrorism Threat Monitor*, May 14, 2015, http://www.memrijttm.org/in-new-audio-speech-islamic-state-isis-leader-al-baghdadi-issues-call-to-a rms-to-all-muslims.html.
35. Ibid.
36. Ibid.
37. Ibid.
38. Ibid.
39. Abu Bakr al Baghdadi, "Even if the Disbelievers Despites Such," *Insite Blog on Terrorism and Extremism*, November 11, 2014, http://news.siteintelgroup.com/blog/index.php/categories/jihad/entry/310-is-leader-abu-bakr-al-baghdadi-rallies-fighters,-welcomes-new-pledges.
40. Ibid., "Islamic State Leader Encourages Emigration."
41. Ibid.
42. Ibid.
43. Ibid., "Islamic State Leader Issues Call to Arms."
44. Ibid., "Islamic State Leader Encourages Emigration."
45. Ibid., "Islamic State Leader Issues Call to Arms."
46. Rowland and Theye, "The Symbolic DNA of Terrorism."
47. "Alleged Baghdadi Appears in Video as 'Caliph,'" Al-Arabiya News, July 5, 2014, http://english.alarabiya.net/en/News/middle-east/2014/07/05/Video-purportedly-shows-extremist-leader-in-Iraq.html.
48. S. J. Prince, "ISIS Releases News Video Explaining the Structure of the Caliphate," *Heavy*, July 7, 2016, http://heavy.com/news/2016/07/new-isis-islamic-state-daesh-al-furqan-media-amaq-news-pictures-videos-the-structure-of-the-khilafah-full-uncensored-youtube-video-mp4-download/.
49. Kenneth Burke, "The Rhetoric of Hitler's Battle," in Thomas W. Benson (ed.) *Landmark Essays on Rhetorical Criticism* (Davis, CA: Hermagoras Press, 1989), 49.
50. Perry and Long, "Why Would Anyone Sell Paradise," 1–17.

51. Jon Levine, "If You Hear President Obama and John Kerry Call ISIS 'Daesh' Here's Why," *News.Mic*, November 15, 2015, https://mic.com/articles/128599/if-you-hear-president-obama-and-john-kerry-call-isis-daesh-here-s-why#.gQSVWItJD.

52. Zeba Khan, "Words Matter in 'ISIS' War, so Use 'Daesh,'" *Boston Globe*, October 9, 2014, https://www.bostonglobe.com/opinion/2014/10/09/words-matter-isis-war-use-daesh/V85GYEuasEEJgrUunodMUP/story.html.

53. Ford, "How Daesh Uses Language in the Domain of Religion," 24.

54. For a further discussion, see Ford, ibid.; Long and Wilner, "Delegitimizing Al-Qaeda."

55. "Countering Daesh (ISIS) Recruitment Propaganda Through Mobilization of Muslim Leaders and Media," *Carter Center*, https://www.cartercenter.org/peace/conflict_resolution/countering-isis.html.

56. Brian R. Moore and Sim Vireak, "Get Ready to Fight ISIS's 'Virtual Caliphate,'" *National Interest*, June 27, 2016, http://nationalinterest.org/feature/get-ready-fight-isiss-virtual-caliphate-167462016.

57. Ford, "How Daesh Uses Language in the Domain of Religion," 24.

58. Roy, "The Construction and Scapegoating of Muslims," 330.

Bibliography

Abizadeh, Arash. "Historical Truth, National Myths and Liberal Democracy: On the Coherence of Liberal Nationalism." *Journal of Political Philosophy* 12 (2004): 291–313. https://doi.org/10.1111/j.1467-9760.2004.00201.x.

Adak, Hiram. "National Myths and Self-Narrations: Mustafa Kemal's *Nutuk* and Halide Edib's *Memoirs* and *The Turkish Ordeal*." *South Atlantic Quarterly* 12 (2003): 509–527.

Al-Arabiya News. "Alleged Baghdadi Appears in Video as 'Caliph.'" July 5, 2014. http://english.alarabiya.net/en/News/middle-east/2014/07/05/Video-purportedly-shows-extremist-leader-in-Iraq.html.

al-Baghdadi, Abu Bakr. "Even If the Disbelievers Despise Us." *Insite Blog on Terrorism and Extremism*, November 11, 2014. http://news.siteintelgroup.com/blog/index.php/categories/jihad/entry/310-is-leader-abu-bakr-al-baghdadi-rallies-fighters,-welcomes-new-pledges.

al-Baghdadi, Abu Bakr. "Islamic State Leader Abu-Bakr al-Baghdadi Encourages Emigration, Worldwide Action." *Insite Blog on Terrorism and Extremism*, July 1, 2014. https://news.siteintelgroup.com/Jihadist-News/islamic-state-leader-abu-bakr-al-baghdadi-encourages-emigration-worldwide-action.html.

al-Baghdadi, Abu Bakr. "Islamic State Leader al-Baghdadi Issues Call to Arms to All Muslims." *MEMRI Jihad and Terrorism Threat Monitor*, May 14, 2015. http://www.memrijttm.org/in-new-audio-speech-islamic-state-isis-leader-al-baghdadi-issues-call-to-a rms-to-all-muslims.html.

Baker, Aryn. "The Nightmare Returns." *Time*, January 20, 2014, 30–36.

Bostdorff, Denise M. "George W. Bush's September 11th Rhetoric of Covenant Renewal: Upholding the Faith of the Greatest Generation." *Quarterly Journal of Speech* 89 (2003): 293–319.

Bulliet, Richard. "It's Good to Be the Caliph." *Politico Magazine*, July 7, 2014. http://www.politico.com/magazine/story/2014/07/its-good-to-be-the-caliph-108630.

Burke, Kenneth. "The Rhetoric of Hitler's Battle." In *Landmark Essays on Rhetorical Criticism*, edited by Thomas W. Benson, 33–50. Davis, CA: Hermagoras Press, 1989.

Calabresi, Massimo. "Abu Bakr al-Baghdadi: The Head of ISIS Exports Extreme Violence and Radical Beliefs Around the Globe." *Time*, December 21, 2015, 100–103.

Carter Center. "Countering Daesh (ISIS) Recruitment Propaganda through Mobilization of Muslim Leaders and Media." May 2017. https://www.cartercenter.org/peace/conflict_resolution/countering-isis.html.

Cauthen, Bruce. "The Myth of Divine Election and Afrikaner Ethnogenesis." In *Myths and Nationhood*, edited by Geoffrey Hosking and George Schopflin, 107–131. New York: Routledge, 1997.

Danforth, Nick. "The Myth of the Caliphate." *Foreign Affairs*, November 19, 2014. https://www.foreignaffairs.com/articles/middle-east/2014-11-19/myth-caliphate.

Diab, Khaled. "The Caliphate Fantasy." *New York Times*, July 2, 2014. http://www.nytimes.com/2014/07/03/opinion/the-caliphate-fantasy.html?_r=0.

Dorsey, Leroy G. "The Frontier Myth in Presidential Rhetoric: Theodore Roosevelt's Campaign for Conservation." *Western Journal of Communication* 59 (1995): 1–19.

Dorsey, Leroy G., and Rachel L. Harlow. "'We Want Americans Pure and Simple': Theodore Roosevelt and the Myth of Americanism." *Rhetoric & Public Affairs* 6 (2003): 55–79.

Edwards, Jason A. "The Demonic Redeemer Figure in Political Myth: A Case Study of Vladimir Zhirinovsky." *Journal of the Wisconsin Communication Association* 32 (2000): 17–32.

Edwards, Jason. A. "The Mythology of Suffering and Redemption in Al-Qaeda's Discourse." In *Myth, Ideology, and Culture*, edited by John Perlich and David Whitt, 83–101. Jefferson, NC: McFarland, 2014.

Fatoohi, Louay. "The Islamic Caliphate Between Past Myths and Present Delusions." September 5, 2014. http://www.louayfatoohi.com/2014/09/islam/the-islamic-caliphate-between-past-myths-and-present-delusions/.

Ford, Theresa. "How Daesh Uses Language in the Domain of Religion." *Military Review* 96 (2016): 16–27.

Fulmer, Hal W. "Mythic Imagery and Irish Nationalism: Henry Grattan Against Union, 1800." *Western Journal of Speech Communication* 50 (1986): 144–157.

Gustainis, J. Justin. "John F. Kennedy and the Green Berets: The Rhetorical Use of the Hero Myth." *Communication* Studies 40 (1989): 1–13.

"ISIS and Myths of History: Did the Caliphate Solve Poverty?" Quilliam Foundation, April 21, 2015. http://www.quilliamfoundation.org/blog/isis-and-myths-of-history-did-the-caliphate-solve-poverty/.

Kelley-Romano, Stephanie. "Myth-Making in Alien Abduction Narratives." *Communication Quarterly* 83 (2006): 383–406.

Khan, Zeba. "Words Matter in 'ISIS' War, So Use 'Daesh.'" *Boston Globe*, October 9, 2014. https://www.bostonglobe.com/opinion/2014/10/09/words-matter-isis-war-usedaesh/V85GYEuasEEJgrUunodMUP/story.html.

Levine, Jon. "If You Hear President Obama and John Kerry Call ISIS 'Daesh' Here's Why." *News.Mic*, November 15, 2015. https://mic.com/articles/128599/if-you-hear-president-obama-and-john-kerry-call-isis-daesh-here-s-why#.gQSVWItJD.

Long, Jerry Mark, and Alex Wilner. "Delegitimizing al-Qaida: Defeating an Army 'Whose Men Love Death.'" *International Security* 39 (2014): 126–164. https://doi.org/10.1162/ISEC_a_00167.

Moore, Brian R., and Sim Vireak. "Get Ready to Fight ISIS's 'Virtual Caliphate.'" *National Interest*, June 27, 2016. http://nationalinterest.org/feature/get-ready-fight-isiss-virtual-caliphate-167462016.
Moore, Mark P. "Rhetorical Criticism of Political Myth: From Goldwater Legend to Reagan Mystique." *Communication Studies* 41 (1991): 295–308.
Nimmo, Dan, and James E. Combs. *Subliminal Politics: Myths and Mythmakers in America*. Englewood Cliffs, NJ: Prentice Hall, 1980.
Noon, David Hoagland. "Operation Enduring Analogy: World War II, the War on Terror, and the Uses of Collective Memory." *Rhetoric & Public Affairs* 7 (2004): 339–365.
Perry, Samuel, and Jerry Mark Long. "'Why Would Anyone Sell Paradise?' The Islamic State in Iraq and the Making of a Martyr." *Southern Journal of Communication* 81 (2016): 1–17. https://doi.org/10.1080/1041794X.2015.1083047.
Prince, S. J. "ISIS Releases News Video Explaining the Structure of the Caliphate." *Heavy*, July 7, 2016. http://heavy.com/news/2016/07/new-isis-islamic-state-daesh-al-furqan-media-amaq-news-pictures-videos-the-structure-of-the-khilafah-full-uncensored-youtube-video-mp4-download/.
Ritter, Kurt W. "The Myth-Making Functions of the American Revolution: Frances Hopkinson as a Case Study." *Today's Speech* 23 (1975): 25–30.
Rowland, Robert, and Kirsten Theye. "The Symbolic DNA of Terrorism." *Communication Monographs* 75 (2008): 52–85.
Roy, Abhik. "The Construction and Scapegoating of Muslims as 'Other' in Hindu Nationalist Rhetoric." *Southern Communication Journal* 69 (2004): 320–332.
Roy, Abhik, and Robert Rowland. "The Rhetoric of Hindu Nationalism: A Narrative of Mythic Redefinition." *Western Journal of Communication* 67 (2003): 225–248.
Rushing, Janice Hocker, and Thomas Frentz. "The Mythic Perspective." In *The Art of Rhetorical Criticism*, edited by Jim A. Kuypers, 241–265. New York: Allyn & Bacon, 2005.
Schopflin, George P. "The Functions and Taxonomy of Myths." In *Myths and Nationhood*, edited by Geoffrey Hosking and George Schopflin, 19–35. New York: Routledge, 1997.
Smith, Anthony. "The Myth of the Golden Age and National Renewal." In *Myths and Nationhood*, edited by Geoffrey Hosking and George Schopflin, 36–59. New York: Routledge, 1997.
Wood, Graeme. "What ISIS Really Wants." *The Atlantic*, March 2015. http://www.theatlantic.com/magazine/archive/2015/03/what-isis-really-wants/384980/.

JASON A. EDWARDS is a Professor of Communication Studies at Bridgewater State University and a Research Fellow with BSU's Center for Democratic Governance and Leadership. He is the author of *Navigating the Post-Cold War World: President Clinton's Foreign Policy Rhetoric*, and coeditor of *The Rhetoric of American Exceptionalism: Critical Essays*, and *The Rhetoric of Civil Religion: Symbols, Sinners, and Saints.*

2 Time, Space, and Communication

A Preliminary Comparison of Islamic State to the Mongol Hordes and the Khmer Rouge

Marwan M. Kraidy
John Vilanova

Time and space, in Immanuel Kant's famous reckoning in *Critique of Pure Reason*, are "a priori intuitions"; *a priori* in the sense that they shape our perception prior to experience, and *intuitions* from the perspective that time and space conjure a fundamental relation between humans and objects in the world.[1] Time and space were also basic dimensions undergirding Harold Innis's theory of empire and communication and the role of media in perpetuating and challenging epistemologies throughout human history. Focusing media technology's role in Western civilization, Innis argues that "Large-scale political organizations such as empires must be considered from the standpoint of two dimensions, those of space and time, and persist by overcoming the bias of media which overemphasize either dimension."[2] In Innis's framing, time-emphasizing media are the hefty relics—the clay and stone of Angkor Wat. Space-emphasizing media are more portable—paper and perhaps the *paiza*, the engraved metal tablet carried by riders along the Mongolian Yam.

This chapter builds on the idea that Islamic State's way of war and life rests on a strategic articulation of time and space.[3] It is a preliminary exploration of how time and space, as fundamental analytical categories, can help us understand Islamic State in a comparative perspective. Against claims that the Islamic State is an unprecedented phenomenon, our analysis uses two case studies, the Mongol hordes and the Khmer Rouge, to give Islamic State a historical comparative grounding. Though these selections are to some extent arbitrary, parallels among the three groups struck us as intuitive and theoretically generative. So, rather than an ironclad comparison with narrow parameters that would ferret out a list of similarities, this chapter attempts to answer a more general question: what can we learn about Islamic State from scholarly literature on the Mongol hordes and the Khmer Rouge? In grappling with that question, we are particularly interested in the role of communication in the processes of self-definition and self-organization. Moving past the obsession with Islamic State's prowess with digital media, we seek to understand how predigital communication may have shaped warrior formations of the past.

As Kant, Innis, and many others have shown, time and space are indeed fundamental dimensions of our existence. Though philosophical perspectives on time and space are legion and often in disagreement with each other, our approach can be broadly characterized as phenomenological. Rather than speaking of time and space as objective and measurable dimensions, we consider these categories as broadly subjective and thus refer to them in terms of *temporality* and *spatiality*, which enable our preliminary analysis to include not only the human lived experience of temporal and spatial dimensions but also the ideological, rhetorical, or representational manipulations of time and space in which groups like Islamic State, the Mongol hordes, and the Khmer Rouge, among others, have engaged. For purposes of analytical clarity and textual concision, we have coupled Islamic State with the Mongol hordes for our analysis of spatiality and with the Khmer Rouge for our analysis of temporality.

June 2014 was a crucial month for the rise of Islamic State. As eight hundred militant fighters waving black flags bearing a rough approximation of the Prophet's seal took Mosul, Iraq's second-largest city, Islamic State's cyberwarriors deployed a Twitter app called The Dawn of Glad Tidings to spam tens of thousands of tweets, robotically amplifying the group's online presence to forty thousand Twitter accounts and spreading disturbing imagery across global networks.[4] On June 29, 2014, Abu Muhammad al-'Adnani, the group's spokesman, officially announced the return of the caliphate, the ascension of Abu Bakr al-Baghdadi as caliph, and the declaration of the Islamic State as a polity with global and exclusive ambition. "The legality of all emirates, groups, states and organisations becomes null by the expansion of the caliph's authority and the arrival of its troops to their areas," the speech declared, as it spread across networks in various languages.[5] Together, these actions—occupying Mosul, announcing the caliphate, declaring the Islamic State, mobilizing attention online—vaulted Islamic State onto the global stage.[6] They also suggest that Islamic State, a hybrid of guerilla group, terrorist actor, and institution builder, has a peculiar understanding of space and time, one that is both external to and overlaps with the prevailing world order of nation-state and the spatio-temporal organization of that global order.

To accomplish this curiosity-driven contextualization and conceptualization of Islamic State, this chapter pairs Islamic State with the Mongol hordes of the thirteenth century and the revolutionary Khmer Rouge regime, which seized power in Cambodia in 1975, as historical analytical equivalents. This does not mean that the three groups are *similar*, only that they present heuristic *overlaps* and *connections*, much like Wittgenstein's metaphor of family resemblances, where members of an extended family share resembling traits in unpredictable and asymmetrical configurations.[7] The Mongols, who operated in a pre-Westphalian context, model a decentralized and modular statecraft that echoes the construction and spatial representation and articulation of the Islamic State. The Khmer Rouge, a more contemporary case, implemented an orthodox, brutal, and ostensibly anti-Western program, which operationalized and deployed a notion of time. This use of time enables a deeper comparative understanding of Islamic State's own temporality, which disorients and reroutes historical time in the service of apocalyptic aims.

This chapter, then, is not intended to be prescriptive or definitive, and we should emphasize that neither the Mongol hordes nor the Khmer Rouge is intended to be a strict one-to-one comparison to Islamic State. Rather, we seek to set otherwise ontologically distinct, geographically scattered, and historically distant entities in conversation with one another, seeking the partial overlaps, fortuitous affinities, and "family resemblances" that might help us identify connections across time and space and enable a conceptually grounded, historically informed understanding of Islamic State. By executing a comparative-historical analysis grounded in the metatheoretical axis of spatiality-temporality, we hope to chip away at the sensationalism, presentism, and exceptionalism that characterizes public discourse about Islamic State.

Spatial and Strategic Flexibility: Territories and Statecraft

The Great Mongol Khans built a networked empire the purposefulness, flexibility, and adaptability of which echoes Islamic State's state-building and media-making structures. In the early thirteenth century, Chinggis Khan successfully united the warring factions of the various clans and peoples who fell under the loose heading of "Mongols." His reign, formalized in 1206, was said to have augured Pax Mongolica, a cultural and political settling of the region that went along with the consolidation of the largest territory ever controlled by a single group to that point, stretching from the Black Sea to the China Sea. Scholar Eric Voegelin once termed the Mongols an *imperium mundi in statu nascendi*, or an "Empire in the Making" as they spread throughout the continent, gaining vast swaths of territory in their hundred-year heyday.[8] The empire of the thirteenth-century Khans can be considered an "Empire in the *Re*making," a configuration of nomadic warriors moving back and forth across a vast swath of territory, with a modular organization notable as much for the tactical success it yielded on the battlefield as for its logistical fluidity.

As the Golden Horde roamed the Asian continent, conquering new lands, acquiring additional resources, and incorporating "foreign" peoples, the idea of what *Mongol* meant was constantly expanding. In fact, the term *Mongol* itself might be more elastic than presentist understandings of world history suggest: "The 'Mongols,' owing to the elasticity, comprehensiveness, and linguistic and ethnic unconcern of tribalism, were not only Mongolians but Turks and Tunguses and Tibetans. To some extent they were even Georgians, Russians, and Chinese, to name only a few of the non-nomad peoples who participated."[9] So the very term by which the group is named is, to some extent, a misnomer that is buttressed by a retroactive understanding of the empire as a nation-state. In reality, there was in principle no Mongol civilian status outside of one's role within the warmaking apparatus. We might consider individual Mongol life along the same lines that Gilles Deleuze and Félix Guattari describe Go pieces, "elements of a nonsubjectified machine assemblage with no intrinsic properties, only situational ones."[10]

The incorportation of war into everyday life meant that the Mongols' innovative and flexible method of warfare also played out in their approach to governance. As Chinggis and his progeny worked to maintain their growing empire, a diversity of new subjects necessitated adaptability; a singular state and culture would be impossible to maintain as the empire grew in size and cultural, ethnic, and religious diversity. What emerged was a calculus by the Mongols that first appears to be surprising but upon a second look is strategic—consciously making and remaking their empire to both meet the needs of governance and to take from its newly conquered subjects statecraft strategies and practices, in the process building ethnically and linguistically diverse human resources to manage the empire. The Mongols were fierce in battle, but after victory, their new subjects, however captive, often had more autonomy than is assumed, a fact reflected in recent popular representations such as Netflix's *Marco Polo*. *The Encyclopedia of Islam*, drawing on *The Secret History of the Mongols*, the only extant Mongolian work from the time of the Great Khans, outlines the governance strategy.

> The Mongols were prepared to adopt almost any institutional arrangements and to employ any potential servant, as long as this appeared likely to facilitate the maintenance of effective government. This effectiveness was measured chiefly by the revenue receipts. There is little that is identifiably "Mongol" in the governmental institutions of the Mongols' empire, except the way in which they made so extraordinary disparate an assemblage work. The principal constraint was always the consideration that nothing should be done that which might endanger Mongol military supremacy, on which the last analysis the perpetuation of Mongol rule depended.[11]

The Mongols' written alphabet came from the Uyghur alphabet; previously the language was singularly oral. Mongols took certain conceptions, vocabulary, and institutions like the Daruyaci, an all-purpose government official, from the Khitan.[12] It has been suggested that the Mongols installed the Qara-Khitai administrative structure almost wholesale after taking them over in 1218.[13] Even the religious practice of the Mongols, Tenggerism, might be said to represent a strategic flexibility. Tenggerism was a folk religion derived from Mongolian and Turkic nomads that suggested a godlike supreme masculine power in the universe. This is, of course, not a new form, but the timing mattered: Tenggerism was the foundation for divine origin of Khanship and used as a strategic rhetoric, even employed during epistolary wartime back-and-forths with the pope.[14] From this we can conclude that much of Mongol governance structures, cultural practices, and spiritual beliefs emerged in the service of warmaking.

Islamic State's global "workforce" is also a showcase for United Colors of Jihad; your nationality of birth does not matter, as long as you make a life-and-death commitment to the caliphate. The group's propaganda emphasizes this "equality within diversity" aspect, as in the video of French jihadists sitting around a bonfire in which they threw their French passports and declared fealty to Islamic State. Just like the Mongol hordes can be understood as an "Empire in the Making," so can Islamic State be grasped as a caliphate "in-formation," a process that in the case of Islamic State is widely disseminated through digital networks.[15] In spite of its doctrinal rigidity and its adoption of extreme operationalization of religious precepts, Islamic State has shown considerable flexibility.

Ironically, the group itself has warned against *bid'ah*, which in Islamic discourse translates to "innovation" and is frowned upon because it is seen as an attempt to innovate on God's work, while "innovating" in a variety of realms, going as far as justifying the videographed February 2015 Jordanian air force pilot immolation or the reestablishment of slavery, through Scripture.[16] Again, the goal here is not to argue whether we might designate Islamic State policy and action as *bida'* (plural), but instead to illuminate that—by whatever name it goes—this work is part of the caliphate's social, political, and warmaking strategies, which betray an adeptness at merging rigid dogmatism with creative innovation.[17]

But for a group for whom extreme religious observance is seemingly so important, why would they even give the appearance of straying? Because of geopolitical convenience, even necessity. "Islamic State's decision-making is opportunistic, adaptive, and dependent upon its leaderships' shifting propensity to implement its ideology," one analyst, Craig Noyes, writes, suggesting why a group that purports itself to be so rigid is actually more adaptable than it tries to appear. "It is only when Islamic State has adequate governing strength, or a decision cannot provide short-term organizational benefit, or IS's ideological legitimacy and grand strategy are at stake that it pivots to overtly ideological decision-making."[18] The ongoing difficulty of persisting requires adaptability at the expense of sticking to principle. This manifests itself in many ways; Islamic State has collaborated with non-Islamist groups for tactical maneuvers and propaganda purposes, publishing a joint statement with the Free Syrian Army and, Noyes notes, organizing its foreign fighters by country of origin despite its denouncement of the Westphalian nation-state system.[19] As a war machine, Islamic State is destructive but also *creative*—it is an entity that is ontologically creative and shape-shifting.[20]

Islamic State looks to draw its borders by other means. The Mongols too, of course, had no such referent for what an empire or "state" was in the way that we understand it today, nor did they have the vast arsenal of media with a planetary reach deployed by Islamic State. Given their premodern means of drawing national borders, one thing that gave the Mongol Empire its shape was the Yam, a communication and transport system of roads that stretched throughout the continent, uniting a disparate and diverse people. Set up in 1234 by Tolui, Chinggis's youngest son, the Yam combined road-building for the movement of people and culture with a courier service for the movement of information and state administration—the Mongol Empire flowed along the Yam. Riders stationed at waypoints every nine to twelve miles were at the ready, facilitating a relay system that could allow an important message to travel up to 480 miles in a single day.[21] While some have pointed out that it too is possibly another borrowed concept, the Yam is notable for its role in connecting the ends of the Mongol Empire, serving as the unifying connector between disparate cultural and spatial territory.[22] This is similar to Deleuze and Guattari's suggestion that "the nomad only goes from point to point as a consequence and as a factual necessity: in principle, points for him are relays along a trajectory."[23] Each waystation was part of the empire, to be sure, but the beginning and endpoints were the more significant nodes in a networked empire.

The internet might be called the Islamic State's Yam—a space of flow where the aims and subjective reality of self-proclaimed statehood are realized not at its interstices but at its networked nodes. Due in large part to its large-scale media operations, Islamic State is perhaps most tactically realized online, and its warmaking is served by its decentralized web presence and media apparatus. "Known as an 'M-form' hierarchy, the emirs at the *wilayat* (regional) level had significant autonomy to execute policy and guidance developed at the central level, while the central level controlled shared resources (such as foreign fighters) and excess revenue collected from its subordinate units," Craig Whiteside writes in an International Centre for Counter-Terrorism history of the Islamic State's media enterprise.[24] This resonates with the Mongol organization, in which the mobile camps that headquartered the great khans left the more remote new citizens some degree of autonomy. Additionally, the regional offices of the media operation have been shown to focus on specific tasks to which they are most suited.[25]

Islamic State has a fluid relation to territoriality, using a constantly shifting combination of military conquest of actual space with strategic, often counterfactual representation of its virtual dominion of spaces that it may or may not actually control. Its recurrent attacks on the Sykes-Picot colonial agreement that shaped current national borders in the Middle East and its deployment of counterfactual maps of world domination in which current countries, from North America to South Asia, are depicted as provinces of a planetary Islamic State fall within that strategy.[26] Mapping the borders of the Islamic State at any time has not been straightforward, so it is evident to conclude that Islamic State does not control all of its territory equally and that the caliphate "is not so much a coherent territorial entity like Jordan or Belgium as a series of spreading cracks in existing states."[27] The thing that unites the disparate pieces is a set network of roads that connects various populated areas to infrastructure such as military bases and oil resources. But further, the network of roads is the pathway along which Islamic State's mobile dominion—embodied by its convoys of troops riding in the flatbeds of their Toyota trucks—moves through the region.

If we consider the estimated forty-six thousand Islamic State supporter Twitter accounts studied by J. M. Berger and Jonathan Morgan's ISIS Twitter Census, we find people who want to occupy its digital territory.[28] While, of course, the majority (55 percent) of the accounts were found in Syria, Iraq, and Saudi Arabia, the other 45 percent are fodder for further analysis. Just as the remote territories of the Mongol Empire received communications and marching orders via the Yam, the networking capabilities of social media allow Islamic State's operations to stretch far beyond the boundaries of the caliphate. Twitter users living outside of the geographic boundaries of the caliphate have deployed a variety of strategies to take up more digital space than their limited numbers would suggest, including hashtagging and, more significantly, tweet-storming, or rapid-fire bursts of tweets far beyond the number generated by the typical user. Prolific users are even celebrated in Islamic State social media strategy documents as the *mujtahidun* (industrious ones).[29] The fact that these users are more likely to report their location than the average user suggests that the geotagging does the same exaggeration-of-space work as the Mongols, whose numbers of dead were frequently exaggerated beyond the level of possibility.[30] In both cases, it allows the group to claim a greater significance and danger. In the case of Islamic State specifically, wherever a supporter is tweeting, Islamic State claims digital spatial territory. Further, Berger and Morgan find an overrepresentation of the English language in Islamic State tweets.[31] This again suggests a kind of fungibility for strategic purposes—like the Mongols, Islamic State takes up a global lingua franca that would reach the largest possible audience, grow their legitimacy, and build their empire, in this case via potential recruitment and spectacular fearmongering.

Whiteside quotes systems scientist Peter Senge to argue that the Islamic State might be called a "learning organization," a "group of people that continually seek out self-improvement and are responsive to the demand signal from the environment."[32] In the disruptive language of today, Whiteside emphasizes the trial-and-error nature of many of its strategies. He suggests that the changes throughout the history of the media program are "innovative" but does not mention *bid'ah*. It might best serve our purposes to reframe this as well. Rather than thinking of it as a tactical reorganization by choice, consider the possibility that the very nature of Islamic State and the space in which it operates is fluid and amorphous. Islamic State's space of statehood and governance is not dictated by the norms by which statehood is understood in the post–World War II global state system. Instead, Islamic State's relationship to space troubles the idea of what a "state" looks and acts like. In the following sections, we explore how the Khmer Rouge's perspective on time enables us to better understand Islamic State's temporal worldview.

Troubling Temporality: Year Zero and the Strategic Performance of Time

To reiterate, this chapter grows from a book project that considers the Islamic State as a Deleuzian "war machine," suggesting that its articulation of terror, territoriality, and temporality illustrate the radical potential and exteriority of what a "war machine" is in the era of global communication.[33] The contemporary war machine that we can glimpse in Islamic State is a force that is at once destructive and creative, that articulates multiple temporalities not only in the velocity with which it circulates between spaces,[34] but also in its vast apparatus of audiovisual representations of its actions, which it constructs as a global spectacle.[35] This resonates with Justin Mueller's notion of the *time machine*, which suggests that, rather than simply deterritorializing space, time machines help produce anachronarchy, which disrupts stable temporalities, obstructs time-building efforts, and creates new temporal projections.[36] Specifically, these are understood to upset given chronarchies, or times dictated by the ruling class of the globe. In the case of Islamic State, this tracks along the violent extremist ideology the group purports to enact in resistance to Western state ideological and territorial organization—notions of time and history are disrupted for political-ideological gains. Islamic State—as well as the Khmer Rouge, their conceptual-comparative antecedent discussed in this section—reject notions of Western time for strategic purposes, ultimately to disorient the subjective reality of their enemies and people.

Illustrative of the time machine in action is the Khmer Rouge's declaration of "Year Zero," which came on April 17, 1975, as their rebellion took the Cambodian capital city, Phnom Penh. The despot Pol Pot declared a "Prodigious Great Leap Forward," following the "Great Leap Forward" of Maoist China twenty years prior and setting for the new Democratic Republic of Kampuchea (DRK) guidelines outlined by the doctoral dissertation of his advisor and eventual prime minister, Khieu Samphan. Cities were evacuated, all contact with the outside world was cut off, and an isolationist agrarian economy delinked the Khmer nation from colonial oppression. Year Zero was a quintessential dialectical opposition against time itself; the "us-versus-them" trope, where the masses are taught to fear an unseen and foreign enemy, was furthered in its significance and justified by a "now-versus-then" mentality.

The Khmers' restarting of the clock was done for multiple reasons: (1) to suggest a new-old Khmer independence of epistemology that stemmed from Angka Loeu, the central command, and not the foreign colonizers; (2) to further set up a dichotomy between the new/old state and its interaction with the Western colonial powers; and (3) to create a more straightforward version of the historical past to fit their propagandistic messaging purposes regarding the glorious Khmer past and the broader rejection of Western media and history. "We are building socialism without a model. We do not wish to copy anyone; we shall use the experience gained in the course of the liberation struggle," Pol Pot said in a speech at the time. "There are no schools, faculties, or universities in the traditional sense, although they did exist in our country prior to liberation, because we wish to do away with all vestiges of the past."[37]

This move shrank Cambodian and global history, taking all of the complications and possible discrepancies of the modern condition and replacing them with a proto-Marxian narrative of unrelieved class warfare, slavery, and foreign intervention. The metaphor that undergirded Khmer society was of an army at war; military terminology was even used widely to refer to social activities of peacetime such as campaigns to grow rice or dig irrigation canals.[38] Fear of outsiders was preached from central command, with the implication that the modern understanding of history itself was also part of the colonial condition. But to install their new model and make it stick, the government undertook a radical turn-back-the-clock process where the temporal shift reset national knowledge to a time before the intrusion of French colonizers in the mid-nineteenth century.

This was accomplished by a massive antieducation, antimedia campaign with a backdrop where knowledge of a foreign or minority language constituted grounds for execution. All education ceased after a May 1975 conference; Pol Pot would declare teachers "in the pay of the oppressor class" in 1977.[39] All libraries, bookshops, publishing houses, universities, and high schools were closed. The government then destroyed 90 percent of school buildings, with the university campus being turned into a farm and one high school becoming the infamous Tuol Sleng prison.[40] The spaces were not the only targets of the government's readjustment plan: 75 percent of the nation's teaching force, 96 percent of tertiary students, and 67 percent of all elementary and secondary pupils died. According to University of Phnom Penh, eighty-seven out of the country's one thousand academics survived.[41] Any person whose prerevolution professional or personal existence ran contra to the Year Zero declaration was a target of the government.

Meanwhile, the agrarians who were rhetorically positioned as the ideal citizens were "Old People"; Pol Pot positioned them as the root of the revolution, suggesting that anonymous, leaderless peasant masses fought against French colonialism.[42] No such movement existed, further illustrating how the allegedly historical past was nothing more than a propaganda tool. Meanwhile, Samphan suggested that 80 percent of the urban population was unproductive, and urbanity itself became a target—city-dwellers were stripped of their citizenship and termed "17 April People" or, more significantly for our purposes, "New People."[43] They were given the hardest work and the longest hours on the "front lines" of the killing fields.[44] Fawaz Gerges documents an equivalent process of what he called the increasing "ruralization" of Islamic State over time.[45]

The ongoing praxis of the revolution would write the history of the new Cambodia, the party claimed.[46] An early outside report posited a goal of the Year Zero paradigm: "to psychologically reconstruct individual members of society."[47] With no remaining formal education, the constant threat of outsiders, and the promise of government surveillance, the populace was disoriented; their institutions, cultural references, and sense of history had been replaced wholesale.[48] Contemporaneous writers summed up the repositioning thus: "Angka Loeu [The 'Organization on High'] had resolved to annul the past and obliterate the present so as to fashion a future uncontaminated by the influences of either. . . . This process entails stripping away, through terror and other means, the traditional bases, structures and forces which have shaped and guided an individual's life until he is left as an atomised isolated individual unit: and then rebuilding him according to party doctrine by substituting a series of new values, organisations and ethical norms for the ones taken away."[49]

The only history allowed was the party's version of events, where no holiday more than seventeen years old was celebrated save one important path backward: the glorious history of Angkor Wat, the twelfth-century city on which Khmer nationalist identity and visions of grandeur hung. Angkor is viewed as specifically Khmer heritage, a "symbolic coding of Cambodia as Angkor Vat, Apsara, and god-kings," one scholar writes. "These symbols are used to describe the unique right of the Khmer to their land and to perpetuate the idea that 'only members of the historic community can be true citizens, all others being minorities of second-class status in a homeland not their own.'"[50] British anthropologist Kathleen Gough calls this revanchist nativism and makes the compelling argument that the Pol Pot system—agrarian totalitarianism—is based on an almost literal attempt to return the society to the time of Angkor's prominence, mapping its technologies, land-ownership rules, trade system, social class structure, and the experience of constant warfare.[51] The past was no mere model here—it was an effectively millenarian model that led to the deaths of one-fifth of the country's population.

The Khmers' example might help us understand some of Islamic State's orientation to temporality. After all, by invoking the caliphate, Islamic State attempts to bring back a politico-religious system of governance and sovereignty that has not existed since World War I—the caliphate conjured up through *strategic nostalgia*.[52] But we might similarly consider it as a strategic disorientation process and a political strategy to justify its actions and persuade potential recruits to join the caliphate. There are two ways in which Islamic State employs troubled temporality similarly to Pol Pot's DRK. First, they too employ a set of rhetorical techniques that effectively reorganize time by constructing a faith that purports to be fundamentalist Islam but in reality is constructed not only from various *hadith*, or records of the Prophet Muhammad, from various sources, regions, and time periods,[53] but also from a variety of theological and jihadi tracts. This is strategic and calculating in accordance with their millenarian aims—it twists time to create its own historical narrative in the service of its aims. Secondly, their time-turning antimodernity obscures contradictions to persuade potential recruits of the IS's righteousness and to avoid the appearance of hypocrisy. In both cases, time itself is both the enemy and the foundation of ideological reorganization.

Like the Khmer, Islamic State anchors its anti-Western critique in a colonial frame—the Sykes-Picot Agreement (addressed by William Lafi Youmans in this volume).[54] But for more than just political and decolonial purposes, calling for an end to Sykes-Picot also turns back the clock to a time before foreign intervention in the Middle East. And while there is no declaration as stark as "Year Zero" here, the prophesied return of the caliphate tracks similarly—the June 2014 declaration of the restoration of the caliphate reestablished a connection that went as far back as at least 1924, when the last caliphal position was abolished. But the connection runs far deeper, framing Abu Bakr al-Baghdadi as the successor to a caliphal line.

Additionally, a 2015 dispatch from the *Diwan al-Buhuth wa al-Iftaa'*, or the Research and Fatwa Issuing Department, suggests an assault on Western measured time through the rejection of the Gregorian (*miladi*) calendar, in favor of the Islamic lunar calendar, *hijri* dating, that begins counting time when the Prophet Muhammad and his followers moved from Mecca to Madina and founded the first Muslim community. "In the contemporary era the Crusaders have succeeded in appointing idolatrous tyrants loyal to them to whom they have entrusted the implementation of their plans, including making the Muslims follow these disbelievers. Among such matters is the replacement of the Hijri dating with the Miladi dating," the report reads.[55] It also references the writing of Ibn Taymiyyah, the historian and theologian who lived during the thirteenth and fourteenth centuries, who himself had to flee from the Mongol hordes as they descended on his village in what is now Turkey.[56] Ibn Taymiyyah is cited frequently in the Islamic State magazine, *Dabiq*, as justification for policies such as the enslavement of apostate women.[57] His fatwa against the Mongols is cited to justify the killing of Muslims whose faith is not perfectly in line with the Islamic State's specific version of Islam in another issue.[58] The words of speakers from seven hundred years ago are brought to life in the Islamic State's version of religious reality.

That faith is purported to be a global Jihadi-Salafist movement; in a 2007 audio address, then-leader Abu 'Umar al-Baghdadi appealed "to all Sunnis, and to the young men of Jihadi-Salafism [*al-Salafiyya al-Jihadiyya*] in particular, across the entire world."[59] Salafism is a reading of the Scripture that is doctrinally rigorous and preoccupied with purifying the Muslim faith, restoring it to what it was in the days of the Prophet and his companion, stripping it of social, political, and cultural "corruption." Salafis believe to be the singular sect of the faith that is true; all others are guilty of idolatry or insufficient affirmation of God's oneness. It is from Salafism that Islamic State's particular brand of jihad, which is, in the words of one scholar, "absolutely uncompromising on doctrinal matters, prioritizing the promotion of an unforgiving strain of Salafi thought," is drawn.[60] The propagandizing of this extremism is all-encompassing: it extends to written communiqués, social media, billboards, license plates, stationery, and coins, all of which are arrived at by following what they call a "Prophetic Methodology."[61] Salafism brings with it a kind of literalism that is used as anti-Islamic evidence by detractors, but again, what is more significant here is that Salafism provides a doctrinal framework that Islamic State manipulates to turn back the clock. It is how the group creates the discursive and religious space from which it launches attacks on its enemies. Public discourse about Islamic State makes much of Salafism in the Islamic State organization. Consider this example:

> ISIS leaders insist that they will not—cannot—waver from governing precepts that were embedded in Islam by the Prophet Muhammad and his earliest followers. They quote from and rely upon the specific traditions and texts of early Islam. For example, Sheik Abu Muhammad al-Adnani, the Islamic State's chief spokesman, called on Muslims in various western nations to find the infidel and "smash his head with a rock," poison him, run him over with a car, or "destroy his crops." This is language directly from The Prophet's orders of how Muslims in the lands of kuffar, or infidels, are to deal with infidels in an unmerciful manner.[62]

Wood explains that *moderns* is a pejorative term used by the Islamic State to criticize other jihadi groups led by modern secular people with modern political connections. Meanwhile, on the individual level, it is important to the group to maintain the appearance of devout purity in their media creations—there is no joking and no portrayal of things not in alignment with Islamic laws.[63] The way it really resolves any contradictions is that it is every-*when*—operating outside of the linear telos of the "modern" West and putting various contexts to use in the service of its work. The aforementioned article was controversial, not least because it poured fuel on the fire of the often-ideologized debate on whether Islamic State is "Islamic" or not and the essentialist arguments about Islam advanced by some pundits. This discussion is beyond the scope of this chapter. For our purposes, suffice it to say that Islamic State portrays itself through its media products as a devout and violent organization. Like any political, religious, or militant organization, it bends religious doctrine to its more earthly goals. This means manipulating temporal frames to conjure pretend direct doctrinal, social, and political connections to the times of the Prophet and his followers.

In one sense, then, Islamic State operates—or, more accurately *claims* to operate—outside of the linear telos of the "modern" West. This is a major contention that undermines the group's claim to statehood, for it makes it clear that such an entity has no place in the global system of nation-states. But the claim that Islamic State is illegitimate can also be a false victory that ultimately falls into the trap Edward Said warned against when he suggested that "discussions of the Orient or of the Arabs and Islam are fundamentally premised upon a fiction."[64] That fiction he wrote about was an orientalizing one, where Islam was, is, and always has been understood by the West in a framework that renders it premodern and puts it to service as a mediated subject made to be understood by and for a Western gaze. Islamic State emerged in the peculiar context of post-Baathist, post-US-UK invasion, post-UN-sanctions Iraq, and the time-shifting of the group is a product of its radical alterity to the groups mentioned above, as much as it is a geopolitical strategy of dominion.

Conclusion

This chapter offered a preliminary comparative analysis of Islamic State, the Mongol hordes, and the Khmer Rouge. To do so, we relied on the master categories of time and space, understood in terms of temporality and spatiality. We hope that by grounding the Islamic State in a historically deep and geographically wide context of warrior groups that have perpetrated atrocities, whether in the name of ideology or in the name of empire building, or combinations thereof, that we can contribute to a wider understanding of the organization. Our analysis was, from the very beginning, meant to be exploratory, identifying parallels and overlaps among these three groups and making references to theory along the way, rather than a tightly structured comparative analysis. To be clear, nowhere do we make the argument that Islamic State, the Mongol hordes, and the Khmer Rouge are ontologically similar. Rather, we hope to have pinpointed echoes and equivalences among the three formations.

Taken in concert, this triad of case studies shows effective challenges to conventions of time- and space-based media organizations. Empires (Western and otherwise) are vulnerable to time- and space-based attacks that remediate temporal and spatial contexts. The Mongols were everywhere and everything at once thanks to their fluid system of governance and their networked communication pathways; this must be considered in any wholesale appreciation of their dominance of the continent, which was about more than battle skills. The Khmer were nowhere and never, rewriting their own history, time, and relationship to inside/outside space for the purpose of building a civilization from the ground up; rejection of media was key to maintenance of this new temporal and spatial order. Thanks to its media-making, Islamic State holds the potential to be anywhere a radicalizing actor takes up its cause and any-when, based on the time that suits it.

Thus, the reason why it has been so difficult to pin down what the Islamic State *is* in contemporary scholarship is because *what* it *is* is so troubled by *when* and *where* it is. Too few studies of the Islamic State extricate it from an orientalizing dialectical relationality to the modern nation-state system, which understands space and politics in a particular temporal context that privileges certain epistemological organizations. These presumptions reveal the flaws inherent in how the Islamic State is conceived. We hope that our comparative analysis, however preliminary, can help create space against those presumptions of exceptionalism and essentialism, paving the way for more robust, more context-sensitive, and ultimately more illuminating understandings of Islamic State.

Notes

1. Immanuel Kant, *The Critique of Pure Reason*, trans. P. Guyer and A. W. Wood (Cambridge, UK: Cambridge University Press, 1999)
2. Harold Innes, *Empire and Communications* (Oxford, UK: Clarendon Press, 1950).
3. Marwan M. Kraidy, "Terror, Territoriality, Temporality: Hypermedia Events in the Age of Islamic State," *Television & New Media* 18, no. 6 (2017b), 170–176.
4. J. M. Berger, "How ISIS Games Twitter," *The Atlantic*, June 16, 2014, https://www.theatlantic.com/international/archive/2014/06/isis-iraq-twitter-social-media-strategy/372856/.
5. Abu Muhammad al-'Adnani, "The Promise of Allah," *FDD's Long War*, June 29, 2014, http://www.longwarjournal.org/archives/2014/06/isis_announces_formation_of_ca.php.
6. Marwan M. Kraidy, "Fun against Fear in the Caliphate: The Islamic State Spectacle and Counter-Spectacle," *Critical Studies in Media Communication* 35, no. 1 (2018): 40–56.
7. Marwan M. Kraidy and Patrick D. Murphy, "Shifting Geertz: Toward a Theory of Translocalism in Global Communication Studies," *Communication Theory* 18 (2008): 335–355.
8. Eric Voegelin, "The Mongol Orders of Submission to European Powers, 1245–1255," *Byzantion* (1941).
9. John Masson Smith Jr., "Mongol Manpower and Persian Population," *Journal of the Economic and Social History of the Orient* 18, no. 3 (1975): 273.

10. Gilles Deleuze and Félix Guattari, *Nomadology: The War Machine* (New York: Semiotext(e), 1986), 5.

11. C. E. Bosworth, E. van Donzel, W. P. Heinrichs, and Charles Pellat, *Encyclopedia of Islam New Edition* (Liden, NED: Brill, 1993), 234–235.

12. D. O. Morgan, "Who Ran the Mongol Empire?" *Journal of the Royal Asiatic Society of Great Britain and Ireland*, 1 (1982): 124–136.

13. David Morgan, *The Mongols*, 2nd ed. (Hoboken, NJ: Blackwell Publishing, 2007).

14. S. H. Bira, "Mongolian Tenggerism and Modern Globalism: A Retrospective Outlook on Globalisation," *Inner Asia* 5, no. 2 (2003): 107–117.

15. Marwan M. Kraidy, "The Projectilic Image: Islamic State's Digital Visual Warfare and Global Networked Affect," *Media, Culture, and Society* 39, no. 8 (2017a): 1194–1209.

16. *Dabiq*, the Islamic State's magazine, cautioned against *bid'ah* in an article in its March 2015 edition titled "Irja': The Most Dangerous Bid'ah."

17. Kraidy, "Terror, Territoriality, Temporality."

18. Craig Noyes, "Pragmatic Takfiris: Organizational Prioritization Along Islamic State's Ideological Threshold," *Small Wars Journal*, July 26, 2016, http://smallwarsjournal.com/jrnl/art/pragmatic-takfiris-organizational-prioritization-along-islamic-state%E2%80%99s-ideological-threshol.

19. Ibid.

20. Marwan M. Kraidy, "The War Machine in the Age of Global Communication," keynote address, Global Fusion 2016, "Media and the Global City," Philadelphia, October 21, 2016.

21. David Morgan, "Reflections on Mongol Communications in the Ilkhanate," in *Studies in Honour of Clifford Edmund Bosworth Volume II: The Sultan's Turret: Studies in Persian and Turkish Culture*, ed. Carole Hillenbrand (Liden, NED: Brill, 1999), 376–385

22. Syed Anwarul Haque Haqqi, *Chingiz Khan: The Life and Legacy of an Empire Builder* (Delhi, India: Primus Books, 2010)

23. Deleuze and Guattari, *Nomadology*, 44.

24. Craig Whiteside, "Lighting the Path: The Evolution of the Islamic State Media Enterprise (2003–2016)," International Centre for Counter-Terrorism—The Hague, 2016, 10

25. Kareem El Damanhoury, "The Social Media Battle for Mosul: Visual Framing of Daesh's Imagery in Ninawa Province," presentation at "Emerging Work on Communicative Dimensions of Islamic State," Workshop of the Jihadi Networks of Communication and Cultures (JINCS) Research Group, Center for Advanced Research in Global Communication, Annenberg School for Communication, May 4, 2017. See also El Damanhoury's chapter in this volume.

26. Kraidy, "Terror, Territoriality, Temporality."

27. Kathy Gilsinan, "The Many Ways to Map the Islamic 'State,'" *The Atlantic*, August 27, 2014, https://www.theatlantic.com/international/archive/2014/08/the-many-ways-to-map-the-islamic-state/379196/.

28. J. M. Berger and J. Morgan, "The ISIS Twitter Census: Defining and Describing the Population of ISIS Supporters on Twitter," Brookings Project on US Relations with the Islamic World, March 20, 2015, http://www.brookings.edu/~/media/research/files/papers/2015/03/isis-twitter-census-berger-morgan/isis_twitter_census_berger_morgan.pdf.

29. Ibid.

30. Bosworth et al., *Encyclopedia*.

31. Berger and Morgan, "The ISIS Twitter Census."

32. Peter Senge, *The Fifth Discipline: The Art & Practice of The Learning Organization* (New York: Doubleday, 1990). Quoted in Whiteside, "Lighting the Path."
33. Kraidy, "The War Machine in the Age of Global Communication."
34. Kraidy, "Terror, Territoriality, Temporality."
35. Kraidy, "The Projectilic Image."
36. Justin Chandler Mueller, *The Temporality of Political Obligation* (New York: Routledge, 2016).
37. Grant Evans and Kelvin Rowley, *Red Brotherhood at War: Indochina since the Fall of Saigon* (London: Verso, 1984).
38. John Marston, "Metaphors of the Khmer Rouge," in *Cambodian Culture Since 1975: Homeland and Exile*, ed. M. M. Ebihara, C. A. Mortland, and J. Ledgerwood (Ithaca, NY: Cornell University Press, 1994), 105–118.
39. Karl D. Jackson, "The Ideology of Total Revolution," in *Cambodia, 1975–1978: Rendezvous with Death*, ed. K. D. Jackson (Princeton, NJ: Princeton University Press, 1992), 37–79.
40. Thomas Clayton, "Building the New Cambodia: Educational Destruction and Construction under the Khmer Rouge, 1975–1979," *History of Education Quarterly* 38, no. 1 (1998): 1–16.
41. Ibid.
42. David P. Chandler, "Seeing Red: Perceptions of Cambodian History in Democratic Kampuchea," in *Revolution and Its Aftermath in Kampuchea: Eight Essays* (New Haven, CT: Yale University Southeast Asian Studies, 1983), 34–56.
43. Rosemary H. T. O'Kane, "Cambodia in the Zero Years: Rudimentary Totalitarianism," *Third World Quarterly* 14, no. 4 (1993): 735–748; Henri Locard, *Pol Pot's Little Red Book: The Saying of Angkar* (Chiang Mai, Thailand: Silkworm Books, 2004).
44. Loung Ung, *First They Killed My Father: A Daughter of Cambodia Remembers* (New York: HarperCollins, 2000). This is not metaphorical; *Sâmârâphoum muck*, which means "front lines," was the term deployed by the state, according to Marston, "Metaphors," 111).
45. Fawaz A. Gerges, *ISIS: A Short History* (Princeton, NJ: Princeton University Press, 2016).
46. Chandler, "Seeing Red," 34–56
47. Kenneth M. Quinn, "The Khmer Krahom Program to Create a Communist Society in Southern Cambodia," Airgram from US Consulate General Can Tho, February 24, 1974, cited in O'Kane, "Cambodia in the Zero Years."
48. Boreth Ly, "Devastated Vision(s): The Khmer Rouge Scopic Regime in Cambodia," *Art Journal* 62, no. 1 (2003): 66–81.
49. John Barron and Anthony Paul, *Peace with Horror* (London: Hodder and Stoughton, 1977), 59–60, cited in O'Kane, "Cambodia in the Zero Years."
50. Penny Edwards, "Imagining the Other in Cambodian Nationalist Discourse Before and During the UNTAC Period," in *Propaganda, Politics, and Violence in Cambodia: Democratic Transition Under United Nations Peace-Keeping*, eds. S. Heder and J. Ledgerwood (New York: Routledge, 1996), 59.
51. Kathleen Gough, "Roots of the Pol Pot Regime in Kampuchea," *Contemporary Marxism* 12 (1986): 14–48.
52. See Marwan M. Kraidy, *The Naked Blogger of Cairo: Creative Insurgency in the Arab World* (Cambridge, MA: Harvard University Press, 2016), part V.

53. Graeme Wood, "What ISIS Really Wants," *The Atlantic*, March 2015, http://www.theatlantic.com/magazine/archive/2015/03/what-isis-really-wants/384980/.
54. See also Kraidy, "Terror, Territoriality, Temporality."
55. Aymenn Jawad Al-Tamimi, "Unseen Islamic State Treatise on Calendars: Full Text, Translation & Analysis," *Pundicity*, accessed May 15, 2017, http://www.aymennjawad.org/2015/10/unseen-islamic-state-treatise-on-calendars-full.
56. Khwaja Khusro Tariq, "Lessons From Islamic History: Ibn Taymiyyah and the Synthesis of Takfir," *Huffington Post*, May 31, 2016, http://www.huffingtonpost.com/khwaja-khusro-tariq/ibn-taymiyyah-and-the-syn_b_10096820.html.
57. Dabiq, issue 4: "The Failed Crusade."
58. Dabiq, issue 8: "Shari'ah Alone Will Rule Africa."
59. Cole Bunzel, "From Paper State to Caliphate: The Ideology of the Islamic State," analysis paper, Brookings Project on US Relations with the Islamic World (2015).
60. Ibid.
61. Wood, "What ISIS Really Wants."
62. Ibid.
63. Daniel Milton, "Communication Breakdown: Unraveling the Islamic State's Media Efforts," Combating Terrorism Center at West Point United States Military Academy, October 2016.
64. Edward W. Said, "Islam Through Western Eyes," *The Nation*, April 26, 1980, https://www.thenation.com/article/islam-through-western-eyes/.

Bibliography

al-'Adnani, Abu Muhammad. "The Promise of Allah." *FDD's Long War.* June 29, 2014. http://www.longwarjournal.org/archives/2014/06/isis_announces_formation_of_ca.php.

Al-Tamimi, Aymenn Jawad. "Unseen Islamic State Treatise on Calendars: Full Text, Translation & Analysis." *Pundicity.* Accessed May 15, 2017. http://www.aymennjawad.org/2015/10/unseen-islamic-state-treatise-on-calendars-full.

Barron, John, and Anthony Paul. *Peace with Horror.* London: Hodder and Stoughton, 1977.

Berger, J. M. "How ISIS Games Twitter." *The Atlantic*, June 16, 2014. https://www.theatlantic.com/international/archive/2014/06/isis-iraq-twitter-social-media-strategy/372856/.

Berger, J. M., and Jonathon Morgan. "The ISIS Twitter Census: Defining and Describing the Population of ISIS Supporters on Twitter." Brookings Project on US Relations with the Islamic World. March 20, 2015. http://www.brookings.edu/~/media/research/files/papers/2015/03/isis-twitter-census-berger-morgan/isis_twitter_census_berger_morgan.pdf.

Bira, S. H. "Mongolian Tenggerism and Modern Globalism: A Retrospective Outlook on Globalisation." *Inner Asia* 5, no. 2 (2003): 107–117.

Bosworth, C. E., E. van Donzel, W. P. Heinrichs, and Charles Pellat. *Encyclopedia of Islam, New Edition.* Leiden, NED: Brill, 1993.

Bunzel, Cole. "From Paper State to Caliphate: The Ideology of the Islamic State." Analysis paper. Brookings Project on US Relations with the Islamic World, 2015.

Chandler, David P. "Seeing Red: Perceptions of Cambodian History in Democratic Kampuchea." In *Revolution and Its Aftermath in Kampuchea: Eight Essays*, edited by

David P. Chandler and Ben Kiernan, 34–56. New Haven, CT: Yale University Southeast Asian Studies, 1983.

Chandler, David P. *The Tragedy of Cambodian History: Politics, War, and Revolution Since 1945*. New Haven, CT: Yale University Press, 1991.

Clayton, Thomas. "Building the New Cambodia: Educational Destruction and Construction under the Khmer Rouge, 1975–1979." *History of Education Quarterly* 38, no. 1 (1998): 1–16.

Dabiq, issue 4: "The Failed Crusade."

Dabiq, issue 8: "Shari'ah Alone Will Rule Africa."

Deleuze, Gilles, and Félix Guattari. *Nomadology: The War Machine*. New York: Semiotext(e), 1986.

Edwards, Penny. "Imagining the Other in Cambodian Nationalist Discourse Before and During the UNTAC Period." In *Propaganda, Politics, and Violence in Cambodia: Democratic Transition Under United Nations Peace-Keeping*, edited by S. Heder and J. Ledgerwood, 50–72. New York: Routledge, 1996.

El Damanhoury, Kareem. "The Social Media Battle for Mosul: Visual Framing of Daesh's Imagery in Ninawa Province." Conference presentation, "Emerging Work on Communicative Dimensions of Islamic State," Center for Advanced Research in Global Communication, Annenberg School for Communication, May 4, 2017.

Evans, Grant, and Kelvin Rowley. *Red Brotherhood at War: Indochina since the Fall of Saigon*. London: Verso 1984.

Gerges, Fawaz A. *ISIS: A Short History*. Princeton, NJ: Princeton University Press, 2016.

Gilsinan, Kathy. "The Many Ways to Map the Islamic 'State.'" *The Atlantic*, August 27, 2014. https://www.theatlantic.com/international/archive/2014/08/the-many-ways-to-map-the-islamic-state/379196/.

Gough, Kathleen. "Roots of the Pol Pot Regime in Kampuchea." *Contemporary Marxism* 12 (1986): 14–48.

Haqqi, Syed Anwarul Haque. *Chingiz Khan: The Life and Legacy of an Empire Builder*. Delhi, India: Primus Books, 2010.

Innes, Harold. *Empire and Communications*. Oxford, UK: Clarendon Press, 1950.

Jackson, Karl D. "The Ideology of Total Revolution." In *Cambodia, 1975–1978: Rendezvous with Death*, edited by K. D. Jackson, 37–79. Princeton, NJ: Princeton University Press, 1992.

Khusro Tariq, Khwaja. "Lessons from Islamic History: Ibn Taymiyyah and the Synthesis of Takfir." *Huffington Post*, December 6, 2017. http://www.huffingtonpost.com/khwaja-khusro-tariq/ibn-taymiyyah-and-the-syn_b_10096820.html.

Kraidy, Marwan M. *The Naked Blogger of Cairo: Creative Insurgency in the Arab World*. Cambridge, MA: Harvard University Press, 2016.

Kraidy, Marwan M. "The War Machine in the Age of Global Communication." Keynote address, Global Fusion 2016, "Media and the Global City," Philadelphia, October 21, 2016.

Kraidy, Marwan M. "The Projectilic Image: Islamic State's Digital Visual Warfare and Global Networked Affect." *Media, Culture, and Society* 39, no. 8 (2017a): 1194–1209.

Kraidy, Marwan M. "Terror, Territoriality, Temporality: Hypermedia Events in the Age of Islamic State." *Television & New Media* 18, no. 6 (2017b): 170–176.

Kraidy, Marwan M. "Fun against Fear in the Caliphate: The Islamic State Spectacle and Counter-Spectacle." *Critical Studies in Media Communication* 35, no. 1 (2018): 40–56.

Kraidy, Marwan M., and Patrick D. Murphy. "Shifting Geertz: Toward a Theory of Translocalism in Global Communication Studies." *Communication Theory* 18 (2008): 335–355.

Locard, Henri. *Pol Pot's Little Red Book: The Saying of Angkar.* Chiang Mai, Thailand: Silkworm Books, 2004.

Ly, Boreth. "Devastated Vision(s): The Khmer Rouge Scopic Regime in Cambodia." *Art Journal* 62, no. 1 (2003): 66–81.

Marston, John. "Metaphors of the Khmer Rouge." In *Cambodian Culture Since 1975: Homeland and Exile*, edited by M. M. Ebihara, C. A. Mortland, and J. Ledgerwood, 105–118. Ithaca, NY: Cornell University Press, 1994.

Milton, Daniel. "Communication Breakdown: Unraveling the Islamic State's Media Efforts." Combating Terrorism Center at West Point United States Military Academy, October 2016.

Morgan, David. "Who Ran the Mongol Empire?" *Journal of the Royal Asiatic Society of Great Britain and Ireland* 1 (1982): 124–136.

Morgan, David. "Reflections on Mongol Communications in the Ilkhanate." In *Studies in Honour of Clifford Edmund Bosworth, Volume II: The Sultan's Turret: Studies in Persian and Turkish Culture*, edited by Carole Hillenbrand, 376–385. Liden, NED: Brill, 1999.

Morgan, David. *The Mongols.* 2nd ed. Hoboken, NJ: Blackwell Publishing, 2007.

Mueller, Justin Chandler. *The Temporality of Political Obligation.* New York: Routledge, 2016.

Noyes, Craig. "Pragmatic Takfiris: Organizational Prioritization along Islamic State's Ideological Threshold." *Small Wars Journal*, July 26, 2016. http://smallwarsjournal.com/jrnl/art/pragmatic-takfiris-organizational-prioritization-along-islamic-state%E2%80%99s-ideological-threshol.

O'Kane Rosemary H. T. "Cambodia in the Zero Years: Rudimentary Totalitarianism." *Third World Quarterly* 14, no. 4 (1993): 735–748.

Quinn, Kenneth M. "The Khmer Krahom Program to Create a Communist Society in Southern Cambodia." Airgram from US Consulate General Can Tho. February 24, 1974.

Said, Edward W. "Islam through Western Eyes." *The Nation*, April 26, 1980. https://www.thenation.com/article/islam-through-western-eyes/.

"Sayyid Qutb and the Ideology of Isis" (pamphlet). Salafi Publications, November 2015. http://www.bidah.com/articles/jnyihml-leaflet-sayyid-qutb-and-the-ideology-of-al-qaeda-and-isis.cfm.

Senge, Peter. *The Fifth Discipline: The Art and Practice of the Learning Organization* (New York: Doubleday, 1990).

Smith, Jr., John Masson. "Mongol Manpower and Persian Population." *Journal of the Economic and Social History of the Orient* 18, no. 3 (1975): 271–299.

Ung, Loung. *First They Killed My Father: A Daughter of Cambodia Remembers.* New York: HarperCollins, 2000.

Voegelin, Eric. "The Mongol Orders of Submission to European Powers, 1245–1255," *Byzantion*, 15 (1941): 378–413.

Whiteside, Craig. "Lighting the Path: The Evolution of the Islamic State Media Enterprise (2003–2016)." International Centre for Counter-Terrorism—The Hague, 2016.
Wood, Graeme. "What ISIS Really Wants." *The Atlantic*, March 2015. http://www.theatlantic.com/magazine/archive/2015/03/what-isis-really-wants/384980/.

MARWAN M. KRAIDY is Anthony Shadid Chair in Media, Politics, and Culture, and Director of the Center for Advanced Research in Global Communication at the Annenberg School for Communication, University of Pennsylvania. His latest book is *The Naked Blogger of Cairo: Creative Insurgency in the Arab World.*

JOHN VILANOVA is a Professor of Practice in Journalism and Africana Studies at Lehigh University.

3 The Islamic State's Passport Paradox

William Lafi Youmans

SHORTLY AFTER ISIS announced its rebranding as Islamic State (IS), two images of purported passports circulated on social media.[1] In August 2014, Swedish terrorism analyst Magnus Ranstorp posted a photo of four passports strewn across a table. Their covers bore the group's famous flag under the word "PASSPORT" (fig. 3.1). There are several reasons these were likely not official documents, starting with the cheap, shiny laminate on the covers. At the very top, the group's name was written in English, an odd language choice. Also, it was not quite the group's actual name in English. "Islamic State of Al Khilafa" is awkwardly spelled; it should be *khalifah* and is also redundant, since it means Islamic State of the Islamic State. Perhaps these pretend passports were made by a supporter to express his exuberance at the announcement of state formation or they were the group's attempt at "psychological warfare," as Ranstorp believed.[2] Or it was simply an exercise in branding through a picture likely to be spread widely on social media—as it was.[3]

During that same summer, an image of a supposed ISIS passport's ornate cover composed of bound leather with a sophisticated, emblazoned insignia made the rounds on social media.[4] This one (fig. 3.2) appeared more consistent with such state documents. One unverified report claimed it was assigned to eleven thousand citizens who lived near the Iraq-Syria border. According to *Al Arabiya*, the group was using a captured Iraqi government "Identification and Passport Center" in Mosul to create the documents. Even if this report is valid, it is apparent the documents never were deployed to all of ISIS's subjects.

Why ISIS or the group's many online fans would create passports seems obvious. Ranstorp interpreted the creation of passports as one way the group tries "to endow themselves with an illusion of statehood . . . to project themselves as a state." For a transnational militant political movement aspiring to statehood—and actualized sovereignty—ISIS would be expected to issue its very own passport to everyone living within the borders, even if the boundaries were fluid and the group always aimed to expand them. However, it never issued such documents, even though it engaged in the formal administration of travel consistent with normal statehood practices. Zooming in on passports, real and imagined, is valuable; such an artifact of the regulatory documentation of identity and travel

Fig. 3.1 Image of Islamic State "passports" circulating online in 2014.

Fig. 3.2 Islamic State passports allegedly dispersed to people living near the Iraq-Syria border.

allows a closer rendering of how ISIS wrestled with enacting abstract and ultimately conflicting notions of sovereignty. In other words, tensions are produced by the problem of making material the immaterial, idealist precepts of the ISIS project.

Passports and Sovereignty

As one of the tangible documents with which states administer their populations, a national passport carries both the practical functions and symbolic resonance of statist aims. On the one hand, a passport officially records individual subjects' formal identities, identifying when and where they were born, as well as representing physical markers with a recent photograph. National membership is thus linked with the individual who bears the passport. As James Scott noted, the issuance of passports and other identification documents was integral to governments making citizenry "legible," that is measurable, observable, and thus governable.[5] It is an instrument of governance whose purpose is to facilitate states' control and tracking of popular movement through national borders. As a document of mobility, it is essential to the maintenance and preservation of the international state system, and thus, the global order.[6] As John C. Torpey wrote, "passports and other documentary controls on movement and identification have been essential to states' monopolization of the legitimate means of movement."[7]

Such a document enacts more than just functions for population and transportation management. For the passport holder, it is testament to her individual mobility in the world, evincing a status to move internationally; this means passports also vary in value. The passport affords the most powerful countries' citizens more privileges, just as it entails more burdens like enhanced scrutiny and travel restrictions for those from the weakest, poorest, or most unstable countries. It is a reflection of the disparities in international prestige, power, and wealth. A passport's purchase on free travel often depends on bilateral, intergovernmental agreements around the terms of travel (for example, whether a visa is required for a given passport holder's entry). A passport also bears a communicative power, signaling the juridical status and desirability of the holder, as well as being an assertion of the authority of the issuing government, which beckons recognition by outsiders—the culmination of state formation.[8]

Fundamentally, the passport is a vital material artifact of sovereignty. For state formation projects that are contested, incomplete, or still in process, the passport could serve as an aspirational political symbol; it lets a burgeoning or weak authority claim a congealed and delineated national membership as its basis and is therefore a claim of jurisdictional authority over a given territory and its residents. Furthermore, issuing a passport is a claim to belonging in the world's community of nations. For the state whose imprimatur is impressed on the cover, a valid, recognized passport is a monument to its recognizable legitimacy, and so issuing them—or not—is as much a performance of sovereignty as is deciding which passport holders may or may not enter through ports of entry.

Islamic State's Competing Notions of Sovereignty

Critical scholars interested in "political theology" have largely built on Carl Schmitt's notion that religious concepts are embedded in the DNA of political thought. As he famously declared, "All significant concepts of the modern theory of the state are secularized theological concepts." That means "theology" is woven into Western "theory of the state." As an example, "the omnipotent God became the omnipotent lawgiver."[9] The notion of sovereignty as the highest and absolute form of authority is an instance of God embodied on earth. This lineage gives the state the nearly transcendental symbolic hegemony status it enjoys in the West. Scholars of political theology strive to unpack the hermeneutic stakes of this linkage and how it concretizes power.

However, in Islamic political thought, the term *political theology* is literal.[10] A caliphate is described in the Quran as God's vice-regency on earth. As Andrew F. March argued, this literalism leaves those studying "theistic political cultures" like Islam in an inverse posture, seeking to "uncover the secular, the mundane, and the human underneath what explicitly travels as the sacred or the theological."[11] His observation drives this chapter's interest in passports as the material expressions of ISIS's conceptualizations of its own sovereignty and justifications.

For many in the West, ISIS was reduced to its unrepentant religious fundamentalism combined with its grotesque, seemingly inexplicable brutality—which many see as mystifying, antimodern, and completely alien to the contemporary world. However, as international relations scholar Stephen Walt observed, ISIS seeks "to build the rudiments of a genuine state in the territory it controls."[12] He also cited a German journalist who visited ISIS-held areas in 2014 and concluded that "ISIS is a country now." At its core is a political objective, a project to assert sovereignty. Letting the group's horrific violence shock the senses obfuscates its underlying program of state formation, a process that historically entailed the ruthless deployment of spectacular violence in modern states such as France, the United States, Algeria, Australia, Israel, and Indonesia, among others. Just as each had its own analyzable historical context and ideological groundings from their very inception point, so did ISIS.

In his article on Islamic "genealogies of sovereignty," March usefully presented several models in which modern Islamic polities have taken, and could yet take, form. Also pertinent to the present discussion is how he foregrounds these models by examining some of the larger challenges to Islamic governance. The high ideal of *hakimiyya*, or the notion of "God's exclusive sovereignty," which modern Sunni Islamists such as Muslim Brotherhood leader Sayyid Qutb proclaimed as a sort of utopian standard, does not provide direct guidance on state formation.[13] This divine sovereignty would need to reflect in human institutions, presenting the perennial dilemma of institutionalization. Humanity's inevitable fallibility means political logics manifestly corrupt the sacred, with all its perfection. The sanctity of such political theology depends on several critical presumptions.

March showed how in early Muslim political thought, authority could be granted to the ummah's leadership by divine designation, but lacking that degree of clarity from above, it could be accomplished by receiving a quasicontractual pledge of oath (*bay'a*) from Muslims—a recognition of the practicality of popular consent. Another important aspect was that divine sovereignty articulated not through "the person of the imam or caliph but in the corpus of the divine law."[14] This put a natural check on authority by raising the prospects of secondary authority of religious experts or clerics who command understanding of this law. Later thinkers sought to rein in authority by getting leaders of the political realm to comply with sharia, as a means to their Islamic legitimacy, and by scoping out a domain of theological jurisdiction distinctly for clerical rule.[15] March argued that these logics allow a "temporal" polity to work on the basis of religious legitimacy. The buffer between real political administration and religious authority—as in Saudi Arabia—prevents or minimizes the politicization of the sacred. A model such as Iran's, however, where the clerics effectively rule, risks a "legitimacy crisis" because both spheres are invested in the same figure, easily leading to the "sacralization of the political" whereby "the sacred is reduced to the political."[16] The survival of the human-made state, for instance, becomes constructed as a matter of divine mandate, which opens it up to accusations of sacrilege; also, calls for political reform are treated as heretical. This appears at odds with what Iran's constitution pledges, that God "made man master of his own social destiny" (Article 56).[17]

Nevertheless, in both of these models, popular sovereignty is weakly institutionalized, completely subordinate to religious doctrine. Many have questioned this on theological and pragmatic grounds. Some politicians, scholars, and jurists—Rashid al-Gannushi, Muhammad Khatimi, Hasan Turabi, Abdullahi An-Na'im, and Khaled About El Fadl—have argued that the divine and popular sovereignties are commensurable, though they differ about the extent to which popular will can check religious imperatives and the degree to which religious governance should be distinct from general authority.[18] Khatami, the former Iranian president, belied that "popular will [is] a main condition for the establishment and durability of the state."[19] Still, the most common position is that in a Muslim "political community," the will of the people must ultimately conform within a range of acceptability determined by "divine law" when it comes to matters in which religious directives preside.[20]

As March and Mara Revkin argued, ISIS adopted a similar model to Saudi Arabia's, one that put a buffer between spheres of life and society clearly governed by Islamic law and the areas of public policy that could be carried out autonomously without violating religious principles.[21] Unlike Saudi Arabia, which is content as a mere state rather than a divinely sanctified Islamic authority, the group claimed the caliphate mantle, and it did so when it changed its name from ISIS to the Islamic State in June 2014. The term *caliphate* or *khalifa* refers to the accepted successor of previous Muslim empires as God's vice-regency on earth. God deputized the first caliphate as his earthly ruler, and its successors inherited this mandate. By calling itself caliphate, it asserted theopolitical ascendency above all existing Muslim polities—both the states that fashion themselves as Islamic, like Iran and Saudi Arabia, and those that are merely Islamized, such as Malaysia and Pakistan.[22] As the statement ISIS released when it declared itself the caliphate demanded: "It is incumbent upon all Muslims to pledge allegiance to (him) and support him. . . . The legality of all emirates, groups, states, and organizations, becomes null by the expansion of the khalifah's authority and arrival of its troops to their areas."[23]

Other Islamist groups, most ambitiously al-Qaeda, would be expected to submit to the khalifa's rule as well. This was a problem, since the group did not approve of the declaration, claiming it was necessary to unite Muslims and obtain popular support first.[24] This highlights the importance of popular will and consent in uniting factions that even share proximate political theologies. Islamic State disavowed al-Qaeda's exception in its declaration and sought to impose its rule over all.

ISIS's appeal to legitimacy rests on the unavoidably dualistic nature of Islamic governance, by which the sacred is necessarily matched with what Raja Bahlul calls "factual sovereignty"—the in-effect, empirical possession of highest authority that gives a group of people "the power to act in accordance with its will."[25] Both are essential to the Islamic State's demonstration of rule. The claim to the sacred begins with the group's integration of the Quran and the witnessed sayings and actions of the Prophet Muhammad and his followers as the basis for its actions and policies. In one announcement by the spokesman in April 2014, he spoke to God, saying, "A state of Islam rules by your book and by the tradition of your Prophet." This grounded it in divine sovereignty. Then the spokesman called for the state to be made a caliphate, fulfilling "the prophetic method" of establishment. This was just months before the actual declaration of al-Baghdadi as caliph. It was a reference to an apparent prophecy espoused by the Prophet himself—an ambiguous one that ISIS interpreted as narrating the end of days.

Underpinning its theological legitimation are essentially two main moves. The first is its claim to resurrect the polity of earliest Islamic caliphates. This seemingly retrograde move was consistent with Salafi theology, which sees in the past practices of early Islam the highest ideal of purity, when caliphal power was completely undivided, as Fred Donner noted.[26] It was what they believe was a religiously pristine authority, before the return of *jahaliyya* (a period of ignorance). The belief is there was no politicization of the sacred or sacralization of the political. It was, for them, a perfect unity. The polity completely reflected the religiosity of the community, with special dispensations for people of the book—other monotheists in the Abrahamic tradition. Theologians who support the group noted that the declared caliph, ISIS's head, Abu Bakr al-Baghdadi, did "meet conditions outlined in Sunni law—being a Muslim adult man of Quraysh descent [related to the Prophet Muhammad]; exhibiting moral probity and physical and mental integrity; and having *'amr*, or authority"—the last point of which argues the necessity of practical sovereignty.[27]

A young Bahraini, Turki ibn Mubarak al-Bin'ali, who joined the group in 2013, saw ISIS's leaders at the "nucleus of the anticipated rightly-guided caliphate," and that it began with the necessary accomplishment of "power, authority and control of territory."[28] These are the bases for the empirical sovereignty necessary to claim statehood. From this standpoint, the Islamic State would seek the oaths of other Sunni Muslims and groups. In this way, the Islamic State is an earthly phenomenon. It could only arise in the power vacuum of established states' failure through invasion and civil war. The group's short-lived reign is a "symptom of the conditions that have been created, where sovereignty has slowly eroded and fragmentation of the state increased" in Iraq and Syria.[29] It managed to grow both due to the failures and neglect of the al-Maliki government in Baghdad and as an intentional policy of al Assad's regime in Damascus. Even as the Islamic State was announced, an estimated 90 percent of the Syrian airstrikes hit the other rebel groups, allowing ISIS to flourish.[30] It was clear the regime prioritized defeating the Syrian rebel groups first. The group's early allure was as a source of control and stability to beleaguered people; it pledged to help those who "struggle to meet basic needs."[31] In many places, it was welcomed initially as a source of earthly law and order by repressing thieves, clamping down on corrupt practices, and issuing quick decisions on matters of governance.[32] The group did not rule entirely based on repression; it had welfare provisions, sought to reestablish governance, and provided legal mechanisms of resource allocation and dispute adjudication.

Given the great deal of writing that takes an interest in Islamic State's theology, in particular its apocalyptic discourses, it is vital to recall what March observed about the inversion of political theology. Scholars of religious politics are attentive to how the sacred travels above and through "the secular, the mundane, and the human." It is in this second element of Islamic governance—"*'amr*, or authority"—that we see that no matter how much Islamic State tries to escape Westphalian sovereignty, the group cannot help but emulate the practices of modern statehood, even while disavowing them. The Islamic State may have emerged from the cracks of the fraught Arab state system, claiming to reject the international system through a rearward mission to resurrect a long-lost imperial caliphate, but their imaginations of what states do are inescapably grounded in modern statecraft, more so than in the old practices of the historic caliphates ISIS sought to emulate.

Passports in Caliphal History

Historically, royal authorities around the globe issued documents to facilitate travel into, out of, and within a territory. In the Middle Ages, European monarchs issued "safe conducts" to grant "visiting negotiators . . . the promise of a safe passage" as well as a "kings license" that permitted its bearer to exit a country.[33] For Craig Robertson, these documents are part of a longer "history of sovereignty and the policing of territory, or a history of state formation."[34] Mercantile trade was essential to Islamic history. Amira Bennison referred to economic trade as Islam's "lifeblood" and observed early empires were perfectly positioned to facilitate intercontinental trade.[35] Flows of people, products, and resources are defining elements of Islam's history. Caliphs were incentivized to administer and facilitate the movement of people for purposes of economy and proselytization, though this was done to varying degrees of tolerance at different times.

Umayyad governors had the authority to manage populations through certified travel documents that functioned as work permits. In Egypt, administrators issued "safe-conduct passes, or 'passports.'"[36] Two remaining papyrus documents from AD 722 and 731 licensed identified villagers to travel to other districts for work.[37] They directed the tax administrators to treat the holders of the documents favorably. After all, such passports were often granted for those seeking work who needed money to pay their taxes (*jizya*). In certain areas, such as near the River Nile, anyone operating or embarking on or off boats had to possess a passport by law.[38] Like passports today, such travel documents were granted for fixed periods, described physical traits of the holder, and cost money to replace, since authorities charged fees. Throughout Islamic history, travelers from abroad were allowed to visit the territory and conduct business as well. Rulers in the sixteenth century granted safe conducts to "infidels" including Florentine traders in furtherance of commercial activity.[39] Islamic authorities allowed networks of hotels to arise, and some business rules and laws relating to the rights of foreign merchants were negotiated through treaties.[40] However, they were also used to monitor and conduct surveillance on Christians and to prevent them from smuggling illegal migrants or spies.[41]

Citing Umayyad practices in a chapter about the Islamic State is not entirely helpful, for several reasons. First, there is no real institutional linkage between Islamic empires of the past and Islamic State as a modern political formation.

Second, and equally important, ISIS largely rejected their legacy, seeing them as corrupt and all too accommodating to the world. That is why the group demolished shrines to Umayyad's caliphs.[42] However, papyrus travel documents were also issued by the Abbasids, and physical evidence of forms issued to Egyptian Christians survives.[43] This was a practice in the earliest days of the Abbasid Empire, which William McCants argues ISIS leaders strive to own as their model for a "rightly guiding caliphate."[44] Far from an exhaustive overview of how early caliphates facilitated and regulated movement, this section was only meant to offer a baseline for the historical model Islamic State claimed to rejuvenate as a basis for the legitimacy of its sovereign aspirations. As we examine ISIS's multidimensional treatment of the passport, we come to see how the divine, the historical, and the practical collide and complement in the group's attempts to wield sovereign power.

The Secular in the Sacred: Administering Human Movement

A researcher who has extensively chronicled the Islamic State from a distance, Aymenn Al-Tamimi obtained and published documents that were captured after battles or leaked by people living under the group's rule. In his 2016 article for a US military publication, "A Caliphate under Strain: The Documentary Evidence," he featured a litany of such artifacts.[45] A few of them revealed how ISIS administered movement within, as well as in and out of, the territories it held. What emerged was a picture of a bureaucratically organized system of forms and official records, consistent with the notion of the group as undertaking a project of state formation by attempting to institutionalize modes of governance. While they frequently gesture toward the sacred, by bearing Quranic inscriptions or symbols, they are fundamentally concerned with replicating the practices of mobility administration in ways required by modern states and consistent with the models of Islamic rule in the past.

While ISIS did not issue passports for everyone and presumptively banned leaving the territory, it created exceptions to allow travel in and out of their territory for special circumstances. As Aymenn Jawad Al-Tamimi chronicled on his personal website, the Al-Buhuth wa al-Eftaa' Committee determined that selling passports depended on the underlying purposes of the traveler, though it was generally forbidden because emigration was seen as a wrong.[46] The fatwa's reasoning behind an outward travel ban was that it is "without gain for anyone who wants to travel to the land of disbelief" and therefore "it is not permitted to have the citizens of the Islamic State" go "to the land of disbelief." By default, then, the citizens were banned from traveling. "Thus," it concluded, "it is not permitted to sell the passport that is tantamount to the identity that makes it possible for its owner to travel to that land."[47] Then it added "and to the means apply the ruling of intentions," which means the necessary instruments (passports) of committing a wrong (leaving) are prohibited.[48] However, if there was a necessary and temporary reason that was permissible, the traveler must "show disavowal of the disbelievers and hatred of idolatry, disbelief and its people with a hatred that has no affection in it, and not to take them as friends/helpers." Travelers must be devout Muslims who truthfully "display the rituals of Islam perfectly" and do not partake in "nationalist, idolatrous occasions of joy." The opinion commanded that "you are not to concord with them inwardly or outwardly." There was a very high standard to gain exit permission.

Consistent with this opinion, the group declared that "those living in Islamic State territory must obtain a permit from the Diwan al-Hisba in whatever *wilaya* [province] they live in if they wish to travel outside Islamic State territory for a limited period of time."[49] Another document Al-Tamimi featured on his personal website, a request for an exit visa, identified as "Specimen 2J," was issued by the Amir al-Hisba of Wilayat al-Kheir.[50] The applicant sought travel permission to Kuwait. Also, dated according to the Islamic calendar, the note written on letterhead bore the common Muslim invocation, "In the name of God, the Compassionate, the Merciful," the phrase that begins all the Quran's chapters but one—again situating this practical authority symbolically within the divine. The form's body shows that permission was requested "to go to the lands of disbelief 'Kuwait'." Such a form replaced the exit function of a passport. Vitally, however, was the reference to Kuwait—in quotation marks—as within the "lands of disbelief." The nations beyond the caliphate were deemed an all-encompassing enemy in their nomenclature. For ISIS, even Muslim-majority countries are "lands of disbelief" and are therefore not to be recognized as equal with the caliphate. In fact, ISIS saw all the countries with current or past Muslim populations as targets of future conquest. Yet, they had to be identified and distinguished for practical purposes. Thus, the form must name Kuwait by necessity, with the name in quotation marks to signify an absence of recognition. The traveler could ultimately only gain admission to the Gulf country using a Syrian passport, as Kuwait would reject any ISIS documentation. In this one document, we see the tensions among administering mobility for practical purposes, the strict adhesion to pretenses of divinity, and the grand historical ambitions of resurrecting the caliphate—and it betrays the group's inability to gain wider legitimacy. Even though the granting of permission to travel out is a normal practice of secular sovereignty, for those living under ISIS's rule, it could only be accomplished with a passport recognized by an authority in the "land of disbelief." Thus, an ISIS passport would be illogical within the international order the group envisioned.[51]

Other Countries' Passports

Examining how Islamic State treated other countries' passports is instructive. If it were to enact a regime premised on divine sovereignty, it would seem to have no purpose for these earthly documents. There is no such thing as nationality in the eye of the sacred. Islamists would see the caliphate as God's only representative, so no other nationality has any standing. Yet, the sorts of past caliphates that ISIS revered and claimed to model issued and recognized travel documents to and from foreign, nonbelieving lands. Thus, there is a tension in ISIS's handling of other countries' passports (a reflection of its sovereign disposition); the theological and the historical visions do not align in their given guidance on passports, and both come to a head with certain practical necessities given the objective of actualizing a state out of a larger transnational network of supporters. Thus, Islamic State charted its own course, wavering between the symbolic repudiation of foreign passports based on its fantasy of theological purity, conditional recognition of travel documentation premised on historical logics, and the practical imperatives of appropriating them for further militant activity.

Early on, foreign arrivals to the areas ISIS held made a show of lighting their passports aflame. French fighters burned their documents, as shown in a video produced by Al-Hayat Media Center. Its title, "What Are You Waiting For?" demonstrated the mobilizing and inspirational intention behind this act of forgoing citizenship and the secular privileges of movement in the world it affords.[52] In another video, "Jayl al-Malahim," ISIS depicted Indonesian and Malaysian fighters burning their passports.[53] A leader of an ISIS-allied group, Millatu-Ibrahim, reneged his Austrian citizenship in a video, calling it a "toxic" society; he then set his passport on fire.[54] The background photo of an article in the tenth issue of *Dabiq* depicted a small pile of various Western passports on the ground. They were riddled with bullet holes and adorned with spent gun shells. There were multiple other examples. Through such acts, ISIS rejected the prospects of supplementing preexisting citizenships by supplanting the entire notion of secular citizenship represented by passports. This rejects the aspirations of the dual citizen or the sovereign citizen who seeks to collect as many passports as possible in order to exploit the privileges of being a globalized interstitial elite. Rather, it is an assertion that there is only one true polity, an echo of the unity and oneness of God, and is therefore in a sense an expression of divine sovereignty. All other authority was deemed illegitimate. The rejection of their prior national membership underscored their total commitment to the project and served as a statement of full investment in their arrival as subjects of this new divine entity. They and ISIS as an organization publicized these dramatic shows of commitment, in order to inspire other Muslims elsewhere to leave behind their places in the lands of hostility and disbelief throughout the rest of the world. The new state was being built, and it would offer a theologically constituted substitute for secular citizenship.[55]

Yet, Islamic State was too practical to let all its members destroy all their prior passports. ISIS frequently repossessed the passports of newcomers, keeping them with the human resources departments, in order to prevent easy return and to use them toward their own purposes.[56] Therefore, nullification of one's passport was far from the norm or standard practice suggesting a unified policy. There was an eventual realization that although performed destruction of the passports was symbolically potent, it was wasteful from the perspective that passports are instruments of value. They grant individuals what ISIS membership nullifies: the ability to move as freely as possible in the world.

As the state fragmented and began losing territory to a broad coalition of enemies, the group began to resort to a different strategy of direct attacks on civilians in Western countries. This threat was something ISIS knew Western officials worried about. One issue of ISIS's magazine, *Dabiq* (issue 4), featured a pull quote from Secretary of Defense Chuck Hagel in a section called "The Enemy's Words." He expressed concern about those with Western passports: "Thousands of foreign fighters, including Europeans and more than 100 Americans have travelled to Syria. With passports that give them relative freedom of movement, these fighters can exploit ISIL's safe haven to plan, coordinate and carry out attacks against the United States and Europe."[57] The Western passports that had been burned or riddled with bullets were now construed as potential weapons themselves.

This fear was heightened with reports that various ISIS entities and affiliates raided government facilities and acquired blank official passport books.[58] Western authorities were alarmed that they would print fake passports to be used by infiltrators for attacks—especially as the state dissolved and the threat of such violent attacks against civilians would heighten. It was telling that ISIS, which had tried to emulate statehood, would use phony passports to survive as an organization. However, forgery was not an adequate method for use of real passports. As Michael Degerald observed, "It is far easier to use a real passport of someone you resemble than it is to counterfeit it completely."[59] The use of scannable chips, he added, makes reproducing them virtually impossible.

There was one notable issue with the possible counterfeiting strategy. Islamic State had prohibited the forgery of passports. It is a well-known saying of the Prophet that "false testimony" is one of the worst sins. As one of Al-Tamimi's analyzed documents showed, a passport forger was subject to a "lesson" in sharia from Diwan Al-Hisba, the religious police that enforces public morality.[60] If the reports were correct and it was going to forge passports, ISIS would have to reconcile its theological judgment forbidding the faking of passports with the utility of forgery in advancing the Islamic State's military objectives to attack the land of disbelief through infiltration and subterfuge operations. There was therefore a conflict between the protocols of divine sovereignty and the practical tactics of preserving the beleaguered organization.

This surfaced in the November 2015 attack in Paris that killed 130 people. Seven attackers, mainly of French and Belgian origin, unleashed a deadly rampage at the Bataclan Theater and other sites within the city. One of the perpetrators was believed to have entered Europe among Syrian refugees. A man carrying a Syrian passport for Ahmad Al Mohammad, born in Idlib, was the first to set off a suicide bomb at the Stade de France after failing to gain entry to the soccer match taking place there.[61] His fingerprints matched those of a supposed asylum seeker who entered the continent through Greece in early October, around two months before, using the same passport. According to Federica Mogherini of the European Union, this attacker was likely an EU citizen who relied on a fake passport because he was on a watch list.[62] There is not much publicly available evidence to bring to bear on this. *Blic*, a Serbian newspaper, reported that another migrant had used a passport with the same exact name and details. The BBC reported this would suggest "both men bought fake documents from the same counterfeiter."[63] While this episode is still unclear, making analysis speculative, Degerald summarized a lingering question about this fake passport: "What was it doing there in the first place? Was it deliberately taken by one of the attackers and left at the scene of the bombing in the expectation that many would blame refugees?"[64] ISIS has a clear incentive to prevent Europe from taking Syrian refugees, as the exodus diminished its own population of subjects.

Passport as Trophy of Violence

Foreign passports also figured into Islamic State propaganda for several different reasons. First, the images of identification cards were produced as proof of violent conquest, in particular the taking of foreign lives. Very often, *Dabiq* published photos of passports and other identification cards of those the group captured or killed. This substantiated their claims of successful attacks, executions, and other coercive acts meant to demonstrate command over others' lives. In issue 12, the magazine showed several Russian passports after the group's bombing of a Russian airliner, which killed all 224 people on board.[65] The magazine reported that "the mujahadin" on the ground in Sinai fished the passports out of the plane's wreckage. In issue 6, it showed the passport and employee ID of an American oil worker an ISIS affiliate kidnapped and murdered in Sinai.[66] One reason for such attacks was to strike fear in foreign populaces' hearts with the aim of altering their governments' policies, namely diminishing their war efforts against ISIS. A side objective of this outward fear-stoking was to reduce tolerance for Muslim citizens, in order to compel them to emigrate to ISIS; that is, narrow the so-called "gray zone." To have such impacts, the group needed to show they were behind the attacks. Passports had, therefore, a forensic function.

Second, in other cases, victims' passports helped the group advance a strategic narrative. In issue 6, the group proudly portrayed Moaz al-Kasasbeh's Jordanian Air Force ID. The card bore the Jordanian flag. He was, according to the magazine, the "apostate pilot flying for the crusader alliance." Islamic State seized him after shooting down his plane in December 2014. After holding him for months, they burned him alive as he was blindfolded in a metal cage.[67] The grisly execution was meant to reenact the effect of bombs falling on Muslims. Islamic State tried to frame it as just recourse for aerial attacks on its fighters and subjects.

At other times, the passport was not present with ISIS victims but later used for propaganda points. In one issue of *Dabiq*, the group published a photo of the executed American journalist Steven Sotloff's Israeli passport.[68] They obtained its image from another source they identified as a "Jewish newspaper." The group was apparently unaware of his dual nationality. While Sotloff was in captivity, his friends and family got the Israeli government's press censors and even the *New York Times* to prevent news of his dual nationality from getting out, in fear it would have doomed him to even worse punishment.[69] The magazine ran a letter he penned to his mother blaming the United States for his captors' anger. The letter said his fate was in President Obama's hands. He would be killed, the writer added, because the United States was attacking ISIS. In his letter, he mentioned that they knew Sotloff was a journalist, but they told him they do not differentiate between civilians and combatants because US bombs do not. However, after learning the American reporter was also an Israeli citizen, the *Dabiq* writer realized another justification. They wrote that his Israeli citizenship undermined those "who portray western journalism and humanitarian aid as purely innocent, for this man was a Jew and citizen of the Jewish state" who "work[ed] for crusader media." They used Sotloff and his passport to narrativize their grievances and to rationalize their brutality as mere reciprocation of American and Israeli violence levied against Muslims.

Third, there is another hermeneutic to consider when analyzing how ISIS made propaganda use of victims' passports. The group's use of national documents is an assertion of sovereignty. Displaying the passports of those captured and killed allows ISIS to proclaim a negation of other sovereign entities and to assert their right to rule. Waving these personal artifacts of governance could be seen as invalidating the protective powers, and therefore the legitimacy, of the national authorities that vest their power in those documents. That is, ISIS used these passports as both tokens of it's prowess and to weaken other states' claims to what Michel Foucault called "pastoral power" over the lives of their subjects.[70] Pastoral power refers to the management of the movement of the many individuals making up the population under care. Such power was thought of as "beneficent," fundamentally concerned with the people's salvation and subsistence, thus it takes the first form of "keeping watch" over them. As much as it is about protecting the people in the macro, it is an "individualizing power" that attends to the safety and security of each member of the flock.

Further, using passports as tokens of crimes is a repudiation of the international order the passport system was meant to represent and further facilitate.

On the one hand, Islamic State is able to show itself as outside this system, which is seemingly consistent with its self-conceived identity as an expression of divine sovereignty. While it is against the pastoral powers of other sovereigns, however, it arguably sought to regulate the population and its morality in ways consistent with aspects of pastoral power—from quantitatively administering the population to handing out sharia lesson cards to punishing individuals violating Islamic norms, as well as engaging in charitable redistribution measures. It therefore also expressed the sort of bureaucratic paternalism of past caliphates. Finally, at the same time, the forensic uses of these trophies was an effort at regime survival, a gruesome method of national defense steeped in a statist logic.

Sovereign Responses: Denationalization as Punishment

In the United Kingdom, UKIP's (United Kingdom Independence Party) Paul Nuttall has called for punishing any citizens who even support Islamic State by revoking their passports, banning them from entry, and in effect denationalizing them.[71] Prime Minister Theresa May echoed this, thinking it would be a deterrent.[72] American senator Ted Cruz proposed a similar punishment for "an American citizen [who] travels abroad and joins a terrorist group waging jihad on America, attempting to murder innocent Americans."[73] Traditionally, such measures were taken in the most exceptional circumstances, and this was not often posed during the era of al-Qaeda. It is likely that ISIS's claims to sovereignty and its supporters' expressed willingness to renounce their prior citizenship has diminished states' long-established commitment to these conventions. It might also be due to the globalization of the war on terror; no longer does jurisdiction rest on citizenship, making it more expendable for law-enforcement purposes.[74]

There have been numerous reports of Islamic State partisans losing their citizenship. Australia took away a fighter's citizenship.[75] The decision was based on a 2015 law that allowed the government to "strip dual nationals of their citizenship if they are found to have carried out militant acts or been members of a banned organization." A court in Denmark took away another ISIS fighter's citizenship in 2017. The year before, the country's supreme court rescinded a Danish-Moroccan bookseller's citizenship for "inciting terrorism."[76]

Denationalization as a punishment unintentionally and implicitly recognizes ISIS's nationality as a sort of substitute, albeit governments may expect the high probability that it results in the death of the expatriated, given the state of war in ISIS's territories. While there is a security rationale, denationalization as punishment comports with Islamic State's notion of either-or belonging, its rejection of the gray zone, and furthers its goal of luring as many Muslims as possible. However, ISIS's recruits would not care about such a punishment. As the group made clear in one Friday sermon dictated for the Ninawa Province Mosques in February 2015, there is a theologically derived "obligation" for

Muslims to "emigrate from the abode of disbelief to the abode of Islam."[77] A researcher who examined fighters in Syria found that the reactions to Theresa May's threat to take away ISIS passports indicate the redundancy of the measure. He told *Vice News* that "some of these foreign fighters on Facebook and Twitter came out and said, 'So what? We're here to establish an Islamic state.'"[78] In an ISIS video, one armed fighter replied similarly to his original country, Bahrain's, denationalization policy: "Don't you know that you, your citizenship, your laws, your constitutions and your threats are under our feet? Don't you know that we are the soldiers of the Islamic State in Iraq and Syria and that our state will expand until it removes the thrones that you sold your religion for?"[79] For many, then, denationalization was received as an empty gesture.

On the other hand, it also marks them as beyond the flock, no longer under the care of the state as shepherd, and in a way exiled from the domestic political community (and the international order). They become what Giorgio Agamben called *Homo sacer*, a man who can be killed without being sacrificed, executed without significance or punishment—unlike when a state kills its own citizen (which is highly formalized and ceremonial).[80] Denationalization allows an ISIS fighter to be killed by his former state unexceptionally. This is an inversion of ISIS's conceptualization of itself as an expression of divine sovereignty. The group's adherents care not for the realm of secular law, seeing themselves only answerable to God. One state's *Homo sacer* is therefore an Islamic State's martyr. The calls to denationalize them, to invalidate their passports, plays precisely into their self-conception as actors extending the sacred. As dramatic a punishment as denationalization is in the pragmatic dimension, determining one's ability to move in the world, it is not as subversive as those in the West construe it as for the truest believers among ISIS's foot soldiers and supporters.

Conclusion

Due to the manifold dimensions of the ISIS project, its passport and travel policies faced complex and conflicting impulses:

- ISIS asserted as a basis for state legitimacy a divine sovereignty while rejecting other countries as "lands of disbelief."
- ISIS sought to emulate a model of the earliest caliphates, although the group recognized, allowed travel to and from, and managed passports from, nonbelieving countries.
- ISIS's own supporters imaginatively designed ISIS passports and destroyed their old documents as expressions of desired statehood.
- There were practical reasons passports matter for the management of people's movement in and out of the territory, as well as for its militant operations against civilian populations in other countries.

- ISIS's political leadership did not desire recognition by the nonbelieving countries of the world, since it would encourage the outward exodus of its citizens in the making anyway. Denationalization, which ISIS fighters welcomed, made this moot either way.

Islamic State and its backers engaged in contorted symbolic and practical maneuvers around the incomplete issue of its own passport (only distributed in limited numbers) and other countries' passports. Issuing an official passport would have forced ISIS to inscribe a coherent discourse of its sovereignty into a material artifact, when it entirely lacked such a clarity of self-conception. This incoherence stemmed from the uncertain desire to project itself as a peculiar historically rooted and divine formation that stands outside of the international state system. Yet, the symbolic and practical demands of passport issuance are unavoidable for any entity aspiring to statehood in the world today. Even as its religious authorities ruled travel outward forbidden and expressed theological justifications, it granted internal travel documents and permissions to leave the territory and promulgated numerous rules around individual mobility in furtherance of its claims to sovereignty. Closely examining passports and travel in the Islamic State reveals the various tensions between the divine, timeless sovereignty ISIS articulated and the secular, modern sovereignty that unavoidably defines sustainable, territorial political organization in the contemporary era.

The complexities embedded within ISIS's administration of mobility are most starkly juxtaposed when we consider the foreign fighters or those who emigrated to it from elsewhere. In 2011, before ISIS rose to prominence and years before it declared itself the Islamic State, Thomas Hegghammer observed that "foreign fighters constitute an intermediate actor category lost between local rebels, on the one hand, and international terrorists, on the other."[81] He concluded they "are insurgents in every respect but their passports." With Islamic State, however, this changed. Their insurgency was precisely about passports. Passports provided a material means through which the group became localized, rejecting the secular transnational to advance a divine project that historically reconstructed a notion of the glorious caliphate of yesteryear.

Notes

1. Thanks to Michael Degerald, Kareem Eldamanhoury, Libby Anker, Rosemary Pennington, and Marwan Kraidy for insights and inspiration for this chapter.

2. Terrorism expert Magnus Ranstorp tweeted an image of these passports in 2014. Magnus Ranstorp (@MagnusRanstorp), "Illusions of a Caliphate. ISIS issue passports as part of psychological warfare," Twitter, August 11, 2014, 11:55 p.m., https://twitter.com/MagnusRanstorp/status/499086698203340800/photo/1. For how journalists covered the

circulation of these passports, see "Are Alleged ISIS Passports a Hoax?," Public Radio International, August 14, 2014, https://www.pri.org/stories/2014-08-13/are-alleged-isis-passports-hoax.

3. Ranstorp attributed the photo to a Scandinavian IS supporter's website. He said, "I don't know if it's real. I cannot verify that from the picture. I just know it came from someone who is connected to ISIS." Chris Köver, "Fake or Not, These Passports Are a Branding Win for the Islamic State," Vice, August 15, 2014, https://news.vice.com/article/fake-or-not-these-passports-are-a-branding-win-for-the-islamic-state.

4. IS Issues Passports for "Citizens," *Al Arabiya*, July 5, 2014, http://english.alarabiya.net/en/News/middle-east/2014/07/05/ISIS-allegedly-issues-caliphate-passport.html.

5. James C. Scott, *Seeing Like a State: How Certain Schemes to Improve the Human Condition Have Failed* (New Haven, CT: Yale University Press, 1998), 220.

6. Not that passport policies and practices are universalized and standard; there remains variation in both rules and rigor of enforcement among countries.

7. John C. Torpey, *The Invention of the Passport: Surveillance, Citizenship, and the State* (Cambridge, UK: Cambridge University Press, 2018), 3.

8. Craig Robertson wrote that for the passport "to be a way to manage international mobility, it had to successfully function as a communication medium, as an identification document." Craig Robertson, *The Passport in America: The History of a Document* (Oxford, UK: Oxford University Press, 2010), 2.

9. Carl Schmitt, *Political Theology: Four Chapters on the Concept of Sovereignty* (Chicago: University of Chicago Press, 2006), 36.

10. Andrew F. March, "Genealogies of Sovereignty in Islamic Political Theology," *Social Research: An International Quarterly* 80, no. 1 (2013): 293–320.

11. March, "Genealogies of Sovereignty in Islamic Political Theology," 294.

12. Stephen M. Walt, "ISIS as Revolutionary State," *Foreign Affairs* 94 (2015): 42.

13. March, "Genealogies of Sovereignty in Islamic Political Theology," 295.

14. Ibid., 297.

15. Ibid., 298–299.

16. Ibid., 307.

17. Ibid., 306.

18. Raja Bahlul, "People vs. God: The Logic of 'Divine Sovereignty' in Islamic Democratic Discourse," *Islam and Christian-Muslim Relations* 11, no. 3 (2000): 287–297.

19. Ibid., 297.

20. Ibid., 296.

21. Andrew F. March and Mara Revkin, "Caliphate of Law," *Foreign Affairs*, April 15, 2015, https://www.foreignaffairs.com/articles/syria/2015-04-15/caliphate-law.

22. To understand Islamization as a distinct process by which secular states adopt religious legitimacy, see Seyyed Vali Reza Nasr, *Islamic Leviathan: Islam and the Making of State Power* (Oxford, UK: Oxford University Press, 2001).

23. "ISIS Changes Name, Declares Islamic 'Caliphate,'" *Haaretz*, June 29, 2014, http://www.haaretz.com/middle-east-news/1.602008.

24. William McCants, *The ISIS Apocalypse: The History, Strategy, and Doomsday Vision of the Islamic State* (New York: St. Martin's Press, 2015), 115.

25. Raja Bahlul, "People vs. God," 296.

26. Fred M. Donner, "The Formation of the Islamic State," *Journal of the American Oriental Society* 106, no. 2 (1986), 295.

27. Graeme Wood, "What ISIS Really Wants," *The Atlantic*, March 2015, https://www.theatlantic.com/magazine/archive/2015/03/what-isis-really-wants/384980/.

28. McCants, *The ISIS Apocalypse*, 116.

29. Simon Mabon and Stephen Royal, *The Origins of ISIS: The Collapse of Nations and Revolution in the Middle East* (New York: I. B. Tauris, 2017), 129.

30. McCants, *The ISIS Apocalypse*, 98.

31. Simon Mabon and Stephen Royal, *The Origins of ISIS*, 162.

32. McCants, *The ISIS Apocalypse*, 89.

33. Robertson, *The Passport in America*, 3.

34. Ibid.

35. Amira K. Bennison, *The Great Caliphs: The Golden Age of the 'Abbasid Empire* (New Haven, CT: Yale University Press, 2009), 137.

36. Lennart Sundelin, "Introduction: Papyrology and the Study of Early Islamic Egypt," in *Papyrology and the History of Early Islamic Egypt*, eds. Petra A. Sijpesteijn and Lennart Sundelin (Leiden, NED: Brill, 2004), 8.

37. Donner, "The Formation of the Islamic State," 286.

38. Frank R. Trombley, "Sawirus ibn al-Muqaffa' and the Christians of Umayyad Egypt: War and Society in Documentary Context," in *Papyrology and the History of Early Islamic Egypt*, eds. Petra A. Sijpesteijn and Lennart Sundelin (Leiden, NED: Brill, 2004), 205.

39. John Wansbrough, "The Safe-Conduct in Muslim Chancery Practice," *Bulletin of the School of Oriental and African Studies* 34, no. 1 (1971): 25–29.

40. Olivia Remie Constable, *Housing the Stranger in the Mediterranean World: Lodging, Trade, and Travel in Late Antiquity and the Middle Ages* (Cambridge, UK: Cambridge University Press, 2004).

41. Frank R. Trombley, "Sawirus ibn al-Muqaffa' and the Christians of Umayyad Egypt," 208.

42. Brian L. Steed, *ISIS: An Introduction and Guide to the Islamic State* (Santa Barbara, CA: ABC-CLIO, 2016), 144.

43. Petra M. Sijpesteijn, *Shaping a Muslim State: The World of a Mid-Eighth-Century Egyptian Official* (Oxford, UK: Oxford University Press, 2013), 311.

44. McCants, *The ISIS Apocalypse*, 131.

45. Aymenn Al-Tamimi, "A Caliphate under Strain: The Documentary Evidence," *CTC Sentinel* 9, no. 4 (2016): 1–8, https://ctc.usma.edu/a-caliphate-under-strain-the-documentary-evidence/.

46. Aymenn Jawad Al-Tamimi, "Archive of Islamic State Administrative Documents," *Pundicity*, January 27, 2015, http://www.aymennjawad.org/2015/01/archive-of-islamic-state-administrative-documents.

47. Al-Tamimi analyzed this fatwa as complementing "the unified Friday sermon for Ninawa Province mosques (Specimen 1Q) on the necessity of migrating to the Dar al-Islam [abode of Islam] and abandon the Dar al-Kufr [abode of disbelief], and also with the general notification of Specimen W urging for people not to be sent to Turkey to seek synthetic body parts." He argues the common objective it "to discourage any potential migration out of IS territory." Al-Tamimi, "Archive."

48. Al-Tamimi wrote that the "phrase 'and to the means apply the ruling of intentions' (*al-wasa'il laha ahkam al-maqasid*) . . . is employed in fatwas as the following line of reasoning: if I have to do/need X to accomplish Y, where Y is a forbidden act, then X is forbidden. So e.g. if I want a passport to go to a place to commit theft, then it is forbidden for me to obtain that passport or for someone to sell it to me." Al-Tamimi, "Archive."

49. Al-Tamimi, "A Caliphate under Strain," 4.
50. Al-Tamimi, "Archive."
51. Other mobility documents Al-Tamimi gathered included: a travel toll receipt from near Kirkuk that identified vehicles, their owners, their travels, and the taxes on movement they paid ("Specimen 6H"); a permission that granted tribe members to return to their home ("Specimen 2K"); a permission of internal travel for the purpose of medical treatment ("Specimen 6K"); a memo to those at checkpoints informing them to check student IDs for anyone going to non-IS Syria to take exams ("Specimen 7R"); a form for requests to travel externally for medical reasons ("Specimen 12B"); administrative guidelines and a fatwa regarding women traveling within and from the IS ("Specimen M" and "Specimen 1Y"). Al-Tamimi, "Archive."
52. Thanks to Kareem El Damanhoury for directing me to this video.
53. Jasminder Singh and Muhammad Haziq Jani, "Al-Fatihin: Islamic State's First Malay Language Newspaper," *RSIS Commentaries*, no. 155, 2016, http://hdl.handle.net/10220/40793.
54. "Millatu Ibrahim Leader Burns Austrian Passport, Renounces Citizenship," Site Intelligence Group, March 15, 2013, https://ent.siteintelgroup.com/Multimedia/millatu-ibrahim-leader-burns-austrian-passport-renounces-citizenship.html.
55. Murat Yeşiltaş and Tuncay Kardaş, "The New Middle East, ISIL and the 6th Revolt Against the West," in *Non-State Armed Actors in the Middle East*, eds. Murat Yeşiltaş and Tuncay Kardaş (Cham, Switzerland: Palgrave Macmillan, 2018), 160–161.
56. Michael Weiss, "Confessions of an ISIS Spy," *The Daily Beast*, November 15, 2015, https://www.thedailybeast.com/confessions-of-an-isis-spy.
57. "The Enemy's Words," *Dabiq* 4 (2014): 46, https://clarionproject.org/docs/islamic-state-isis-magazine-Issue-4-the-failed-crusade.pdf.
58. Brian Ross, Michele McPhee, and Lee Ferran, "ISIS Has Whole Fake Passport 'Industry,' Official Says," *ABC News*, January 25, 2016, http://abcnews.go.com/International/isis-fake-passport-industry-official/story?id=36505984.
59. Michael Degerald, "Borders, Passports, and Daesh: How the Global System of Passports and Movement Helped Shape Both Daesh and the Refugee Crisis," *Medium*, January 21, 2016, https://medium.com/@MENAhistorian/borders-passports-and-daesh-how-the-global-system-of-passports-and-movement-helped-shape-both-2d1a41focfac.
60. The card was issued for the "forging (of) travel [passes/passports]." Al-Tamimi, "Archive of Islamic State Administrative Documents," January 27, 2015.
61. Anthony Faiola, "The Mystery Surrounding the Paris Bomber with a Fake Syrian Passport," *Washington Post*, November 18, 2015, https://www.washingtonpost.com/world/europe/the-mystery-surrounding-the-paris-bomber-with-a-fake-syrian-passport/2015/11/17/88adf3f4-8d53-11e5-934c-a369c80822c2_story.html?utm_term=.899314049638.
62. Ben Farmer, "Who Is Salah Abdeslam and Who Were the Paris Terrorists? Everything We Know about the Isil Attackers," *The Telegraph*, March 18, 2016, http://www.telegraph.co.uk/news/worldnews/europe/france/11996120/Paris-attack-what-we-know-about-the-suspects.html.
63. "Paris Attacks: Who Were the Attackers?" *BBC News*, April 17, 2016, http://www.bbc.com/news/world-europe-34832512.
64. Degerald, "Borders, Passports, and Daesh."

65. Lizzie Dearden, "Isis Plane Attack: Egypt Admits 'Terrorists' Downed Russian Metrojet Flight from Sharm el-Sheikh for First Time," *The Independent* (UK), February 24, 2016, http://www.independent.co.uk/news/world/africa/isis-plane-attack-egypt-terrorists-downed-russian-metrojet-flight-from-sharm-el-sheikh-islamic-state-a6893181.html.

66. Louisa Loveluck, "Egyptian Jihadis Claim Responsibility for Killing American Oil Worker William Henderson." *The Telegraph*, December 14, 2014, http://www.telegraph.co.uk/news/worldnews/africaandindianocean/egypt/11264664/Egyptian-jihadis-claim-responsibility-for-killing-American-oil-worker-William-Henderson.html.

67. This was an act that many argued violated Islamic precepts, and supporters of the group replied with their own theological justifications. Jenna McLaughlin, "Islamic Teachings Explicitly Forbid Death by Burning, But ISIS Did It Anyway," *Mother Jones*, February. 5, 2015, http://www.motherjones.com/politics/2015/02/why-burning-worse-beheading-muslims/.

68. *Dabiq*, 4 (2014): 47, https://clarionproject.org/docs/islamic-state-isis-magazine-Issue-4-the-failed-crusade.pdf.

69. Alexandra Zavis and Batsheva Sobelman, "Friends, Supporters Worked to Keep Steven Sotloff's Israel Ties Secret," *Los Angeles Times*, September 5, 2014, http://www.latimes.com/world/middleeast/la-fg-sotloff-israel-20140906-story.html.

70. Michel Foucault, *Security, Territory, Population: Lectures at the Collège de France, 1977–78* (New York: Palgrave MacMillan, 2007), 125–130.

71. "UKIP's Paul Nuttall Says Party 'Vindicated' on Immigration," *BBC News*, June 6, 2017, http://www.bbc.com/news/election-2017-40171947.

72. Hollie McKay, "London Terror Attack: British Officials Eye Burka Ban and Stripping Citizenship" *Fox News*, June 4, 2017, http://www.foxnews.com/world/2017/06/04/london-terror-attack-british-officials-eye-burka-bans-and-stripping-citizenship.html.

73. Joel Gehrke, "Cruz in Push to Revoke Citizenship from Americans Who Join Islamic State," *Washington Examiner*, February 14, 2017, https://www.washingtonexaminer.com/cruz-in-push-to-revoke-citizenship-from-americans-who-join-islamic-state.

74. Furthermore, citizenship itself offers fewer protections. For example, the United States was willing to assassinate US citizens such as the cleric Anwar Al-Awlaki under the cover of the war on terror.

75. "Islamic State Fighter Is First Australian Stripped of Citizenship: Report," *Reuters*, February 11, 2017, www.reuters.com/article/us-australia-islamic-state-idUSKBN15Q05K?il=0.

76. "Danish Court Strips Islamic State Fighter of Citizenship," *Reuters*, March 31, 2017, www.reuters.com/article/us-denmark-islamic-state-idUSKBN1721VF.

77. Al-Tamimi, "Archive of Islamic State Administrative Documents," January 27, 2015.

78. Alice Speri, "Syria's Foreign Fighters Are There to Stay," *Vice News*, April 18, 2014, https://news.vice.com/article/syrias-foreign-fighters-are-there-to-stay.

79. Scott Shane and Ben Hubbard, "ISIS Displaying a Deft Command of Varied Media," *New York Times*, August 30, 2014, https://www.nytimes.com/2014/08/31/world/middleeast/isis-displaying-a-deft-command-of-varied-media.html?_r=0.

80. Giorgio Agamben, *Homo Sacer: Sovereign Power and Bare Life* (Stanford, CA: Stanford University Press, 1998).

81. Thomas Hegghammer, "The Rise of Muslim Foreign Fighters: Islam and the Globalization of Jihad," *International Security* 35, no. 3 (2010): 55.

Bibliography

Agamben, Giorgio. *Homo Sacer: Sovereign Power and Bare Life*. Stanford, CA: Stanford University Press, 1998.

Al-Tamimi, Aymenn. "A Caliphate under Strain: The Documentary Evidence." *CTC Sentinel* 9, no. 4 (2016): 1–8. https://ctc.usma.edu/a-caliphate-under-strain-the-documentary-evidence/.

Al-Tamimi, Aymenn Jawad. "Archive of Islamic State Administrative Documents." *Pundicity*, January 27, 2015. http://www.aymennjawad.org/2015/01/archive-of-islamic-state-administrative-documents.

"Are Alleged ISIS Passports a Hoax?" Public Radio International, August 14, 2014. https://www.pri.org/stories/2014-08-13/are-alleged-isis-passports-hoax.

Bahlul, Raja. "People vs. God: The Logic of 'Divine Sovereignty' in Islamic Democratic Discourse." *Islam and Christian-Muslim Relations* 11, no. 3 (2000): 287–297.

Bennison, Amira K. *The Great Caliphs: The Golden Age of the 'Abbasid Empire*. New Haven, CT: Yale University Press, 2009.

Constable, Olivia Remie. *Housing the Stranger in the Mediterranean World: Lodging, Trade, and Travel in Late Antiquity and the Middle Ages*. Cambridge, UK: Cambridge University Press, 2004.

"Danish Court Strips Islamic State Fighter of Citizenship." *Reuters*, March 31, 2017. www.reuters.com/article/us-denmark-islamic-state-idUSKBN1721VF.

Dearden, Lizzie. "Isis Plane Attack: Egypt Admits 'Terrorists' Downed Russian Metrojet Flight from Sharm el-Sheikh for First Time." *The Independent* (UK), February 24, 2016. http://www.independent.co.uk/news/world/africa/isis-plane-attack-egypt-terrorists-downed-russian-metrojet-flight-from-sharm-el-sheikh-islamic-state-a6893181.html.

Degerald, Michael. "Borders, Passports, and Daesh: How the Global System of Passports and Movement Helped Shape Both Daesh and the Refugee Crisis." *Medium*, January 21, 2016. https://medium.com/@MENAhistorian/borders-passports-and-daesh-how-the-global-system-of-passports-and-movement-helped-shape-both-2d1a41focfac.

Donner, Fred M. "The Formation of the Islamic State." *Journal of the American Oriental Society* 106, no. 2 (1986): 283–296.

"The Enemy's Words." *Dabiq*, 4. p. 46. https://clarionproject.org/docs/islamic-state-isis-magazine-Issue-4-the-failed-crusade.pdf.

Faiola, Anthony. "The Mystery Surrounding the Paris Bomber with a Fake Syrian Passport." *Washington Post*, November 18, 2015. https://www.washingtonpost.com/world/europe/the-mystery-surrounding-the-paris-bomber-with-a-fake-syrian-passport/2015/11/17/88adf3f4-8d53-11e5-934c-a369c80822c2_story.html?utm_term=.899314049638.

Farmer, Ben. "Who Is Salah Abdeslam and Who Were the Paris Terrorists? Everything We Know about the Isil Attackers." *The Telegraph*, March 18, 2016. http://www.telegraph.co.uk/news/worldnews/europe/france/11996120/Paris-attack-what-we-know-about-the-suspects.html.

Foucault, Michel. *Security, Territory, Population: Lectures at the Collège de France, 1977–78*. New York: Palgrave MacMillan, 2007.

Gehrke, Joel. "Cruz in Push to Revoke Citizenship from Americans Who Join Islamic State." *Washington Examiner*, February 14, 2017. https://www.washingtonexaminer.com/cruz-in-push-to-revoke-citizenship-from-americans-who-join-islamic-state.

Hegghammer, Thomas. "The Rise of Muslim Foreign Fighters: Islam and the Globalization of Jihad." *International Security* 35, no. 3 (2010): 53–94.
"ISIS Changes Name, Declares Islamic 'Caliphate.'" *Haaretz*, June 29, 2014. http://www.haaretz.com/middle-east-news/1.602008.
"Islamic State Fighter Is First Australian Stripped of Citizenship: Report." *Reuters*, February 11, 2017. www.reuters.com/article/us-australia-islamic-state-idUSKBN15Q05K?il=0.
Köver, Chris. "Fake or Not, These Passports Are a Branding Win for the Islamic State." *Vice*, August 15, 2014. https://news.vice.com/article/fake-or-not-these-passports-are-a-branding-win-for-the-islamic-state.
Loveluck, Louisa. "Egyptian Jihadis Claim Responsibility for Killing American Oil Worker William Henderson." *The Telegraph*, December 14, 2014. http://www.telegraph.co.uk/news/worldnews/africaandindianocean/egypt/11264664/Egyptian-jihadis-claim-responsibility-for-killing-American-oil-worker-William-Henderson.html.
Mabon, Simon, and Stephen Royal. *The Origins of ISIS: The Collapse of Nations and Revolution in the Middle East*. New York: I. B. Tauris, 2017.
March, Andrew F. "Genealogies of Sovereignty in Islamic Political Theology." *Social Research: An International Quarterly* 80, no. 1 (2013): 293–320.
March, Andrew F., and Mara Revkin. "Caliphate of Law." *Foreign Affairs*, April 15, 2015. https://www.foreignaffairs.com/articles/syria/2015-04-15/caliphate-law.
McCants, William. *The ISIS Apocalypse: The History, Strategy, and Doomsday Vision of the Islamic State*. New York: St. Martin's Press, 2015.
McKay, Hollie. "London Terror Attack: British Officials Eye Burka Ban and Stripping Citizenship." *Fox News*, June 4, 2017. http://www.foxnews.com/world/2017/06/04/london-terror-attack-british-officials-eye-burka-bans-and-stripping-citizenship.html.
McLaughlin, Jenna. "Islamic Teachings Explicitly Forbid Death by Burning, but ISIS Did It Anyway." *Mother Jones*, February 5, 2015. http://www.motherjones.com/politics/2015/02/why-burning-worse-beheading-muslims/.
"Millatu Ibrahim Leader Burns Austrian Passport, Renounces Citizenship." *Site Intelligence Group*, March 15, 2013. https://ent.siteintelgroup.com/Multimedia/millatu-ibrahim-leader-burns-austrian-passport-renounces-citizenship.html.
Nasr, Seyyed Vali Reza. *Islamic Leviathan: Islam and the Making of State Power*. Oxford, UK: Oxford University Press, 2001.
"Paris Attacks: Who Were the Attackers?" *BBC News*, April 17, 2016. http://www.bbc.com/news/world-europe-34832512.
Robertson, Craig. *The Passport in America: The History of a Document*. Oxford, UK: Oxford University Press, 2010.
Ross, Brian, Michele McPhee, and Lee Ferran. "ISIS Has Whole Fake Passport 'Industry,' Official Says." *ABC News*, January 25, 2016. http://abcnews.go.com/International/isis-fake-passport-industry-official/story?id=36505984.
Schmitt, Carl. *Political Theology: Four Chapters on the Concept of Sovereignty*. Chicago: University of Chicago Press, 2006.
Scott, James C. *Seeing Like a State: How Certain Schemes to Improve the Human Condition Have Failed*. New Haven, CT: Yale University Press, 1998.
Shane, Scott, and Ben Hubbard. "ISIS Displaying a Deft Command of Varied Media." *New York Times*, August 30, 2014. https://www.nytimes.com/2014/08/31/world/middleeast/isis-displaying-a-deft-command-of-varied-media.html?_r=0.

Sijpesteijn, Petra M. *Shaping a Muslim State: The World of a Mid-Eighth-Century Egyptian Official*. Oxford, UK: Oxford University Press, 2013.

Singh, Jasminder, and Muhammad Haziq Jani. "Al-Fatihin: Islamic State's First Malay Language Newspaper." *RSIS Commentaries*, no. 155, 2016. http://hdl.handle.net/10220/40793.

Speri, Alice. "Syria's Foreign Fighters Are There to Stay." *Vice News*, April 18, 2014. https://news.vice.com/article/syrias-foreign-fighters-are-there-to-stay.

Steed, Brian L. *ISIS: An Introduction and Guide to the Islamic State*. Santa Barbara, CA: ABC-CLIO, 2016.

Sundelin, Lennart. "Introduction: Papyrology and the Study of Early Islamic Egypt." In *Papyrology and the History of Early Islamic Egypt*, edited by Petra A. Sijpesteijn and Lennart Sundelin, 1–20. Leiden, NED: Brill, 2004.

Torpey, John C. *The Invention of the Passport: Surveillance, Citizenship, and the State*. Cambridge, UK: Cambridge University Press, 2018.

Trombley, Frank R. "Sawirus ibn al-Muqaffa' and the Christians of Umayyad Egypt: War and Society in Documentary Context." In *Papyrology and the History of Early Islamic Egypt*, edited by Petra A. Sijpesteijn and Lennart Sundelin, 199–226. Leiden, NED: Brill, 2004.

"UKIP's Paul Nuttall Says Party 'Vindicated' on Immigration." *BBC News*, June 6, 2017. http://www.bbc.com/news/election-2017-40171947.

Walt, Stephen M. "ISIS as Revolutionary State." *Foreign Affairs* 94 (2015): 42.

Wansbrough, John. "The Safe-Conduct in Muslim Chancery Practice." *Bulletin of the School of Oriental and African Studies* 34, no. 1 (1971): 20–35.

Weiss, Michael. "Confessions of an ISIS Spy." *The Daily Beast*, November 15, 2015. https://www.thedailybeast.com/confessions-of-an-isis-spy.

Wood, Graeme. "What ISIS Really Wants." *The Atlantic*, March 2015. https://www.theatlantic.com/magazine/archive/2015/03/what-isis-really-wants/384980/.

Yeşiltaş Murat, and Tuncay Kardaş. "The New Middle East, ISIL, and the 6th Revolt Against the West." In *Non-State Armed Actors in the Middle East*, edited by Murat Yeşiltaş and Tuncay Kardaş, 147–167. Cham, Switzerland: Palgrave Macmillan, 2018.

Zavis, Alexandra, and Batsheva Sobelman. "Friends, Supporters Worked to Keep Steven Sotloff's Israel Ties Secret." *Los Angeles Times*, September 5, 2014. http://www.latimes.com/world/middleeast/la-fg-sotloff-israel-20140906-story.html.

WILLIAM LAFI YOUMANS is Associate Professor at George Washington University's School of Media and Public Affairs. He is the author of *Unlikely Audience: Al Jazeera's Struggle in America*.

4 Picturing Statehood during ISIS's Caliphal Days

Kareem El Damanhoury

Visual imagery is a powerful means of argumentation. Images argue and counterargue,[1] shape collective memory,[2] and imply a proximity to the truth and an ability to prove claims.[3] An image can be an ideal carrier of messages not only at the national level but also across borders, languages, and cultures.[4] In the context of established state actors like the United States, for example, some images have created identity and bolstered citizenship by serving as iconic photographs that model citizenship and reproduce ideology[5] and as representational forms that define cultural boundaries.[6] For nonstate actors, however, images can stimulate imagination and create a "political state of being."[7]

As a nonstate actor that claims statehood, ISIS disseminated its visual imagery in multiple-language publications to reach a wider range of audience groups. In its heyday, ISIS produced several publications targeting an English-speaking audience (*Dabiq* magazine), a French-speaking audience (*Dar al-Islam* magazine), a Turkish-speaking audience (*Konstantiniyye* magazine), and a Russian-speaking audience (*Istok* magazine) between summer 2014 and summer 2016. As ISIS transitioned into another phase marked by territorial losses, it condensed its publications into one monthly magazine, *Rumiyah*, that was produced in ten different languages, including English, French, German, Turkish, Ughur, Urdu, and Pashto, between September 2016 and September 2017. In its thirteen issues, ISIS used almost the same imagery and infographics across the different versions of each issue, targeting diverse audience groups with a seemingly one-publication-fits-all strategy. Nonetheless, a key audience group was always missing in *Rumiyah* and its predecessors: the Arabic-speaking audience. However, ISIS has targeted this audience group with an Arabic-language weekly online newsletter, *al-Naba'*, since late 2015. Even with all its non-Arabic publications stalled since September 2017 and with the territorial losses it has suffered in Iraq and Syria[8], ISIS still manages to produce and disseminate *al-Naba'*. ISIS has always segmented its local and global networks, using *al-Naba'* to target the former and *Dabiq*, *Rumiyah*, and others to target the latter.

ISIS's Visual Campaign

Visual imagery has been particularly salient in ISIS's communication campaign, yet it has not been sufficiently studied comparatively between English and Arabic publications. ISIS disseminated more than fifty thousand images on Twitter between January 2015 and August 2016, making up 90 percent of its visual media products[9] and used an average of one hundred images per *Dabiq* issue.[10] Under immense military pressure, imagery also constituted the majority of ISIS's media products in late 2016 and early 2017.[11] Meanwhile, unofficial pro-ISIS groups put out several thousand images per month.[12] To examine ISIS's imagery, many researchers focus on its English-language magazines, highlighting *Dabiq*'s glossiness and its similarities with al-Qaeda's *Inspire* magazine;[13] comparing *Dabiq* images with those appearing in the English version of *Rumiyah* magazine and Rayat al-Tawhid's online materials,[14] tracing the origin of *Dabiq* images and the incorporation of mainstream media's imagery,[15] comparing the adaptation of the about-to-die visual trope in *Dabiq* and *al-Naba'* images,[16] and grouping *Dabiq* images according to visual frames, purpose, and/or narrative theme.[17] Two other studies focus exclusively on *al-Naba'* infographics by examining the arguments of authority and depictions of statehood.[18] Several other studies examine ISIS's media products, including videos, photo reports, and audio productions, on Twitter or Telegram by grouping various media products into themes and frames, yet without focusing exclusively on images.[19] ISIS's Arabic publication has not received as much attention, despite its strategic role as both an online and reportedly offline newsletter distributed in the group's claimed territories.

This chapter expands on previous work by comparing the way ISIS utilized visual arguments to bolster its state status in the English-language magazine, *Dabiq*, and Arabic-language newsletter, *al-Naba'*, when it controlled territory in Iraq and Syria. To do so, the chapter explores the similarities and differences in ISIS's visual depiction of statehood across almost two thousand images. After highlighting international norms for statehood as a global framework to evaluate ISIS's visual arguments, reviewing the history of the group's state project, and laying out the study's mixed-methods approach, I will then compare the relationship between visuals and statehood in *Dabiq* and *al-Naba'* through the lens of the Montevideo Convention and discuss its implications for counter-messaging campaigns. As the analysis will show, ISIS's appropriation of the international norms of statehood differed in its visual arguments when targeting an English-speaking audience versus an Arabic-speaking audience.

International Norms of Statehood

Despite ISIS's apparent violations of international law, its statehood claims can be examined through the framework of international norms, as with previous attempts in the twentieth century by Manchuria, Rhodesia, Croatia, and Bosnia and Herzegovina. The Montevideo Convention has been a prominent framework for defining statehood. In December 1933, the United States and nineteen Latin American countries met in Montevideo, Uruguay, and approved four criteria for statehood: "a) a permanent population; b) a defined territory; c) government; and d) capacity to enter into relations with the other states."[20] The Montevideo Convention asserted that any entity that meets all four statehood criteria has the right to "legislate upon its interests, administer its services, and to define the jurisdiction and competence of its courts,"[21] even if no other state recognizes it. The Montevideo Convention's adopted standards have become part of customary international law and benchmarks for identifying statehood ever since.[22]

Despite the lack of recognition by any nation-state, ISIS arguably met all four criteria for statehood for a period of time.[23] The declaration of the Islamic State of Iraq (ISI) in 2006 was a form of self-representation as a state, despite not meeting the criteria for statehood. Almost a decade later, however, the group was in a quite different position. First, by 2015, ISIS-controlled areas had a prewar population ranging between 2.8 million and 5.3 million people.[24] Second, ISIS controlled and practiced some form of governance over its territories in Iraq and Syria.[25] Third, ISIS exhibited a capacity to enter into relations with other states by reportedly exporting oil through Turkey, selling antiquities internationally, and receiving funds.[26] Since the self-declaration of the caliphate in summer 2014, ISIS has highlighted its governance capabilities over claimed territories through announcements of ministries and depictions of social services, economic activities, law enforcement, education, and health care. Whereas over one-fourth of ISIS's online media products highlighted governance, *da'wah* (preaching), and *hisba* (moral policing) activities in April 2015,[27] over half of its media products depicted a utopia that is characterized by social services, justice, prosperity, and religiosity a few months later.[28] Similarly, almost one-fourth of *Dabiq* images depicted a utopian state, using images of orphanages, schools, workshops, hospitals, clinics, and sharia courts.[29]

ISIS is not the first militant group to claim statehood, but it had created the most successful model during its three-and-a-half-year tenure as a self-declared caliphate (and over ten years as a self-declared state) until the loss of its heartland in Iraq and Syria in 2017. Despite the death of many of its leaders, the depletion of its resources, and the loss of its territory, ISIS achieved what no other Islamist militant group could do.[30] Although al-Qaeda (AQ) Central is reluctant to declare statehood anywhere until it wins the hearts and minds of Muslims and controls vast territory, al-Qaeda in Iraq declared the Islamic State of Iraq (ISI) in 2006 before achieving either. Other AQ affiliates followed suit and declared statehood, such as al-Shabab in Somalia, al-Qaeda in the Arabian Peninsula (AQAP) in Yemen, and al-Qaeda in the Islamic Maghreb (AQIM) in Mali. But they all rapidly crumbled due to their harsh implementation of sharia law and provocation of local tribes and/or other countries.[31] ISIS, however, set the establishment of a state as a priority over global terrorism.[32] Thus, it reversed the win-hearts-and-minds tactic by first declaring the so-called ISI. Despite its weakness between 2007 and 2009, ISI was keen on projecting and preserving its statehood image by announcing two cabinets of ministers in April 2007 and September 2009 and maintaining an online presence.[33] Following its expansion in Syria, the group adopted the name ISIS in April 2013.

After the declaration of the caliphate in June 2014, ISIS reportedly released a blueprint on how to consolidate power in its territories and expand further, according to a document that was leaked to and translated by Aymen Al-Tamimi.[34] Chapters five, six, and seven of the master plan explain some of ISIS's state-building projects to organize the provinces by securing oil and gas resources, use gold as currency, preserve the natural assets, administer wealth and projects by using specialists, secure trade routes between provinces, break through monopolies, increase local production, and implement new investment projects. Through such balance, ISIS was able to avoid the fates of earlier statehood attempts by AQIM, al-Shabab, and AQAP for an extended period of time. This chapter examines ISIS's efforts in utilizing visual arguments to create and maintain its statehood image in both *Dabiq* and *al-Naba'* publications.

Methodology

To obtain a better understanding of ISIS's visual statehood arguments and how it markets itself to English- and Arabic-speaking audiences in *Dabiq* and *al-Naba'* respectively, this study employed a mixed-methods approach, using content and visual framing analyses. The study examined a total of 1,966 images appearing in the first fifteen issues of *Dabiq*, issued from July 2014 to July 2016, and the first twenty-six available online issues of *al-Naba'*, issued from December 2015 to June 2016. Three female and two male coders from Egypt, China, and the United States coded the entire sample of images after devising a coding instrument, conducting a pilot study, and revising the instrument accordingly.

Content and Visual Framing Analyses

The study started with a quantitative content analysis to examine the visual semiotics, including the viewer's perceived distance, camera angle, direct eye contact, facial expressions, and size. Visual semiotics constitute the visual grammar to understand the message an individual image conveys.[35] The viewer's perceived distance, or proxemics, influence the viewer's connection with the photo subject. The intimate, personal, social, and public distances can distinguish among intimates, friends, acquaintances, and strangers in the image.[36] In that sense, close and medium shots tend to personify and prompt connection with photo subject(s), compared to long shots that depersonify and depict them as types.[37] The camera angle, or viewer position, depicts symbolic power and influences the viewer's evaluations of characters. Low camera angles tend to imply the subject's superiority and symbolic power, compared to eye-level angle that implies equality and visual parity with the viewer and high angles that imply inferiority and symbolic weakness.[38] Further, direct eye contact has been used to establish an imaginary connection with the photo subject, and the subject sends a message to and makes a demand from the viewer.[39] Understanding that message or demand requires an examination of the immediate visual context and the photo subject's facial expressions. Moreover, the size of the image influences the viewer's attention and perception of the covered issue.[40] These variables were added to a preliminary coding instrument.

Then, the material underwent an inductive, qualitative analysis of the choice of visual frames, which were selected based on the recurring themes and patterns regarding the state-related elements contained within the images. The study applied Robert M. Entman's definition of framing,[41] a process in which communicators select certain aspects of an issue and make them more salient in order to "promote a particular problem definition, causal interpretation, moral evaluation, and/or treatment recommendation" to images.[42] Accordingly, a statehood coding category was added to the coding instrument to examine the visual depiction of social services, law-enforcement activities, maps, economic activities, natural landscapes, pledges of allegiance, and media promotion/distribution, as well as a mixed option for images depicting more than one component. After being trained on the coding instrument and applying it in a pilot study, the coders revised the instrument to guide the entire coding process. Two coders coded each *Dabiq* and *al-Naba'* issue, yielding an overall intercoder reliability of .915 using Cohen's Kappa. Table 4.1 includes the intercoder reliability levels achieved on each of the coding categories. A third coder resolved all discrepancies between the pairs of coders.

Statehood Visual Frames

Statehood images are prevalent in both *Dabiq* and *al-Naba'* publications, yet the types of images differ between the two. The statehood images are broken down into seven main visual frames, ranging from social services, law enforcement, tribes, and populations pledging allegiance to ISIS, media promotion/distribution, economic activities, and maps of territories to natural landscapes. The social services frame depicts the provision of services in ISIS-claimed territories, such as education, electricity restoration, street-cleaning services, eldercare, orphanages, and *zakat* (tidings) distribution. The law enforcement frame depicts efforts to maintain law and order in ISIS territories by implementing its interpretation of

Table 4.1. Intercoder Reliability of Coding Instrument.

Variable	Percent Agreement	Cohen's Kappa
Size	99.02	0.97
Distance	90.95	0.88
Viewer Position	94.64	0.87
Facial Expressions	95.98	0.91
Eye Contact	95.94	0.93
Nonmilitary Activity	96.10	0.93

Intercoder reliability between coders on each variable examined in this chapter.

sharia law—stoning for adultery, throwing off buildings for homosexuality, cutting hands for robbery, execution for banditry and treachery—as well as carrying out *hisba* activities, such as leveling graves; confiscating *haram* materials; and burning cigarettes, alcohol, and drugs. The pledging-allegiance frame depicts tribes and individuals joining the group and declaring their loyalty to ISIS and its leader, al-Baghdadi. The media distribution/promotion frame depicts the availability and accessibility of ISIS's media products through images showing media kiosks in its territories and the distribution of videos, publications, and literature. The economic-activities visual frame depicts the prosperity in ISIS-controlled lands by showing trade and busy markets. The maps frame depicts the territory ISIS allegedly controlled or was fighting over, mainly in Iraq and Syria. Finally, the natural-landscapes visual frame depicts the beauty and serenity of ISIS-controlled lands and territories.

Dabiq *Magazine*

Statehood images constitute a prevalent visual strategy in *Dabiq* online magazine, with a special emphasis on its governance capability. Out of 1,475 images, 307 (21 percent) display a nonmilitary statehood activity. Averaging 20 statehood images per issue, ISIS promotes its self-proclaimed state predominantly in Iraq and Syria as a so-called utopian Islamic caliphate that is pristine, geographically established, economically sufficient, and media savvy, with established social services and an infrastructure for implementing sharia law.

Government

ISIS's depiction of statehood relies on each of the Montevideo Convention's four criteria of statehood (see table 4.2). First, the images of law enforcement, social services, economic activities, and state propaganda promote the *topos* of a functioning government. *Dabiq* photo editors visually emphasize law enforcement as the most important component of its so-called state, which foregrounds the

Table 4.2. Size of *Dabiq* Statehood Images.

Statehood	Full Page	Half Page	Less than Half	Expands over Two Pages	Total
Social Services	7	3	63	0	73
Law Enforcement	6	18	74	0	98
Maps	3	1	8	0	12
Economy	4	1	11	0	16
Natural Landscape	10	3	19	2	34
Pledging Allegiance	0	3	20	0	23
Media Promotion/Distribution	6	2	36	0	44
Mixed	0	0	7	0	7
Total	36	31	238	2	307

The types and sizes of statehood images varied in *Dabiq*, with the majority consisting of images of less than half a page in size.

group's capability to provide a semblance of law and order in an area ravaged by war. About one-third of statehood images show law-enforcement activities, such as arrests, public executions, and punishments for civil crimes. Executions of locals constitute the most prominent type of law-enforcement images in *Dabiq*, despite not garnering as much attention in Western media as the executions of foreigners.

According to one study, out of seventy-four foreigners executed by ISIS between January 2015 and April 2016, seventy executions were covered by Western media, while only 165 out of 1,134 executions of locals were covered.[43] Almost 36 percent of full-page and half-page statehood images emphasize ISIS's punitive actions against enemies, including the immolation of Jordanian pilot Muaz al-Kasasbeh, the beheading of James Foley, the shooting of a spy working for the Israeli Mossad, and the execution of an officer in the Syrian army. In that sense, quite similar to Western media's emphasis on the executions of foreigners,[44] ISIS visually emphasizes the executions of foreign hostages, despite their relatively rare occurrence compared to executions of locals. A total of twenty-nine law-enforcement images, or almost 41 percent of all statehood images shot from a high angle, look down on and belittle enemies as ISIS militants execute them; sinners as hisba agents punish them according to the group's interpretation of sharia to expiate their sins (as the group puts it); and prohibited substances as hisba agents confiscate and burn them. The depiction of enemies and sinners as inferior beings is reinforced with their recurring negative facial expressions of fear and desperation and their gaze looking downward or directly to the viewer. As many as 85 percent of all statehood images using such negative expressions and more than 60 percent of images showing the photo subjects looking

{And do not dispute and [thus] lose courage and [then] your strength would depart} [Al-Anfal: 46].

It's important to note that the forces of kufr and apostasy have understood that they are further weakened when divided. As such, they regularly hasten to set aside their differences for the sake of waging war against the truth, for just as Shaytān incites the children of Ādam to split and divide along racial, ethnic, and tribal lines in order to divert them from maintaining the firm bond of walā' and barā', so too does he incite them to set aside such petty differences for the sake of uniting them in waging war against Islam. His incitement of the kuffar and tawāghīt to that end has today culminated in the formation of an alliance of over 60 nations to fight the Islamic State! And as Allah informs us, the answer to any coalition of disbelievers seeking to wage war against Islam and the Muslims is for the Ummah to strengthen its walā' and barā'.

{And those who disbelieved are allies of one another. If you do not do so, there will be fitnah on earth and great corruption} [Al-Anfal: 73].

So let every Muslim who wishes to taste the sweetness of walā' and barā' follow the example of Ibrāhīm and declare enmity towards the kuffar amongst his own people – whether black, white, Arab, or non-Arab – and then march forth and wage war against them with whatever means are available to him.

DABIQ 21

Fig. 4.1 A full-page image of a hostage about to be executed in *Dabiq* issue 11.

downward or directly to the camera are in the law-enforcement visual frame (see fig. 4.1). Overall, law-enforcement images visualize the consequences of violating ISIS's penal code and hence use high angles, negative facial expressions, direct or downward gaze of those being punished, and the size of the image to showcase the violators' weakness, emphasize ISIS's authority, and warn potential violators.

Dabiq images highlight social services as the second-most-emphasized statehood activity. Almost one-quarter of the statehood images show services operating within ISIS-controlled territories, such as health care, education, *zakat* to the poor and needy, and building of infrastructure (e.g., laying electricity cables, installing streetlights, and paving roads). About half of social service images relate to health care. They display health workers aiding civilians after the airstrikes in Raqqa, eldercare homes in the Ninawa Province, and hospitals in both Syria and Iraq. As many as 80 percent of social services images are shot at a social/public distance (greater than four feet), which prioritizes the exhibition of various "types" of services over personifying photo subjects.[45] The third-most-frequent category of statehood images features the ISIS government's public-information apparatus. Fourteen percent of the *Dabiq* statehood images advertise ISIS's media products: *Dabiq* magazine, Islamic State Report (ISR) newsletters, news of the caliphate hashtags, al-Bayan radio, and the al-Hayat Media Center's video series, for example. Whereas ISIS's promotional posters often appear on less than half a page in *Dabiq*, almost one-fifth of them place more emphasis on *Dabiq*, al-Bayan radio, and central video releases by promoting them on either a full or half page. Five percent of the statehood images depict economic activities in ISIS's claimed territories to establish the economic vibrancy and sustainability of the state. Over half of economic-related images display ISIS's new gold dinar to announce the return of the currency of the early Islamic caliphate. Emphasizing on the notion of economic independence and autonomy, more than 80 percent of the economy images display the dinar or people trading in markets at a close to medium distance (less than four feet), while one-fourth of the images display the new dinar on full pages. Together, the social services, economic activities, and ISIS's media visual frames complement the law-enforcement frame to depict ISIS as a functioning government and a prosperous state capable of providing services, boosting its economy, and operating its own public-information apparatus.

Territory

Second, images of maps and natural landscapes deploy another line of argument for statehood established at Montevideo: the physical geographic territory of the ISIS state. More than one in every ten of the statehood images visualizes natural scenery in ISIS-claimed territories to establish the "Islamic State" as a pristine landscape with expansive possibilities. Emphasizing beauty and serenity, ten natural landscape images appear on full pages, making up over one-fourth of all statehood full-page images. For example, an image of a garden appears on a full page in the eighth issue, complementing a prophetic hadith that predicts the emergence of a caliphate in the Holy Land. Another image of farmland with dozens of sheep and a dog protecting them expands over two pages in the first issue, complementing an article that explains the concept of *Imamah* (leadership). More than 90 percent of such landscapes are shot from a social/public distance to display their various types within ISIS-claimed territory, ranging from sunset, sunrise, valleys in Qawqaz, and deserts of Arabia to seas and oceans. ISIS also uses maps to display its territory or what it claims to be Muslim lands that should be acquired. Consistent with the group's disregard for borders, ISIS uses a full-page borderless map on the cover page of *Dabiq*'s first issue. The unlabeled map, which shows the Arabian Peninsula and parts of the Levant and Egypt, reinforces the group's notions of territorial fluidity, expansionism, and defiance

Fig. 4.2 A full-page image of a borderless map on the cover of *Dabiq* issue 1.

of geographical boundaries (see fig. 4.2). Taken together, natural landscape and map visual frames serve as a signifier of ISIS's territorial control and aspirations as well as the pristine nature of these lands.

Population and Capacity to Enter into Relations

Third, the remainder of the images highlight both the Montevideo Convention criteria of a permanent population and the capacity to enter into relations with other groups and tribes. About 7 percent of state images showcase ISIS's expanding population and relationships with tribes and distant militant groups. The pledging allegiance (*bay'ah*) images depict different tribes, Kurdish villagers, members of the Iraqi government, members of other factions in Iraq and Syria, and militant groups in other locations pledging lifelong allegiance to ISIS leader Abu Bakr al-Baghdadi—all of which suggest ISIS has a strong relationship with its allied groups. With all pledging allegiance images appearing on half pages or less, over 78 percent display at least one person at an intimate/personal distance, hence personifying and prompting connection with those who have taken the decision to join ISIS. The pledging allegiance visual frame displays different groups of people as they come together to announce their loyalty to ISIS's leader. These images suggest that the populations living in ISIS-controlled lands are increasing, with more people pouring in. The scene of these images expands beyond ISIS's former strongholds in Iraq and Syria to Libya, Algeria, Pakistan, Afghanistan, Somalia, and Nigeria, thus signifying a continually expanding population.

Taken together, the statehood images in *Dabiq* employ the four topoi for statehood. The images portray a functioning government ruling over a defined territory where a permanent population resides and is capable of entering into lasting relationships with other groups and tribes.

Al-Naba' Newsletter

Statehood images also constitute a prevalent visual strategy in the *al-Naba'* newsletter for its Arabic-speaking audience. Out of 491 images, almost one-quarter display statehood activities, including maps of controlled/disputed territories, media promotion/distribution, social services, law enforcement, and pledges of allegiance. Averaging 4.5 statehood images per issue, ISIS promotes a self-proclaimed state that is quite different from the one depicted in its English-language publication. ISIS's promotion of its statehood in *al-Naba'* imagery evokes the Montevideo Convention's topoi of state government but does so in a more limited way than in *Dabiq*.

Government

Al-Naba' narrows the scope of the visual argument for a functioning government when targeting its Arabic-speaking audience. Only 9 percent of the newsletter's statehood images visualize executions of reported spies and local enemies, and none display any other law-enforcement activities (i.e., threat prevention or the punishments for civil crimes). The executions of foreign individuals are absent in the *al-Naba'* publication, unlike in *Dabiq*. Using intimate/personal distance, law-enforcement images bring the jurists of local enemy groups, *sahwa* rebels, and alleged spies closer to the viewer in 80 percent of the images, while in positions of submission, weakness, and desperation (see fig. 4.3). Additionally, the wide variety of social services imagery in *Dabiq*—educational facilities, elder homes, hospitals, and building infrastructure—does not appear in *al-Naba'*. Instead, about 12 percent of *al-Naba'* statehood images highlight social services, mostly focusing on the payment of *zakat* to the poor and needy, sharia courses, public proselytizing events, and media kiosks where civilians can read, watch, and

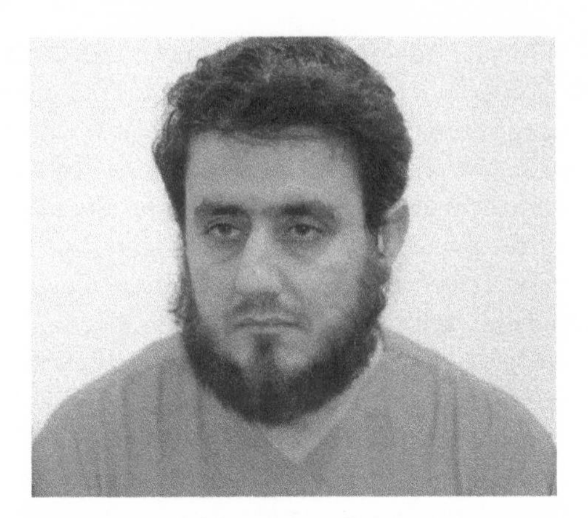

Fig. 4.3 Muhammad Tabshu, the jurist for the Levantine Front group, before his execution in *al-Naba'* issue 11.

listen to ISIS media products. According to an interview with its media agents in the twenty-first issue of *al-Naba'*, ISIS operated more than sixty media kiosks in Ninawa Province, thirty-nine in Dijla Province, and twenty-five in Raqqa Province as of March 2016. The group does not emphasize its social-services imagery in *al-Naba'*, with all such images appearing on less than half a page each. Unlike images of social services in *Dabiq*, which are mostly shot at a social/public distance, 70 percent of social-services images in *al-Naba'* place at least one photo subject closer to the viewer at an intimate/personal distance, depicting civilians as they receive zakat money, gather at a media point, or attend public events. The ISIS state pictured in *al-Naba'* appears neither economically vibrant nor sustainable, with only one image shot from a social/public distance and showing men, teenagers, and fully covered women walking and checking clothes displayed in the market. The image accompanies an article titled "The Regulations for Muslim Women Going Out to the Market" in the twenty-eighth issue. In the meantime, *al-Naba'* photo editors extensively highlight the public-information apparatus, with about 44 percent of statehood images advertising Arabic-language media products, such as *al-Himma* Library publications (e.g., posters, flyers, and books), *al-Naba'* newsletter, *Istok* Russian publication, *Dar al-Islam* French publication, *al-Bayan* radio programming, and banners promoting provincial videos. While the majority of state propaganda images are doctored graphically to display various photo subjects on video banners and flyers, very few images display a single photographed scene. For example, one image appears in the twenty-first issue showing several civilians lining up at a window, where a man sits on a computer and distributes the fifteenth issue of the *al-Naba'* newsletter to the people. If viewers accept the visual argument of *al-Naba'*, they can rely on ISIS as a reliable information source. Despite the restrained representation of law and order and social services in *al-Naba'*, with an average of almost one image per issue, the visualization of the government criterion is largely dependent on promoting ISIS's public-information apparatus, with an average of two images per *al-Naba'* issue. The group's capacity to achieve other government functions, however, remains more elusive in the imaginary.

Territory

Al-Naba' images also regularly feature the statehood topos of physical territory but again do so in a way that differs from *Dabiq*. With greater emphasis than *Dabiq*, more than one-third of statehood images in *al-Naba'* visualize mapped territory of ISIS-claimed lands and sites of military operations. Whereas 91 percent of maps appear as small images in *al-Naba'* pinpointing areas of ISIS's operations, three maps appear as full-page infographics listing the suicide attacks against security forces and *shi'a* civilians in Syria and Lebanon in the sixteenth issue, highlighting the major attacks against Russian security forces and civilians across the provinces in the thirty-fourth issue, and historicizing conquests and operations by the early Muslims in the month of Ramadan during the life of the Prophet Muhammad in the thirty-fifth issue. Just like in *Dabiq*, the maps in *al-Naba'* usually omit the borders between countries to depict lands of Muslim-majority populations as legitimate territory for the so-called caliphate. The large display of maps depicts ISIS as a powerful militant group capable of controlling land and fighting simultaneously on multiple fronts. However, unlike the *Dabiq* imagery, *al-Naba'* does not romanticize ISIS-claimed physical territory; instead, it avoids shots of pristine, natural landscapes altogether.

Population and Capacity to Enter into Relations

Al-Naba' imagery generally avoids visual arguments for permanent populations or relationships with other states, tribes, and other members of the population. Only two images in *al-Naba'* depict pledges of allegiance by groups of militants in the Philippines and Khurasan, leaving the lasting population status of the state in doubt. One image, accompanying the article "Emirs of the Mujahideen Battalions Meet in the Philippines Islands and Announce their Pledge of Allegiance to the Caliph of Muslims" in the twelfth issue, displays more than twenty fighters in the Philippines gathered to pledge allegiance to Abu Bakr al-Baghdadi, with weapons in their hands and ISIS's black flag in the background. The other image, accompanying an interview with the self-declared *Wali* (ruler) of Khurasan in the seventeenth issue displays several fighters gathered in Khurasan to pledge their allegiance to al-Baghdadi as their leader reads the pledge from a small piece of paper. No images of tribes, villagers, and civilians pledging their allegiance to al-Baghdadi appear in *al-Naba'*. Thus, the pledge of allegiance visual frame in *al-Naba'* narrows down the population expansion only to a number of dispersed militants in distant locales.

The newsletter portrays an aspirational militant group that extensively promotes its public information apparatus, constantly fights for control over physical territory, and occasionally enters into relations with distant militants. Less clear is whether the group can provide social services and maintain control over a permanent population. In that sense, the visualization of ISIS's statehood in *al-Naba'* does not live up to the standards set in *Dabiq* imagery.

Segmented Visual Campaigns

The analysis of statehood depictions in ISIS's English and Arabic publications highlights the importance of argumentative context in its strategic communication campaign and finds that the group used a segmented visual campaign of statehood with differential visual arguments to target different audience groups. Although violent and militaristic imagery was frequent in *Dabiq* and *al-Naba'*, the group constantly balanced such imagery with statehood depictions. Targeting an Arab audience in a region mostly ravaged by conflict, the group used *al-Naba'* to shed light on its aspirations, capability, and persistence to win over other warring factions, and hence presented a localized, militaristic insurgency that is fighting off Arab states—Iraq, Syria, Libya, Yemen, Egypt, Algeria, Tunisia, Saudi Arabia, and Somalia—and other militant groups. *Al-Naba'* imagery foregrounded ISIS-claimed and contested territories in maps and its public information apparatus in promotional material. Using borderless maps appearing in *al-Naba'*, ISIS blurred the line between territorial control and territorial aspirations, implying the legitimacy of acquiring Muslim lands. It also positioned itself as the only credible and Islamic voice to be heard through its wide-ranging media products. However, with limited law-enforcement and social-services capacity as well as an inability to expand its population, *al-Naba'* imagery failed to present a functioning state. By doing so, ISIS adopted a less utopian, more realistic approach when targeting the local Arab audience who are closer in proximity to the group's former heartland. Hence, ISIS's local, realistic approach was arguably more consistent and aligned with actual conditions on the ground, falling short of the four criteria for statehood.

On the other hand, targeting a global English-speaking audience that is far from ISIS-claimed territories, *Dabiq* imagery romanticized life under ISIS's rule and depicted an all-encompassing, fully functional caliphate that supersedes nation-states, implements sharia law, engages in a global conflict, and emphasizes individual agency by calling on Muslims to join voluntarily. *Dabiq* foregrounded the group's capability to govern and control a population and highlighted the breadth and serenity of its controlled lands. The English-language publication visualized ISIS's law-enforcement and social-services capacity at the time as well as its aspirations to expand further to lands once ruled by the Ummayyad and Abbasid Muslim empires in medieval times. Images of pledges of allegiance and economic prosperity complemented the group's visual argument for a sustainable Islamic state. By doing so, *Dabiq*'s visual argument globalized the conflict and presented a viable alternative to living in the West by instilling high expectations and incentivizing immigration in search of a self-fulfilling life under the banner of a newly declared utopian caliphate. Taken together, this comparative study helps explain how ISIS deployed segmented, cross-cultural visual arguments that likely influenced the decisions of at least forty thousand foreign fighters who traveled to Iraq and Syria to become part of the nascent state.[46]

With ISIS utilizing audience segmentation strategies based on the audience's language and/or proximity to the group's militant activity, a one-size-fits-all countermessaging campaign is likely to fail. Although ISIS might have temporarily lost its statehood appeal after defeat in Iraq and Syria, it still adopts segmentation strategies that must be considered when developing alternative and counternarratives. At this transitional period, ISIS is operating as an insurgency with its militants fighting a guerilla warfare in Iraq, Syria, Sinai, Afghanistan, and Yemen. Targeting its Arab audience, ISIS still releases the *al-Naba'* newsletter, provincial videos, and imagery to document its militant activity in the region. This as the group's weakened state has largely hindered its ability to conduct large-scale attacks in Western countries, such as the Paris and Brussels attacks, and thus it is now dependent on inspired lone actors to terrorize the West. Targeting its English-speaking audience, ISIS continues to release videos calling for more attacks in Western countries in support of the caliphate. Further, ISIS has left behind an accessible online archive of multilingual publications and videos that document its caliphal legacy, prompt nostalgia among supporters, and provide instructions for lone-actor attacks.

Countering ISIS's segmented messaging necessitates the development of alternative and equally compelling narratives that can address the differential argumentative contexts to effectively reach different audience groups. A focus solely on the group's brutality, for example, would be a statement of the obvious for many ISIS supporters. Instead, exposing the incompetency of ISIS's state project, for example, could help shatter the idealized spectacle and narrative the group has created over the past few years. Without providing compelling, localized, and contextual alternatives to potential ISIS supporters, however, a narrative would have nothing to offer. To guide the development of such narratives, future studies can examine the visual and textual frames and strategies employed in ISIS's multilingual media products and track the shifts in its strategic communication campaign after the loss of its territory.

Notes

This chapter expands on a brief essay by the author in the 2017 Alta Argumentation Conference proceedings.

1. See D. S. Birdsell and L. Groarke, "Toward a Theory of Visual Argument," *Argumentation and Advocacy* 33 (1996): 1–10; Catherine Helen Palczewski, "Argument in an Off Key: Playing with the Productive Limits of Argument," *Arguing Communication and Culture* (2002): 1–23; M. Hardin, S. L. Walsdorf, K. Walsdorf, and B. Hardin, "The Framing of Sexual Difference in SI for Kids Editorial Photos," *Mass Communication and Society* 5, no. 3 (2002): 341–359; and L. Rodriguez and D. V. Dimitrova. "The Levels of Visual Framing," *Journal of Visual Literacy* 30, no. 1 (2011): 48–65.
2. Robert Hariman and John Lucaites, *No Caption Needed: Iconic Photographs, Public Culture, and Liberal Democracy* (Chicago: University of Chicago Press, 2007).
3. See Paul Messaris and Linus Abraham, "The Role of Images in Framing News Stories," in *Framing Public Life: Perspectives on Media and Our Understanding of the Social World*, edited by S. D. Reese, O. H. Gandy, and A. E. Grant (Mahwah, NJ: Lawrence Erlbaum, 2001), 215–226; and R. Barthes, *Camera Lucida: Reflections on Photography* (New York: Hill and Wang, 1981).
4. See Attila Kovacs, "The 'New Jihadists' and the Visual Turn from Al-Qa'ida to ISIL /ISIS/Da'ish," *Biztpol Affairs* 2, no. 3 (2015): 47–70.
5. Hariman and Lucaites, *No Caption Needed.*
6. Janis L. Edwards and Carol K. Winkler, "Representative Form and the Visual Ideograph: The Iwo Jima Image in Editorial Cartoons," *Quarterly Journal of Speech* 83, no. 3 (1997): 289–310.
7. Ariella Azoulay, *Civil Imagination: A Political Ontology of Photography* (London: Verso Books, 2015), 3.
8. Iraqi PM Media Office, 2017, "Victory Speech." https://www.facebook.com/IraqPM MediaOffice/posts/805121279672569.
9. Daniel Milton, "Communication Breakdown: Unraveling the Islamic State's Media Efforts," Combating Terrorism Center at West Point, 2016, https://ctc.usma.edu /communication-breakdown-unraveling-the-islamic-states-media-efforts/.
10. Carol Winkler, Kareem El Damanhoury, Aaron Dicker, and Anthony Lemieux, "The Medium Is Terrorism: Transformation of the About to Die Trope in Dabiq," *Journal of Terrorism and Political Violence* 31, no. 2 (2016): 224–243.
11. See Charlie Winter, "ICSR Insight: The ISIS Propaganda Decline," *ICSR*, March 23, 2017, http://icsr.info/2017/03/icsr-insight-isis-propaganda-decline/; Kareem El Damanhoury, Carol Kay Winkler, Wojciech Kaczkowski, and Aaron Dicker, "Examining the Military -Media Nexus in ISIS's Provincial Photography Campaign," *Dynamics of Asymmetric Conflict* 11, no. 2 (2018): 89–108. doi:10.1080/17467586.2018.1432869.
12. George Washington Univeristy's Progrem on Extremism tracked the distribution of such images by ISIS from June 2017 to September 2018 via its "Telegram Tracker," https:// extremism.gwu.edu/isis-online
13. See Frank Furedi, "Islamic State Propaganda Buys into Western Culture of Victimhood," *The Australian*, July 25, 2016, http://www.frankfuredi.com/article/islamic _state_propaganda_buys_into_western_culture_of_victimhood; see also Kovacs, "The New Jihadists."

14. See Peter Wignell, Sabine Tan, Kay L. O'Halloran, and Rebeca Lange, "A Mixed-Methods Empirical Examination of Changes in Emphasis and Style in the Extremist Magazines *Dabiq* and *Rumiyah*," *Perspectives on Terrorism* 11, no. 2 (2017): 19, http://www.terrorismanalysts.com/pt/index.php/pot/article/view/592/1169; see also Peter Wignell, Sabine Tan, and Kay L. O'Halloran, "Under the Shade of AK47s: A Multimodal Approach to Violent Extremist Recruitment Strategies for Foreign Fighters," *Critical Studies on Terrorism* 10, no. 3 (2017): 429–452.

15. "Overview of Daesh's Online Recruitment Propaganda Magazine, *Dabiq*," Carter Center, 2015, http://www.cartercenter.org/resources/pdfs/peace/conflict_resolution/countering-isis/dabiq-report-12-17-15.pdf.

16. Winkler, El Damanhoury, Dicker, and Lemieux, "The Medium Is Terrorism;" Damanhoury, Winkler, Kaczkowski, and Dicker, "Examining the Military."

17. Shahira Fahmy, *Visual Framing in the Islamic State* (report prepared for NATO, 2016); Kareem El Damanhoury and Carol Winkler, "Picturing Law and Order: A Visual Framing Analysis of ISIS's Dabiq Magazine," *Arab Media & Society* 25 (2018): 1–25; Stratcom Centre of Excellence, *Daesh Information Campaign and Its Influence* (2016), http://www.difesa.it/SMD_/CASD/IM/IASD/65sessioneordinaria/Documents/DaeshInformationCampaignanditsInfluence.pdf.

18. Michael Degerald, "Where Media Meets Statecraft: Daesh Promotion of Governmental Competence through Its Media," *Gobal-E* 10, no. 68 (2017), https://www.21global.ucsb.edu/global-e/october-2017/where-media-meets-statecraft-daesh-promotion-governmental-competence-through; Carol Winkler, Kareem El Damanhoury, and Anthony Lemieux, "Validating Extremism: Strategic Use of Authority Appeals in Al-Naba' Infographics," *Journal of Argumentation in Context* 7, no. 1 (2018): 33–71, https://benjamins.com/catalog/jaic.17014.win.

19. See Charlie Winter, "Apocalypse, Later: A Longitudinal Study of the Islamic State Brand," *Critical Studies in Media Communication* 35, no. 1 (2018): 103–121; Aaron Y. Zelin, "Picture or It Didn't Happen: A Snapshot of the Islamic State's Official Media Output," *Perspectives on Terrorism* 9, no. 4 (2015): 85–97.

20. Montevideo Convention 1933, "Convention on Rights and Duties of States," http://avalon.law.yale.edu/20th_century/intam03.asp.

21. Ibid., article 3.

22. Thomas D. Grant, "Defining Statehood: The Montevideo Convention and Its Discontents," *Columbia Journal of Transnational Law* 37, no. 403 (1998): 404–457, http://heinonlinebackup.com/hol-cgi-bin/get_pdf.cgi?handle=hein.journals/cjtl37§ion=19.

23. David Kilcullen, *Quarterly Essay (58) Blood Year: Terror and the Islamic State* (Melbourne: Schwartz, 2015).

24. Eli Berman and Jacob N Shapiro, "Why ISIL Will Fail on Its Own," *Politico*, November 29, 2015, http://www.politico.com/magazine/story/2015/11/why-isil-will-fail-on-its-own-213401.

25. Aaron Y. Zelin, "The Islamic State's Territorial Methodology," January 2016, http://www.washingtoninstitute.org/uploads/Documents/pubs/ResearchNote29-Zelin.pdf; Aymenn Al-Tamimi, "Archive of Islamic State Administrative Documents," *Aymennjawad.Org*, 2015, http://www.aymennjawad.org/2015/01/archive-of-islamic-state-administrative-documents.

26. Kilcullen, *Quarterly Essay.*

27. Zelin, "The Islamic State's Territorial Methodology."
28. Winter, "Apocalypse, Later."
29. Shahira Fahmy, "What ISIS Wants You to See," *Ahramonline*, February 7, 2016, http://english.ahram.org.eg/NewsPrint/186884.aspx; see also Stratcom Centre of Excellence, *Daesh Information Campaign*, 2016, https://www.stratcomcoe.org/daesh-information-campaign-and-its-influence.
30. Hassan Hassan and William McCants, "Experts Weigh In (Part 7): Is ISIS Good at Governing?" *Brookings*, April 18, 2016, http://www.brookings.edu/blogs/markaz/posts/2016/04/18-experts-weigh-in-isis-governance-hassan-mccants.
31. William McCants, *The ISIS Apocalypse: The History, Strategy, and Doomsday Vision of the Islamic State* (London: Macmillan, 2015).
32. Eric Heyl, "The Pathology of ISIS," *Trib Live*, February 21, 2015, http://triblive.com/opinion/qanda/7773945-74/isis-west-qaida.
33. Al-Furqan Media, "Announcement of Ministry Formation for the Islamic State of Iraq," *Archive.Org*, 2007, https://archive.org/details/The_Islamic_State_of-Iraq; see also Al-Furqan Media, "Second Ministry Formation for the Islamic State of Iraq," *Archive.Org*, 2009, https://archive.org/details/Al-Tashkeelah-2-Le-Dwla-Iraq-Islamic.
34. "The Isis Papers: A Masterplan for Consolidating Power," *The Guardian*, December 7, 2015, http://www.theguardian.com/world/2015/dec/07/islamic-state-document-masterplan-for-power.
35. Gunther Kress and Theo van Leeuwen, *Reading Images: The Grammar of Visual Design*, 2nd ed. (London: Rouletdge, 1996).
36. Edward T. Hall, *The Hidden Dimension* (Garden City, NY: Doubleday, 1966).
37. Carey Jewitt and Rumiko Oyama, "Visual Meaning: A Social Semiotic Approach," in *Handbook of Visual Analysis*, 7th ed., edited by Theo van Leeuwen and Carey Jewitt (London: Sage, 2008), 1:134–156; Jonathan Cohen, "Mediated Relationships and Media Effects: Parasocial Interaction and Identification," in *The Sage Handbook of Media Processes and Effects* 2, edited by R. L. Nabi and Mary Beth Oliver (Thousand Oaks, CA: Sage, 2009), 223–236.
38. Shahira Fahmy, "Picturing Afghan Women: A Content Analysis of AP Wire Photographs during the Taliban Regime and after the Fall of the Taliban Regime," *International Communication Gazette* 66, no. 2 (2004): 91–112; Robert N. Kraft, "The Influence of Camera Angle on Comprehension and Retention of Pictorial Events," *Memory & Cognition* 15, no. 4 (1986): 291–307, doi:10.3758/BF03197032; L. M. Mandell and D. L. Shaw, "Judging People in the News—Unconsciously: Effect of Camera Angle and Bodily Activity," *Journal of Broadcasting* 17 (1973): 353–362.
39. Kress and van Leeuwen, *Reading Images.*
40. Wayne Wanta, "The Effects of Dominant Photographs: An Agenda-Setting Experiment," *Journalism Quarterly* 65, no. 1 (1988): 107–111; Mario R. Garcia and Pegie Stark, *Eyes on the News* (St. Petersburg, FL: Pointer Institute for Media Studies, 1991).
41. Robert M. Entman, "Framing: Toward Clarification of a Fractured Paradigm," *Journal of Communication* 43, no. 4 (1993): 51–58.
42. Ibid., 52.
43. Judith Tinnes, "Counting Lives Lost—Statistics of Camera-Recorded Extrajudicial Executions by the 'Islamic State,'" Stratcom Centre of Excellence, http://www.terrorismanalysts.com/pt/index.php/pot/article/view/483/DATA.

44. Ibid.
45. Jewitt and Oyama, "Visual Meaning."
46. Mike Giglio and Munzer Al-Awad, "How ISIS Members Fled the Caliphate, Perhaps to Fight Another Day," *BuzzFeed News*, December 19, 2017, https://www.buzzfeed.com/mikegiglio/how-isis-members-fled-the-caliphate-perhaps-to-fight?utm_term=.fsZgbRG6n#.xyq61xXLA.

Bibliography

Al-Furqan Media. "Announcement of Ministry Formation for the Islamic State of Iraq." *Archive.Org*, 2007. https://archive.org/details/The_Islamic_State_of-Iraq.

Al-Furqan Media. "Second Ministry Formation for the Islamic State of Iraq." *Archive.Org*, 2009. https://archive.org/details/Al-Tashkeelah-2-Le-Dwla-Iraq-Islamic.

Al-Tamimi, Aymenn. "Archive of Islamic State Administrative Documents." *Aymennjawad.Org*, 2015. http://www.aymennjawad.org/2015/01/archive-of-islamic-state-administrative-documents.

Azoulay, Ariella. *Civil Imagination: A Political Ontology of Photography.* London: Verso Books, 2015.

Barthes, Ronald. *Camera Lucida: Reflections on Photography.* New York: Hill and Wang, 1981.

Berman, Eli, and Jacob N Shapiro. "Why ISIL Will Fail on Its Own." *Politico*, November 29, 2015. http://www.politico.com/magazine/story/2015/11/why-isil-will-fail-on-its-own-213401.

Birdsell, D. S., and L. Groarke. "Toward a Theory of Visual Argument." *Argumentation and Advocacy* 33 (1996): 1–10.

Cohen, Jonathan. "Mediated Relationships and Media Effects: Parasocial Interaction and Identification." In *The Sage Handbook of Media Processes and Effects* 2, edited by R. L. Nabi and Mary Beth Oliver, 223–236. Thousand Oaks, CA: Sage, 2009.

Damanhoury, Kareem El, and Carol Winkler. "Picturing Law and Order: A Visual Framing Analysis of ISIS's *Dabiq* Magazine." *Arab Media & Society* 25 (2018): 1–25.

Damanhoury, Kareem El, Carol Kay Winkler, Wojciech Kaczkowski, and Aaron Dicker. "Examining the Military-Media Nexus in ISIS's Provincial Photography Campaign." *Dynamics of Asymmetric Conflict* (2018): 1–20. doi:10.1080/17467586.2018.1432869.

Degerald, Michael. "Where Media Meets Statecraft: Daesh Promotion of Governmental Competence through Its Media." *Gobal-E* 10, no. 68 (2017). https://www.21global.ucsb.edu/global-e/october-2017/where-media-meets-statecraft-daesh-promotion-governmental-competence-through

Edwards, Janis L., and Carol K. Winkler. "Representative Form and the Visual Ideograph: The Iwo Jima Image in Editorial Cartoons." *Quarterly Journal of Speech* 83, no. 3 (1997): 289–310. doi:10.1080/00335639709384187.

Entman, Robert M. "Framing: Toward Clarification of a Fractured Paradigm." *Journal of Communication* 43, no. 4 (1993): 51–58. doi:10.1111/j.1460-2466.1993.tb01304.x.

Fahmy, Shahira. "Picturing Afghan Women: A Content Analysis of AP Wire Photographs during the Taliban Regime and after the Fall of the Taliban Regime." *International Communication Gazette* 66, no. 2 (2004): 91–112. doi:10.1177/0016549204041472.

Fahmy, Shahira. "Visual Framing in the Islamic State." Report prepared for NATO, 2016a.

Fahmy, Shahira. "What ISIS Wants You to See." *Ahramonline.* February 7, 2016. http://english.ahram.org.eg/NewsPrint/186884.aspx.

Furedi, Frank. "Islamic State Propaganda Buys into Western Culture of Victimhood." *The Australian,* July 25, 2016. http://www.frankfuredi.com/article/islamic_state_propaganda_buys_into_western_culture_of_victimhood.

Garcia, Mario R., and Pegie Stark. *Eyes on the News.* St. Petersburg, FL: Pointer Institute for Media Studies, 1991.

George Washington University Program on Extremism. "Telegram Tracker." Washington, DC, 2017–2018. https://extremism.gwu.edu/isis-online.

Giglio, Mike, and Munzer Al-Awad. "How ISIS Members Fled the Caliphate, Perhaps to Fight Another Day." *BuzzFeed News,* December 19, 2017. https://www.buzzfeed.com/mikegiglio/how-isis-members-fled-the-caliphate-perhaps-to-fight?utm_term=.fsZgbRG6n#.xyq61xXLA.

Grant, Thomas D. "Defining Statehood: The Montevideo Convention and Its Discontents." *Columbia Journal of Transnational Law* 37, no. 403 (1998): 404–457. http://heinonlinebackup.com/hol-cgi-bin/get_pdf.cgi?handle=hein.journals/cjtl37§ion=19.

Guardian, The. "The Isis Papers : A Masterplan for Consolidating Power." *The Guardian,* December 7, 2015. http://www.theguardian.com/world/2015/dec/07/islamic-state-document-masterplan-for-power.

Hall, Edward T. *The Hidden Dimension.* Garden City, NY: Doubleday, 1966.

Hardin, M., S. L. Walsdorf, K. Walsdorf, and B. Hardin. "The Framing of Sexual Difference in SI for Kids Editorial Photos." *Mass Communication and Society* 5, no. 3 (2002): 341–359.

Hariman, Robert, and John Lucaites. *No Caption Needed: Iconic Photographs, Public Culture, and Liberal Democracy.* Chicago: University of Chicago Press, 2007.

Hassan, Hassan, and William McCants. "Experts Weigh in (Part 7): Is ISIS Good at Governing?" *Brookings,* April 18, 2016. http://www.brookings.edu/blogs/markaz/posts/2016/04/18-experts-weigh-in-isis-governance-hassan-mccants.

Heyl, Eric. "The Pathology of ISIS." *Trib Live,* February 21, 2015. http://triblive.com/opinion/qanda/7773945-74/isis-west-qaida.

Iraqi PM Media Office. "Victory Speech." 2017. https://www.facebook.com/IraqPMMediaOffice/posts/805121279672569.

Jewitt, Carey, and Rumiko Oyama. "Visual Meaning: A Social Semiotic Approach." In *Handbook of Visual Analysis,* 7th ed., edited by Theo van Leeuwen and Carey Jewitt, 134–156. London: Sage, 2008. doi:10.1017/CBO9781107415324.004.

Kilcullen, David. *Quarterly Essay (58) Blood Year: Terror and the Islamic State.* Melbourne: Schwartz, 2015.

Kovacs, Attila. "The 'New Jihadists' and the Visual Turn from Al-Qa'ida to ISIL/ISIS/Da'ish." *Biztpol Affairs* 2, no. 3 (2015): 47–70.

Kraft, Robert N. "The Influence of Camera Angle on Comprehension and Retention of Pictorial Events." *Memory & Cognition* 15, no. 4 (1986): 291–307. doi:10.3758/BF03197032.

Kress, Gunther, and Theo van Leeuwen. *Reading Images: The Grammar of Visual Design,* 2nd ed. London: Rouletdge, 1996.

Mandell, L. M., and D. L. Shaw. "Judging People in the News—Unconsciously: Effect of Camera Angle and Bodily Activity." *Journal of Broadcasting* 17, no. 3 (1973): 353–362.

McCants, William. *The ISIS Apocalypse: The History, Strategy, and Doomsday Vision of the Islamic State*. London: Macmillan, 2015.

Messaris, Paul, and Linus Abraham. "The Role of Images in Framing News Stories." In *Framing Public Life: Perspectives on Media and Our Understanding of the Social World*, edited by S. D. Reese, O. H. Gandy, and A. E. Grant, 215–226. Mahwah, NJ: Lawrence Erlbaum Associates, 2001.

Milton, Daniel. "Communication Breakdown: Unraveling the Islamic State's Media Efforts." Combating Terrorism Center at West Point, 2016. https://ctc.usma.edu /communication-breakdown-unraveling-the-islamic-states-media-efforts/

Montevideo Convention. "Convention on Rights and Duties of States." 1933. Text available at: http://avalon.law.yale.edu/20th_century/intam03.asp.

"Overview of Daesh's Online Recruitment Propaganda Magazine, *Dabiq*." Carter Center, 2015. http://www.cartercenter.org/resources/pdfs/peace/conflict_resolution /countering-isis/dabiq-report-12-17-15.pdf.

Palczewski, Catherine Helen. "Argument in an Off Key: Playing with the Productive Limits of Argument." *Arguing Communication and Culture* (2002): 1–23.

Rodriguez, L., and D. V. Dimitrova. "The Levels of Visual Framing." *Journal of Visual Literacy* 30, no. 1 (2011): 48–65.

Russian MoD. "Statement of the Chief of the General Staff of the Russian Armed Forces—First Deputy Defence Minister General of the Army Valery Gerasimov." 2017. https:// www.facebook.com/mod.mil.rus/posts/2016575361918543.

Stratcom Centre of Excellence. "Daesh Information Campaign and Its Influence." 2016. http://www.difesa.it/SMD_/CASD/IM/IASD/65sessioneordinaria/Documents /DaeshInformationCampaignanditsInfluence.pdf.

Tinnes, Judith. "Counting Lives Lost—Statistics of Camera-Recorded Extrajudicial Executions by the 'Islamic State.'" 2016. http://www.terrorismanalysts.com/pt/index .php/pot/article/view/483/DATA.

Wanta, Wayne. "The Effects of Dominant Photographs: An Agenda-Setting Experiment." *Journalism Quarterly* 65, no. 1 (1988): 107–111.

Wignell, Peter, Sabine Tan, and Kay L O'Halloran. "Under the Shade of AK47s: A Multimodal Approach to Violent Extremist Recruitment Strategies for Foreign Fighters." *Critical Studies on Terrorism* 10, no. 3 (2017): 429–452. doi:10.1080/17539153.2 017.1319319.

Wignell, Peter, Sabine Tan, Kay L. O'Halloran, and Rebeca Lange. "A Mixed Methods Empirical Examination of Changes in Emphasis and Style in the Extremist Magazines *Dabiq* and *Rumiyah*." *Perspectives on Terrorism* 11, no. 2 (2017): 19. http://www .terrorismanalysts.com/pt/index.php/pot/article/view/592/1169.

Winkler, Carol, Kareem Damanhoury, Aaron Dicker, and Anthony F. Lemieux. "Images of Death and Dying in ISIS Media: A Comparison of English and Arabic Print Publications." *Media, War & Conflict* (2018). doi:10.1177/1750635217746200.

Winkler, Carol, Kareem El Damanhoury, Aaron Dicker, and Anthony Lemieux. "The Medium Is Terrorism: Transformation of the About to Die Trope in Dabiq." *Journal of Terrorism & Political Violence* 31, no. 2 (2016): 224–243. http://dx.doi.org/10.1080/09546 553.2016.1211526.

Winkler, Carol, Kareem El Damanhoury, and Anthony Lemieux. "Validating Extremism: Strategic Use of Authority Appeals in Al-Naba' Infographics." *Journal of*

Argumentation in Context 7, no. 1 (2018): 33–71. https://benjamins.com/catalog/jaic.17014.win.

Winter, Charlie. "Apocalypse, Later: A Longitudinal Study of the Islamic State Brand." *Critical Studies in Media Communication* 35, no. 1 (2018): 103–121. doi:10.1080/15295036.2017.1393094.

Winter, Charlie. "Documenting the Virtual 'Caliphate.'" Quilliam Foundation, 2015. http://www.quilliamfoundation.org/wp/wp-content/uploads/2015/10/FINAL-documenting-the-virtual-caliphate.pdf.

Winter, Charlie. "ICSR Insight: The ISIS Propaganda Decline." *ICSR*, March 23, 2017. https://icsr.info/2017/03/23/isis-propaganda-decline/

Zelin, Aaron Y. "The Islamic State's Territorial Methodology." Washington Institute, January 2016. http://www.washingtoninstitute.org/uploads/Documents/pubs/ResearchNote29-Zelin.pdf.

Zelin, Aaron Y. "Picture or It Didn't Happen: A Snapshot of the Islamic State's Official Media Output." *Perspectives on Terrorism* 9, no. 4 (2015): 85–97.

KAREEM EL DAMANHOURY is Assistant Professor in the Department of Media, Film, & Journalism Studies at the University of Denver.

Part II

Mediating Terror

5 ISIS's Media Ecology and Participatory Activism Tactics

Michael Krona

During the sociopolitical revolutions in Syria, Libya, Egypt, and other countries in the MENA region, the so-called Arab Spring of 2011 and onward, the strategic use of social media by activists was widely recognized and celebrated.[1] Concepts like "liberation technologies" and "technologies of freedom"[2] emerged in both political and academic spheres to describe the democratic and liberating function of social media. This glowing embrace of technological innovation and the practice of ascribing value and qualities to technology itself seems to return every time a new media technology emerges.

Such a celebration of contemporary participatory media cultures and online engagement has been prevalent in recent years. However, the same characteristics and mechanisms used by organizations promoting liberating and democratic aspects of social change through the use of media technologies—the foundation of media activism—have simultaneously been adopted by extremist organizations and antidemocratic groups with a completely different agenda. Such a reality suggests the need for a richer understanding of the media activism tactics and practices now deployed by several terrorist organizations—with none more explicit or successful than the Islamic State.

Media technologies change and redefine the nature of conflict at a rapid pace, but basic strategies for hybridized and mediated warfare have been seen throughout history. When German forces managed their Blitzkrieg against Poland and France during World War II, they significantly changed the pace of contemporary warfare. The international community was astonished by how quickly the Germans took over territory, and history has revealed that it was partly the result of the close coordination of radio transmissions and military strategy. The media technology was used to not only shape public perceptions of German forces but also to strategically connect those perceptions to military operations on the ground. It was a breakthrough in war tactics at the time and has been a vital ingredient in the hybridized warfare of late modern society. Radio allowed German forces to speed up their military advancement, while simultaneously allowing the Germans to incite fear among adversaries. Seven decades later, ISIS utilizes similar tactics in social media.

In early 2014, seemingly out of the blue and at a rapid pace, several major cities in northern Iraq were captured by ISIS fighters, with Iraqi government forces either abandoning their posts, killed, or captured. The brutal organization's military campaign on the ground was accompanied by a hashtag campaign on social media platforms. The #AllEyesOnISIS campaign coincided with one of the most unexpected and fastest seizure of cities, territory, and populations ever. Even if it would be an exaggeration to say that ISIS managed to seize Mosul because of their massive online campaigning, it raises an important point concerning the way the Islamic State wages war. Only two weeks before the fall of Mosul, ISIS had released a video in the series "Clanging of the Swords," a typical jihadist production meant to exhibit power and incite fear.[3] Images from this video and others were attached to the #AllEyesOnISIS hashtag and spread intensively both internationally and locally in the region. After the defeat of the Iraqi army in Mosul and Fallujah, it became clear that ISIS's mediated exploitation of atrocities also had worked to promote a sense of fear among populations and soldiers, even before the seizure of the cities began, which in turn helped the speed up the pace of ISIS's territorial expansion. The aftermath of this seizure also clarified another aspect of ISIS's hybridized warfare, namely how their operations on the ground were deeply connected to the group's online messaging.

This chapter seeks to advance the understanding of ISIS's global media endeavors as a) intersectional media strategies combining a decentralized technical infrastructure with a simultaneously highly centralized messaging practice, and b) an ecological process in which the relationships between the central organization and its supporters are manifested through forms of media activism, including tactics for disseminating propaganda attracting and targeting mainly Muslim youth around the world. After introducing an overview of the most fundamental ISIS media outlets used and a general reflection on their global propaganda strategies, the chapter explores how the media ecology of ISIS, defined as a media environment in which "a profound connectivity through which places, events, people, and their actions and inactions, seem increasingly connected"[4] plays out through forms of media activist tactics deployed by the organization in order to make platforms and sympathizers tools in ISIS's virtual universe and warfare.

New Media and ISIS Activism

One of the most significant aspects of ISIS's entire propaganda effort is the balance of content that aims to be defiant and oppositional to enemies with content meant to promote the caliphate as an attractive religious and political alternative to the West. In comparison to previous Salafi jihadist groups, the communication of this competitive system of meaning and utopian vision marks a clear break from earlier narratives. To promote this positive notion of their brand, ISIS puts extreme emphasis on levels of participation, for combatants as well as long-distance supporters.

In 2016, ISIS released a doctrine for information warfare, and it reveals much about the aim, implementation, and purposes of what ISIS considers "media jihad" with the help of "media operatives." Charlie Winter at ICSR explains ISIS's use of supporters and mainstream media platforms this way: "it is first worth examining what precisely the Islamic State means by the term 'media operative.' Crucially, the group uses it with extreme exibility—indeed, the moniker refers as much to frontline cameramen as it does to self-appointed social media disseminators. 'Everyone,' the document's authors hold, 'that participate[s] in the production and delivery' of propaganda should be regarded as one of the Islamic State's 'media *mujahidin*.'"[5]

Like no other terrorist organization, previous or present, ISIS has managed to attract and recruit tens of thousands of supporters to the caliphate in the wake of its declaration. Figures of exactly how many foreign fighters have joined ISIS since 2014 vary, but a fair assessment is that roughly 7,700 Western fighters heeded ISIS's call, together with 35,000 extremists—in total representing around 120 countries.[6] Even if considerably few academic studies so far have addressed the role of media propaganda and online radicalization in the decision to join, one can assume that the content and dissemination strategies of ISIS's media propaganda enterprise have been significant factors. There are, however, numerous studies on the actual content,[7] the financing of the organization and media enterprise,[8] and overall global propaganda strategies.[9] Reasons for this research imbalance are certainly connected to the difficulties of ethnographic and qualitative interview studies of supporters, something that would be required to reach a better understanding of the significance of media and propaganda in ISIS's success. What we have been able to do is analyze media infrastructures,[10] strategies, and content in relation to each other, working to create a holistic approach to the study of ISIS's media practices, with the hope that this understanding may help prevent further escalation of contemporary terrorist organizations' growth in the virtual realm as well as curb their ability to conduct and inspire attacks.

Approaching the operations and strategies of ISIS as a type of media activism may at first glance seem far-fetched. However, when contextualizing select features of their global digital warfare through a lens of technological adaptation (infrastructure, decentralization of messaging for instance) in combination with the mediation of a competitive system of meaning (propaganda content), it becomes apparent that ISIS deliberately adopted tactics, forms, and genres highlighted as activist practices usually anchored in discourses of improving society.[11] Media operatives within the organization, as well as supporters in the digital realm have also been referred to as "media activists" in parts of the propaganda and in internal documents.[12]

The theoretical framework of media activism as it concerns social and digital platforms takes a point of departure in the strategic use of new media technologies. Here, three main factors are involved in framing new media, namely a) devices (smartphones, cameras, etc.), b) activities (the use of the devices), and c) organizations (how the use is structured and organized).[13] ISIS has managed to synergize these three factors into one successful formula, combining it with an activism meant to challenge established structures—be they world orders, sectarian conditions, mainstream media practices, or religious doctrines. A theoretical framework of media activism would seem useful to understanding ISIS strategies within the virtual sphere, not least of all if that activism is seen as an endeavor that "makes or changes history."[14]

Previous Groups

This chapter examines the strategy behind, and deployment of, central information operations[15] in combination with an extensive global network of supporters and followers, as media activism practices and as significant parts of ISIS's cyber- and information warfare. Terrorist organizations utilizing media channels and platforms as part of operational warfare is not a new phenomenon. For instance, the mujahidin in Afghanistan in the 1980s used audiocassettes and several jihadist organizations as well as right-wing movements utilized the internet in the 1990s. In addition, in 1999 Hamas launched the Palestinian Information Center and helped generate online information favorable to the organization in different languages. Evidence also shows that groups imitate, adapt, and learn from each other.[16]

The use of videos, particularly beheading videos, as propaganda has been held up as a unique product of ISIS; however, such videos were utilized by rebel groups during the Chechen War in the early 2000s.[17] Al-Qaeda, the organization ISIS grew out of, was another early adopter of media technologies to control its messaging.[18] This can be seen in the production of the magazine *Inspire*, which was first released in 2011 and has since developed into an important outlet for the currently expanding group.[19] Al-Qaeda's branch in Syria (Hay'at Tahrir al-Sham, HTS) started another magazine called *Al-Haqaqi* in 2017, which compiles news from al-Qaeda-affiliated media offices like *Fursan Al Sham Media* and *Bilad Al Sham Media*.

Both right-wing and jihadist organizations also extensively used electronic billboards and Web 2.0 during the early 2000s;[20] however, social media has proven to be a particularly fertile ground for messaging. A recent example of a contemporary terrorist organization's strategic deployment of social media campaign is Somalia-based *Al-Shabaab*'s 2013 attack on a shopping mall in Nairobi, Kenya. During the attack, the group started tweeting live messages and images of "the carnage."[21] Accounts operated by the militants inside the mall were quickly suspended by Twitter; however, they immediately started new ones. This made clear both the significance of the online presence of terror organizations as well as the difficulties in censoring them.

ISIS of today has refined what previous groups have done, taken advantage of technological developments, and enforced use of both online and offline media strategies through which their narratives and competitive system of meaning are still deployed. What stands out is the massive media output, including media infrastructure and content, as well as the storytelling techniques and audience targeting in the videos, magazines, and other publications they produce. These elements are extensively discussed in other parts of this book. From here on, this chapter will mainly focus on ISIS's media ecology and infrastructure, the network and role of sympathizers, and how these networks serve different functions in the overall global propaganda strategy of ISIS.

Media Foundations and Platforms Utilized

A reasonable explanatory model for the success of ISIS, not least in terms of its wide global outreach and extensive virtual networks of support, is to look at the intersections between, and integration of, three dimensions: *access*, *information*, and *inspiration*. The process of making followers feel part of ISIS, regardless of geographic distance, through their online presence and participation, is a result of a synergy among these three factors.

In terms of access, ISIS has put emphasis on making its propaganda and messaging structure come as close as possible to people's everyday lives—particularly in terms of social media and mobile applications. Services like YouTube, Facebook, Twitter, Instagram, Kik, Snapchat, archive.org, justpaste.it, sendspace.com, and more recently, Telegram, Wikr, Threema, Chatsecure, WhatsApp, RocketChat, and Signal, have all been widely exploited by the organization as vehicles for information dissemination as well as spaces of interaction for recruiters and supporters.[22] Because of this extensive online presence, it's not difficult for ideologically like-minded individuals to get in touch with each other or find support from recruiters. By 2018, the main outlet for ISIS messaging had become Telegram,[23] and to some extent parts of ISIS's virtual universe can be described as a 24/7 helpdesk.

The second key factor is information. With its massive volume of content, the variety of narratives and forms, the intricate storytelling techniques and visual imagery, and the extent of languages for publications, ISIS's information and messages are easily adopted and interpreted. Information about operations and propaganda are spread and circulated on a sometimes incomprehensible number of platforms, applications, and forums. Information about the Islamic State, its ideology and vision, news updates and instructions, are not only accessible but are also sophisticated in their design and narrative structure. This creates an appealing form of communication, with information that can be found by basically anyone with a smartphone and thereby integrated into leisure end everyday life media practices.

The third and final factor concerns inspiration. With the layout (textual and visual) and specificities of the propaganda in mind, there are clear indications of inspirational appeals over the course of the last four years (2014–2018). Not only does ISIS make the information about everything from ideology and organizational structure to DIY terrorists attacks accessible, it also produces content meant to inspire supporters to not only embrace the ideology but to act on it, to live it. These three factors are essential to ISIS and have of course all been significant in the past, but ISIS's current synergy surpasses the infrastructural and content-related strategies that came before and illustrates the difficulties of countering ISIS online.

As of 2018, the research community monitoring and tracking ISIS's information operations has largely been shifting focus to the mobile application Telegram, as the organization in early 2016 deliberately moved much of its operations to this application, due to increased censorship efforts on more open media platforms. The move resulted in ISIS implementing a more encrypted communication practice.[24] Telegram allows them to conduct media raids more under the radar and then disseminate content back into surface web platforms. This shift is important to understanding ISIS's networks as a fluid, media-saturated environment where supporters online can not only form relationships with each other but also with the organization itself.

But before this move to Telegram, the media industry behind the organization was developed over a long period of time. The establishment and eventual restructuring of ISIS's media enterprise dates back more than a decade.[25] One of its core media organs, al-Furqan, was officially established in 2006 when al-Qaeda in Iraq (AQI) together with other insurgency groups became Islamic State in Iraq (ISI) and the seed of what later formed into ISIS really started to grow. Internal documents from this time suggest that al-Furqan's main purpose was to publish material that was "creative, innovative, and economical and to attempt at attracting people to such products."[26] This signified a dynamic change in comparison to al-Qaeda. In the years after the September 11 attacks, al-Qaeda's production of videos and other propaganda products was more focused on reaching a homogenous and global audience, rather than targeting specific groups for recruitment. After ISIS later broke ties with al-Qaeda in 2013, the media strategy of targeting audiences, coupled with careful attention to multimodal messaging and platforms, emerged as a fundamental part of their communication strategy. This ambition can be seen in part in the establishment of several media wings tied to the organization.

One of the first was al-I'Tisam, which focused on different social media domains, spreading content about the organization (at the time still ISI) to enhance recruitment, increase fundraising, and strengthen the brand. On the same trajectory, al-Hayat Media Center has for years been a central media organ, producing and distributing propaganda videos and other publications in Arabic as well as several other languages. For instance, one of al-Hayat's flagships, the online magazine *Rumiyah*, published its tenth issue (released in June 2017) in ten different languages. Al-Furat is a media wing with a focus on disseminating material to non-Arab supporters. In terms of attention to modalities, al-Ajnad is a rather specific media organ being developed as main producer of *anāshīd* (religious a cappella songs), often used as background in many gruesome execution videos in turn produced by other media wings.[27] Besides these major official outlets, there are a number of unofficial agencies and foundations, like Dawa al-Haqq News Agency and al-Battar Media that in different ways have helped (or still help) ISIS with translation services or other additional work.

From these core media organizations follow a number of regional and provincial media bureaus. Because of ongoing territorial advances and setbacks, the actual number of regional ISIS media bureaus is hard to determine. However, a fair estimation would be that during 2015–2016 it peaked to between twenty and twenty-five provincial bureaus. These have mainly been located in Iraq and Syria but also include media offices in countries like Libya, Yemen, and Afghanistan. During 2018, official visual propaganda, videos, and photo stories, marked with which province (*wilayat*) they've been produced in, have indicated a drastic stagnation of media-producing wilayats to around five to ten. In fact, in July 2018 there was an official communique coming out of official ISIS channels on Telegram declaring that there are now only two wilayats remaining from the 2014-defined caliphate: Wilayat al-'Iraq and Wilayat al-Sham (Iraq and Syria).[28]

But apart from the regional aspects of media production, there are more central media outlets that are vital in the media ecology of ISIS. First are the al-Bayan radio broadcasts with more or less daily updates both within the caliphate and as digital audio files online. The station produces broadcasts that are collectively consumed in media kiosks on the ground by the local and controlled populations.[29] Second is the *al-Naba* weekly online newspaper. To date, more than 170 issues have been published, and the paper packages stories and updates from the previous week, including updates on events or attacks that may or may not have connection to ISIS, as well as featuring more in-depth reports on military progress and political developments.

The founding of Amaq News Agency in 2014 is an example of ISIS's need to not only adapt to Western news cycles and forms but also to initiate news-management practices. Directly controlled by the Islamic State, Amaq is increasingly integrated with the propaganda apparatus of ISIS, even if they are officially not part of the media industry.[30] It was initially an experiment to contextualize "scoops" and offer news flashes, mainly for those who distrust mainstream

Western media outlets. It is a bit ironic to see how the stories from Amaq are often referred to and displayed by the same mainstream media channels, especially in relation to claims of attacks, which will be discussed later in this chapter.

The content from these propaganda outlets is disseminated through a wide variety of channels. From 2013 to 2018, the strategies and platforms have naturally changed. At its peak in terms of propaganda quantity and frequency of publication in August 2015, the number of official visual media products being published reached 761 (including photo stories, photographs attached in Twitter posts, and videos), and during several months of 2015, the number stayed above seven hundred.[31] Without a doubt, this "is massive and impressive for an organization operating out of a very active conflict zone."[32] Even if these numbers have been reduced substantially since then, it is fair to say that ISIS, in order to reach this volume of content, has put tremendous effort and focus on its media wings and operations.

A 2015 study from the Brookings Institute shows that during the first months following the declaration of the caliphate in 2014, ISIS supporters managed at least forty-six thousand Twitter accounts, although the authors emphasize that this is a low estimate, and it could have been as many as seventy thousand accounts.[33] These accounts and numbers only present the infrastructural pretext from which ISIS propaganda is disseminated. Hidden in this estimation is a smaller number of highly active core accounts, individuals operating across different platforms and with several networks of supporters.[34] These "credibility nodes" can be seen as catalysts for a more efficient spread of official propaganda and show how this takes place at the intersection of centralized (from media wing outputs through core accounts) and decentralized (replicated by distant supporters) communication practices. The core accounts and individuals can also be seen as "daily harvesters" and can be defined as individuals or groups affiliated with ISIS who collect, repackage, compile, and publish between forty and eighty pages of briefings, containing a vast amount of propaganda material.[35] These packages are then added to so-called paste websites, primarily justepaste.it and addpost.it. They then get shared by supporters and followers in new networks, making the daily volume of content disseminated online difficult to censor as it is continuously shared on new and multiple platforms.

It is something of a misconception to believe that the Islamic State only relies on a decentralized structure of communication where supporter networks are the main platforms for dissemination,[36] though it is true that ISIS benefits greatly from their ability to engage and include supporters in its external propaganda. There is evidence of a highly centralized chain of communication. In terms of the timing of certain publications on different platforms, roughly two weeks after a drowned Syrian boy was found on a Turkish beach (whose death was held up in Western media as an example of the tragedy of the Syrian refugee crisis), thirteen different regional ISIS media bureaus produced and spread videos over a two-day period addressing the ongoing refugee situation, attempting to convince people to stay in Syria instead of leaving the country.[37] Even if a central command for this type of timing and shared production narrative is hard to prove, it does suggest that the ISIS ministry of media may dictate the production at regional media bureaus at times. ISIS does use a number of central media wings to produce content and then relies heavily on core accounts and channels for dissemination, hoping the content will be amplified by online followers around the world—integrating the centralized and decentralized organization of messaging.

From this overview of ISIS media infrastructure, the following sections of this chapter illustrate dominant media activism practices and genres utilized by ISIS since it declared its caliphate. The practices are *participatory journalism*, *alternative computing*, *mediated mobilization*, and *cultural jamming* and are considered significant parts of ISIS's process of using media and sympathizers as symbolic weapons.[38]

Participatory Journalism and News Management

There are several examples of the purposeful development of both organizational media structure as well as content-related strategies in ISIS's virtual universe. Both videos and magazines like *Dabiq* and *Rumiyah* contain several segments and articles that take the form of journalistic narrative. The content is a mixture of storytelling through arguments, religious justification, and overall a presentation of a worldview that not only opposes that of adversaries but also forcefully embraces the ideological core of the Islamic State.

A common denominator in the media operations of ISIS is the implementation of strategies that not only seem to understand and follow international news cycles and logics but also attempt to control and challenge them. Within media activism, this tactic can be understood through the concept of participatory (or citizen) journalism.[39] Fundamentally—and this is the case with many extremist organizations—it comes down to enforcing and communicating a system of meaning, ideology, or worldview opposing the hegemonic structures of, in this case, Western news media. And through its widespread network of sympathizers, ISIS has shown the ability to not only pinpoint what is on Western political and media agendas but also integrate their own messaging as a response to that, almost like a form of "management of visibility."[40] The Amaq news agency has been particularly useful to that end.

In the aftermath of attacks, claims of responsibility usually come through Amaq and its encrypted Android application as well as the ISIS Telegram channel.[41] Amaq works like a totalitarian state news agency, and its visual layout is similar to that of mainstream news organizations (see fig. 5.1). By using rather short and simple digital stickers with only a few sentences, Amaq's visual statements are easily shared in social media and help strengthen their legitimacy in news media spheres.

Fig. 5.1 Amaq agency advertisement for application. SOURCE: Author's copy.

When Amaq is used to claim an attack, the validity and logic of these claims is widely discussed among researchers and analysts,[42] especially as ISIS, at times, has appeared to claim basically any attack regardless of connection to the organization itself. This is, of course, far from the truth and the result of other contributing factors. Mainly, the logic of claiming is based on the potential political or financial benefit of the attack. If ISIS leadership are confident an attack will provide a certain reaction among its adversaries or further financial support from donors or supporters, there is most certainly a claim. In other cases, there is not. Another reason for the importance of having very official and streamlined claims can be that it makes it harder for other groups to make false claims in ISIS's name and thereby damage its reputation.

Another important outlet is Nashir, which can be considered the official channel or direct voice of ISIS leadership. Currently, ISIS releases statements and claims about attacks and operations via Nashir (simultaneously with Amaq publications), but the main focus of Nashir is to advertise forms of official propaganda and publish official material of different sorts. Having these two major networks on Telegram, ISIS deploys an infrastructure of messaging that helps them manage the image of the organization.

ISIS aspires to sustain momentum in the Western news media through "news management"—an umbrella concept for various techniques of spin and influencing news coverage. When implemented by groups like ISIS, it is, however, more a result of understanding current media logics, what clicks for journalists and editors and what doesn't, as well as what type of messages and headlines they could profit from. In the aftermath of the declaration of the caliphate in June 2014, a number of gruesome videos of Western journalists and aid workers appeared online. These videos were orchestrated and purposefully disseminated during the initial phases of ISIS's advancement in Iraq and Syria and functioned as marketing for the group, garnering global attention.[43] James Foley, Steven Sotloff, David Haines, Alan Henning, and Peter Kassig were among the first kidnapped Westerners (after al-Baghdadi's declaration) whose filmed beheadings were spread online between August and November of 2014. Their executions resulted in headlines depicting ISIS as murderers, barbarians, and monsters, with the deaths and videos serving their purpose from the organization's perspective—they were an exhibition of power as well as attempts to provoke Western powers.

As the executions circulated, the media wings of ISIS produced and disseminated high numbers of other videos with a completely different narrative. The same day the caliphate was declared (June 29, 2014), several videos were released with, for instance, a strong political narrative and justification for the caliphate and its vision ("The End of Sykes-Picot" and "Breaking the Border"). This, in combination with the release of the first issue of monthly magazine *Dabiq* (July 4), displayed ISIS's multiplatform and multinarrative approach, which would only expand as time went by. This combination of different platforms and publications with several layers of narrative and messages separates ISIS from previous groups, though it does have its antecedents in a media industry dating back to 2003, a media enterprise with both financial and labor resources.[44]

Alternative Computing

Deriving from the hacking culture of the 1960s, alternative computing is a form of media activism usually associated with hacker groups (for lack of a better term) using software and engineering skills to push the boundaries of principled democracy. WikiLeaks and Anonymous are perhaps two of the most recognized examples of groups with subjective agendas using online spaces to either promote causes like freedom of information or aid in closing down the accounts of extremist groups, as Anonymous did during a campaign in 2015.

Alternative computing, in which individuals "design, build, and 'hack' or reconfigure systems with the purpose of resisting political, commercial, and state restraints on open access to information and the use of information technologies,"[45] has been promoted by ISIS through its crowdsourcing of supporters. Developing applications for mobile phones, as well as extensions to web browsers, is perhaps the most significant use of coding and software computing that ISIS's participatory media universe has collectively engaged in.[46] One of the first applications, designed to enhance the outreach and spread of official propaganda, was Fajr al-Bashaer (Dawn of Glad Tidings; see fig. 5.2). Available in 2014 for Android platforms during a limited time on the Google Play store, and for PC, the application functioned as a generator of tweets and facilitated posts to accounts belonging to ISIS supporters.[47]

When the application was downloaded, the user automatically approved ISIS to post tweets through the user's account and simultaneously through every

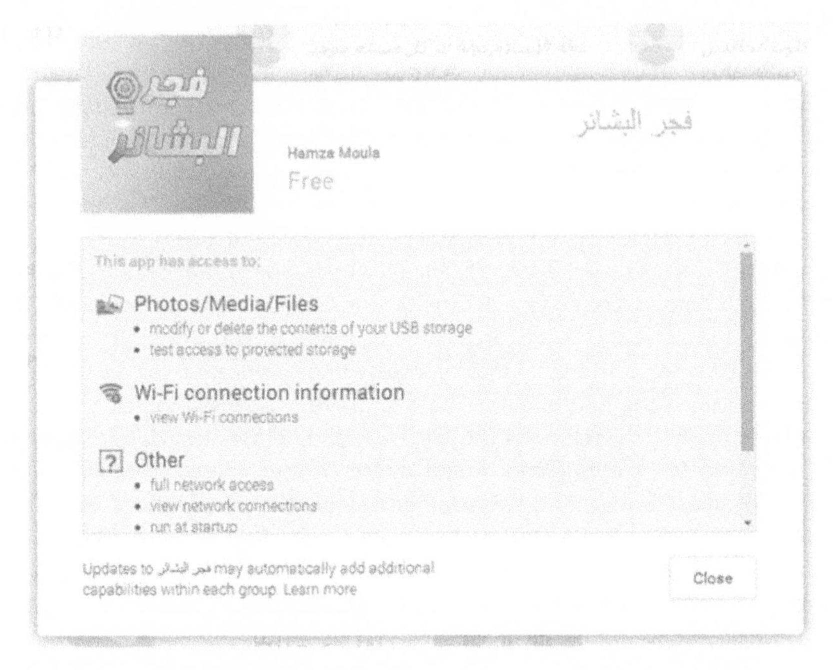

Fig. 5.2 Screenshot of Android application Fajr al-Basaer (Dawn of Glad Tidings). SOURCE: AlArabiya English.

other registered account, which means that one single message reached a huge number of Twitter users.[48] This massive circulation of tweets not only amplified a message, it also made it harder for Twitter to detect accounts worth suspending.

The Amaq News Agency launched its own Android application in late 2014, providing supporters with the ability to follow news and updates about ISIS operations. As an extension of this service, in August 2016 ISIS developed and launched a Firefox browser plug-in for Amaq and uploaded instructions and installation files on one of its Telegram channels (see fig. 5.3).

This enabled supporters to follow the ISIS news from Amaq directly via their browser.[49] This instructional, consumer-friendly approach further strengthens the idea of the organization's 24/7 help-desk strategy and care for the details of audience experience, as well as enhancing the multiplatform approach through alternative computing.

In addition to the focus on the overall user experience, ISIS also works to target specific audiences, nationalities, and ages. Another mobile application, Huroof, was released on several ISIS Telegram channels in May 2016.[50] This was the first application aimed at children, and its content was designed for learning the Arabic alphabet and pronunciations. But as with other applications, Huroof

Fig. 5.3 Screenshot of instructions to install Amaq browser plug-in, shared over Telegram. SOURCE: Author's copy.

was filled with jihadist terminology and images, strategically woven into the educational aspects of the application (see fig. 5.4). For instance, the elementary words children learn though the application include "tank," "gun," "caliphate," and "ammunition." In the background, they hear anasheeds filled with jihadist terminology and content. The visual imagery is colorful and playful, but the content is obviously connected to ISIS's larger ideology.

The development of mobile and desktop applications by ISIS stretches its reach to a wide demographic and age span. This tactic of alternative computing is adopted from common Western media practices and thereby accessible to a large audience because of its familiarity. Political approaches to media literacy and the digital divides of the world, where access to technology is not equivalent to the competence to use it, tend to lack the latter dimension, and solutions are often presented in terms of granting access and investing in technological infrastructure, rather than securing a competence to engage with technology.[51] ISIS does not only provide easy access to a platform or application itself; they also design the media content in such a way that very little is required from the user in terms of capability to interact or consume it.

Fig. 5.4 Screenshots of Haroof application. SOURCE: Author's copy.

Mediated Mobilization and Hashtag Hijacking

In June 2014, a group of German ISIS supporters created an online campaign via Facebook to encourage people around the world to express their support. One of the initiators explained, "Just write 'One Billion Muslims to Support the Islamic State' on an individually designed piece of cardboard. Add your home country, in this case 'Support from Germany', or some trademark of the country. . . . This is an international campaign to thank the lions of our state. . . . So get involved in shaa Allah! May Allah azza wa jall reward you, amin."[52] The attached images had different layouts, as was encouraged, with the title and logo appearing one way or another. Together with attached hashtags like #Dawla and #DawlaIslamiyya (state, Islamic State), the campaign went more or less viral and illustrated the participatory engagement of the networks of supporters so crucial, and deliberately cultivated, by ISIS central media command.

The intersections between the centralized communication practices of ISIS and the decentralized practices of supporters is made visible through the tactic of mediated mobilization. Using media platforms to organize, prepare, and execute campaigns or incite support for a cause is perhaps the most widely applied activist tactic deployed by social movements. The term *clicktivism* is sometimes used to describe this participatory activity in media, where participation can be reduced to a minimum of effort when compared, for instance, with developing mobile applications.

The goal of this strategy is to mobilize support and sometimes transfer online engagement into the physical space, something that can be achieved through different means by both ISIS and their supporters. These include bottom-up campaigns initiated by sympathizers (the German example above), top-down campaigns initiated by the central organization (the #AllEyesOnISIS campaign mentioned earlier), as well as mixed campaigns that combine both of these approaches. Sometimes it is hard for analysts to fully know the organizational background of the execution of so-called "hashtag-hijacking"—a now-widespread tactic for mobilizing support online and exposing large audiences to propaganda content. But there are several examples of rather open encouragement from core accounts within the ISIS social media spheres, hence a top-down model of mobilization, some of which have been reported in journalistic outlets.

> Another propaganda operative called Abdulrahman al-Hamid asked his 4,000 followers on Twitter for the highest trending topics in the UK and popular account names they could jump on to get the required uplift. Writing in Arabic under the now-suspended handle @Abu_Laila, he wrote: "We need those who can supply us with the most active hashtags in the UK. And also the accounts of the most famous celebrities. I believe that the hashtag of Scotland's separation from Britain should be the first."
>
> Replies from followers advised using #andymurray, #scotland, #scotlandindependence, #VoteNo and #VoteYes and linking to David Cameron's twitter handle. "Please work hard to publish all the links," Hamid urged. At the same time @With_baghdadi told Isis supporters to "invade" the #voteno hashtags "with the video of the british prisoner."[53]

Considering the amount of social media accounts affiliated with the organization, this openness in communication practices rests heavily on a notion of pride in being part of the organization and not only aiding its operations but doing it publicly as well. To further stimulate followers to assist in dissemination, many of the official videos coming out of ISIS media wings are uploaded on a vast amount of servers and platforms and then posted for download or to stream in different resolutions on other platforms.

This multiplatform strategy of dissemination and engaging follower involvement is clearly related to how core accounts or "daily harvesters" package and facilitate propaganda for further spread. When content is uploaded on many platforms, it is downloaded and uploaded again on the networks of supporters, making it practically impossible for censors to remove it. Mediated mobilization, using networked technologies to facilitate change and pragmatic action,[54] is perhaps the most extensively used media activist practice by ISIS.

Cultural Jamming

As should be obvious at this point, both from this and other chapters in this book, ISIS does not hesitate to make explicit references to mainstream popular culture in its messaging in general and in visual imagery in particular. But producing content mimicking the special effects of Hollywood blockbuster movies is not the same as the type of twists of cultural references entailed in the media activist form of cultural jamming.[55] As the name suggests, it is a matter of stretching limits, pushing boundaries, experimenting with cultural references, and recontextualizing them in order to promote a message opposite to what was originally intended. Adbusters is perhaps the most well-known organization using this type of media activism, usually attacking large corporations. By reversing messages through the recontextualization of identifiable cultural references, cultural jamming has become a central piece of modern-day activist practices.

When it comes to ISIS, this type of technique can be seen in both official as well as supporter-generated content. In August 2014, an official video called "Eid Greetings from the Land of Khilafah" played like a television travel show, with utopian stories featuring interviews with foreigners who had joined, describing the caliphate as a safe and harmonious place, filled with images of happy children, and ending with one participant saying, "I wish you were here."[56] By using recognizable formats from television programming, something Al-Hayat has been doing for a long time, ISIS creates an instant shortcut into the interpretative processes of the targeted audience. This recontextualization also takes place by using visual material from major news agencies and channels. Not only do various form of news footage become integrated in videos, but the first Issue of *Dabiq* magazine (released July 2014) also contained a Photoshopped 2010 Reuters image taken in Afghanistan, showing wounded US soldiers (see fig. 5.5). The photo is used in the magazine to fit the narrative of ISIS's strength and to suggest that US soldiers are unable to endure the battle.

This "jamming" of not only Western news material but also symbolically charged visuals is a recurrent theme in ISIS information operations. In addition to this official side of the propaganda, similar yet even more creative techniques are used by supporters who constantly replicate official propaganda and create posters as textual and visual artifacts. These posters usually appear shortly after attacks and thereby have cities or countries (including symbolic buildings or monuments) as part of the visual layout. London and Paris are cities that have been widely exploited in these posters, largely due to ISIS's continual use of the UK and France in some political narratives (the Sykes-Picot Agreement) as well as the increasing number of attacks in these countries.

This type of sociological propaganda, following in the digital wake of official content, can be understood from a participatory media culture perspective. In such a perspective, the interplay between popular culture (or other types of cultural) references and forms and the subversion of such forms helps transform these posters from art into expressions of media activism. By recontextualizing and transforming aspects of mainstream media culture, ISIS supporters help

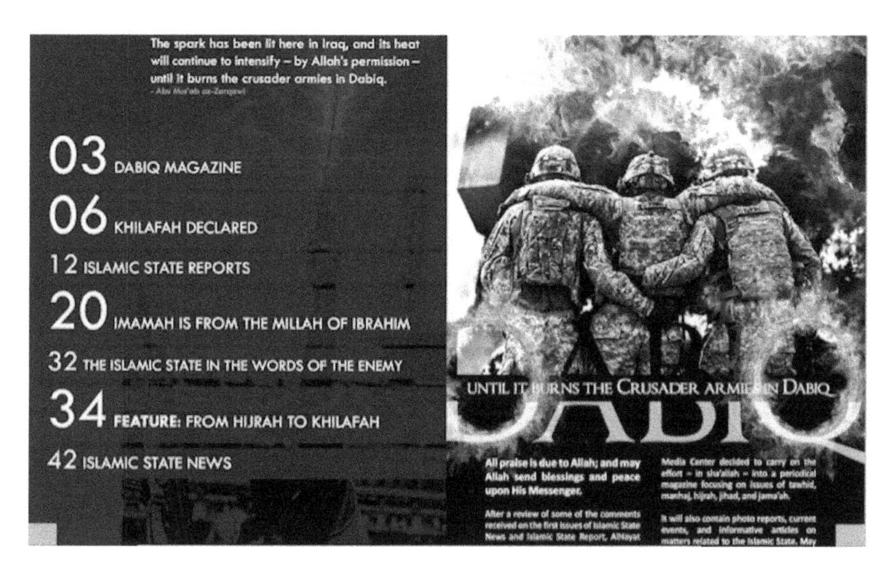
The spark has been lit here in Iraq, and its heat will continue to intensify – by Allah's permission – until it burns the crusader armies in Dabiq.

03 DABIQ MAGAZINE
06 KHILAFAH DECLARED
12 ISLAMIC STATE REPORTS
20 IMAMAH IS FROM THE MILLAH OF IBRAHIM
32 THE ISLAMIC STATE IN THE WORDS OF THE ENEMY
34 FEATURE: FROM HIJRAH TO KHILAFAH
42 ISLAMIC STATE NEWS

UNTIL IT BURNS THE CRUSADER ARMIES IN DABIQ

All praise is due to Allah; and may Allah send blessings and peace upon His Messenger.

After a review of some of the comments received on the first issues of Islamic State News and Islamic State Report, AlHayat Media Center decided to carry on the effort – in sha'allah – into a periodical magazine focusing on issues of tawhid, manhaj, hijrah, jihad, and jama'ah.

It will also contain photo reports, current events, and informative articles on matters related to the Islamic State. May

Fig. 5.5 *Dabiq* issue 1, pp. 2–3, July 2014.

make manifest an accessible and inclusive method of participation in the virtual universe and war of the Islamic State—clearly illustrating the relationship between official and sociological propaganda.

Participatory Ecology

This chapter is an attempt not only to present the main foundation of ISIS's media ecology since 2014 but also to generate knowledge about how it has been, and still is, the catalyst for the production of different propaganda tactics. It has also worked to shed light on how these practices can help supporters around the world feel like part of the organization. The synergizing effect of official central communication practices and decentralized dissemination is only possible when supporter networks buy into the strategy and the ideological framework—when they identify with it.

A Canadian citizen, Andre Poulin, who was a petty criminal with a minor criminal record in his home country, traveled to Syria to join ISIS. He was put in an al-Hayat recruitment video targeting international audiences ("The Chosen Few of Different Lands") and given the name Abu Muslim al Canada, which can be translated to and interpreted as the father of Muslims in Canada. In addition to being the main figure in the video, his identity was elevated to that of a role model, a hero, a true believer, and a devoted Muslim who could inspire other Muslims back home to join or feel part of ISIS. Even the title of the video suggests he was one of "the chosen few," hence special and indicates that whomever is watching can become special as well.

There are reasons to argue that a larger revolution is happening in the context of global jihadism and organizations' use of media. The savvy exploitation of social media and propaganda that ISIS has implemented has the additional effect of inspiring other groups to mimic their strategies—and not just designated terrorist organizations, but even groups as wide-ranging as minor criminal networks, major military forces, and political regimes and administrations are taking cues from ISIS's use of media. It would be hyperbolic to claim that ISIS started this revolution, but it is fair to argue that their efforts have served as a kind of proof of concept to others of how such a media strategy, a media ecology, might function and thrive.

Concerning ISIS's future, the development and support of this media ecology working in combination with the Islamic State's reliance on supporter networks presented in this chapter, the group has increased its possibilities of growing in other parts of the world. Beginning with airstrikes in 2015 in Iraq and Syria, which strongly contributed to the crippling of the physical caliphate, ISIS has witnessed a loss of territory—but a loss they may have foreseen as they worked to make online supporters feel like part of their so-called state. This nurturing of the virtual caliphate is perhaps the most significant lesson to learn from ISIS's global media industry and may also prove to be the greatest challenge for future interventions. The combination of centralized and decentralized communication, applied through recognized media activism practices, has resulted in geographical support in many parts of the world where ISIS, after withdrawal and regrouping from losses in Iraq and Syria, may reenter the stage, even more prepared than last time.

Notes

1. Michael Krona and Måns Adler, "Emerging Publics and Interventions in Democracy," in *Making Futures: Marginal Notes on Innovation, Design, and Democracy*, eds. P. Ehn, E. Nilsson, and R. Topgaard (Cambridge, MA: MIT Press, 2014), 324–325.

2. See Giovanni Ziccardi, *Resistance, Liberation Technology, and Human Rights in the Digital Age* (London: Springer, 2013).

3. Michael Weiss and Hassan Hassan, *ISIS: Inside the Army of Terror*, 2nd ed. (New York: Regan Arts, 2016), 174.

4. Akil N. Awan, Andrew Hoskins, and Ben O'Loughlin, *Radicalization and Media: Connectivity and Terrorism in the New Media Ecology* (London: Routledge, 2011), 5.

5. Charlie Winter, *Media Jihad: The Islamic State's Doctrine for Information Warfare* (London: The International Centre for the Study of Radicalisation and Political Violence, 2017), 12.

6. Lorenzo Vidino, Francesco Marone, and Eva Entenmann, "Fear Thy Neighbor: Radicalization and Jihadist Attacks in the West," *ICCT* Report, 2017, https://icct.nl/wp-content/uploads/2017/06/FearThyNeighbor-RadicalizationandJihadistAttacksintheWest.pdf.

7. See, for instance, Charlie Winter, "Documenting the Virtual Caliphate," Quilliam Foundation Report, 2015, http://www.quilliaminternational.com/wp-content/uploads/2015/10/FINAL-documenting-the-virtual-caliphate.pdf.

8. See Craig Whiteside, "Lighting the Path: The Evolution of the Islamic State Media Enterprise (2003–2016)," ICCT Research Paper, 2016, https://icct.nl/wp-content/uploads/2016/11/ICCT-Whiteside-Lighting-the-Path-the-Evolution-of-the-Islamic-State-Media-Enterprise-2003-2016-Nov2016.pdf.

9. See Gabi Siboni, Daniel Cohen, and Tal Koren, "The Islamic State's Strategy in Cyberspace," *Military and Strategic Affairs* 7, no. 1 (2015); and Daveed Gartenstein-Ross, Nathaniel Barr, and Bridget Moreng, "The Islamic State's Global Propaganda Strategy," ICCT Research Paper, 2016, https://www.icct.nl/wp-content/uploads/2016/03/ICCT-Gartenstein-Ross-IS-Global-Propaganda-Strategy-March2016.pdf.

10. The concept of "infrastructure" is here applied in line with how Geoffrey. C. Bowker and Susan Leigh Star present the term in their book, *Sorting Things Out: Classification and Its Consequences* (Cambridge, MA: MIT Press, 2000), namely as a form of precondition for what is taking place, in this case how architectual design of platforms are pretexts for what is communicated via these platforms, and how each platform and outlet of ISIS media is part of a larger network and connects the organization, its supporters, and the propaganda.

11. Ziccardi, *Resistance, Liberation Technology.*

12. See Winter, "Documenting the Virtual Caliphate."

13. Leah Lievrouw, *Alternative and Activist New Media* (Cambridge, MA: Polity Press, 2011), 7.

14. Bart Cammaerts and Nico Carpentier, eds. *Reclaiming the Media: Communication Rights and Democratic Media Roles* (Bristol, UK: Intellect, 2017), 217.

15. See Haroro Ingram, "The Strategic Logic of Islamic State Information Operations," *Australian Journal of International Affairs* 69, no. 6 (2015): 729–752

16. Michael Horowitz, "Nonstate Actors and the Diffusion of Innovations: The Case of Suicide Terrorism," *International Organization* 64 (2010): 33–64.

17. IntelCenter, "Evolution of Jihadi Video EJV," report published May 11, 2005.

18. Philip Seib, "The al-Qaeda Media Machine," *Military Review* 88, no. 3 (2008): 74.

19. Harleen Gambhir, "The Strategic Messaging of the Islamic State," paper for Institute for The Study of War, 2014, http://www.understandingwar.org/dabiq-strategic-messaging-islamic-state-0.

20. Akil N. Awan, "Virtual Jihadist Media," *European Journal of Cultural Studies* 10, no. 3 (2007): 390.

21. Brian Reis, "Twitter's Terrorist Policy," *The Daily Beast*, September 24, 2013, http://www.thedailybeast.com/articles/2013/09/24/twitter-s-terrorist-policy.html.

22. Bill Goodwin, "Islamic State Supporters Shun Tails and Tor Encryption for Telegram," *Computer Weekly*, June 2017, http://www.computerweekly.com/news/450419581/Islamic-State-supporters-shun-Tails-and-Tor-encryption-for-Telegram?utm_content=bufferfc08f&utm_medium=social&utm_source=twitter.com&utm_campaign=buffer.

23. Ahmet S. Layla and Anne Speckhard, "Telegram: The Mighty Application That ISIS Loves," International Center for The Study of Violent Extremism, brief report, May 9, 2017, http://www.icsve.org/brief-reports/telegram-the-mighty-application-that-isis-loves/.

24. A good overview of ISIS's use of Telegram is presented by Mia Bloom, Hicham Tiflati, and John Horgan in "Telegram: Navigating ISIS' Preferred Platform," *Terrorism and Political Violence* 29 (2017): 1–13.

25. This process is described in detail in Daniel Milton, "Communication Breakdown: Unraveling the Islamic State's Media Efforts," *CTC Westpoint*, October 2016, https://www.ctc.usma.edu/v2/wp-content/uploads/2016/10/ISMedia_Online.pdf.

26. Ibid., 4.

27. Craig Whiteside, "Lighting the Path: The Evolution of the Islamic State Media Enterprise (2003–2016)," ICCT Research Paper (2016): 18. https://icct.nl/wp-content/uploads/2016/11/ICCT-Whiteside-Lighting-the-Path-the-Evolution-of-the-Islamic-State-Media-Enterprise-2003-2016-Nov2016.pdf.

28. At the time of writing this chapter (July 2018), it remains unclear how this restructuring and rebranding of wilayats will influence the production and distribution of propaganda.

29. See Winter, "Documenting the Virtual Caliphate."

30. See, for instance, Rukhmani Callimachi, "A News Agency with Scoops Directly from ISIS, and a Veneer of Objectivity," *New York Times*, January 15, 2016, https://www.nytimes.com/2016/01/15/world/middleeast/a-news-agency-with-scoops-directly-from-isis-and-a-veneer-of-objectivity.html; as well as Alex Kassirir, "The Rise of an ISIS Affiliated Media Unit: A'maq," *Flashpoint*, 2016, https://www.flashpoint-intel.com/blog/terrorism/the-rise-of-an-isis-affiliated-media-unit-amaq/.

31. Milton, "Communication Breakdown."

32. Ibid., 21.

33. J. M. Berger and Jonathon Morgan, "The ISIS Twitter Census: Defining and Describing the Population of ISIS Supporters on Twitter," Brookings Project on US Relations with the Islamic World, analysis paper no. 20, March 2015, https://www.brookings.edu/wp-content/uploads/2016/06/isis_twitter_census_berger_morgan.pdf.

34. See also Joseph Shaheen, *Network of Terror: How Daesh Uses Adaptive Social Networks to Spread Its Message*, NATO Centre of Excellence Strategic Communications, 2015, https://www.stratcomcoe.org/download/file/fid/3312.

35. Lorand Bodo and Anne Speckhard, "How ISIS Disseminates Propaganda over the Internet Despite Counter-Measures and How to Fight Back," *Modern Diplomacy*, April 23, 2017, https://moderndiplomacy.eu/2017/04/23/how-isis-disseminates-propaganda-over-the-internet-despite-counter-measures-and-how-to-fight-back/.

36. Milton, "Communication Breakdown," 16.

37. Ibid.

38. These forms of activism are argued for and defined in Lievrouw, *Alternative and Activist New Media*, and also include others; however, the four forms presented in this chapter are chosen and implemented to enhance the theoretical understanding of ISIS media strategies explicitly.

39. Lievrouw, *Alternative and Activist New Media*, 120.

40. See Keren Tenenboim-Weinblatt, "The Management of Visibility: Media Coverage of Kidnapping and Captivity Cases around the World," *Media, Culture & Society* 35, no. 7 (2013): 791–808.

41. There are two official networks of channels that ISIS uses as official outlets on Telegram (July 2018), and these are *Amaq* channels and *Nashir* channels. Amaq distributes news updates and claims of attacks, while Nashir spreads the same updates but also official propaganda products like videos, photo stories, links to al-Bayan radio bulletins, etc.

42. Max Abrahms and Justin Conrad, "The Strategic Logic of Credit Claiming: A New Theory for Anonymous Terrorist Attacks," *Security Studies* 26, no. 2 (2017): 279–304.

43. See also Imogen Richards, "'Flexible' Capital Accumulation in Islamic State Social Media," *Critical Studies on Terrorism* 9, no. 2 (2016): 205–225.
44. Whiteside, "Lighting the Path."
45. Lievrouw, *Alternative and Activist New Media*, 98.
46. This excludes pro-ISIS hacker groups like United Cyber Caliphate, which regularly advertises themselves online and on Telegram as working for the organization, however are not recognized officially.
47. Siboni, Cohen, Tal Koren, "The Islamic State's Strategy in Cyberspace," 134.
48. According to Berger (2014), approximately forty thousand tweets were sent though the application on the day ISIS seized Mosul.
49. Lisa Daftari, "ISIS Releases Web-Browser Plugin for 24/7 News Updates," *The Foreign Desk*, August 9, 2016, http://www.foreigndesknews.com/world/middle-east/isis-releases-web-browser-plugin-247-news-updates/.
50. Caleb Weiss, "Islamic State Launches Mobile App for Children," *The Long War Journal*, May 11, 2016, http://www.longwarjournal.org/archives/2016/05/islamic-state-launches-mobile-app-for-children.php.
51. See Krona and Adler, "Emerging Publics."
52. Henri Tartaglia, "German ISIS Supporters Started a Jihadi Facebook Campaign," *VICE*, June 22, 2014, https://www.vice.com/sv/article/german-jihadi-internet-meme-campaign.
53. Shiv Malik, "Isis in Duel with Twitter and YouTube to Spread Extremist Propaganda," *The Guardian*, September 24, 2014, https://www.theguardian.com/world/2014/sep/24/isis-twitter-youtube-message-social-media-jihadi.
54. Lievrouw, *Alternative and Activist New Media*, 149.
55. Ibid., 73.
56. Steve Rose, "The Isis Propaganda War: A Hi-Tech Media Jihad," *The Guardian*, October 7, 2014, https://www.theguardian.com/world/2014/oct/07/isis-media-machine-propaganda-war.

Bibliography

Abrahms, Max, and Justin Conrad. "The Strategic Logic of Credit Claiming: A New Theory for Anonymous Terrorist Attacks." *Security Studies* 26, no. 2 (2017): 279–304.

Aly, Anne, Stuart Macdonald, Lee Jarvis, and Thomas M. Chen. "Introduction to the Special Issue: Terrorist Online Propaganda and Radicalization." *Studies in Conflict & Terrorism* 40, no. 1 (2017): 1–9.

Awan, Akil. N. "Virtual Jihadist Media: Function Legitimacy, and Racializing Efficacy." *European Journal of Cultural Studies* 10, no. 3 (2007): 389–408.

Awan, Akil. N., Andrew Hoskins, and Ben O'Loughlin. *Radicalization and Media: Connectivity and Terrorism in the New Media Ecology*. London: Routledge, 2011.

Berger, J. M. "How ISIS Games Twitter." *The Atlantic*, June 16, 2014. https://www.theatlantic.com/international/archive/2014/06/isis-iraq-twitter-social-media-strategy/372856/.

Berger, J. M. and J. Horgan. "The ISIS Twitter Census: Defining and Describing the Population of ISIS Supporters on Twitter." Brookings Project on US Relations with the Islamic

World, analysis paper no. 20. March 2015. https://www.brookings.edu/wp-content/uploads/2016/06/isis_twitter_census_berger_morgan.pdf.

Blaker, Lisa. "The Islamic State's Use of Online Social Media." *Military Cyber Affairs* 1, no. 1 (2015).

Bloom, Mia, Hicham Tiflati, and John Horgan. "Navigating ISIS' Preferred Platform: Telegram." *Terrorism and Political Violence* 29 (2017): 1–13.

Bodo, Lorand, and Anne Speckhard. "How ISIS Disseminates Propaganda over the Internet Despite Counter-Measures and How to Fight Back." *Modern Diplomacy*, April 23, 2017. https://moderndiplomacy.eu/2017/04/23/how-isis-disseminates-propaganda-over-the-internet-despite-counter-measures-and-how-to-fight-back/.

Bowker, Geoffrey C., and Susan Leigh Star. *Sorting Things Out: Classification and Its Consequences*. Cambridge, MA: MIT Press, 2000.

Callimachi, Rukmani. "A News Agency with Scoops Directly from ISIS, and a Veneer of Objectivity." *New York Times*, June 14, 2016. https://www.nytimes.com/2016/01/15/world/middleeast/a-news-agency-with-scoops-directly-from-isis-and-a-veneer-of-objectivity.html.

Cammaerts, Bart, and Nico Carpentier, eds. *Reclaiming the Media: Communication Rights and Democratic Media Roles*. Bristol, UK: Intellect, 2007.

Daftari, Lisa. "ISIS Releases Web-Browser Plugin for 24/7 News Updates." *The Foreign Desk*, August 9, 2016. http://www.foreigndesknews.com/world/middle-east/isis-releases-web-browser-plugin-247-news-updates/.

Gambhir, Hareleen. "The Strategic Messaging of the Islamic State." Paper for Institute for The Study of War, 2014. http://www.understandingwar.org/dabiq-strategic-messaging-islamic-state-0.

Gartenstein-Ross, Daveed, Nathaniel Barr, and Bridget Moreng. "The Islamic State's Global Propaganda Strategy." ICCT Research Paper, March 2016. https://www.icct.nl/wp-content/uploads/2016/03/ICCT-Gartenstein-Ross-IS-Global-Propaganda-Strategy-March2016.pdf.

Goodwin, Bill. "Islamic State Supporters Shun Tails and Tor Encryption for Telegram." *Computer Weekly*, June 2017. http://www.computerweekly.com/news/450419581/Islamic-State-supporters-shun-Tails-and-Tor-encryption-for-Telegram?utm_content=bufferfc08f&utm_medium=social&utm_source=twitter.com&utm_campaign=buffer.

Horowitz, Michael. C "Nonstate Actors and the Diffusion of Innovations: The Case of Suicide Terrorism." *International Organization* 64, no. 1 (2010): 33–64.

Ingram, Haroro. J. "The Strategic Logic of Islamic State Information Operations." *Australian Journal of International Affairs* 69, no. 6 (2015): 729–752.

IntelCenter. "Evolution of Jihadi Video EJV." Report published May 11, 2005. https://intelcenter.com/EJV-PUB-v1-0.pdf.

Kassirir, Alex. "The Rise of an ISIS Affiliated Media Unit: A'maq." *Flashpoint*, 2016. https://www.flashpoint-intel.com/blog/terrorism/the-rise-of-an-isis-affiliated-media-unit-amaq/.

Krona, Michael, and Måns Adler. "Emerging Publics and Interventions in Democracy." In *Making Futures: Marginal Notes on Innovation, Design, and Democracy*, edited by Pelle Ehn, Elisabeth Nilsson, and Richard Topgaard, 323–344. Cambridge, MA: MIT Press, 2014.

Layla, Ahmet S., and Anne Speckhard. "Telegram: The Mighty Application That ISIS Loves." International Center for The Study of Violent Extremism, brief report, May 9, 2017. http://www.icsve.org/brief-reports/telegram-the-mighty-application-that-isis-loves/.
Lievrouw, Leah A. *Alternative and Activist New Media*. Cambridge, UK: Polity Press, 2011.
Malik, Shiv, Sandra Laville, Elena Cresci, and Aisha Gani. "Isis in Duel with Twitter and YouTube to Spread Extremist Propaganda." *The Guardian*, September 24, 2014. https://www.theguardian.com/world/2014/sep/24/isis-twitter-youtube-message-social-media-jihadi.
Milton, Daniel. "Communication Breakdown: Unraveling the Islamic State's Media Efforts." *CTC Westpoint*, October 2016. https://ctc.usma.edu/communication-breakdown-unraveling-the-islamic-states-media-efforts/
Reis, Brian. "Twitter's Terrorist Policy." *The Daily Beast*, September 24, 2013. http://www.thedailybeast.com/articles/2013/09/24/twitter-s-terrorist-policy.html.
Richards, Imogen. "'Flexible' Capital Accumulation in Islamic State Social Media." *Critical Studies on Terrorism* 9, no. 2 (2016): 205–225.
Richardson, Louise. *What Terrorists Want: Understanding the Enemy, Containing the Threat*. New York: Random House, 2006.
Rose, Steve. "The ISIS Propaganda War: A Hi-Tech Media Jihad." *The Guardian*, October 7, 2014. https://www.theguardian.com/world/2014/oct/07/isis-media-machine-propaganda-war.
Seib, Philip. "The al-Qaeda Media Machine." *Military Review* 88, no. 3 (2008): 74–80.
Shaheen, Joseph. *Network of Terror: How Daesh Uses Adaptive Social Networks to Spread Its Message*. NATO Centre of Excellence Strategic Communications, 2015. www.stratcomcoe.org/download/file/fid/3312.
Siboni, Gabi, Daniel Cohen, and Tal Koren. "The Islamic State's Strategy in Cyberspace." *Military and Strategic Affairs* 7, no. 1 (2015): 127–144.
Tartaglia, Henri. "German ISIS Supporters Started a Jihadi Facebook Campaign." *VICE*, June 22, 2014. https://www.vice.com/sv/article/german-jihadi-internet-meme-campaign.
Tenenboim-Weinblatt, Keren. "The Management of Visibility: Media Coverage of Kidnapping and Captivity Cases around the World." *Media, Culture & Society* 35, no. 7 (2013): 791–808.
Vidino, Lorenzo, Francesco Marone, and Eva Entenmann. "Fear Thy Neighbor: Radicalization and Jihadist Attacks in the West." *ICCT* Report, released June 14, 2017. https://icct.nl/wp-content/uploads/2017/06/FearThyNeighbor-RadicalizationandJihadistAttacksintheWest.pdf.
Weiss, Caleb. "Islamic State Launches Mobile App for Children." *The Long War Journal*, May 11, 2016. http://www.longwarjournal.org/archives/2016/05/islamic-state-launches-mobile-app-for-children.php.
Weiss, Michael, and Hassan Hassan. *ISIS: Inside the Army of Terror*, 2nd ed. New York: Regan Arts, 2016.
Whiteside, Craig. "Lighting the Path: The Evolution of the Islamic State Media Enterprise (2003–2016)." ICCT Research Paper, 2016. https://icct.nl/wp-content/uploads/2016/11/ICCT-Whiteside-Lighting-the-Path-the-Evolution-of-the-Islamic-State-Media-Enterprise-2003-2016-Nov2016.pdf.
Winter, Charlie. "Documenting the Virtual Caliphate." Quilliam Foundation Report, 2015. http://www.quilliaminternational.com/wp-content/uploads/2015/10/FINAL-documenting-the-virtual-caliphate.pdf.

Winter, Charlie. *Media Jihad: The Islamic State's Doctrine for Information Warfare*. London: The International Centre for the Study of Radicalisation and Political Violence, 2017.
Yayla, A. S., and A. Speckhard. "Telegram: The Mighty Application that ISIS Loves." International Center for the Study of Violent Extremism, brief report, May 9 2017. http://www.icsve.org/brief-reports/telegram-the-mighty-application-that-isis-loves/.
Ziccardi, Giovanni. *Resistance, Liberation Technology, and Human Rights in the Digital Age*. London: Springer, 2013.

MICHAEL KRONA is Assistant Professor in Media and Communication Studies and Visual Communication at Malmö University, Sweden. He works within a nationally funded research project in Sweden exploring Salafi-jihadist information operations, with particular focus on ISIS communication practices.

6 Video Verité in the Age of ISIS

Kathleen German

For four hundred years, developments in communication technologies have accelerated political and economic change—from the printing press, which contributed to the Protestant Revolution, to the Twitter revolution that observers say fueled the Arab Spring. Information and communication technologies have transmitted the information and images critical to each of these social movements. In the past, social movements took decades to develop, partially because the communication necessary to coalesce support was slow. The American Revolution, for example, was twelve years in the making. The abolition of slavery took decades to mature, as did the overthrow of British rule in India. In these and other cases, diverse groups, sometimes with different languages and cultures, faced barriers of distance and time, making it difficult to garner support for social, economic, or political change.

New technologies have shortened the communication cycle. While combatants in World War II measured communication in days, and even the conflict in Afghanistan was often hampered by communication delays, today digital data spread viral messages to warring factions in seconds.[1] Contemporary social movements such as those in the wake of the Arab Spring have been transformed by new information and communication technologies that allow widespread public access to agitators' images and rhetoric. For example, Lashkar-e-Taiba employed cyber technologies such as Google Earth and mobile phones in its 2008 assault on Mumbai. In September 2013, al-Shabaab used Twitter to coordinate its attack on the Westgate Mall in Nairobi. Later, the same media platform became the site for intimidation of its enemies and boasting to its followers.[2] Social movements have been revolutionized by the almost instantaneous digital connections now possible between local and global communication systems.

Information and communication technologies have introduced new possibilities for public communication, especially among the young, whose enthusiastic adoption of social media demonstrates its possibilities as an agent of social change.[3] Contemporary social media are porous and dynamic, allowing people to participate in constructing messages outside of the constraints of economic or political institutions. As a result, individuals and marginalized groups can often wrestle the initiative from traditional, entrenched media as they share visual texts that become the common denominators that condense and transmit the ideologies of social movements.[4] This chapter examines the persuasive function of viral images, the exploitation of discursive opportunities afforded by information and communication technologies, and the implications of these technologies for the evolving nature of warfare using the contemporary case of ISIS.

Images in Contemporary Viral Media Texts

Contemporary media texts are dominated by images. Instantaneous internet communication foregrounds images because images are immediate, able to simultaneously communicate multiple meanings, and able to function effectively in an increasingly fragmented media landscape. Visual texts are more effective than other message types in communicating ideas. Research reveals that people remember 10 percent of what they read, 30 percent of what they hear, and 80 percent of what they see.[5] Since retention is critical to influencing attitudes and behavior, images are more likely than other modes of communication to result in persuasion.

The power of images is not a recently discovered phenomenon. For centuries, the potency of images has been recognized by communication scholars from Aristotle (384–332 BC), who linked beauty to form and matter, to Francois Fenelon's (1651–1715) idea of language as "portraiture," to Kenneth Burke's (1897–1993) focus on symbols as "terministic screens." The turn to the visual has surfaced in the works of various contemporary scholars.[6] Neville Bolt[7] draws the link between images and the perceptions that fuel social movements: "And increasingly it is pictures, images triggering crystallised messages that resonate with popular memories of grievance and injustice. In today's overcrowded marketplace of ideas and communications, they offer clarity . . . [acting] as a lightning rod for collective memory."[8]

The contemporary turn to the visual by proponents of marginalized ideas is enhanced by information and communication technologies that offer the possibility of immediate, relatively unimpeded digital sharing with millions of potential participants. Advocates of social change can solidify their core of supporters while simultaneously frightening members of entrenched institutions who scramble for effective countermeasures. According to recent public opinion research, American fears of terrorism now parallel those in the wake of 9/11, suggesting that the rhetoric of social movements has had an impact on American life.[9] The unique feature of information and communication technologies is that they conform to multiple contexts. It is the technology itself, heavily dependent on compelling imagery, that accounts for the rapid upsurge of some recent social movements like ISIS. As Emerson T. Brookings and P. W. Singer claim, "The principles that have guided the Islamic State's viral success are the same ones used to publicize a new Taylor Swift album or the latest Star Wars movie."[10] For both kinds of promotional messages, information and communication technology is cheap and readily available, it lends itself to theatrical display, and it has intensified displays of nationalism.

The use of visual images that has become part of the strategy of contemporary social movements is rooted in the experiences of twentieth-century world war combatants who exploited the power of visual propaganda. The visualizations of Allied and Axis filmmakers like Frank Capra and Leni Riefenstahl resulted in controversial but potent films. They effectively articulated national ideologies and created unity among diverse participants because their images condensed abstract concepts of nationalism into immediately understandable symbols that transcended the limitations of language. As Michael Krona detailed in the previous chapter, partisans have weaponized digital media and widened the battle front to include cyberspace.

Images of conflict, especially those of death, have transfixed viewers for generations, further illustrating the power of the visual image. For example, the New England Execution Sermon, which flourished from 1660 to 1800, used the spectacle of the condemned individual facing the gallows with an open coffin at its foot to draw moral lessons for onlookers. Thomas Edison electrocuted Topsy the elephant in 1903 for advertising purposes, and Robert Capa's September 5, 1936, photograph, "The Falling Soldier" documented a Spanish Civil War soldier's moment of death and still mesmerizes viewers. Each of these images utilizes a common theme. The visual depiction of death serves to shape attitudes and behaviors by gaining attention, offering moral lessons, and constraining behavior.

As these examples reveal, images of death vividly punctuate human memory. More recent public displays of death share these features when social media images replace text, quickly circulating among millions of participants online. Such images are characterized by fragmentation as well as immediacy, ultimately configuring the modern political landscape. Although the spectacle of death mesmerizes viewers, the real power of shared images lies not in their focus on death but rather, "it is the uncluttered simplicity of the images, stripping out any extraneous distraction that might complicate the intended message. As reality is transformed into iconographic representation, the greater chance of prolonging its life and freezing the moment forever. In short, the more likely it is to anchor memory."[11] The last seconds of Neda Agha Soltan's life remain etched in our minds, along with the silhouette of Buddhist monks engulfed in flames in protest of American occupation of South Vietnam. These images join others—the planes bursting into flames as they strike the Twin Towers, the frantic efforts of the caged Jordanian pilot to escape the flames racing toward him, the glint of the Japanese sword raised to strike the neck of the captive Australian pilot in World War II—as simple and unerringly immediate representations of death.

Recent public memory is organized around the spectacle of pictures. Images anchor public memory and form the cornerstone of historical experience. The result of emphasizing the visual shifts the importance of the message to action—what we do becomes more important than what we say. Action becomes the compelling performance of ideology registered in images. Particularly violent images such as the online suicide of Pennsylvania treasurer Budd Dwyer or the public beating of Rodney King induce a cultural aftershock that resonates across individuals and communities. The gruesome nature of these images functions as spectacle and commands attention by the very nature of their content. They can also trigger associations with past grievances. When violent images are linked to social injustices, even ones long past, the opportunity arises for changing the social narrative. The violence of such images captures a moment that "fractures the continuities of hegemonic myths and narratives only to assert the continuity of revolutionary narrative constructed from its own discontinuities."[12] In this case, the revolutionary narrative can overwhelm and supplant existing institutions.

Two functions of images contribute to their impact: images have a *documentary* element as well as a *suasory* component. The documentary element appears to be passive, capturing and recording events as they transpire. It is rooted in the assumption of historical authenticity, much like the actualities that dominated the first few years of filmmaking or the video verité style of some documentary films. Visual representations were assumed to be accurate, conveying documentary truth with the force of verisimilitude. It is this impulse that dominates the cell phone video recording of the death of Eric Garner, for example. The recording was spontaneous, with no immediate purpose other than to capture events. The camera operator coincidentally was at the scene and not part of a larger, more elaborate network of participants or grassroots initiative to document civil rights violations. The original video was later coopted as performance for persuasive purposes. The video was ultimately circulated to support accusations of police brutality, probably because it resonated with existing public sentiment. In this transformation, the video shifted from documentary to suasory in its function.

The cell phone recordings of the death of Iranian bystander Neda Agha Soltan form another case of spontaneously recorded videos being coopted for political purposes.[13] The recordings of Soltan's death became a rallying point for Iranians protesting perceived election fraud in 2009. As such, visual recordings of her death took on a suasory function that condensed the arguments, ideologies, and beliefs of Iranian protestors into a single compelling image that functioned much like the rhetorical ideograph or political condensation symbol.[14] As Neville Bolt maintains, "Ideologies are conveyed as mediated spectacles."[15] As spectacle, images perform a suasory function for millions of viewers. Images circulated via the internet invite participation because of the nature of the medium, as participants actively choose to view, post, repost, and otherwise participate. As Michael McGee claims, the physical resources available to revolutionary groups and their respondents are less important than its beliefs, attitudes, values, and especially self-identities.[16] For this reason, images are a critical element in manipulating these features of revolutionary identity.

Extending the paradigm, Kevin DeLuca argues that a key component of any successful social movement is the "image event" that is staged to gain significant attention from media—especially global public media such as television, social media, and internet sources of news.[17] The reason is articulated by Bruce E. Gronbeck, who writes, "If confrontational dramas are played out before cameras, they are accorded significance and cultural importance by viewers in their very specularity and 'newsworthiness.'"[18] The shared visual image becomes a common denominator in the persuasion of the social movement, condensing and transmitting its ideological position. In this way, images become instrumental, symbolic communication that articulate the ideology and goals of the social movement.[19] The recent online visual presence of ISIS illustrates the successful suasory function of images in the development of a social movement.

The Suasory Function of ISIS Images

ISIS has made newsworthy use of social media for a variety of purposes, from soliciting financing to recruiting fighters, establishing legitimacy, and instilling fear in its adversaries. The group produces professional promotional media that are distributed in a wide variety of formats, including online magazines, blogs, internet forums, and YouTube videos. These messages spawn others, such as the "one billion campaign," which calls on Muslims to post messages, photos, and videos on Twitter, Instagram, and YouTube in support of ISIS. They also use more informal but still highly orchestrated social media such as initiating a Twitter hashtag in Arabic that translates to #theFridayofsupportingISIS, asking supporters around the world to wave the ISIS flag in public, film themselves, and upload the clips on social media platforms. Another free internet application called The Dawn of Glad Tidings automatically posts approved tweets to the accounts of the application's subscribed users. During periods of military clashes, as many as forty thousand tweets have been posted in a single day. In one post, for example, an armed jihadist gazed at the ISIS flag flying over Mosul with the inscription in Arabic: "We are coming, Baghdad." Images such as this are promoted by ISIS leaders for their strong potential "presumably to create fear among its enemies and win the admiration of other radical groups."[20] While the format of messages varies widely, compelling images are always featured.

The images are ambiguous and fluid, allowing disparate and diverse receivers to construct their own identities around them.[21] At the same time, as receivers reinterpret the images, they incorporate them into their own hierarchy of thinking. ISIS positions itself as more fundamentally true to its roots than other competing social movements such as al-Qaeda; in doing so, it offers an ideological statement that challenges the viability and value of rival movements.[22] ISIS is positioned as the honest apostle of the sovereign faith, a real agent of change grounded in social justice that avenges the wrongs suffered by the faithful. Demonstrations of strength such as the swift justice meted out to infidels through graphic executions accompanied by compassion for the elderly, children, and kittens reinforce this message. The messages create their own narrative, boost morale, attract supporters and financing, and demoralize the enemy. To date, counter-messages have been largely ineffective because they do not address the fundamental psychological appeal of the ISIS narrative.[23]

Visual messages are more likely to be shared actively across social media. It is estimated, for example, that forty-five thousand active ISIS Twitter accounts were operating in 2015.[24] High visibility affects the success of messages that are engaged in competition with hundreds of other messages for the attention of media users. As the gruesome nature of ISIS videos increased, viewer attention skyrocketed. One additional feature of the videos suggests a sophisticated adaptation to woo viewers. The visual sequences have shortened over the last decade to entice viewers. Videos now average twenty minutes. Originally, between 1998 and 2001, they were fifty-three minutes in length. The average time reduced to thirty-five minutes (2001–06), thirty-two minutes (2006–08), and twenty minutes (2008–09). Shorter average production times suggest greater sensitivity to a generation of consumers fluent in digital technologies and multiple media platforms that attract viewers impatient with lengthy visuals.[25] Videos also mimic popular video games like Grand Theft Auto and Call of Duty by using first-person point of view and rapid editing to create immersion in alternative reality.

Despite the random look of ISIS's social media visuals, closer examination reveals that the visual materials are purposeful, well-financed, and carefully choreographed. Rather than media generated spontaneously by individuals, these messages are well-conceptualized productions that sometimes strategically mimic poor production quality to imply grassroots origins.[26] It has been estimated that as many as forty media organizations are engaged in generating audio, video, and print messages, continually adapting to the evolving media context. On multiple occasions, for example, ISIS soldiers going into battle were equipped with GoPro cameras strapped to their helmets and remotely operated drones followed the armed clashes. Later, the footage was used in videos distributed through various internet and communication technologies. This is just one instance of a coordinated media strategy that serves the mission of the caliphate. Compared to other social movements, Julianne Pepitone concludes, "The scale and relative professionalism of ISIS' management of social media and other PR platforms has been far superior."[27] The overall goal of ISIS is to manipulate public sentiment and coalesce political-military power via sophisticated media that form part of its strategy of warfare.

The conclusion that ISIS's media use is purposeful, despite its homespun "video verité" look, is also supported by observations rooted in the practices of media production.[28] The video images are staged dramatic performances with carefully selected camera placements; effective theatrical blocking of subjects; and attention to lighting, sound, and other aesthetics important for producing effective messages. Image sequences are clearly edited to engage viewers. In one instance, the destruction of the temples and arches in Palmyra required special wide-angle lenses and strategic camera placement, as well as impeccable timing coordinated to capture the action. In addition, the footage is designed to work equally well across multiple media formats, suggesting preproduction planning, professional-quality production, and postproduction sophistication, with an understanding of the confluence of multiple media channels. Witnesses report that one particularly bloody mass beheading was carefully choreographed, with victims and executioners spaced so that camera operators could move easily among the victims and executioners to record the action from the best close-up angles.

ISIS's media use exhibits flexibility as it adapts messages to distinct target audiences. Messages adapt both to the potential viewing group and to the flow of unfolding events as they describe battles, territory taken, and even offer an online speed-dating service for fighters looking for jihadist brides.[29] By far, the largest number of followers who access ISIS through Twitter accounts are located in Syria and Iraq, although one in five ISIS supporters selected English as their primary language.[30] ISIS promotes itself especially to youthful viewers using high-level production techniques in short mash-ups that play "like a trailer for an action movie, with slow-motion explosions and flames engulfing American troops."[31] Images are shared on platforms like Twitter, Facebook, Kik, Telegram, and WhatsApp to reach their target audience in appealing youth-oriented language while exploiting popular hashtags to disseminate these messages.

It is likely that Western ISIS recruits promote the cause to their peers, as Matthew Pascarella discusses, in part, in his chapter of this volume; this recruitment has also at times emphasized the need to recruit teen girls. Sash Havlicek, chief executive of the Institute for Strategic Dialogue, observes, "We're seeing young women from across Western countries both expressing their support for and migrating to Syria now in totally unprecedented numbers. And I would say this is the result really of an extremely sophisticated propaganda recruitment machinery that's targeting young women very specifically."[32]

Although there are no reliable figures, it is estimated that 10 percent of foreigners who voluntarily entered the Islamic State are women, and ISIS is actively seeking to increase its appeal to young, computer-literate women.[33] According to Aqsa Mohmood, a Scottish teenager who traveled to join ISIS in 2013, his devotion was rewarded with the gift of "a house with free electricity and water provided to you due to the Khilafah [the caliphate or state] and no rent included."[34] His blogs to other teens considering the trip, reassure women, "You can find shampoos, soaps and other female necessities here, so do not stress if you think you will be experiencing some cavewoman life here."[35] Mohmood appeals to the belief that ISIS is helping its citizens, and he urges his internet followers to become part of that dream.

Other ISIS bloggers rely on fantasy to attract women with suggestive storylines, gauzy images, and hidden romances. A celebrity culture has even emerged around some ISIS fighters popularly known as "jihotties," like the French recruit known as Guitone.

The proliferation of internet social media messages among younger users of social media is fostered partially because they are interacting with their peers. Shahed Amanullah, a former senior adviser at the State Department, explains, "Part of the reason it is so effective is because it is organic, it's from the audience that it is going after. These young people understand youth frustration, they understand the fascination with violence, they understand that imagery and graphics that you see in Hollywood will attract these people." The results are obvious, as messages propagate quickly through the internet. Although followers rarely number more than fifty thousand per site, they actively forward images and text at a higher rate than conventional users. Amanullah draws this comparison with government counter-messages, which "don't percolate through the Internet in the same way. The kumbaya message does not fly through the Internet the way a beheading video does."[36] The messages court the undecided by displaying the heroic nature of the fighters, strengthen Muslim resolve by situating the fighting as a defense of daily life, and threaten the West by revealing the consequences of their resistance to the infidel.[37] It is clear to Lint Watts of the Foreign Policy Institute that social media "accelerate the radicalization of recruitment" partially through visual images in video, immersing potential recruits in a very engaging way, and through repetition as video messages pop up in many places across multiple platforms—something ISIS has done more successfully than any other group.[38]

The media productions are multilayered, which is important to successful social movements.[39] There are simultaneous hard and soft activities. Western analysts have labeled ISIS media use as schizophrenic because images of fighters holding kittens, sharing family photos, or describing their meals are juxtaposed with the gruesome spectacles of beheadings, immolations, and other brutalities.[40] But the appearance of inconsistency on the surface belies a more sophisticated media mixture of hard and soft messages whose complexity appeals to the target audiences.[41] The underlying theme of swift justice on behalf of those who have suffered justifies both violent and compassionate images. The credibility of the messages is reinforced as the sources are perceived as genuinely human in their daily activities and devotion to the cause. The authenticity of the messages derives from the documentary, video verité style of its framing. For example, the internet magazine The Islamic State Report details life within an idyllic Islamic state. The magazine explains that "caring for the residents of Wilayat Ar-Raqqah [Province of Ar-Raqqah] is a goal of the Islamic State."[42] For this reason, Islamic services committees composed of multiple departments are formed. From this base, Abu Salih Al-Ansari, the head of the Consumer Protection Office, tells the magazine reader, "Our teams go out every day, split up on the streets of the city and examine the restaurants, wholesale outlets and shopping centers. We also conduct direct medical supervision of the slaughterhouses in order to ensure that they are free of any harmful substances. We will soon be holding a seminar (God willing) to teach the proper Islamic method of slaughter. We hold surprise inspections on a daily basis at varying times."[43]

Throughout its media, ISIS offers the spectacle of violence that delivers justice to unbelievers, alongside the demonstration of a fully functioning state that rewards believers with the fruits of their faith. As several analysts conclude, the early manifestations of jihadist philosophy expressed by al-Qaeda have matured into a viable nation in the rhetoric of the Islamic State.[44]

ISIS has been highly successful at evading the censorship of traditional media that privilege news generated to represent establishment viewpoints. Traditional media tend to centralize control in the hands of business and political elites whose news offerings are shaped by advertiser interests and political needs. These, in turn, feature entertaining content, avoid basic challenges to entrenched institutions, and promote establishment interests. According to Robert McChesney, the challenge comes as insurgents operate outside the system of media production but remain fully part of the viewer's community, albeit a more critically engaged segment of it.[45] We have entered an age of discontinuity, where traditional economic, political, and ideological boundaries dictated by traditional top-down media controlled by entrenched interests have given way to a participatory culture where competing messages blur the lines between producer and consumer in a process that is increasingly iterative and reciprocal.[46] Previous boundaries among television, radio, and print are now reconfigured as converged messages that flow freely among traditional media outlets and new information and communication technologies.

The advantage of fluidity offered by digitalized messages is accompanied by unpredictability in a highly ephemeral context. Neville Bolt points out the challenge for revolutionaries: "What insurgents need is sustainable development of memory to challenge state or media hegemony. Viral flows muster rapid support around particular ideas, but they dissipate as fast as they appear."[47] Known as "swarmcasts," these multiplatformed, multimodal, multisourced social media events have proven to be difficult to eradicate. They have stretched traditional definitions of media, as Ali Fisher concludes: "It marks a shift from the hierarchical and broadcast models of communication during conflict to a new dispersed and resilient form which embraces the strength of emergent behaviour."[48] By turning to information and communication technologies, social movements have introduced a new form of digital conflict that exploits the advantages of cyberspace.

The Exploitation of Discursive Opportunities

The most important feature of mediated messages is that they capture viewer attention. ISIS's media messages have accomplished this goal by exploiting discursive opportunities through visibility, resonance, and the creation of legitimacy.[49] The potency of visual images allows insurrectionists to insert themselves between potential viewers and mainstream media by staging dramatic visual actions and commanding attention using internet and communication technologies. Contemporary media platforms thrive on clear tensions most often found in binary themes. Binary themes are easier to package as visual material because images can capture good and evil more effectively than gradations. The complexities of context, competing opinions, and historical innuendos rarely often come across with visual immediacy or clarity. Most audiences negotiate simple binary frameworks for understanding with greater ease than the more tedious process of comprehending multilayered issues. Such binary themes dominate ISIS videos, including forgiveness/vengeance, heroism/cowardice, honor/dishonor, life/death, ours/theirs, and truth/falsehood.[50] This binary structure leads quickly to the clear division between ISIS and others, allowing little middle ground for negotiating alternative configurations. Uncritical viewers, swept up in the pathos of the videos, may be less likely to discern the binary framework of the visual messages.

In addition, ISIS messages reflect value issues that "thrive on two-valued logics that allow for no compromise but for this very reason heighten their attractiveness as image events for the news camera."[51] The problem is compounded because news reporting flourishes on less complex issues, especially those with good visuals. As a result, reports on ISIS in Western media sometimes crowd out less appealing and more complex news stories on the economy and other complicated topics. Messages initiated by ISIS and posted online create a ripple effect as traditional media access and spread the narratives. As media attention resonates across the West, ISIS derives a form of legitimacy from international attention.

Resonance. Whether coverage is positive or negative, the simple fact that ISIS attracts the attention of Western media enhances the spread of its message. News

reports make salient the existence of ISIS and thereby perpetuate the salience of its message through traditional media outlets. Even though ISIS appeals most often to leaderless Syrian and Palestinian youth, European nations have reacted to the threat, sometimes disproportionately, probably magnifying the actual threat of ISIS. Social media act in conjunction with traditional media as messages leak from one forum to others. Social media sharing offers the potential for greater resonance as individuals access videos that might otherwise have more limited circulation if subject to traditional news media editorial gatekeeping and conventional distribution channels.

Images shared via social media are likely to have a direct impact on behavioral tendencies. Multiple studies have documented a link between observing violent images and subsequent violent behavioral tendencies in youth.[52] While a direct causal relationship between viewing violent images and subsequent acts of violence is a simplistic model, since intermediate variables are likely to complicate human behavior, professional organizations like the US Surgeon General, the American Psychiatric Association, and the American Medical Association have warned about the long-term impact of violent images, especially among highly impressionable and young viewers. Thus, images of violence perpetuated in the messages of ISIS may increase the danger of more frequent violent outbursts, which further alarms nations bordering ISIS whose youth are the direct targets of its persuasion, as well as more remote targets like the United States and Britain.

Legitimacy. The degree to which media attention grants ISIS any degree of importance in world events supports the movement's goals to recruit financial and individual contributions and to issue a warning to other nations. Julianne Pepitone outlines these goals in more detail: "ISIS is even more brutal than most social movements to create its own authentic narrative, boost the morale of its followers by establishing their righteousness, recruit money, men, and materiel, and demoralize its enemies by positioning them outside the movement."[53]

These functions further underscore the complex nature of social media videos produced under the auspices of ISIS that sometimes appear almost contradictory. They are designed with distinct aims to work on multiple viewers simultaneously. For this reason, ISIS can recruit voluntary contributions at the same time it threatens other onlookers. Those who accept the ISIS ideological position can be seduced, while outsiders are distressed because the same message operates on different planes as a polysemic message.[54] The alarm is so great in some cases that it has spread to the battlefield. There is evidence that the unstoppable image of ISIS perpetuated online was "clearly a factor in encouraging people to leave their posts as ISIS was advancing."[55]

Symbolic Action. The gruesome reality of the blood sacrifice in videos of beheadings, immolation, mass execution, and other violence distributed through social media functions as incipient action.[56] Participation in the video verité messages through viewing or sharing online forms an initial commitment to act as the symbolic events displayed become part of the viewer's reality. As Neville Bolt explains, "Narrative of historic grievance and suffering that 'allowed insurgents to use violent political acts not just as kinetic or symbolic deeds but as systemic triggers for memory of political-economic grievance and stories that tapped deep into communities' spiritual lives.'"[57]

Online and communication technologies, especially images, provide an alternative to hegemonic messages that dominate establishment rhetoric. Often, the shock appeal of graphic images reinforces their credibility because they establish a counter-reality that is compelling because of its resonance with the viewer's experience. The videos craft narratives rooted in past grievances negotiated with the present in a way that taps personal experience. Thus, cultural and historical memories become entwined with the social-movement ideology of ISIS as the values of marginalized individuals and groups are reflected. Personal experience is further reinforced as reality through online participation. Social media participation becomes vicarious lived experience, part of participatory culture dependent on the immediacy of social media.

Implications

The powerful rhetorical function of social media videos promulgated by ISIS is apparent in several ways. First, there are the immediate, practical results visible in international support for its cause. Both recruitment and financial backing have flourished as a direct result of ISIS's online media presence. For the *New York Times*, Eric Schmitt and Somini Senguptasept report that "Nearly 30,000 foreign recruits have now poured in Syria, many to join the Islamic State, a doubling of volunteers in just the past 12 months and stark evidence that an international effort to tighten borders, share intelligence and enforce antiterrorism laws in not diminishing the ranks of new militant fighters."[58]

While the fortunes of the Islamic State have been challenged on the battlefield in recent months and the final outcome of the struggle is still unpredictable at the time of this writing, ISIS still maintains a vigorous media presence and influences so-called "lone wolf" attacks that occur periodically.[59] The shift in focus from recruiting soldiers to influencing terrorist attacks has altered the dynamics of recruitment. Frank Cilluffo, director of the George Washington University Homeland Security Policy Institute, explains, "At the end of the day, they don't need big numbers. They're trying to appeal to small numbers, which unfortunately in the terrorism business is all it takes."[60] Instead of more generic appeals, ISIS recruiters can establish personal relationships with online contacts, providing the motivation and information necessary to encourage local acts of terrorism. Potential recruits share online narratives of heroic nationalism with practical advice on evading detection as they aspire to act on their ideological commitments. The online magazine *Inspire*, formerly published by al-Qaeda in the Arabian Peninsula (AQAP) and aimed at British and American youth, for example, mashes reader-submitted photos and stories with messages from Islamic leaders, accounts of attacks on infidels, and recipes for bombs. Such online material melds practical advice with ideological rants against Western nonbelievers that attracts and inspires readers.

Even with cyberspace countermeasures, the recruitment trend has continued upward. Tina S. Kaidanow, top counterterrorism official for the US State Department, concluded that "the Islamic State's unprecedented ability to recruit and to radicalize followers over the Internet and on social media" will continue that trend.[61] As ISIS has vowed to export the fight to other nations, the internet has served as an invaluable tool in the radicalization of supporters.[62] And the role of information and communication technologies has evolved according to the needs of the social movement. Adherents could gather virtually undetected online without geographical constraints to solidify their ideological leanings and enact their beliefs through participation in the internet community of like-minded supporters whose anger is rooted in religious justification, economic displacement, and history. Online participation has proven highly effective at mobilizing and directing anger at the enemy "other." The link is made vivid by Patrick Kingsley, who draws this comparison: "In wars gone by, advancing armies smoothed their path with missiles. ISIS did it with tweets and a movie."[63]

Changes in their messages have corresponded with their tactical changes in social media use as messages have shifted from encouraging the physical journey, known as *hijrah* (the Arabic reference to Prophet Muhammad's journey to escape persecution in Mecca) to serving Islam by striking at the enemy in situ. As travel to Syria has become increasingly difficult and as anti-ISIS groups become more adept at identifying and detaining aspiring jihadists, urging supporters to strike at the enemy at home was a practical solution. Internet recruiters played a vital role in recruiting, inspiring, and enabling terrorism at home. As Abu Muhammad al-Adnani said in a message released in May 2017, "If the tyrants have closed in your faces the door of hijrah, then open in their face the door of jihad."[64] Clearly, the role of internet and communication technologies has adjusted to the new realities facing the Islamic State.

The implications for future use of social media to support the goals of social movements are staggering, and hints of such use are already present. Islamic State handlers operating online were heavily implicated, from recruitment to the final planning stages in the Hyderabad strike as well as other attacks.[65] In at least ten recent attacks, recruits were in direct contact with their online coaches until minutes before the attack was launched. Experts who have examined plots carried out in the name of ISIS suggest that for the past three years, such "enabled attacks" through online applications such as ChatSecure, Pidgin, Tutanota, and the Tails operating system have grown as a percentage of the military operations. Online contacts targeted and recruited individuals, guided them through radicalization, and provided the knowledge and materials to execute the strike.[66] According to terrorism analyst Bridget Moreng, "this is the future of ISIS."[67] This method of operations is simply an extension of the group's tendency to invest heavily in people rather than infrastructure.[68] As airstrikes increase and geographic holdings erode, it is wise to resist creating targets such as buildings and other structures that can easily be captured or destroyed. Mobile personnel, including internet experts, are much more difficult to eliminate.[69] Amid billions of social media accounts worldwide, it is safer, easier, and more effective for ISIS recruiters to hide, using skillfully crafted videos as "clickbait" to lure future recruits.

As a highly successful revolutionary social movement, ISIS uses visual metaphor in order to establish the legitimacy of its claims and to coalesce opinion behind its leadership. The striking image is paramount to this process because it is an expression of the rights of the rebels and a claim to revolt. The graphic, bloody nature of the images promoted by ISIS simultaneously combines these messages in one horrific metaphor shared by millions of viewers through social media. Through images, ideologies are conveyed as mediated spectacles.

Conclusion

In predicting the future of social media, Peter W. Singer, director of the Center for 21st Century Security and Intelligence, drew this comparison: "Just as the Crimea War was the first war reported by telegraph and Vietnam the first TV war, we are now seeing wars in places like Syria and Iraq, just like the broader use of media technology, playing out online."[70] And, just as the introduction of the new technologies of the telegraph and television altered the way audiences participated in warfare, the latest information and communication technologies have once again changed the relationship of audiences to war.

Contemporary internet media are dominated by images as the visual is increasingly privileged over print. Online media function as a new strategic concept, shaping individual participation in their communities and political institutions. Groups such as ISIS can efficiently solidify their base of support, gather adherents, promulgate their ideology, and recruit finances and fighting personnel. Although ISIS began as a relatively small social movement, it rapidly emerged as a threat to surrounding nations and world powers alike. The advent of new, ubiquitous information and communication technologies requires that we adjust old models of political and social change as social movements like ISIS enthusiastically embrace social media to promote their ideological agendas.

In the future, social movements will undoubtedly continue to crop up as advocates challenge institutions and practices. Information and communication technologies will probably contribute to the success or failure of these social movements. Increasingly, whatever we know about our society or about the world in which we live, we know through the mass media. While archaeologists are more likely to use the phrase "in situ" to describe an artifact found in its original resting place, a renewed critical focus on "situation" and "context" is given fresh inertia by the promotion of social-movement ideology in cyberspace. To fully appreciate the shifting contexts of revolutionary social movements, critics must embrace the emerging technologies of netwar. The spectacular images that swirl across digital forums have become an important part of twenty-first-century conflict, allowing advocates to exploit the participatory nature of social media culture and thereby bring revolution directly into our lives.

Notes

1. See N. Bolt, *The Violent Image: Insurgent Propaganda and the New Revolutionaries* (New York: Columbia University Press, 2012); E. T. Brooking and P. W. Singer, "War Goes Viral: How Social Media Is Being Weaponized," *The Atlantic* 318, no. 4 (2016): 72–83; and A. Speckhard, A. S. Yayla, and A. Shajkovci, "Defeating ISIS on the Battle Ground as Well as in the Online Battle Space: Considerations of the 'New Normal' and Available Online Weapons in the Struggle Ahead," *Journal of Strategic Security* 19, no. 4 (2016): 1–10.
2. James P. Farwell, "The Media Strategy of ISIS," *Survival: Global Politics and Strategy* 56, no. 6 (2014): 449–455.
3. *Information and communication technologies* is used here as a broad category that includes varied internet platforms such as blogs, Facebook, YouTube, Instagram, and many others. These platforms often share converged content and are easily accessed through cell phones, computer links, and various other digital devices.
4. In this chapter, social movements are defined as any group that opposes an institutional base of power over a period of time with some form of organizational structure. For a more formal definition of social movements and a discussion of the hierarchy of social movement communication strategies, see Bowers and Ochs, *The Rhetoric of Agitation and Control*.
5. P. Lester, "Syntactic Theory of Visual Communication," *Visual Communication Images with Messages* (Boston: Wadsworth, 2003).
6. See L. C. Olson, C. A. Finnegan, and D. S. Hope, eds., *Visual Rhetoric* (Los Angeles: Sage, 2014).
7. Bolt, *The Violent Image*.
8. Ibid., 7.
9. Brooking and Singer, "War Goes Viral."

10. Ibid., 76.
11. Ibid., 115.
12. Ibid., 77.
13. See Kathleen M. German, "Social Media and Citizen Journalism in the 2009 Iranian Protests: The Case of Neda Agha-Soltan," *Mass Communication and Journalism* 4, no. 195 (2015): 104–115; J. Malkowski, "Streaming Death: The Politics of Dying on YouTube," *Jump Cut* 54 (2012). jc54.2012/malkowskiYoutubeDeaths/.
14. See M. C. McGee, "The Ideograph: The Link between Rhetoric and Ideology," *Quarterly Journal of Speech* 66, no. 1 (1980): 1–16; D. A. Graber, *Media Power in Politics* (Washington, DC: Congressional Quarterly Press, 2011).
15. Bolt, *The Violent Image*, 50.
16. M. C. McGee, "Social Movements as Meaning," *Communication Studies* 31, no. 1 (1983): 74–77.
17. K. M. DeLuca, *Image Politics: The New Rhetoric of Environmental Activism* (New York: Guilford Press, 1999).
18. B. E. Gronbeck, "The Rhetoric of Agitation and Control Confronts Movement Theory and Practice," *Poroi: An Interdisciplinary Journal of Rhetorical Analysis and Invention* 9, no. 2 (2013): 4.
19. John Bowers and Donovan Ochs defined rhetoric as "instrumental, symbolic behavior" in their 1971 analysis of the rhetoric of social movements, *The Rhetoric of Agitation and Control.*
20. F. Irshaid, "How ISIS Is Spreading Its Message Online," BBC, June 19, 2014, http://www.bbc.com/news/world-middle-east-27912569.
21. Bolt, *The Violent Image*; Graber, *Media Power in Politics.*
22. See Sam Garin, "Pop Terrorism: ISIS' Media Campaign," *Harvard Political Review*, June 11, 2015, http://harvardpolitics.com/world/pop-terrorismismediacampaignM/; J. Pepitone, "Why ISIS' Social Media Campaign Is 'Even More Brutal' Than Most," *NBC News*, June 16, 2014, http://www.nbcnews.com/storyline/iraq-turmoil/why-isis-social-media-campaign-even-more; Jessica Stern and J. M. Berger, *ISIS: The State of Terror* (New York: HarperCollins, 2015).
23. M. Mazzetti and M. R. Gordon, "ISIS Is Winning the Social Media War, US Concludes," *New York Times*, June 12, 2015, http://www.nytimes.com/2015/06/13/world/middleeast/isis-is-winning-message-war-us-concludes.
24. Brookings Institution's Project on US. Relations with the Islamic World, 2016, https://www.brookings.edu/project/u-s-relations-with-the-islamic-world/.
25. Bolt, *The Violent Image.*
26. G. Siboni, D. Cohen, and T. Koren, "The Islamic State's Strategy in Cyberspace," *Military and Strategic Affairs* 7, no. 1 (2015): 127–144.
27. Pepitone, "Why ISIS' Social Media Campaign."
28. Siboni et al., "The Islamic State's Strategy in Cyberspace."
29. S. Smith, "ISIS Offers 5-Minute Speed Dating Service to Help Militants Find Jihadi Brides," *Christian Post*, January 9, 2015, http://www.christianpost.com/news/isis-offers-5-minute-speed-dating-service-to-help-militants-find-jihadi-brides-132361/#BdSLcASh1lro3JOj.99.
30. J. M. Berger and J. Morgan, "The ISIS Twitter Census: Defining and Describing the Population of ISIS Supporters on Twitter," The Brookings Project on US Relations with the Islamic World Analysis Paper, no. 20, 2015.

31. A. Perrucci, "ISIS Takes to Internet to Target Teens," *WGNO*, February 25, 2015, http://wgno.com/2015/02/25/isis-takes-to-internet-to-target-teens/.
32. Ibid.
33. H. Khelghat-Doost, "Women of the Caliphate: The Mechanism for Women's Incorporation into the Islamic State," *Perspectives on Terrorism* 11, no. 1 (2017), http://www.terrorismanalysts.com/pt/index.php/pot/article/view/574/html.
34. Perrucci, "ISIS Takes to Internet."
35. Ibid.
36. L. Walker, "Inside the ISIS Social Media Campaign," *Newsweek*, March 6, 2015, http://www.newsweek.com/inside-isis-social-media-campaign-312062.
37. Garin, "Pop Terrorism."
38. S. Simon, "ISIS Runs a Dark Media Campaign on Social Media," *NPR*, September 6, 2014, http://www.npr.org/2014/09/06/3452992/isis-runs-a-dark-media-campaign-on-social-media. See also Stern and Berger, "The State of Terror."
39. J. W. Bowers and D. Ochs, *The Rhetoric of Agitation and Control* (Reading, MA: Addison-Wesley Publishing Company, 1971).
40. Simon, "ISIS Runs a Dark Media Campaign."
41. Garin, "Pop Terrorism."
42. M. Ajbaili, "How ISIS Conquered Social Media," *Al Arabiya News*, June 24, 2014, http://english.alarabiya.net/en/media/digital/2014/06/24?How-had-ISIS-conquered-social-media.
43. Ibid.
44. William McCants, *The ISIS Apocalypse: The History, Strategy, and Doomsday Vision of the Islamic State* (New York: Picador, 2015); Stern and Berger, "The State of Terror."
45. Quoted in Bolt, *The Violent Image*, 139.
46. P. Drucker, *The Age of Discontinuity* (New York: Harper & Row, 1969).
47. Bolt, *The Violent Image*, 144.
48. A. Fisher, "Swarmcast: How Jihadist Networks Maintain a Persistent Online Presence," *Perspectives on Terrorism* 9, no. 4 (2015): 8, http://www.terrorismanalysts.com/pt/index.php/pot/article/view/445/html.
49. R. Koopmans, "Movements and Media: Selection Processes and Evolutionary Dynamics in the Public Sphere," *Theory and Society* 33, no. 3–4 (2004): 367–391.
50. Bolt, *The Violent Image*.
51. B. E. Gronbeck, "The Rhetoric of Agitation and Control Confronts Movement Theory and Practice," *Poroi: An Interdisciplinary Journal of Rhetorical Analysis and Invention* 9 (2013): 2–8.
52. S. L. Smith, E. Moyer-Guse, and E. Donnerstein, "Media Violence and Sex: What Are the Concerns, Issues, and Effects?" in *The Sage Handbook of Media Studies*, ed. J. D. H. Downing (Thousand Oaks, CA: Sage, 2004).

53. Pepitone, "Why ISIS' Social Media Campaign."
54. J. Fiske, *Television Culture* (New York: Routledge, 1987).
55. P. Kingsley, "Who Is Behind ISIS's Terrifying Online Propaganda Operation?" *The Guardian*, June 23, 2014, http://www.theguardian.com/world/2014/jun/23/who-behind-isis-propaganda-operation-iraq.
56. K. Burke, *A Grammar of Motives* (Berkeley: University of California Press, 1945).
57. Bolt, *The Violent Image*, 50.

58. E. Schmitt and S. Senguptasept, "Thousands Enter Syria to Join ISIS Despite Global Efforts," *New York Times*, September 27, 2015: A1.

59. See T. Arango, "Grim Toll in Mosul Reflects New Urgency in ISIS Fight," *New York Times*, March 28, 2017: A1 & A9; B. Hubbard and M. R. Gordon, "US War Footprint Grows in Middle East, with No Endgame in Sight," *New York Times*, March 29, 2017: A1, A9.

60. F. Ciluffo, "A Blueprint for Cyber Deterrence: Building Stability through Strength," *Military and Strategic Affairs* 4, no. 3 (2014): 6.

61. Cited by Schmitt and Senguptasept, "Thousands Enter Syria," A1.

62. Stern and Berger, "The State of Terror."

63. Kingsley, "Who Is Behind ISIS's Terrifying Online Propaganda Operation?"

64. R. Callimachi, "Not 'Lone Wolves' After All: How ISIS Guides World's Terror Plots from Afar," *New York Times,* February 4, 2017, https://www.nytimes.com/2017/02/04/world/asia/isis-messaging-app-terror-plot.html?emc=edit_ta_20170204&nl=top-stories&nlid=69281225&ref=cta&_r=0.

65. Ibid.

66. Ibid.

67. B. Moreng, "ISIS' Virtual Puppeteers: How They Recruit and Train "Lone Wolves," *Foreign Affairs*, September 21, 2016, https://www.foreignaffairs.com/articles/2016-09-21/isis-virtual-puppeteers.

68. S. Almukhtar, "ISIS Finances Are Strong," *New York Times*, May 19, 2015, https://www.nytimes.com/interactive/2015/05/19/world/middleeast/isis-finances.html.

69. Ibid.

70. Quoted in Ajbaili, "How ISIS Conquered Social Media."

Bibliography

Ajbaili, M. "How ISIS Conquered Social Media." *Al Arabiya News*, June 24, 2014. http://english.alarabiya.net/en/media/digital/2014/06/24?How-had-ISIS-conquered-social-media.

Almukhtar, S. "ISIS Finances Are Strong." *New York Times*, May 19, 2015. https://www.nytimes.com/interactive/2015/05/19/world/middleeast/isis-finances.html.

Arango, T. "Grim Toll in Mosul Reflects New Urgency in ISIS Fight." *New York Times*, March 28, 2017, A1, A9.

Berger, J. M., and J. Morgan. "The ISIS Twitter Census: Defining and Describing the Population of ISIS Supporters on Twitter." The Brookings Project on US Relations with the Islamic World Analysis Paper, no. 20, 2015.

Bolt, N. *The Violent Image: Insurgent Propaganda and the New Revolutionaries*. New York: Columbia University Press, 2012.

Bowers, J. W., and D. Ochs. *The Rhetoric of Agitation and Control*. Reading, MA: Addison-Wesley Publishing Company, 1971.

Brooking, E. T., and P. W. Singer. "War Goes Viral: How Social Media Is Being Weaponized." *The Atlantic* 318, no. 4 (2016): 72–83.

Brookings Institution's Project on US Relations with the Islamic World, 2016. https://www.brookings.edu/project/u-s-relations-with-the-islamic-world/.

Burke, K. *A Grammar of Motives*. Berkeley: University of California Press, 1945.

Callimachi, R. "Not 'Lone Wolves' After All: How ISIS Guides World's Terror Plots from Afar." *New York Times*, February 4, 2017. https://www.nytimes.com/2017/02/04/world/asia/isis-messaging-app-terror-plot.html?emc=edit_ta_20170204&nl=top-stories&nlid=69281225&ref=cta&_r=0.
Cilufflo, F. "A Blueprint for Cyber Deterrence: Building Stability through Strength." *Military and Strategic Affairs* 4, no. 3 (2014): 3–23.
DeLuca, K. M. *Image Politics: The New Rhetoric of Environmental Activism*. New York: Guilford Press, 1999.
Drucker, P. *The Age of Discontinuity*. New York: Harper & Row, 1969.
Farwell, J. P. "The Media Strategy of ISIS." *Survival: Global Politics and Strategy* 56, no. 6 (2014): 449–455.
Fisher, A. "Swarmcast: How Jihadist Networks Maintain a Persistent Online Presence." *Perspectives on Terrorism* 9, no. 4 (2015). http://www.terrorismanalysts.com/pt/index.php/pot/article/view/445/html.
Fiske, J. *Television Culture*. New York: Routledge, 1987.
Garin, S. "Pop Terrorism: ISIS' Media Campaign." *Harvard Political Review*, June 11, 2015. http://harvardpolitics.com/world/pop-terrorismismediacampaign/.
German, Kathleen M. "Social Media and Citizen Journalism in the 2009 Iranian Protests: The Case of Neda Agha-Soltan." *Mass Communication and Journalism* 4, no. 195 (2015): 104–115.
Graber, D. A. *Media Power in Politics*. Washington, DC: Congressional Quarterly Press, 2011.
Gronbeck, B. E. "The Rhetoric of Agitation and Control Confronts Movement Theory and Practice." *Poroi: An Interdisciplinary Journal of Rhetorical Analysis and Invention* 9 (2013): 2–8.
Hubbard, B., and M. R. Gordon. "US War Footprint Grows in Middle East, with No Endgame in Sight." *New York Times*, March 29, 2017: A1, A9.
Irshaid, F. "How ISIS Is Spreading Its Message Online." *BBC*, June 19, 2014. http://www.bbc.com/news/world-middle-east-27912569.
Khelghat-Doost, H. "Women of the Caliphate: The Mechanism for Women's Incorporation into the Islamic State." *Perspectives on Terrorism* 11, no. 1 (2017). http://www.terrorismanalysts.com/pt/index.php/pot/article/view/574/html.
Kingsley, P. "Who Is Behind ISIS's Terrifying Online Propaganda Operation?" *The Guardian*, June 23, 2014. http://www.theguardian.com/world/2014/jun/23/who-behind-isis-propaganda-operation-iraq.
Koopmans, R. "Movements and Media: Selection Processes and Evolutionary Dynamics in the Public Sphere." *Theory and Society* 33 (2004): 367–391.
Lester, P. "Syntactic Theory of Visual Communication." *Visual Communication Images with Messages*. Boston: Wadsworth, 2003.
Malkowski, J. "Streaming Death: The Politics of Dying on YouTube." *Jump Cut* 54 (2012). jc54.2012/malkowskiYoutubeDeaths/.
Mazzetti, M., and M. R. Gordon. "ISIS Is Winning the Social Media War, US Concludes." *New York Times*, June 12, 2015. https://www.nytimes.com/2015/06/13/world/middleeast/isis-is-winning-message-war-us-concludes.html.
McCants, W. *The ISIS Apocalypse: The History, Strategy, and Doomsday Vision of the Islamic State*. New York: Picador, 2015.
McGee, M. C. "The Ideograph: The Link between Rhetoric and Ideology." *Quarterly Journal of Speech* 66, no. 1 (1980): 1–16.

McGee, M. C. "Social Movements as Meaning." *Communication Studies* 31, no. 1 (1983): 74–77.
Moreng, B. "ISIS' Virtual Puppeteers: How They Recruit and Train 'Lone Wolves.'" *Foreign Affairs*, September 21, 2016. https://www.foreignaffairs.com/articles/2016-09-21/isis-virtual-puppeteers.
Olson, L. C., C. A. Finnegan, and D. S. Hope, eds. *Visual Rhetoric*. Los Angeles: Sage, 2014.
Pepitone, J. "Why ISIS' Social Media Campaign Is 'Even More Brutal' Than Most." *NBC News*, June 16, 2014. https://www.nbcnews.com/storyline/iraq-turmoil/why-isis-social-media-campaign-even-more-brutal-most-n132321.
Perrucci, A. "ISIS Takes to Internet to Target Teens." *WGNO*, February 25, 2015. http://wgno.com/2015/02/25/isis-takes-to-internet-to-target-teens/.
Schmitt, E., and S. Senguptasept. "Thousands Enter Syria to Join ISIS Despite Global Efforts." *New York Times*, September 27, 2015: A1.
Siboni, G., D. Cohen, and T. Koren. "The Islamic State's Strategy in Cyberspace." *Military and Strategic Affairs* 7, no. 1 (2015): 127–144.
Simon, S. "ISIS Runs a Dark Media Campaign on Social Media." *NPR*, September 6, 2014. http://www.npr.org/2014/09/06/3452992/isis-runs-a-dark-media-campaign-on-social-media.
Smith, S. "ISIS Offers 5-Minute Speed Dating Service to Help Militants Find Jihadi Brides." *Christian Post*, January 9, 2015. http://www.christianpost.com/news/isis-offers-5-minute-speed-dating-service-to-help-militants-find-jihadi-brides-132361/#BdSLcASh1lro3JOj.99.
Smith, S. L., E. Moyer-Guse, and E. Donnerstein. "Media Violence and Sex: What Are the Concerns, Issues, and Effects?" In *The Sage Handbook of Media Studies*, edited by J. D. H. Downing. Thousand Oaks, CA: Sage, 2004.
Speckhard, A., A. S. Yayla, and A. Shajkovci. "Defeating ISIS on the Battle Ground as Well as in the Online Battle Space: Considerations of the 'New Normal' and Available Online Weapons in the Struggle Ahead." *Journal of Strategic Security* 19, no. 4 (2016): 1–10.
Stern, J., and J. M. Berger. *ISIS: The State of Terror*. New York: HarperCollins, 2015.
Walker, L. "Inside the ISIS Social Media Campaign." *Newsweek*, March 6, 2015. http://www.newsweek.com/inside-isis-social-media-campaign-312062.

KATHLEEN GERMAN is a Professor in the Department of Media, Journalism, and Film at Miami University in Oxford, Ohio. She is the author of *Promises of Citizenship: Film Recruitment of African Americans in World War II*, *The Ethics of Emerging Media*, *Queer Identity/Political Reality*, and *Principles of Public Speaking*.

7 Brand of Brothers

Marketing the Islamic State

Brian Hughes

In the span of only a few years, the so-called Islamic State (ISIS) grew from a marginal al-Qaeda affiliate fighting a war of attrition in northern Iraq into an international force capable of holding key cities in both Iraq and Syria and executing shocking terror plots abroad. In that time, the group would stake its claim as the agent of a renascent Islamic purity, honing its message to potential recruits through a suite of tactics belonging to the world of commercial marketing and brand management, and spreading its words and iconography through the media of networked digital communication to a fascinated and frightened public. Though today ISIS's territorial claims have diminished drastically, the Islamic State continues to occupy physical, virtual, and psychic space through effective use of old and new media, by turns lurking and posturing, and then rearing into action in moments of spectacular brutality.[1]

The Islamic State was able to leverage a sophisticated understanding of brand messaging, positioning, and image-craft—formally identical to methods of contemporary commercial marketing—into tacit, explicit, military, and monetary support for its self-proclaimed caliphate. Indeed, one cannot completely understand the success of the Islamic State without addressing the brand-marketing dimension of its rise. And yet, by the very use of these tactics and instruments, ISIS reveals the incoherence of its claims to fundamentalist integrity. In the first place, this very insistence on an organic Islamic order reveals its own base impossibility, rooted and motivated as it is in intractable social heterogeneity. Perhaps more significantly, it is the quasi-commercial process by which ISIS would forge and distribute its claims that demonstrates how the appeal of ISIS speaks not to the devoted religious traditionalist but more appropriately to the spiritually bereft consumer subject.

The brand-marketing approach preferred by ISIS in its propaganda and outreach efforts is snugly enveloped by industry-standard practices for cultivating consumer loyalty. By understanding it as such, a new mode for challenging the still-prevalent "conveyor belt" model of radicalization theory is revealed. Such an understanding divorces counterradicalization discourse from the presumption that Islam is itself constitutive of radicalism, while offering new opportunities to develop strategies for intervening in the radicalization process. By interpreting the group's communication and outreach practices through the lens of brand-marketing strategies, a clearer understanding of ISIS—and whatever groups may follow in its wake—may better be pursued, all while reducing the unjust targeting of Muslim communities in the West.

Brand ISIS and the Impossibility of Religious Integralism

Ironically, despite its use of cutting-edge media and orthodox marketing tactics, ISIS has always set as its goal the eradication of the very contemporary global order that birthed these technologies and techniques. This contradiction of means and ends is no mere oversight; it is an unavoidable condition of movements such as the Islamic State. As Slavoj Zizek describes in *Living in the End Times*, the reactionary passion for organic social integrity is itself symptomatic of an intractable social heterogeneity. To movements such as the Islamic State, "the shift from the organic Whole to Universality . . . from particular spiritualized lifeworlds to a global secular order [is] a freakish idiosyncrasy in the history of the human species . . . the root . . . of crisis."[2] The Islamic State seeks an organic unity, wherein "there is no cure for khilaf (differing) other than the Khilafah [caliphate]."[3] However, as Zizek points out, such a search inevitably "reveals itself to be the mode of appearance of its opposite, of inherent instability [for] the 'secret' of despotic societies is that they never find their '*inneres Gestalt*,' their inner form."[4] In other words, the Islamic State's dream of an eternally stable, organic society is the outcome of such a dream's very impossibility. Far from representing a true Islamic inneres gestalt, the Islamic State was "always already" a collage of instability and ideological and practical contradiction.[5]

As a player on the global stage, communicating through the organs and via the forms of commercial media, the Islamic State would remain a participant in the global capitalist order, and "no matter how much we see ourselves as embedded in a particular culture, the moment we participate in global capitalism, this culture is always already de-naturalized, effectively functioning as one specific and contingent 'way of life.'"[6] So, while the Islamic State proclaimed itself the realization of a caliphate foretold and ever imminent since the days of the Prophet, it would (and will) amount to nothing more than another expression of a contemporary global order in which "mediation of nationhood is closely linked to the process of commercialization, production, and consumption of services and goods" and "even the 'authentic' practices and spheres of social and cultural life, such as national identity, citizenship, creativity, politics, and religion are subjected to branding."[7]

On a more prosaic level, it is appropriate to treat the Islamic State as a branding and marketing entity for the simple fact that ISIS treats itself this way, insofar as it makes the effort to engage and attack the contemporary global order on its own turf. Postmodernity has seen the weakening of the once-powerful unifying intersubjectivity of nationalism, while "in recent decades, national communities have been increasingly eclipsed by tribes of customers who do not know one another intimately but share the same consumption habits and interests, and therefore feel part of the same consumer tribe." Modernity has also witnessed the inverse of this trend, a giving-over of the national intersubjectivity to the tactics and practices of marketing and branding.[8]

To some extent, this giving-over simply applies a contemporary label to the process of imagined community construction that characterized the nationalist project.[9] However, the shift from nationalist myth-making to nation-branding is not exclusively semantic. Nations continually rebrand themselves as their reality changes, with this rebranding being both explicit and implicit and aimed at external and internal audiences.[10] Like corporations, nations are not immutable. The ongoing reinvention of the nation takes place within the ecosystem of communicative media and therefore operates at the pace of contemporaneous media. The speed of global communications and its impact on the pace of contemporary geopolitics has perhaps necessitated this shift from myth-making to the speedier and more self-consciously constructed ethos of branding and advertising. Such questions of causality are beyond the scope of this chapter. Suffice it to say that within the contemporary order of meaning, wherein the figure of the markets has subsumed the political and cultural fields that once contained them, states increasingly treat themselves as brands in a global marketplace of competing nation-states.[11]

For a would-be polity like the nascent Islamic State, lacking recognized borders while seeking new citizens transnationally, the high-speed, self-defining ethos of the branded nation-state was nearly an ideal situation. Whereas most transitional countries "are more concerned with internal affairs at the beginning of their transition and only after a few years . . . start to pay more attention to their external images,"[12] the Islamic State relied on reversing this process. ISIS would attempt to market itself beyond the specific geopolitical realities relative to which its ambitions would always fall short.

The very emergence of the Islamic State would come about partly in the mode of a corporate rebranding. Manto Gotsi and Constantine Andriopoulos, writing in the journal *Corporate Communications*, offer a convenient schema for understanding the quality and motivation of corporate rebranding: "In cases of mergers and acquisitions, strategic alliances, partnering, spin offs and image related problems, corporate rebranding often involves revolutionary creations of new corporate names, underpinned by a new corporate brand vision and new corporate brand values."[13]

As in the prototypical corporate rebrand they describe, the change from al-Qaeda in Iraq (AQI) to the Islamic State occurred as a result of merger, alliance, and partnership, and was undertaken to reflect the group's renewed mission, while overcoming problematic brand legacy. This shift was both organic—a bottom-up evolution—and top-down, a hierarchically instituted program for change originating at the leadership level. When Abu Musab al-Zarqawi, the head of al-Qaeda in Iraq, was killed in an airstrike in the summer of 2006,[14] his de facto successor, Abu Ayyoub al-Masri, "emerged as the new leader, espousing the cause of an Islamic State of Iraq (ISI)."[15] This move was, in part, an attempt to assimilate the remaining forces of AQI, the Mujahedeen Shura Council in Iraq, and Jund al-Sahhaba (Soldiers of Prophet's Companions)—a merger, in corporate terms.[16]

The name change also offered al-Masri a chance to reposition the group in relation to a string of atrocities, what in brand-management terms would be called "reputation management" responding to "image-related problems." Between 2004 and 2008, al-Qaeda bombings took the lives of 3,010 people. Of those, 2,649 were non-Westerners. Excluding the London and Madrid bombings of that period, the proportions are even starker.[17] "The overwhelming majority of al Qa'ida victims are Muslims living in Muslim countries, and many are citizens of Iraq, which suffered more al Qa'ida attacks than any other country courtesy of the al Qa'ida in Iraq (AQI) affiliate."[18] By the time of al-Zarqawi's death, the name of al-Qaeda was perhaps more likely to inspire terror in an Iraqi Muslim[19] than a non-Muslim American. However, rather than rebranding as a means of distancing AQI from these atrocities, al-Zarqawi, and later al-Masri, initiated the break from al-Qaeda *as a means of affirming them*. Al-Qaeda, they believed, was "too tepid and tolerant of theological lapses" in pursuing its aim to unify Muslims worldwide against the West.[20] Zarqawi, Masri, and those who followed them were not above "making enemies on all sides."[21] And they wanted the world to know it.

The repositioning from AQI to the Islamic State represented a change in core organizational mission. In the language of branding, al-Qaeda's "unique selling proposition" had been to rally Muslims globally, to drag the West into an unwinnable war, and to ruin the West financially.[22] The al-Qaeda leadership had long embraced the strategy of "mobilizing a popular Muslim front,"[23] prioritizing attacks on the centers of so-called infidel power—the United States and Europe—over seizing political power at home. This ideology drove al-Qaeda's aggressive strategy from the post-Soviet 1990s until the American occupation of Iraq. In a 1998 statement foretelling the 9/11 attacks to come, Osama bin Laden wrote, "The ruling to kill the Americans and their allies—civilians and military—is an individual duty for every Muslim who can do it in any country in which it is possible to do it."[24] To accomplish this, al-Qaeda pursued a strategy of drawing the United States into Afghanistan, to suffer the fate of the Soviet Union a decade before. In contrast to al-Qaeda, the Islamic State, by its very name, repositioned its mission as regional and sectarian. Its fight was not *against* the United States per se, but *for* the establishment of an ultra-Salafist caliphate in the Middle East, and later the world. This constitutes ISIS's foundational act of positioning—"designing an organization's offering and image to occupy a distinctive place in the target market's mind"[25]—in contrast to al-Qaeda. With its position officially established, ISIS "has created a 'brand ecosystem' presenting itself 'as the one truly incorruptible force that can avenge the grievances of Muslims everywhere.'"[26]

Print Apocalypse: Old Media, New Caliphate

Early issues of the Islamic State's flagship magazine, *Dabiq*, graphically reinforced the group's established brand position. The now-defunct *Dabiq* was a semimonthly PDF-format magazine, published in multiple languages from July 2014 (one month following the announcement of the caliphate) until July 2016.[27] The magazine format, as a medium predating the digital age's read/write expectations, was uniquely qualified to conjure and carry the ISIS brand's claims to pure Salafist Islam, building relationships with readers at little risk of losing control of its message. The magazine medium's unique mode of address "offers an effective way to present a coherent set of ideas through its editorial voice and community-building capability."[28] Multiple audiences may be addressed around an issue's sustained theme, and ongoing topics may be covered from issue to issue, while editorial voice ensures ideological and tonal consistency. *Dabiq*'s PDF format and digital distribution method permitted infinite replication, while rendering alteration prohibitively difficult. This last characteristic was critical to securing the integrity of the *Dabiq* message, ensuring that unlike a website or social media platform, the magazine would be immune from outside attempts at detournement or spoofing. As such, *Dabiq* belongs to the same category of marketing as al-Masri's original rebranding act: an organized, top-down initiative aimed at shaping public perception and setting an organizationwide agenda.

The Jamestown Foundation, a Washington think tank whose directors have included Bruce Riedel and Zbigniew Brzezinski, identified *Dabiq*'s purpose as threefold: "to call on Muslims to come help the new caliph"; to tell "the story of the Islamic State's success"; and to "explain and justify the nature of the caliphate, its intentions, legitimacy and political and religious authority over all Muslims."[29] As a political marketing vehicle, *Dabiq*'s aim was "the creation of coherent and consistent images and messaging designed to appeal to target audiences to encourage their participation despite adversaries' attempts to undermine those messages/images."[30] In accomplishing the threefold purpose articulated by the Jamestown Foundation, *Dabiq* rigorously represented the ISIS brand while simultaneously defining and reaching out to the organization's target market.

Dabiq's explicit justification for the caliphate and its military endeavors was completed through basic propagandistic reportage. Relations between the Islamic

State and local religious/political leaders are portrayed in glowing terms, the better to paint a picture of an organically emergent, seamlessly integrated caliphate. A feature in issue number one describes a meeting between representatives of ISIS's public relations department and local imams: "The head of Tribal Affairs began the meeting with words of welcome, respect and thanks for the invitation. He then spoke about the fact that the mission of the Islamic State is neither local nor regional, but rather global. Furthermore, he called to implementing [*sic*] the Shari'ah, establishing the religion, promoting virtue and preventing vice."[31]

The following page depicts young men clasping hands and kneeling in prayer.[32] While such language would hardly be out of place in a weekly suburban newspaper, it is the visual language and the quality of the rhetoric just pages away that turn *Dabiq* from banal mouthpiece to violent extremist marketing platform.

Turning the page, the reader encounters photo spreads intended to affirm identification with the Islamic State. The first spread depicts the mangled corpses of alleged Sunni civilians (portrayed as an atrocity), while the second shows murdered Shia soldiers (portrayed as justice). In the first spread, Sunni victims are pictured in humanizing, everyday clothing: Adidas track pants, T-shirts. A hand caresses the cheek of a Sunni man with a bullet hole to the head. The dead man's face displays an expression of peaceful sadness, a martyr beatified by the camera's lens. Beneath it reads the caption "Sunnis murdered by the Sawafis."[33] Contrast that with the following page, where Shia bodies in paramilitary garb lie half-exposed in body bags. "Rafidi[34] soldiers killed by the Mujahidin."[35] The dead Shia are thoroughly dehumanized; at first glance, their burned and abused bodies look like rocks or clumps of soil, not men. Finally, on the last page of the spread, the black flag of the Islamic State flies proudly in a Photoshop-azure sky.[36]

Through such stark delineation of its ingroup/outgroup distinctions, the Islamic State vindicates the thesis of extremist media and terrorism expert Donald Holbrook: "The ideational dimensions of terrorist PR initiatives . . . combine to create a narrative designed to rationalize and promote violent activity in the name of the cause, sustain the terrorist movement and enhance its impact."[37] The visual and written language of *Dabiq* paints Shia as positively subhuman and ISIS-allied Sunni as beatific martyrs. This implicitly builds justification for the Islamic State's violent activities while creating a brand cult of the very highest stakes.

Digital Detournement: Transgressive Marketing for Reactionary Ends

While the magazine format helped establish and protect the Islamic State's brand image and position, ISIS's recruitment strategies branched further out into "an integrated system of recruitment communications that combine elements of public relations, social media marketing, digital content production and online messaging."[38] These digital and social media communications would engage supporters and recruits at early stages of potential recruitment. Social channels can be especially effective in promoting outré messaging; the interactive conceits of these channels offer users an opportunity not only to encounter transgressive perspectives such as ISIS's but to experimentally assume them as their own: "In the virtual environment, individuals can be free of many constraints they face in real-world interactions, and in fact, can experiment with new, perhaps risky, ideas and expressions of self that would not readily emerge in the more threatening, adversarial and perhaps legally challenging communications found in real-world encounters."[39]

In contrast to *Dabiq*, the Islamic State would (and continues to) relinquish a great deal of control over its communications when those messages enter the digital sphere in the form of tweets, memes, videos, etc. However, the messages it disseminates are, for a variety of reasons, resistant to alteration or coopting (although Rosemary Pennington discusses in a later chapter how one group has attempted to coopt their messages), even as they spread virally. The content of ISIS's digital transmissions tends toward greater extremity, both in shows of brutality and, paradoxically, humor. Brevity and exaggeration are qualities to which the cluttered, ultra-fast medium of the internet seems to lend itself. But whether by intention or not, these more extreme transmissions appear less vulnerable to third-party reappropriation. In the case of extremely violent or hateful material, content tends to attract an audience more willing to simply relay the content along social channels, rebroadcasting it intact out of respect for the authority of the source. In the case of its humorous content—particularly its memes—the Islamic State at the height of its media heyday often engaged in detournement, "the reuse of preexisting artistic elements in a new ensemble."[40] Through this practice of appropriating and reordering artistic elements from online commercial and pop-cultural discourse, ISIS rendered "second-order" satire exceedingly difficult, as attempts to reorder any act of detournement simply indicate the original object of reuse. Hence, despite its relinquishing direct control over these messages, the Islamic State's digital ephemera have proven remarkably robust and resilient.

The Islamic State has used myriad channels to spread its content: message boards on jihadi-hosted websites, photo-sharing sites such as Flickr, crowdsourced Q&A sites such as Ask.fm, instant messengers such as Kik, and other social media, including Facebook and Twitter. (The myriad outlets ISIS uses are discussed in chap. 5 of this volume.) ISIS launched the app Dawn of Glad Tidings, which offers access to users' accounts to the ISIS media team. This allowed the ISIS social media team to tweet a single message from all app users' accounts in unison, effectively turning all app users into a chorus for the caliphate. Indeed, an entire book could be written on just the diversity and breadth of ISIS's social media strategy. For the purpose of this chapter, however, we will focus on its most high-profile outlet: Twitter.

The Triviality of Evil: Tweeting Terror

Until its suspension in July 2015, the Twitter account @ISILCats was among the most well-known quasi-official Islamic State social media accounts. The account began operation in late June 2014, tweeting photos of kittens and their "mewjahid" in moments of play and repose. With @ISILCats, ISIS hijacked the internet's most beloved meme—one very likely to find audience purchase, particularly among young people—and used it as the pathogenic vehicle of viral media transmission. "The uncanny power of these images radiates from the gap between the familiar and the foreign, the domestic and the wild. These images are weapons—they disarm not by dividing the 'Western' spectator from the ISIS militant, but by playing in 'the grey zone,' staging an intimate, yet conflicted relationship between them."[41] By locating ISIS's message adjacent to the most beloved internet meme of all time (the LOLcat), on a popular—and indeed, particularly psychologically addictive media platform—the door to audience absorption was opened.[42]

What few violent images do appear in the @ISILCats archive are presented in sentimental tones. A Palestinian child lies in a hospital bed, innocent and vulnerable. A dead soldier wears a beatific Mona Lisa smile beneath the caption "How can we defeat them when their death is this beautiful?" Despite their seeming incongruity, these juxtapositions of war verité and LOLcat memes are all of a piece, suggesting a profound and deeply rooted affective complex, wherein protectiveness, affection, and sadism quietly coexist: "There's sadism in the process by which we render an animal cute, and a latent potential for cruelty and violence within the cute animal itself, qualities that are constitutive of its cuteness. As theorist Sianne Ngai argues in *Our Aesthetic Categories*, cuteness is 'an aesthetic response to the diminutive, the weak, and the subordinate [that] depends entirely on the subject's affective response to an imbalance of power between herself and the object.'"[43]

@ISILCats summoned the affective complex already present in the LOLcat meme, amplifying its elements of latent sadism and protectiveness with images of bloodshed and collateral damage, in a process of affective direction toward ISIS's project of violent extremism and the construction of the caliphate.

ISIS's widely circulated Call of Duty parody image presents another example of ISIS hijacking the language and imagery of popular internet culture, reordering its elements in a new ensemble and spreading the mutation via social media. "This is our Call of Duty," the image reads, in familiar, CoD brand-appropriate font, "and we respawn in Jannah."[44] As an act of detournement, the parodic meme is "first of all a negation of the value of the previous organization of expression."[45]

As such, it reappropriates a video game brand celebrating American military prowess and reorients it to underline American military fallibility, "subsuming western-style propaganda into a particular religio-political agenda."[46] Moreover, the meme seizes an existing relationship—that of young men to a popular video game—and redirects it to the greater glory of violent extremism. We see this in the juxtaposition of jargons—"respawn," a video-gaming term meaning to start over after losing, and "Jannah" an Arabic word indicating Islamic conceptions of heaven. The meme promises a "new and improved" Call of Duty, one where the reward is heaven, the guns are real, and the graphics are flesh and blood. This meme's detourned advertising imagery thereby underlines the artificiality of the gamer's valor, even while using that artifice to mask the unpleasant realities of the experience it is itself advertising.

One is reminded of George Lois's legendary recycling of his Maypo Oatmeal slogan, "I want my Maypo!" for the nascent MTV Network—"I want my MTV."[47] In both the Call of Duty meme and the @ISILcats Twitter feed, the searching and unaffiliated individual is greeted by tropes that are at once familiar—comfortable, even routine. "Terrorist organizations often subvert conventional broadcasting norms" write Bhui and Ibrahim, "products may be more persuasive if they match the personality of target users or are similar in other ways."[48] Reflexive resistance to a marketing message is softened by preexisting trust in the figures and commercial brands subject to ISIS's detournement, and thus the potential consumer or potential violent extremist is rendered more amenable to convincing.

These messages present a fascinating paradox. They seize Western media icons, beloved by youth the world over, and subvert them to convey a message of antagonism against the West. In his seminal *Subculture: The Meaning of Style*, Dick Hebdige cites sociologist Phil Cohen: "[Subculture is] a compromise solution between two contradictory needs: the need to create and express autonomy and difference from parents . . . and the need to maintain the parental identifications."[49] While ISIS was never a musical subculture in the mode of Hebdige, the Islamic State would nevertheless function to *feed and be fed by* a population of disaffected Western youth, seeking to carve out a role that both identifies with and rebels against that of their immigrant parents and grandparents.

On one hand, such youth identify with their parents' religious faith but embrace the popular media of their adopted homes. Conversely, they mimic the consumptive patterns of their parents' assimilationist tendencies while rejecting the moderating compromises their parents make in order to live in the West. The advertising and marketing of ideology work best when bypassing the conscious logic of the mind, as "successful campaigns compete in the marketplace of emotions rather than in the marketplace of ideas."[50] By connecting with paradox and cognitive dissonance, these messages, whether intentionally or not, become all the more powerful.

Even more portentous may have been the benefits conferred on ISIS by Western corporate media censorship. By banning the very worst of the Islamic State, such as beheading and other execution videos, while permitting more moderate and even likable voices to remain, outlets like Twitter and YouTube were, for a time, doing ISIS's media buying work for it.[51] Audiences encountered difficulty accessing ISIS content in direct proportion to the extremity of the message, ensuring that casual onlookers would be treated mainly to appealing content, shielded from those repellant materials that would—rightly—prejudice them against ISIS.

The Conversion Career: A Marketing Process of Radicalization

The boundary dividing the morbidly curious from the potential Islamist radical is by no means a clear one. Even to speak of such distinctions—between seeker and radical, sympathizer and terrorist—is to indulge in a definitional absolutism, one that is not borne out by real-world examples. Yet, judgments must nevertheless be made. For the purposes of counterterrorism, deradicalization, and sparing the innocent from state and social harassment, we must be able to identify when individuals are moving in the direction of violent extremism, as well as those watersheds of choice that constitute escalation in this process and the points of no return. This goal requires the development and application of multiple models and heuristics, tailored for specific use cases. The concluding portion of this chapter intends to suggest such an interpretive tool, based around ISIS's established role as a branding and marketing apparatus.

In her book *Brands of Faith*, Mara Einstein argues that the process of religious conversion follows a process similar to that of commercial brand purchase and loyalty: "The religious seeker or shopper goes through a multistage process in coming to accept a religious practice. The steps are: (1) pre-affiliation (potential members who have not yet committed to a group); (2) affiliation (formal membership); (3) conversion; and finally (4) confession (committed membership)."[52]

Einstein adds to this a stage preceding *preaffiliation*—that of spiritual awareness. By including this prefatory step, Einstein's expanded conversion career may be compared point by point to the classic five-point marketing relationship curve.[53] The stage of spiritual awareness is analogous to the marketing relationship curve's introductory stage: problem recognition. In both models, this first stage represents the moment during which a potential consumer realizes something is missing—whether that something is a better whitening toothpaste or the discipline and metaphysical certainty of totalitarian fundamentalism. Indeed, "in the marketing relationship curve, that need could be religious or secular, it really makes no difference. In the conversion career, it is strictly religious or spiritual."[54]

Einstein's religious conversion career is valuable to the study of Islamic State recruitment content, precisely for its fidelity to an orthodox understanding of marketing and brand loyalty. By treating the Islamic State primarily as an organization engaged in branding and marketing, such an approach attacks ISIS's communication and outreach in the manner and mode to which it committed itself. Moreover, a conversion career approach to radicalization estranges ISIS's beliefs and actions from those of ordinary Muslims worldwide. From tweets to fatwas, ISIS communication "is in essence a form of outreach, framed as Islamic, aimed at propagating the group's ultra-conservative Salafi jihadist views."[55] The conversion career denies ISIS the right to claim definitional authority over Islam, while also offering a superior model for achieving the moral and strategic imperatives of targeting only potential violent extremists and not innocent people.

Much has been written about the so-called "process of radicalization." In the "conveyor-belt" theory of radicalization that characterized so much early deradicalization discourse,[56] "religious belief forms a slippery slope or a conveyor belt that leads to radicalism. The first step is ostensibly practicing the faith or adherence to 'radical' forms of Islam like Salafism with its literalist bent."[57] According to this reckoning, traditionalist Muslims are practically born on the cusp of Einstein's third stage (affiliation with the Islamic state). This, even though "no causal relationship can be definitively shown between traditionalists and radicalization."[58]

Far from being born on the cusp of radicalization, it is more accurate to assume that a devoted traditionalist is not even "spiritually aware"—not in the sense of being irreligious, but in the sense of not feeling a problem or lack in the practice of their faith. There is, so to speak, no consumer need to which the ISIS brand may offer a solution. On a conversion career that demands as its final stage "confession"—a state of total loyalty characterized by actions that are often referred to, both theologically and commercially, as "evangelization"—the already-devoutly religious are among the *least* likely to take the journey from awareness to confession.

This matches anecdotally with the many high-profile terrorists. Bataclan conspirators Salah and Brahim Abdeslam, Westminster machete attacker Khalid Masood, and Nice truck attacker Mohamed Lahouaiej-Bouhlel were reportedly heavy drinkers and drug users.[59] Boston bomber Tamerlan Tsarnaev, Chattanooga shooter Mohammad Yousouf Abdulazeez, and suicide truck bomber Pierre Choulet were all involved in competitive combat sports.[60] ISIS soldier and spokesman Denis "Deso Dogg" Mamadou Gerhard Cuspert toured with gangsta rapper DMX in the 2000s.[61] These behaviors bear little in common with the habits of devout Muslims. However, they do match quite closely with the most common type of hate criminal, the "thrill seeker."[62] It is far more likely that the spiritual awareness and problem recognition that inaugurate these men's journeys to violence originate in thrill seeking and the delight of violence—not religiosity.

If we inspect the Islamic State's communication materials, it soon becomes apparent that in spite of its quasi-Islamic rhetoric, ISIS media has always marketed just those thrills. Certainly, this was the case in the Call of Duty parody, and as Cornell argues, it is also the subtext for the entire @ISILCats feed. Other marketing messages continue this thrill-seeking theme, including "sequences of video, such as the fast-moving scenes of violence . . . [and] reference to video games, such as *Grand Theft Auto.*"[63] Even the first issue of *Dabiq*, which focused on positioning ISIS as the purest expression of Islam, reveals a roughly four-to-one ratio of violent and victorious images versus images of worship.[64]

Based on the faulty assumptions of conveyor belt radicalization theory, programs such as Great Britain's Prevent, NYPD's Muslim Surveillance Program (MSP), and the FBI's Shared Responsibilities Committees (SRC) focus attention on communities of observant and orthodox Muslims, enlisting advisors and informants from the ranks of congregants and imams.[65] But such efforts seem to have yielded little in the way of thwarted terror plots and much in the way of ill will between devout Muslims and intelligence/law enforcement.[66] Programs like Prevent, MSP, and SRC constitute a process that "constructs Muslims into a 'suspect community,' in which the failure of Muslim individuals or organisations to comply . . . makes them suspect."[67] Muslims in communities targeted by practices such as these report feelings of alienation and resentment toward intelligence and law enforcement.[68] This, in turn, makes ordinary Muslims less eager to cooperate with government organizations, whom they rightly view as targeting them based on arbitrary religious criteria. According to research funded by the US National Science Foundation, there is "a robust correlation between perceptions of procedural justice and both perceived legitimacy and willingness to cooperate among Muslim American communities in the context of antiterrorism policing."[69] Racial and racialized religious profiling violate a basic expectation of fairness in law-enforcement processes, and by doing so construct suspect communities, damaging perceptions of procedural justice, and weakening counterterrorism practice.

Not only does the application of conveyor-belt radicalization theory diminish the likelihood of community cooperation with law enforcement, but "to the extent that government-based counterterrorism strategies outrage participants or energize a base of potential supporters, such strategies may increase the likelihood of further terrorist strikes."[70] Indeed, questions abound as to whether policing policies based on the conveyor-belt theory do not themselves inspire terrorism. A British study of opinions among college-age Muslims found that experiences of discrimination, such as those triggered by applications of conveyor-belt theory "rendered [participants] more sympathetic to others' experience to non-normative forms of political action."[71]

There is ample anecdotal evidence to support this fear as well. The famous case of Yemeni-American cleric Anwar al-Awlaki provides a stark example of this danger. As an imam at the prestigious Dar al-Hijrah mosque in Fall Church, Virginia, the imam's opinions "would not have been out of place at a Republican

National Convention."[72] He was a vocal supporter of President George W. Bush, aided in the training of Muslim military chaplains, and participated in numerous interfaith events around the Washington, DC area. However, following reports that two of the 9/11 hijackers had prayed at a mosque in San Diego where al-Awlaki had presided, the FBI turned its attention to the imam. The FBI "found no evidence that Awlaki was involved in terrorism," yet continued to press the imam, uncovering embarrassing facts about his habit of visiting prostitutes, and using this information as leverage to coerce his cooperation.[73] Hounded by American law enforcement, al-Awlaki departed, first to Britain and later to Yemen. By 2007, al-Awlaki was allied with al-Qaeda in Yemen. His public statements were no longer conservative and ecumenical but violent and extreme.

Prior to his harassment by the FBI, al-Awlaki was precisely the sort of orthodox traditionalist to whom jihadi ideology held no appeal. He comfortably inhabited the confessional stage of conversion, devoted to and preaching a socially conservative but ultimately inclusive and civic-minded practice of Islam. The FBI effectively evicted him from this comfortable position by threatening to expose his sexual frailty. Thus, forcefully returned to a prefatory state of spiritual awareness—in need of an outlet for his religiosity but now positioned antagonistically toward the civil society that he once served—he found his solution in al-Qaeda.[74] What of those young men who are less enfranchised, less devout, and exhibit more of the thrill-seeking/sadistic traits of the hate criminal?[75] The Islamic State would promise these young men a welcoming home with the trappings of spirituality and the thrill of cruelty.

Therefore, rather than focusing blanket social service and law enforcement attention on devout Muslim communities, which has the demonstrated effect of alienating those targeted, the conversion career suggests that resources should be directed toward reaching those thrill-seeking young men who do not demonstrate the discipline of religious devotion and to whom the fast-paced and sadistic messages of a group such as ISIS might appeal.[76] It is in these preliminary stages—awareness and preaffiliation—that we may yet find our greatest success in stopping groups like the Islamic State from attracting young adherents.

It is particularly important to arrest the radicalization of thrill-seeking recruits before they reach the stage of affiliation. At this stage, the effects of interpersonal socialization take hold; deradicalization becomes more difficult, and the likelihood of completing the conversion career becomes most likely. Research jointly funded by the Air Force Office of Scientific Research, the Office of Naval Research, and the Spanish Ministry of Economy and Competitiveness found that "participants who were fused with a kin-like group of friends and considered sharia a sacred value were more willing to make costly sacrifices (including violence and dying) for sharia and were also more likely to support militant jihad, compared to other participants."[77] This tendency carried over into non-Muslims asked about their willingness to make costly sacrifices on behalf of democracy. Those individuals fused with kin or a kin-like group are far more likely to support violence on behalf of their cause.

Commercial marketing has made similar findings (albeit unrelated to political violence). Long-term brand loyalty is often definitively established when consumers come to view themselves as members of a community of brand users. Empirical research shows that this community needn't even be interpersonal; brand commodities mediate the social relationship such that community may be experienced in lieu of person-to-person interaction "even . . . in the entirely nongeographical space of the Internet."[78] Even to this day, the Islamic State's various periodicals and testimonial videos, expressed in the second person, introduce this digitally mediated virtual community. Even the most atomized internet user is therefore able to consider him- or herself a part of the Islamic State.

However, lacking the kinlike group identified by Sheikh et al., such an atomized individual is unlikely to engage in the risky behaviors that ISIS truly seeks from its members. More important to the process of establishing brand community (in pure marketing terms) is "the value of going beyond image-building endeavors to establishing real relationships between the company and customers."[79] Islamic State recruiters trawl message boards and chat rooms, reaching out to those individuals who appear to have reached the stage of preaffiliation/brand awareness, and moving them along the conversion career to affiliation via the establishment of more concrete social bonds. To accomplish this, "hundreds of hours can be spent in Skype conversations and other online dialogue to build an intimate connection."[80] Then, "once the online relationship is established—or has been moved to real-world meetings in support groups—and is friendly and supportive, it becomes easy for discussions to progress to the idea of traveling."[81]

By agreeing to real-world meetings, ISIS recruits enter the second stage of the conversion career, formally affiliating themselves with the group. The function of these real-world meetings is to induce conversion, after which ISIS ideology demands "confession," whether in the form of migration to the caliphate (when it existed) or terroristic violence. Thompson identifies three core elements to the ISIS ideology and by extension its confessional stage: Hijrah (migration), Kalifa (caliphate), and Jihad (holy war).[82] Of these three components, two are effectively social. Thompson likewise identifies four primary promises made to potential ISIS recruits: kinship/power, sexual opportunity, money/comfort, and adventure/ultraviolence; at least half of these promises (kinship and sex) are unambiguously social in nature.

By applying Einstein's conversion career to the Islamic State's communication and recruitment, it becomes clear that the Islamic State has never marketed religious piety but the thrill of ultraviolence and the promise of community. These are the very rewards sought by violent extremists of all persuasions.[83] Racialized religious profiling of the type aimed at Muslim communities is therefore a clear waste of resources and a transgression against civic ethics. Rather than pursuing strategies that alienate citizens, provoke extremists, ignore non-Muslim extremism, and discredit law enforcement, new strategies based on brand marketing understanding of ISIS and groups like it should be pursued.

Conclusion

In spite of its claims to represent a fundamental and organic mode of Islamic living, the self-proclaimed Islamic State was, in fact, always a product of the disintegrative characteristics of postmodernity. Facing the dissolution of national, occupational, religious, and gender identities, ISIS undertook a project shared by many contemporary states, attempting to reestablish its integrity via practices adopted from commercial branding, marketing, and advertising. ISIS employed the old media format of magazines in order to position its "pure Salafist" brand image in a manner resistant to message disruption. Conversely, the group exploited the read/write capabilities of new digital media to reach young people through parody and detournement of popular Western entertainment tropes. Close reading of these messages reveals that while the ISIS brand purports to be one of scrupulous Islamic observance, its marketing is actually aimed at thrill-seekers and sadists. Anecdotal evidence confirms this analysis, as many notable terrorists display behaviors more in line with thrill-seeking hate criminals than with observant traditionalist Muslims.

By applying Einstein's conversion career to our analysis of radicalization, we can further observe how law enforcement resources are often misdirected, targeting innocent, observant Muslims who are unlikely to become radicalized. Such misdirected suspicion is not merely a waste of resources, however. It also poses the risk of alienating Muslim communities, reducing cooperation with law enforcement, and even provoking otherwise unradicalized individuals toward violent extremism. Rather than targeting religiously observant communities, it would be far more effective and ethical to seek radicalization prevention among tenuously religious individuals who demonstrate the thrill-seeking and/or sadistic tendencies of the hate criminal.

Notes

1. Marwan Kraidy, "Terror, Territoriality, Temporality: Hypermedia Events in the Age of the Islamic State," *Television & Media* 19, no. 2 (2018): 170–176.
2. Slavoj Zizek, *Living in the End Times* (New York: Verso, 2011), 279.
3. *Dabiq* 1436: 23.
4. Zizek, *Living in the End Times*, 280.

5. The Islamic State's "despotic secret" would become especially apparent in its internal racial and ethnic friction. While IS would promise "a state where the Arab and non-Arab, the white man and black man, the easterner and westerner are all brothers," (*Dabiq* 1435 AH, 7), the reality was always one of stark racial and ethnic hierarchy, wherein non-Arab pilgrims to the Islamic State faced rampant discrimination and inequality (Jain 2015; Hoyle et. al 2015; Dettmer 2015).

6. Zizek, *Living in the End Times*, 291.

7. Magdalena Kani-Lundholm, "Nation in Market Times: Connecting the National and the Commercial. A Research Overview," *Sociology Compass* 8, no. 6 (2014): 603–613.

8. Wally Olins, "Branding the Nation: The Historical Context," *Journal of Brand Management* 9, no. 4 (2002): 241–248.

9. Benedict Anderson, *Imagined Communities* (London: Verso, 1991).

10. Olins, "Branding the Nation."

11. Peter Van Ham, "The Rise of the Brand State: The Postmodern Politics of Image and Reputation," *Foreign Affairs* 80, no. 5 (2011): 2–6.

12. György Szondi, "The Role and Challenges of Country Branding in Transition Countries: The Central and Eastern European Experience," *Place Branding and Public Diplomacy* 3, no. 1 (2007): 8.

13. Manto Gotsi and Constantine Andriopoulos, "Understanding the Pitfalls in the Corporate Rebranding Process," *Corporate Communications: An International Journal* 12, no. 4 (2007): 342.

14. Dexter Filkins and John F. Burns, "At Site of Attack on Zarqawi, All That's Left Are Questions," *New York Times*, June 11, 2006, http://www.nytimes.com/2006/06/11/world/middleeast/11scene.html.

15. Zana Khasraw Gulmohamad, "The Rise and Fall of the Islamic State of Iraq and Al-Sham (Levant) ISIS," *Global Security Studies* 5, no. 2 (2014): 1.

16. Ibid., 2.

17. Scott Helfstein, Nassir Abdullah, and Muhammad al-Obaidi, "Deadly Vanguards: A Study of al-Qa'ida's Violence Against Muslims," occasional paper series, Combating Terrorism Series at West Point, December 2009, https://ctc.usma.edu/app/uploads/2010/10/deadly-vanguards_complete_l.pdf: 2–3.

18. Ibid.

19. Unfortunately, available statistics do not distinguish between Sunni and Shia civilian casualties.

20. William McCants, "The Feud Between al-Qaeda and the Islamic State, Explained," *Newsweek*, September 25, 2016, http://www.newsweek.com/isis-al-qaeda-feud-499052.

21. Ibid.

22. Daveed Gartenstein-Ross, "Don't Get Cocky, America," *Foreign Policy*, May 2, 2011, http://foreignpolicy.com/2011/05/02/dont-get-cocky-america-2/.

23. McCants, "The Feud."

24. Osama bin Laden, "Jihad Against Jews and Crusaders," fatwa, World Islamic Front, February 23, 1998, https://fas.org/irp/world/para/docs/980223-fatwa.htm.

25. Jean L. Harrison-Walker, "Strategic Positioning of Nations as Brands," *Journal of International Business Research* 10, no. 2 (2011): 135.

26. Chris Galloway, "Media Jihad: What PR Can Learn in Islamic State's Public Relations Masterclass," *Public Relations Review* 42, no. 4 (2016): 588.

27. Harleen K. Gambhir, "The Virtual Caliphate: ISIS's Information Warfare," Institute for the Study of War, 2016.

28. Susan Currie Sivek, "Packaging Inspiration: Al Qaeda's Digital Magazine *Inspire* in the Self-Radicalization Process," *International Journal of Communication* 7 (2013): 584–606.

29. Michale W. S. Ryan, "Hot Issue: *Dabiq*: What Islamic State's New Magazine Tells Us about Their Strategic Direction, Recruitment Patterns, and Guerrilla Doctrine," *Terrorism Monitor*, August 1, 2014, https://jamestown.org/program/hot-issue-dabiq-what-islamic-states-new-magazine-tells-us-about-their-strategic-direction-recruitment-patterns-and-guerrilla-doctrine/.

30. Paul R. Baines and Nicholas J. O'Shaughnessy, "Al-Qaeda Messaging Evolution and Positioning, 1998–2008: Propaganda Analysis Revisited," *Public Relations Inquiry* 3, no. 2 (2014): 165.

31. *Dabiq* Ramadan 1435: 13.

32. *Dabiq* Ramadan 1435: 15.

33. Derogatory term referring to Shias. *Dabiq* Ramadan 1435: 16.

34. In this context, another slur for Shia.

35. *Dabiq* Ramadan 1435: 18.

36. *Dabiq* Ramadan 1435: 19.

37. Donald Holbrook, "Approaching Terrorist Public Relations," *Public Relations Inquiry* 3, no. 2 (2014): 147.

38. Gareth Thompson, "Extremes of Engagement: The Post-Classical Public Relations of the Islamic State," *Public Relations Review* 43, no. 5 (2017): 8.

39. Kamaldeep Bhui and Yasmin Ibrahim, "Marketing the 'Radical': Symbolic Communications and Persuasive Technologies in Jihadist Websites," *Transcultural Psychiatry* 50, no. 2 (2013): 219.

40. Guy Debord, "Détournement as Negation and Prelude," *Internationale Situationniste* no. 3 (1959): 10.

41. Matt Cornell, "Feral Memes," *The New Inquiry* 56, November 2016, https://thenewinquiry.com/feral-memes/.

42. Thompson, "Extremes of Engagagment;" Daria J. Kuss, Antonius J. van Rooij, Gillian W. Shorter, Mark D. Griffiths, and D. van de Mheen, "Internet Addiction in Adolescents: Prevalence and Risk Factors," *Computers in Human Behavior* 29, no. 5 (2013): 1987–1996.

43. Cornell, "Feral Memes."

44. Patrick Kingsley, "Who Is Behind ISIS's Terrifying Online Propaganda Operation?" *The Guardian* (US edition), June 23, 2014, https://www.theguardian.com/world/2014/jun/23/who-behind-isis-propaganda-operation-iraq.

45. Debord, "Détournement as Negation and Prelude," 10.

46. Galloway, "Media Jihad," 584.

47. Jean Bergantini Grillo, "The First Media Brand," *Cablevision* 25, no. 21 (2001): 5A.

48. Bhui and Ibrahim, "Marketing the 'Radical,'" 219.

49. Dick Hebdige, *Subculture: The Meaning of Style* (London: Routledge, 1979), 77.

50. Patrick Butler and Phil Harris, "Considerations on the Evolution of Political Marketing," *Marketing Theory* 9, no. 2 (2009): 155

51. Sean Cubitt, "Distribution and Media Flow," *Cultural Politics* 1, no. 2 (2005): 193–214.

52. Mara Einstein, *Brands of Faith* (Abingdon: Routledge, 2007), 81.

53. The five stages of the marketing relationship curve are: (1) Brand Awareness, (2) Consideration, (3) Conversion, (4) Retention/Loyalty, and (5) Post-Sale Service and Support.

54. Einstein, "Brands of Faith," 83.
55. Galloway, "Media Jihad," 584.
56. Arun Kundnani, *A Decade Lost: Rethinking Radicalisation and Extremism* (London: Claystone, 2015).
57. Cyra Akil Choudhury, "Ideology, Identity, and Law in the Production of Islamophobia," *Dialectical Anthropology* 39, no. 1 (2014): 55.
58. Ibid., 56.
59. BBC, "Paris Attacks: Who Were the Attackers?", April 27, 2016, http://www.bbc.com/news/world-europe-34832512; Peter Beaumont, "Mohamed Lahouaiej-Bouhlel: Who Was the Bastille Day Truck Attacker?" *The Guardian* (US edition), July 15, 2016, https://www.theguardian.com/world/2016/jul/15/bastille-day-truck-driver-was-known-to-police-reports-say; Jason Burke, "Khalid Masood Was a Convert with a Criminal Past. So Far, so Familiar," *The Guardian* (US Edition), March 25, 2017, https://www.theguardian.com/uk-news/2017/mar/25/khalid-masood-was-a-convert-with-a-criminal-past-so-far-so-familiar.
60. Shelly Bradbury, "Who Was Mohammad Youssef Abdulazeez?" *Chattanooga Times Free Press*, July 17, 2015, http://www.timesfreepress.com/news/local/story/2015/jul/17/who-wmohammad-youssef-abdulazeez/315079/; Francoise Chaptal, "Seeking to Kick Jihadi Threat, French Warily Eye Martial Arts Clubs," *Times of Israel*, May 19, 2016, http://www.timesofisrael.com/seeking-to-kick-jihadi-threat-french-warily-eye-martial-arts-clubs/; Andrea Crossan, "Why the Boston Marathon Bombing Made Me Watch Mixed Martial Arts." *Public Radio International*, April 21, 2014, https://www.pri.org/stories/2014-04-21/why-boston-marathon-bombing-made-me-watch-mixed-martial-arts.
61. Sarah Kaplan, "'Jihad Is a Lot of Fun,' Deso Dogg, a German Rapper Turned Islamic State Pitchman Said. Now He's Reportedly Dead from US Air Strike," *Washington Post*, October 30, 2015, https://www.washingtonpost.com/news/morning-mix/wp/2015/10/30/deso-dogg-the-german-rapper-turned-islamic-state-militant-reportedly-killed-in-airstrike/.
62. J. McDevitt, J. Levin, and S. Bennett, "Hate Crime Offenders: An Expanded Typology," *Journal of Social Issues* 58, no. 2 (2002): 303–317.
63. Thompson, "Extremes of Engagement," 6.
64. That is, thirty-eight images of battle, death, or victory parades, and a mere eight images of worship. Images of everyday life in the caliphate appear as well.
65. Trevor Aaronson, *The Terror Factory: Inside the FBI's Manufactured War on Terrorism* (New York: IG Publishing, 2013); Imran Awan, "'I Am a Muslim Not an Extremist': How the Prevent Strategy Has Constructed a 'Suspect Community," *Politics and Policy* 40, no. 6 (2012): 1158–1185; Sara Kamali, "Informants, Provocateurs, and Entrapment: Examining the Histories of the FBI's PATCON and the NYPD's Muslim Surveillance Program," *Surveillance and Society* 15, no. 1 (2017): 68–78.
66. Aaronson, *The Terror Factory.*
67. Arun Kundnani, "Spooked: How Not to Prevent Violent Extremism," Institute of Race Relations, October 17, 2009, http://www.kundnani.org/wp-content/uploads/spooked.pdf: 15.
68. Awan, "'I Am a Muslim Not an Extremist.'"
69. Tom R. Tyler, Stephen Schulhofer, and Aziz Z. Huq, "Legitimacy and Deterrence Effects in Counterterrorism Policing: A Study of Muslim Americans," *Law and Society Review* 44, no. 2 (2010): 365–402.
70. Gary Lafree and Gary Ackerman, "The Empirical Study of Terrorism: Social and Legal Research," *Annual Review of Law and Social Science* 5 (2009): 361.

71. Leda Blackwood, Nick Hopkins, and Stephen Reicher, "From Theorizing Radicalization to Surveillance Practices: Muslims in the Cross Hairs of Scrutiny," *International Society of Political Psychology* 37, no. 5 (2016): 606.

72. Scott Shane, "The Lessons of Anwar al-Awlaki," *New York Times*, August 27, 2015, https://www.nytimes.com/2015/08/30/magazine/the-lessons-of-anwar-al-awlaki.html?.

73. Ibid.

74. ISIS, as such, did not exist during al-Awlaki's moment of crisis. Al-Qaeda's position within his ancestral province of Shabwah in Yemen likely also held appeal for the disgraced al-Awlaki.

75. Less well documented is the case of Mohammed "Jihadi John" Emwazi, whose reported harassment by British Intelligence agency MI5 is blamed by some for his association with IS (Blumenthal 2015).

76. The FBI's Domain Management Program has come under fire for its crude application of big-data analytics, using publicly available consumer data such as regional falafel sales to direct surveillance and informant programs (Aaronson, *The Terror Factory*, 48). These arbitrary categories, a 2011 ACLU complaint alleges, have led the FBI "to gather intelligence on people not suspected of having committed crimes," a clear violation of the norms of procedural justice on which community cooperation is predicated. One can easily imagine a reapplication of the Domain Management's analytics toward nonracialized criminal profiling, derived from consumer information about the thrill-seeking hate criminal type.

77. Hammad Sheikh, Ángel Gómez, and Scott Atran, "Empirical Evidence for the Devoted Actor Model," *Current Anthropology* 57, no. S13 (2016): 206.

78. James H. McAlexander, John W. Schouten, and Harold F. Koenig, "Building Brand Community," *Journal of Marketing* 66, no. 1 (2002): 39.

79. Ibid., 50.

80. Thompson, "Extremes of Engagement," 17.

81. Ibid.

82. Ibid., 4.

83. McDevitt et. al, "Hate Crime Offenders."

Bibliography

Aaronson, Trevor. *The Terror Factory: Inside the FBI's Manufactured War on Terrorism*. New York: IG Publishing, 2013.

Anderson, Benedict. *Imagined Communities*. London: Verso, 1991.

Awan, Imran. "'I Am a Muslim Not an Extremist': How the Prevent Strategy Has Constructed a 'Suspect Community.'" *Politics and Policy* 40, no. 6 (2015): 1158–1185.

Baines, Paul R., and Nicholas J. O'Shaughnessy. "Al-Qaeda Messaging Evolution and Positioning, 1998–2008: Propaganda Analysis Revisited." *Public Relations Inquiry* 3, no. 2 (2004): 163–191.

BBC. "Paris Attacks: Who Were the Attackers?" April 27, 2016. http://www.bbc.com/news/world-europe-34832512.

Beaumont, Peter. "Mohamed Lahouaiej-Bouhlel: Who Was the Bastille Day Truck Attacker?" *The Guardian* (US edition), July 15, 2016. https://www.theguardian.com/world/2016/jul/15/bastille-day-truck-driver-was-known-to-police-reports-say.

Bhui, Kamaldeep, and Yasmin Ibrahim. "Marketing the 'Radical': Symbolic Communications and Persuasive Technologies in Jihadist Websites." *Transcultural Psychiatry* 50, no. 2 (2013): 216–234.
bin Laden, Osama. "Jihad Against Jews and Crusaders," fatwa, World Islamic Front, February 23, 1998. https://fas.org/irp/world/para/docs/980223-fatwa.htm.
Blackwood, Leda, Nick Hopkins, and Stephen Reicher. "From Theorizing Radicalization to Surveillance Practices: Muslims in the Cross Hairs of Scrutiny." *International Society of Political Psychology* 37, no. 5 (2016): 597–612.
Blumenthal, Max. "Did British Security Services Drive 'Jihadi John' to Join ISIS? Emails and Phone Exchanges Raise Serious Questions." *Alternet*, March 9, 2015. http://www.alternet.org/world/did-britains-security-services-drive-jihadi-john-hands-isis-shocking-emails-and-phone.
Bradbury, Shelly. "Who Was Mohammad Youssef Abdulazeez?" *Chattanooga Times Free Press*, July 17, 2015. http://www.timesfreepress.com/news/local/story/2015/jul/17/who-wmohammad-youssef-abdulazeez/315079/.
Burke, Jason. "Khalid Masood Was a Convert with a Criminal Past. So Far, so Familiar." *The Guardian* (US Edition), March 25, 2017. https://www.theguardian.com/uk-news/2017/mar/25/khalid-masood-was-a-convert-with-a-criminal-past-so-far-so-familiar.
Butler, Patrick, and Phil Harris. "Considerations on the Evolution of Political Marketing." *Marketing Theory* 9, no. 2 (2009): 149–164.
Chaptal, Francoise. "Seeking to Kick Jihadi Threat, French Warily Eye Martial Arts Clubs." *Times of Israel*, May 19, 2016. http://www.timesofisrael.com/seeking-to-kick-jihadi-threat-french-warily-eye-martial-arts-clubs/.
Choudhury, Cyra Akil. "Ideology, Identity, and Law in the Production of Islamophobia." *Dialectical Anthropology* 39, no. 1 (2014): 47–61.
Cornell, Matt. "Feral Memes." *The New Inquiry* 56, November 2016. https://thenewinquiry.com/feral-memes/.
Crossan, Andrea. "Why the Boston Marathon Bombing Made Me Watch Mixed Martial Arts." *Public Radio International*, April 21, 2014. https://www.pri.org/stories/2014-04-21/why-boston-marathon-bombing-made-me-watch-mixed-martial-arts.
Cubitt, Sean. "Distribution and Media Flow." *Cultural Politics* 1, no. 2 (2005): 193–214.
Dabiq. "Khilafah Declared." Ramadan, 1435 AH.
Dabiq. "Halab Tribal Assemblies." Ramadan, 1435 AH.
Dabiq. "Tal Afar Liberated." Ramadan, 1435 AH.
Dabiq. "Remaining and Expanding." Muharram, 1436 AH.
Debord, Guy. "Détournement as Negation and Prelude." *Internationale Situationniste*, no. 3 (1959): 10–11.
Dettmer, Jamie. "ISIS Barbarians Face Their Own Internal Reign of Terror." *The Daily Beast*, February 6, 2015. http://www.thedailybeast.com/isis-barbarians-face-their-own-internal-reign-of-terror.
Einstein, Mara. *Brands of Faith*. Abingdon: Routledge, 2007.
Filkins, Dexter, and John F. Burns. "At Site of Attack on Zarqawi, All That's Left Are Questions." *New York Times*, June 11, 2006. http://www.nytimes.com/2006/06/11/world/middleeast/11scene.html.
Galloway, Chris. "Media Jihad: What PR Can Learn in Islamic State's Public Relations Masterclass." *Public Relations Review* 42, no. 4 (2016): 582–590.

Gambhir, Harleen K. *The Virtual Caliphate: ISIS's Information Warfare*. Washington, DC: Institute for the Study of War, 2016.
Gartenstein-Ross, Daveed. "Don't Get Cocky, America." *Foreign Policy*, May 2, 2011. http://foreignpolicy.com/2011/05/02/dont-get-cocky-america-2/.
Gotsi, Manto, and Constantine Andriopoulos. "Understanding the Pitfalls in the Corporate Rebranding Process." *Corporate Communications: An International Journal* 12, no. 4 (2007): 341–355.
Grillo, Jean Bergantini. "The First Media Brand." *Cablevision* 25, no. 21 (2011): 5A.
Gulmohamad, Zana Khasraw. "The Rise and Fall of the Islamic State of Iraq and Al-Sham (Levant) ISIS." *Global Security Studies* 5, no. 2 (2014): 1–11.
Harrison-Walker, L. Jean. "Strategic Positioning of Nations as Brands." *Journal of International Business Research* 10, no. 2 (2011): 135–147.
Hebdige, Dick. *Subculture: The Meaning of Style*. London: Routledge, 1979.
Helfstein, Scott, Nassir Abdullah, and Muhammad al-Obaidi. "Deadly Vanguards: A Study of al-Qa'ida's Violence Against Muslims" (occasional paper series, Combating Terrorism Series at West Point), December 2009. https://ctc.usma.edu/app/uploads/2010/10/deadly-vanguards_complete_l.pdf.
Holbrook, Donald. "Approaching Terrorist Public Relations." *Public Relations Inquiry* 3, no. 2 (2014): 141–161.
Hoyle, Carolyn, Alexandra Bradford, and Ross Frenet. *Becoming Mulan? Female Migrants to ISIS*. London: Institute for Strategic Dialogue, 2015.
Kamali, Sara. "Informants, Provocateurs, and Entrapment: Examining the Histories of the FBI's PATCON and the NYPD's Muslim Surveillance Program." *Surveillance and Society* 15, no. 1 (2017): 68–78.
Kani-Lundholm, Magdalena. "Nation in Market Times: Connecting the National and the Commercial. A Research Overview." *Sociology Compass* 8, no. 6 (2014): 603–613.
Kaplan, Sarah. "'Jihad Is a Lot of Fun,' Deso Dogg, a German Rapper Turned Islamic State Pitchman Said. Now He's Reportedly Dead from US Air Strike." *Washington Post*, October 30, 2015. https://www.washingtonpost.com/news/morning-mix/wp/2015/10/30/deso-dogg-the-german-rapper-turned-islamic-state-militant-reportedly-killed-in-airstrike/.
Kingsley, Patrick. "Who Is Behind ISIS's Terrifying Online Propaganda Operation?" *The Guardian* (US edition), June 23, 2014. https://www.theguardian.com/world/2014/jun/23/who-behind-isis-propaganda-operation-iraq.
Kraidy, Marwan. "Terror, Territoriality, Temporality: Hypermedia Events in the Age of the Islamic State." *Television & Media* 19, no. 2 (2018): 170–176.
Kuss, Daria J., Antonius J. van Rooij, Gillian W. Shorter, Mark D. Griffiths, and D. van de Mheen. "Internet Addiction in Adolescents: Prevalence and Risk Factors." *Computers in Human Behavior* 29, no. 5 (2013): 1987–1996.
Kundnani, Arun. "Spooked: How Not to Prevent Violent Extremism." Institute of Race Relations, October 17, 2009. http://www.kundnani.org/wp-content/uploads/spooked.pdf.
Kundnani, Arun. *A Decade Lost: Rethinking Radicalisation and Extremism*. London: Claystone, 2015.
Lafree, Gary, and Gary Ackerman. "The Empirical Study of Terrorism: Social and Legal Research." *Annual Review of Law and Social Science* 5 (2009): 347–374.

McAlexander, James H., John W. Schouten, and Harold F. Koenig. "Building Brand Community." *Journal of Marketing* 66, no. 1 (2002): 38–54.

McCants, William. "The Feud Between al-Qaeda and the Islamic State, Explained." *Newsweek*, September 25, 2016. http://www.newsweek.com/isis-al-qaeda-feud-499052.

McDevitt, J., J. Levin, and S. Bennett. "Hate Crime Offenders: An Expanded Typology." *Journal of Social Issues* 58, no. 2 (2002): 303–317.

Olins, Wally. "Branding the Nation: The Historical Context." *Journal of Brand Management* 9, no. 4 (2002): 241–248.

O'Shaughnessy, Nicholas J., and Paul R. Baines. "Selling Terror: The Symbolization and Positioning of Jihad." *Marketing Theory* 9, no. 2 (2009): 227–241.

Ryan, Michale W. S. "Hot Issue: *Dabiq*: What Islamic State's New Magazine Tells Us about Their Strategic Direction, Recruitment Patterns, and Guerrilla Doctrine." *Terrorism Monitor*, August 1, 2014. https://jamestown.org/program/hot-issue-dabiq-what-islamic-states-new-magazine-tells-us-about-their-strategic-direction-recruitment-patterns-and-guerrilla-doctrine/.

Shane, Scott. "The Lessons of Anwar al-Awlaki." *New York Times*, August 27, 2015. https://www.nytimes.com/2015/08/30/magazine/the-lessons-of-anwar-al-awlaki.html?.

Sheikh, Hammad, Ángel Gómez, and Scott Atran. "Empirical Evidence for the Devoted Actor Model." *Current Anthropology* 57, no. S13 (2016): S204–S209.

Sivek, Susan Currie. "Packaging Inspiration: Al Qaeda's Digital Magazine *Inspire* in the Self-Radicalization Process." *International Journal of Communication* 7 (2013): 584–606.

Szondi, György. "The Role and Challenges of Country Branding in Transition Countries: The Central and Eastern European Experience." *Place Branding and Public Diplomacy* 3, no. 1 (2007): 8–20.

Thompson, Gareth. "Extremes of Engagement: The Post-Classical Public Relations of the Islamic State." *Public Relations Review* 43, no. 5 (2017): 915–924.

Tyler, Tom R., Stephen Schulhofer, and Aziz Z. Huq. "Legitimacy and Deterrence Effects in Counterterrorism Policing: A Study of Muslim Americans." *Law and Society Review* 44, no. 2 (2010): 365–401.

Van Ham, Peter. "The Rise of the Brand State: The Postmodern Politics of Image and Reputation." *Foreign Affairs* 80, no. 5 (2001): 2–6.

Zizek, Slavoj. *Living in the End Times.* New York: Verso, 2011.

BRIAN HUGHES is a PhD student in the School of Communication at the American University in Washington, DC. He is the author of the *Throwing Rocks at the Google Bus Teacher's Guide.*

8 It's More Than Orange

ISIS's Appropriation of Orange Prison Jumpsuits as Rhetorical Resistance

Patrick G. Richey
Michaela Edwards

A SHAVEN AND MALNOURISHED James Foley, clad in an orange jumpsuit, kneels in the hot desert. On his left flank is an ISIS fighter with his face covered. Foley, who is clearly suffering, states, "I call on my friends, family, and loved ones to rise up against my real killers, the US government, for what will happen to me is only a result of their complacency and criminality." Then the masked militant, who speaks with a British accent, delivers a warning to the US government: "You are no longer fighting an insurgency. We are an Islamic army and a state that has been accepted by a large number of Muslims worldwide." The fighter, soon to be identified as British citizen Mohammed Emwazi (popularly known as Jihadi John, and the subject of chapter 10 of this book) begins to cut at Foley's throat as the picture fades away. The video eventually returns to the scene, revealing a body without a head.

When asked what should happen to two captured men linked to the death of her son, Diane Foley said that if the two were to be sent to Guantanamo Bay, "It would continue the hatred." Drawing parallels between the orange jumpsuits worn by inmates there and the one worn by her son during his execution, Foley's mother continued, "You know, they were executed in orange jumpsuits like [the ones] used in Guantanamo. So, I would be very against that. I think that would be a travesty. I think that would perpetuate this cycle of hatred that I think we need to be above that. And I think we need to show them what justice really looks like."[1]

In speaking of her son's death and the punishment of his captors and executioners, Diane Foley highlighted an important rhetorical tool of ISIS—the orange jumpsuit. This chapter explores ISIS's use of the iconic orange jumpsuit as resistance rhetoric to Western intervention in Muslim countries. It does so by examining photos of prisoners at Abu Ghraib and Guantanamo Bay prisons, which are juxtaposed with images of ISIS prisoners, all of whom wear orange jumpsuits.

The appropriation of this particular article of clothing creates a rhetorical rally point for ISIS. Western audiences view the orange jumpsuit as an insignificant symbol of incarceration; however, it has been utilized as a symbol of humiliation and dehumanization by ISIS and is forced on its prisoners to visually display the group's control over them. The chapter approaches the subject by first examining Michel Foucault's concept of bio-power as it considers the postcolonial rhetorical battleground of the visually iconographic orange jumpsuit. It then engages with Robert Hariman and John Lucaites's work on visual iconography as it considers how the orange jumpsuit can serve as a space of ideological resistance.

Short History of Prison Uniforms

Every day, billions of images and ideas are spread across the world. With the technological boom of the late twentieth century, the flow of information across cultures became a torrent, opening the minds and homes of people in virtually every nation. In many ways, this has had a positive effect on cultural understanding, creating veins of conversation that can foster knowledge and understanding. Much like the balance created in all aspects of life, however, this invisible connection also opens up channels for harm and indoctrination. Within such an environment, an artifact that has been utilized in one way by one culture can be utterly transformed as it is shared and reshared via global information networks. In order to understand how this flow of information can provide moments of cultural appropriation and misappropriation, one can look to a single artifact such as the iconic orange jumpsuit to provide insight.

Prisons have evolved over time. A fear of disorder birthed both the governing bodies and the penal systems seen in most ancient and modern civilizations.[2] The first written code of law comes from ancient Babylon: the Code of Hammurabi.[3] Building upon this and other such codes, criminal law has historically been punitive in nature. Prisoners were often executed or locked up, never to be heard from again.[4] As human rights and issues of equality have gained prominence, incarceration has become increasingly focused on the rehabilitation of citizens, with advocates calling for better living conditions and spaces for social interaction.[5]

As prisoners were increasingly introduced to the social sphere via work and community service, the need to easily identify them arose, creating a need for recognizable clothing.[6] Across history, prisoners have been issued various uniforms as a means of subordination, debilitation, and identification. Some countries in Europe once identified prisoners through their lack of shoes and the use of wrist restraints, leaving them in their civilian clothes.[7] In Asia, many prisoners were given long pieces of cloth as to use as loincloths and dresses, much like what would have been seen on common slaves.[8] Before the prisons of the Victorian Era, prisoners would often be sold into slavery, shipped to faraway territories such as Australia, or killed.[9] As prison sentencing elongated in the Victorian Era, a desire for an identical uniform for prisoners came into style, often in one color, much like scrubs of today.[10] The prison garb of the British crown in the nineteenth century also sported a broad arrow denoting property of the crown. Wherever uniforms were compulsory, the inmates were crown property.[11]

The prison systems of the United States began in 1790.[12] The earliest dressed their inmates in compulsory uniforms of horizontal stripes in muted grays and blacks. This was the common prison uniform in the United States for the whole of the eighteenth and nineteenth centuries. During the enlightenment of the nineteenth century in America, the prison systems went through ideological reform. The idea of purely punitive incarceration shifted to rehabilitative incarceration for those individuals who did not receive capital punishment,[13] as prisons were slowly transformed into a tool for societal control.[14] During this reformation, the muted black and gray stripes became connotatively linked with the shame and disgrace of lifelong criminal status. This connotation did not align with the new corrective and rehabilitative goals emerging at the time. By the early twentieth century, the horizontal stripes were removed and replaced with varying colors of jumpsuits and scrubs.[15] The iconic orange jumpsuit was put into use in this period.

The Orange Jumpsuit

The orange jumpsuit has come to symbolize all inmates in the United States, even though most prisons use a wide range of different methods to clothe and identify prisoners. Jumpsuits may have specific colors and meanings, which can sometimes signify the threat the prisoner poses to society.[16] Different-colored uniforms have also been used to signify particular minority populations in the prison system.[17] The theme of rehabilitative incarceration versus punitive incineration prompted a working class of prisoners who were often dressed in blue jeans and work shirts, a nod to the labor they were required to perform. This can still be seen in United States federal prisons in the form of khaki work pants and shirts.[18]

The color orange has been utilized for its aesthetic purposes. The striking color serves to make escape more difficult. Prisoners dressed in orange scrubs are easy to recognize and spot in public settings.[19] Through media coverage, including courtroom hearings and transfers of prisoners, the orange jumpsuit has become an iconic symbol of imprisonment in the United States. The connection between incarceration and the bright-orange jumpsuit is also strengthened through media such as shows like *Orange Is the New Black* and through news coverage of prisoners of war from the expanding global war on terror. After the

9/11 attacks, high-value military prisoners were confined at the US naval base in Guantanamo Bay, Cuba. At Guantanamo Bay, two color designations are present. Prisoners who behave well and comply with regulations receive white jumpsuits. Prisoners who have behavioral problems receive orange jumpsuits.[20]

However, this is not the image of Guantanamo Bay that the world has seen. Activists who protest the conditions in the camp often cite images of detainees *all* dressed in orange. In Turkey in 2006, a member of al-Qaeda was scheduled to appear before courts for "masterminding" the 2003 Istanbul bombings. In an act of solidarity with those imprisoned at Guantanamo Bay, he chose to wear an orange jumpsuit and was denied trial until 2007 when he was sentenced to sixty-seven life imprisonments.[21]

The rhetorical weight of the orange jumpsuit intensified in 2004 with the release of photos of prisoners being abused at Abu Ghraib, a detainment facility run by US armed forces in Iraq after the Second Iraq War. The images were broadcast by nightly and cable newscasts, they were printed in newspapers, and they were circulated on the internet. Their publication created a worldwide scandal and were held up as evidence of the villainy of American forces. Messages of solidarity with the abused prisoners also circulated globally, and members of extremist Muslim groups used them to help radicalize others. Terrorist groups often dressed their own prisoners in orange jumpsuits in videos and photographs as they demanded the surrender of the Western world and beheaded their victims.[22] All of this together has helped iconize the orange jumpsuit on a global level.[23]

The Ideological History of ISIS

The tensions in the Middle East have been at the forefront of international affairs for more than two decades now. In the 1990s, a man by the name of Abu Musab al-Zarqawi from Jordan traveled to Afghanistan to learn to wage jihad. There he met two men, Mohammad al-Masari and Abu Mohammad al-Maqdisi.[24] Al-Masari was the third in command of al-Qaeda, a group of men sworn to Osama bin Laden and his ideological goals, the foremost of which was to push the "infidel" out of the Middle East.[25] Al-Maqdisi was a different kind of man; he was not a leader of war but a leader of faith. Al-Maqdisi was the principal theological mind to influence al-Zarqawi and set his path toward extremism at a young age.[26]

Al-Zarqawi did not join al-Qaeda in his first visit to Afghanistan; instead he traveled with al-Maqdisi back to Jordan, where they set their sights on freeing Jordan from "infidels" who wished to make deals with the United States and Israel. He and al-Maqdisi were eventually tried and imprisoned for terrorist activity in Jordan.[27] While incarcerated in Jordan, they were able to develop and widely spread their ideology in the prison system. As the conflict in the Middle East continued to develop in severity, so did al-Zarqawi's religious beliefs.[28] By

1998, al-Zarqawi and al-Maqdisi began to quarrel about religious beliefs, primarily the persecution of other Muslims. A rift grew between the mentor and his pupil as al-Zarqawi's religious beliefs became further radicalized, including his thoughts on how to dispose of the infidel.[29]

When power changed hands in Jordan and al-Zarqawi was released on amnesty, his radical following had grown considerably. He traveled to Afghanistan and met with bin Laden, who asked for his allegiance to al-Qaeda. However, the two men were ideologically different; al-Zarqawi believed that all Shiites should be executed as infidels. Bin Laden was more sympathetic to the Shiite people and focused on repelling and annihilating the West. Al-Zarqawi did fight alongside al-Qaeda while he remained in Afghanistan, helping militarily train al-Qaeda members.[30] Al-Zarqawi's aim was to create an army he could move globally to wage jihad. It was in 2001 that al-Zarqawi's force joined with al-Qaeda to fight the US invasion in Afghanistan. After he was injured in an airstrike, he took some three hundred men with him into Iran, where he recruited heavily in the Sunni refugee camps and cities.[31]

In 2003, al-Zarqawi moved his base into the Sunni parts of Iraq, where he began his terrorist activity with fervor. In 2004, al-Zarqawi finally pledged his allegiance to bin Laden and the goals of al-Qaeda. It is speculated that this was done because al-Zarqawi could profit from the organization, while bin Laden needed a stronghold in Iraq. However, this relationship was strained, and al-Zarqawi continued to act outside of bin Laden's wishes, creating a divide between the leaders and their respective followers.[32]

After al-Zarqawi's death in a US airstrike in 2006, his followers separated from al-Qaeda joined together by Abu Bakr al-Baghdadi. As a new group, they proclaimed a caliphate stretching from Aleppo in Syria to Diyala in Iraq.[33] A caliphate is an Islamic state ruled by a caliph, who is proclaimed to be a direct successor to Muhammad. The caliph has absolute power and is both a spiritual and political leader for the state.[34] This Islamic State is considered by its people to be a holy entity, and they have proclaimed their leader, al-Baghdadi, to be a prophet.[35] The organization would come to be known by many names, but the most recognizable is that of ISIS.

ISIS officially cut ties with al-Qaeda in 2014. Since then, they have been launching terrorist initiatives throughout the world and storming through the Middle East, at one time creating strongholds in Syria and Iraq. Foreign countries have come to the aid of the Iraqi government and other various rebel groups fighting against the Islamic State.[36] In 2015, with the aid of United States airstrikes, the Iraqi government was able to push ISIS out of Ramadi and away from the Syrian-Turkish border.[37] However, IS entrenched in Syria and remain there.

In less than a decade, ISIS was able to create a global army through the use of propaganda and religious zealots. Attacks as far away as England, France, Saudi

Arabia, and the United States have been claimed by ISIS and its followers. As has been discussed in several chapters of this book, ISIS's proliferation can be attributed to its use of global media as a propaganda machine.[38] ISIS's use of the orange jumpsuit in such media is not incidental. The choice of the clothing item and color is very specific. While there may be several approaches to understanding the nature of ISIS's use of the orange jumpsuit, this chapter focuses on two—Michel Foucault's concept of bio-power and Robert Hariman and John Lucaites's thoughts on iconography.

Bio-Power

The term *bio-power* is Michel Foucault's conceptualization of the rhetorical power of the body. Foucault defines bio-power as "a number of phenomena that seem to me to be quite significant, namely, the set of mechanisms through which the basic biological features of the human species became the object of political strategy, of a general strategy of power, or, in other words, how, starting from the eighteenth century, modern Western societies took on board the fundamental biological fact that human beings are species."[39]

There is often a misassociation with Foucault's term *bio-politics*. The two terms are separate but not mutually exclusive when examining the body as a being of power. Foucault prefers the concept of bio-power to describe the disciplinary and fear aspects of a society,[40] thus controlling a society's physical actions. Foucault uses the example of the soldier's body. A soldier is conditioned through his or her body. Movements are engrained over repetition. Thought is unnecessary; only the correct action, as prescribed by those in charge. While learning to march has practical uses, it is also a form of discipline. In contrast, bio-politics focuses more on the simple management of society for its betterment. Naturally, authoritarian governments rely on bio-power to a much greater extent than bio-politics. Outright physical control is preferred to political exigence of discourse using the body for advancement. This Machiavellian approach of fear coupled with physical pain controls docile bodies.

Foucault developed the concept of docile bodies in *Discipline and Punish: The Birth of the Prison*.[41] Foucault used the example of soldiers to explain the concept of docile bodies. Soldiers train their bodies with repetitive motions to maneuver in a certain way in combat. Soon their bodies move in flawless motion without thought. This unconscious conditioning is what Foucault claimed society does to its citizens as a form of power over them.

Gary Gutting simplified Foucault's docile bodies and wrote, "Docile bodies are produced through three distinctively modern means."[42] The first is hierarchical observations. Simply put, observations from above influence a person's behaviors. Soldiers unconsciously move their bodies in combat formations because they know their superiors watch them. The same is true of the body. Government entities fine any misappropriation of clothing or unregulated nudity, and some violations may lead to imprisonment. Some people put on clothing without thought, while others do so with conscious effort. Laws decree that women must cover their breasts while men do not, even though uncovered breasts allow for ease of nursing children.

The second means Gutting develops is normalizing judgment.[43] Normalizing judgment goes beyond what is right and wrong, but rank orders actions. Soldiers learn to move flawlessly, without thought, while still maintaining order. The soldier is always trying to be the best within the ranks. The soldier does not want to be abnormal in his or her motions and lose ranking. Society regulates and rank orders almost all aspects of life. "There is no escaping it."[44] The body is also rank ordered. There is a preferable shape and size ascribed to both men and women. Disorders such as bulimia and anorexia relate directly to societal views of the body. Even nudity is rank ordered. Those with "better" bodies readily display more of themselves in public. Sexuality displayed on television by perfect bodies, for example, is the idealized model. Americans obsess over the notion of possessing a physically attractive body. Women, for example, enhance their bodies in various ways in order to better rank in the sexual hierarchy. A conservative group such as ISIS would try to diminish this in women by covering them and pointing to such behavior as an example of Western decadence.

The final means Gutting develops is examination. It is a combination of the first two; hierarchical observations and normalizing judgments create a system that elicits "truth" from individuals and controls their behaviors.[45] Society does this by examining its citizens; this can be done both through written exams and visual examinations. Superiors watch a soldier's maneuvers to see if he or she is competent as a controlled body. Society also regulates the naked body. The government, for example, regulates what people can do with their bodies. Many people consider the unmarked and unpierced as proof of a clean body. Society catalogs and ranks the uses of the body and its exposure and rewards those who wear the prescribed clothes for their ability to conform. This conformity reinforces "proper" dress.

ISIS seeks to normalize its practices on the docile bodies of its constituents while sending a rhetorically powerful message. Persons in areas controlled by ISIS understand that they are under constant surveillance by the caliphate. Individuals living under ISIS rule are forced to conform their physical bodies to the strict standards of ISIS's interpretation of sharia law. Women wear the hijab, and men grow out their beards, partly for religious piety but also to conform their bodies for their ISIS rulers. One of the severest punishments in ISIS territories is death, and ISIS has used the orange jumpsuit as a symbol synonymous with death. ISIS forces condemned prisoners to don this dress as part of the public execution spectacle,[46] making hypervisible the subjugated body of their victims.

Rank ordering their bodies is also important for persons living under ISIS's authority. The gender roles for men and women differ significantly. Again, ISIS's strict interpretation of sharia law prescribes very clear rules. The penalty for stealing could result in lashings or even the severing of an arm or hand.[47] Yet, the penalty for adultery for a married man or woman is death.[48] There are less lethal orderings in the lands ISIS controls. A man's beard is sign of piety and is encouraged. The longer and fuller the beard, the more prestigious and religious ISIS considers a man.[49] Therefore, in a society that strictly regulates dress and body image, clothing is rhetorically significant. Orange jumpsuits are at the bottom of the tiered dress code. The jumpsuit's combined association with the West and its symbolic signification of guilt in ISIS areas serves as a reminder to all who see it of the low status of the jumpsuit's wearer, as well as a warning to those who would try to fight or challenge ISIS's authority or interpretation of Islam.

ISIS clearly uses fear as a key factor in controlling its populace. Foucault's bio-power helps us understand ISIS's governing strategy. The fear of severe bodily repercussions is powerful and effective. ISIS's extreme physical punishments, such as cutting off the hand of a thief for stealing food, are as much about public display for the group as they are about individual punishment. The orange jumpsuit is one powerful way ISIS visualizes the severity of its control of bodies for all to see. Within this environment, the orange jumpsuit becomes associated with bodily pain and suffering; orange is not seen as the warm color it is but instead as a warning.

Iconography

There are aspects of communication that a culture values above others. A word such as *patriotism* is a powerful cultural word. While speakers in a culture may have varied definitions of patriotism, all understand the importance of the word and may place it above other words in their lexicon. This phenomenon is what Michael McGee refers to as ideography. McGee defines ideographs (the focal words/phrases in ideography) as things that "exist in real discourse."[50] The ideograph's connotative meaning is as important as the denotative meaning. Individuals do not create ideographs; culture does. It is the mass agreement in culture that gives ideographs their power. This also means that as culture changes, so do ideographs. Yet, the ideograph is not restricted to the spoken language of a culture. It transcends language and incorporates many communicative acts. The meaning of an ideograph can be communicated visually in an iconograph—these, in turn, serve an important function in a society. Robert Hariman and John Lucaites define iconography as "photographic images produced in print, electronic, or digital media that are widely recognized, are understood to be representations of historically significant events, activate strong emotional response, and are reproduced across a range of media, genres, or topics."[51]

Hariman and Lucaites have examined multiple iconographs in their work, including the flag raising at Iwo Jima,[52] the photographs of a young girl after napalm bombing during the Vietnam War,[53] the Times Square kiss,[54] and multiple images representing aspects of American society.[55] Through this work they have identified five important ways iconographs communicate meaning to those who view them.

First, iconographs reflect social knowledge and dominant ideologies. The flag raising on Iwo Jima in 1945 reflects the struggles, courage, and sacrifice of the American fighting soldier, as well as the war effort at home. Most Americans hold these characteristics dear. When Americans see the image, they reflect upon those sacred characteristics.[56] Second, iconographs shape understanding of specific events and periods. Thus, Hariman and Lucaites's's[57] essay that examined the Times Square kiss only makes sense if the audience knows that the photographer captured the image at the end of WWII after American victory. Iconographs often relate to historically significant events, which are easier for a culture to identify with when seen.

In the third aspect, "iconographs influence political action by modeling relationships between civic actors, themselves cementing the ideograph of patriotism with the visual representation of soldiers raising the flag on Mount Suribachi."[58] Yet, the iconography is not just an issue of the past. It can be used to describe modern events. One such example is Janice Edwards and Carol Winkler's essay that explains that the visual ideograph of the flag raising at Iwo Jima can be used as a basis for modern political discourse, such as in cartoons on subjects as far-ranging as gender and LGBT rights.[59]

Fourth, iconographs provide figural resources for subsequent communicative action. They become the starting point to begin an argument about other ideographs. Hariman and Lucaites's essay that examines the Times Square kiss moved well beyond a young woman and a sailor kissing, to discuss other issues. One issue the authors extrapolate is of two men kissing and how that would be read by an audience if it were photographed in a similar manner.[60] Finally, Hariman and Lucaites explain that iconographs "illustrate the ways visual communication can underwrite polity by providing resources for thought and feeling necessary for constituting people as citizens and motivating identification with and participation in specific forms of collective life."[61] Not only are images important for a modern industrialist society, but iconographs are also. Richey notes that "iconographs become part of the glue that holds society together."[62]

Iconographs manifest the five functions in two ways. The first way is through the embodiment of symbolic resources that are available through media.[63] It is complicated to capture the anguish of a young Vietnamese girl fleeing her village after napalm destroyed it. However, the iconic photograph shows all of the horrific details, to galvanize the incident in the viewer's mind. With ISIS, symbolic messages communicated through media platforms are core to its propaganda campaign. It is interesting to note that while ISIS claims to create a new caliphate to mirror to those of the Islamic golden age, it uses the detested and "morally bankrupt" Western modes of media such as Facebook and Twitter to communicate its message. Photographs and videos of ISIS's "justice" are easy to disseminate in such media and leave little to the imagination.

Second, iconographs can emphasize the limitations of the printed word.[64] Using the example of the young girl in the iconic post-napalm photo, a person would have difficulty putting into words all the emotions felt upon viewing the image. The photograph becomes symbolic of the viewer's emotional attachments to the event. Critics used this photograph as evidence of failed American intervention in Vietnam.

ISIS is very careful when creating its visual self through multiple media platforms, selecting each aspect of its propaganda for maximum impact.[65] Hariman and Lucaites's conceptualization of visual ideography works well to explain one reason ISIS chooses to use the orange jumpsuit in its propaganda videos and photographs. ISIS uses, to their advantage, the knowledge that many in the Middle East see the West as colonizers. By not only using terms such as *crusaders*, but also by dressing their captives in the prison orange jumpsuits associated with Western (particularly American) powers, they further emphasize the otherness of their captives while working to enrage Muslim audiences. As mentioned earlier, orange jumpsuits have become a collective symbol of imprisonment and torture at the hands of the Americans in places such as Abu Ghraib and Guantanamo Bay. ISIS relies on their Muslim audiences to connect their use of the orange jumpsuit with such abuses to create a rhetorically vivid understanding of the Western colonization and subjugation of Muslim peoples.

Roland Barthes emphasizes the importance of visuals as a means of communicating to audiences who may not be literate or who may not be fluent in the dominant language of the message creators[66]—in this case, Arabic for ISIS. Barthes believes photographs are produced through the interaction of three particular experiences: that of operator (photographer), spectator (viewer of photographs), and the target (object of the photographer). "I possessed only two experiences," Barthes wrote, "that of observed subject and that of the subject observing."[67]

Barthes imagines two groups of photographs. The first consists of ordinary and everyday photographs that he calls "studium." The second is made of photographs that differentiate themselves from all others. He calls them "punctum." Barthes suggests that punctum photographs "disturb the studium . . . sting, speck, cut."[68] Writing on this idea, Richey notes that "Barthes develops the concept that photographic images gain rhetorical value because people can physically see photographs but must cognitively piece together what they view from elements present both physically and cognitively. Certain people may see certain aspects of photographs that others may not. Thus, a photograph's meaning cannot be concrete or universal. Some may see the photographs taken at Abu Ghraib prison as just individual events by a group of heinous soldiers, while others may see them as endemic of much larger problems."[69]

ISIS uses this representation of abuse from Abu Ghraib by visually incorporating the orange jumpsuit in their own propaganda. Thus, they use the orange jumpsuit as a rhetorical artifact with the assumption the audience already connects ISIS's prisoners with those at Abu Ghraib as a Hammurabian form of justice. It is the specific events that took place at Guantanamo Bay and Abu Ghraib that help clarify Hariman and Lucaites's second aspect of an iconograph.[70] By understanding the nature of the orange jumpsuit as a symbol of Western imperialism to a Muslim audience, it is clear why ISIS chooses to deploy the visually important object in its media. It serves as a reminder of the group's resistance to Western imperialism.

This leads directly to Hariman and Lucaites's third aspect of an iconograph, the call to political action.[71] ISIS's use of the orange jumpsuit is meant to inflame Muslim audiences and push them to take action of some kind. ISIS's view of Islam is to bring back the caliphate and exterminate Western crusaders and their perceived puppet governments throughout the Holy Lands. ISIS's approach is anything but static. They call for brutal and open resistance. There is very little room for mercy, and the deaths of innocent men, women, and children are of little concern, as long as ISIS gets its desired outcome. ISIS's use of the orange jumpsuit is a visual call to action to entice young men throughout the world to support the Islamic State, either by joining the group directly or by giving their lives in global suicide attacks.

ISIS's use of the orange jumpsuit also ensures future rhetorical usage. One reason the group uses the jumpsuit and the color orange is to serve as a constant reminder to Muslim audiences of Western abuses at Guantanamo Bay and Abu Ghraib; it serves to cut through the detritus of a media-saturated world, communicating to the audience that ISIS seeks justice for Muslims, if they adopt the group's interpretation of Islam. Richey expands Hariman and Lucaites's concept of underwriting and creating social unity and contends that there can be rhetorical resistance to common ideologies that power structures use.[72] Here ISIS twists the Western concepts of justice and freedom by subverting the orange jumpsuit as a countervalue of abuse, therefore appropriating it symbolically to reflect the West and its allies. Thus, not only does ISIS cement its control of its own subjects; it simultaneously calls for others to reject the West and Western allies in Muslim lands. For ISIS, the use of the orange jumpsuit is a win-win rhetorical strategy.

ISIS has mastered the ability to use multiple media to spread their message. By moving beyond text, ISIS is also able to overcome the problem of literacy and the multiple languages spoken in the countries they target. A viewer only needs a cursory knowledge of the events at Abu Ghraib prison or Guantanamo Bay to understand ISIS's use of the orange jumpsuit. ISIS has appropriated the iconic orange jumpsuit from Abu Ghraib and Guantanamo Bay to use as a form of resistance that sends a powerful visual message that suggests ISIS will provide justice for Muslims who have been victimized by Western powers.

Conclusion

By deploying Foucault's concept of bio-power and Hariman and Lucaites's conceptualization of iconographs, the rhetorical nature of the orange jumpsuit is made clear. Whether to control the docile bodies living under ISIS's control or to serve as a resistance message portrayed in its propaganda, the specific choice of the orange jumpsuit is not arbitrary. ISIS carefully chose the orange jumpsuit to maximize its rhetorical impact on ISIS's subjects and to send a clear message to broader global audiences. ISIS rejects modernity because of its strict interpretation of Islam. It uses the orange jumpsuit to resist Western ideology by appropriating iconic images of the West's (America's) abuses of Muslim individuals in the prisons at Guantanamo Bay and Abu Ghraib. The pathos of ISIS's propaganda ensures maximum emotional impact for its limited propaganda apparatus. While one could easily argue, and many do, against ISIS's goals and brutal methods, few could argue against their mastery of visual persuasion.

As scholars continue to grapple with ideology-driven organizations such as ISIS, it becomes imperative to understand the rhetorical power of simple messages. In this instance, the message is wrapped in the orange jumpsuit. However, this chapter's approach is not exclusive to one color, set of clothing, or organization. Rather, this rhetorically investigative approach can help us begin to understand the techniques that organizations use to persuade and even control others. The approach could be used for other artifacts that seem common but contain a deep visual meaning that holds the possibility of controlling people. What may seem ordinary or trivial to one viewer may have the power to terrify or enrage another. Understanding this can allow societies to better counter or combat certain messages or ideologies.

Notes

1. The Associated Press, "Mother of US Journalist Killed by ISIS Reacts to Reports of Capture of Militants," AlArabiya English, February 11, 2018, http://english.alarabiya.net/en/media/print/2018/02/11/Mother-of-US-journalist-killed-by-ISIS-reacts-to-reports-of-capture-of-militants.html.

2. Michel Foucault, *Discipline and Punish: The Birth of the Prison*, A. Sheridan, trans. (New York: Pantheon, 1977).

3. For a discussion of ancient lawmaking, see Stanley A. Cooke, *The Laws of Moses and the Code of Hammurabi* (London: A. and C. Black, 1903) and Henry S. Maine, *Ancient Law: Its Connection with the Early History of Society and Its Relation to Modern Ideas, 1861* (New York: Dorset, 1986).

4. Foucault, *Discipline and Punish.*

5. "A Victorian Prison," The National Archives, 2018, http://www.nationalarchives.gov.uk/education/resources/victorian-prison/.

6. Foucault, *Discipline and Punish.*

7. Philip Priestley, *Victorian Prison Lives: English Prison Biography, 1830–1914* (Cambridge, UK: Cambridge University Press, 1985).

8. Juliet Ash, "The Prison Uniforms Collection at the Galleries of Justice Museum, Nottingham, UK," *Uniforms in Design History* 24, no. 2 (2011): 187–193.

9. J. M. Moore, "Is the Empire Coming Home? Liberalism, Exclusion, and the Punitiveness of the British State," (conference paper, British Criminology Conference, 2014).

10. Michael Ignatieff, *A Just Measure of Pain: The Penitentiary in the Industrial Revolution, 1750–1850* (New York: Pantheon, 1978).

11. "A Victorian Prison."

12. Adam J. Hirsch, *The Rise of the Penitentiary: Prisons and Punishment in Early America* (New Haven, CT: Yale University Press, 1992).

13. Blake McKelvey, *American Prisons: A Study in American Social History Prior to 1915* (Montclair, NJ: Patterson Smith, 1968).

14. Scott Christianson, *With Liberty for Some: 500 Years of Imprisonment in America* (Boston: Northeastern University Press, 1998).

15. Ash, "The Prison Uniforms Collection." For news reporting on this topic, see these stories from the *Hartford Courant*, "Prisons Using Colors to Classify Inmates," http://articles.courant.com/1995-08-06/news/9508060236_1_prison-inmates-highest-security and *The Columbiana*, "Inmate Clothes at Clark County Jail More Than Fashion," http://www.columbian.com/news/2013/jun/16/inmate-clothes-clark-county-jail-threat-level-save/.

16. Christopher Beam, "Orange Alert: When Did Prisoners Start Dressing in Orange?" *Slate*, December 3, 2010, http://www.slate.com/articles/news_and_politics/explainer/2010/12/orange_alert.html.

17. Sharon Dolovich, "Strategic Segregation in the Modern Prison," *American Criminal Law Review* 48, no. 1 (2011): 11–22.

18. John Pratt, *Punishment and Civilization: Penal Tolerance and Intolerance in Modern Society* (Thousand Oaks, CA: Sage, 2002).

19. Beam, "Orange Alert."

20. Adam Brookes, "Inside Guantanamo's Secret Trials," *BBC News*, April 8, 2005, https://www.mlive.com/news/saginaw/index.ssf/2014/07/black_and_white_is_the_new_ora.html.

21. Allen Meek, *Biopolitical Media: Catastrophe, Immunity, and Bare Life* (New York: Routledge, 2016).

22. Ibid.

23. Louie Palu, "Image Control in the Age of Terror," in *Art as Political Witness*, eds. Kia Lindroos and Frank Möller (Opladen, Germany: Barbara Budrich Publishers, 2017).

24. Mary Ann Weaver, "The Short, Violent Life of Abu Musab al-Zarqawi," *The Atlantic*, June 8, 2006, https://www.theatlantic.com/magazine/archive/2006/07/the-short-violent-life-of-abu-musab-al-zarqawi/304983/.

25. Michael Griffin, *Islamic State: Rewriting History* (London: Pluto, 2015).

26. Joas Wagemakers, "Invoking Zarqawi: Abu Muhammad al-Maqdisi's Jihad Deficit," *CTC Sentinel* 2, no. 6 (2009): 14–17.

27. Weaver, "The Short, Violent Life."

28. Jason M. Breslow, "Who Was the Founder of ISIS?" *Frontline*, May 17, 2016, https://www.pbs.org/wgbh/frontline/article/who-was-the-founder-of-isis/.

29. Jim Muir, "Islamic State Group: The Full Story," BBC News, October 17, 2017, https://www.bbc.com/news/world-middle-east-35695648.

30. Weaver, "The Short, Violent Life."

31. Griffin, "Islamic State."

32. Michael Weiss and Hassan Hassan, *ISIS: Inside the Army of Terror* (New York: Regan Arts, 2015).

33. Breslow, "Who Was the Founder of ISIS?"

34. Cole Bunzel, "From Paper State to Caliphate: The Ideology of the Islamic State," The Brookings Project on US relations with the Islamic World, 2016, https://www.brookings.edu/wp-content/uploads/2016/06/The-ideology-of-the-Islamic-State.pdf.

35. Ibid.

36. Weiss and Hassan, *ISIS: Inside the Army of Terror.*

37. Richard Engel, *And Then All Hell Broke Loose* (New York: Simon & Schuster, 2016).

38. Palu, "Image Control in the Age of Terror."

39. Michel Foucault, *Security, Territory, Population: Lectures at The College de France, 1977–1978*, G. Burchell, trans. (New York: Picador, 2007), 1.

40. Michel Foucault, "*Society Must Be Defended: Lectures at The College de France, 1975–1976*, D. Macey, trans. (New York: Picador, 2003).

41. Foucault, *Discipline and Punish.*

42. Gary Gutting, *Foucault: A Very Short Introduction* (New York: Oxford University Press, 2005), 82.

43. Ibid.

44. Ibid., 84.

45. Ibid.

46. Griffin, "Islamic State."

47. Tom Wyke, "ISIS Release Horrific Photos of a Man Having His Hand Amputated for Theft and an 'Assad Spy' Being Crucified in the Streets of Syria," *Daily Mail*, December 19, 2014, http://www.dailymail.co.uk/news/article-2880945/ISIS-release-shocking-photos-man-having-hand-amputated-theft-Assad-spy-crucified-streets-Syria.html.

48. Simon Tomlinson, "Chilling Pictures Show ISIS Militants Savagely Stoning Four Married Men to Death for 'Committing Adultery' in Iraq," *Daily Mail*, June 16, 2016, http://www.dailymail.co.uk/news/article-3645062/Chilling-pictures-ISIS-militants-savagely-stoning-four-married-men-death-committing-adultery-Iraq.html.

49. Amanullah De Sondy, "The Relationship Between Muslim Men and Their Beards Is a Tangled One," *The Guardian*, January 28, 2016, https://www.theguardian.com/commentisfree/2016/jan/28/muslim-men-beards-facial-hair-islam.

50. Michael McGee, "The Ideograph: A Link Between Rhetoric and Ideology," *The Quarterly Journal of Speech* 66, no. 1 (1980): 7.

51. Robert Hariman and John L. Lucaites, "Performing Civic Identity: The Iconic Photograph of the Flag Raising on Iwo Jima," *Quarterly Journal of Speech* 88, no. 4 (2002): 366.

52. Ibid.

53. Robert Hariman and John L. Lucaites, "Public Identity and Collective Memory in US Iconic Photography: The Image of Accidental Napalm," *Critical Studies in Media Communication* 20, no. 1 (2003): 35–66.

54. Robert Hariman and John L. Lucaities, "The Times Square Kiss: Iconic Photography and Civic Renewal in US Public Culture," *Journal of American History* 94, no. 1 (2007b): 122–131.

55. Robert Hariman and John L. Lucaites, *No Caption Needed: Iconic Photographs, Public Culture, and Liberal Democracy* (Chicago: The University of Chicago Press, 2007a).

56. Hariman and Lucaites, "Performing Civic Identity."

57. Hariman and Lucaites, "The Times Square Kiss."

58. Patrick G. Richey, "Unnecessary Evil: An Examination of Abu Ghraib Torture Photographs as Postcolonial Resistance Rhetoric" (doctoral dissertation, Middle Tennessee State University, 2012), 51.

59. Janice L. Edwards and Carol K. Winkler, "Representative Form and the Visual Ideograph: The Iwo Jima Image in Editorial Cartoons," in *Visual Rhetoric: A Reader in Communication and American Culture*, eds. L. C. Olson, C. A. Finnegan, and D. S. Hope (Thousand Oaks, CA: Sage, 2008): 119–137.

60. Hariman and Lucaites, "The Times Square Kiss."

61. Hariman and Lucaites, "Performing Civic Identity," 366.

62. Richey, "Unnecessary Evil," 52.

63. Hariman and Lucaites, "Performing Civic Identity."

64. Ibid.

65. Palu, "Image Control."

66. Roland Barthes, *Image Music Text*, S. Heath, trans. (New York: Hill & Wang, 1977); Roland Barthes, *Camera Lucida: Reflections on Photography*, R. Howard, trans. (New York: Hill & Wang, 1981).

67. Barthes, *Camera Lucida*, 10.

68. Ibid., 27.

69. Richey, "Unnecessary Evil," 47.

70. Hariman and Lucaites, "Performing Civic Identity."

71. Ibid.

72. Ibid.

Bibliography

"A Victorian Prison." The National Archives, 2018. http://www.nationalarchives.gov.uk/education/resources/victorian-prison/.

Ash, Juliet. "The Prison Uniforms Collection at the Galleries of Justice Museum, Nottingham, UK." *Uniforms in Design History* 24, no. 2 (2011): 187–193.

Barthes, Roland. *Image, Music Text.* S. Heath, trans. New York: Hill & Wang, 1977.

Barthes, Roland. *Camera Lucida: Reflections on Photography.* R. Howard, trans. New York: Hill & Wang, 1981.

Beam, Christopher. "Orange Alert: When Did Prisoners Start Dressing in Orange?" *Slate*, December 3, 2010. http://www.slate.com/articles/news_and_politics/explainer/2010/12/orange_alert.html.

Breslow, Jason M. "Who Was the Founder of ISIS?" *Frontline*, May 17, 2016. https://www.pbs.org/wgbh/frontline/article/who-was-the-founder-of-isis/.

Brookes, Adam. "Inside Guantanamo's Secret Trials." *BBC News*, April 8, 2005. https://www.mlive.com/news/saginaw/index.ssf/2014/07/black_and_white_is_the_new_ora.html.

Bunzel, Cole. "From Paper State to Caliphate: The Ideology of the Islamic State." The Brookings Project on US Relations with the Islamic World, 2016. https://www.brookings.edu/wp-content/uploads/2016/06/The-ideology-of-the-Islamic-State.pdf.

Christianson, Scott. *With Liberty for Some: 500 Years of Imprisonment in America*. Boston: Northeastern University Press, 1998.

Cooke, Stanley A. *The Laws of Moses and the Code of Hammurabi*. London: A. and C. Black, 1903.

De Sondy, Amanullah. "The Relationship between Muslim Men and their Beards Is a Tangled One." *The Guardian*, January 28, 2016. https://www.theguardian.com/commentisfree/2016/jan/28/muslim-men-beards-facial-hair-islam.

Dolovich, Sharon. "Strategic Segregation in the Modern Prison." *American Criminal Law Review* 48, no. 1 (2011): 11-22.

Edwards, Janice L., and Carol K. Winkler. "Representative Form and the Visual Ideograph: The Iwo Jima Image in Editorial Cartoons." In *Visual Rhetoric: A Reader in Communication and American Culture*, edited by L. C. Olson, C. A. Finnegan, and D. S. Hope, 119–137. Thousand Oaks, CA: Sage, 2008.

Engel, Richard. *And Then All Hell Broke Loose*. New York: Simon & Schuster, 2016.

Foucault, Michel. *Discipline and Punish: The Birth of the Prison*. A. Sheridan, trans. New York: Pantheon, 1977.

Foucault, Michel. *Security, Territory, Population: Lectures at The College de France, 1977–1978*. G. Burchell, trans. New York: Picador, 2007.

Griffin, Michael. *Islamic State: Rewriting History*. London: Pluto Press, 2015.

Gutting, Gary. *Foucault: A Very Short Introduction*. New York: Oxford Press, 2005.

Hariman, Robert, and John L. Lucaites. "Performing Civic Identity: The Iconic Photograph of the Flag Raising on Iwo Jima." *Quarterly Journal of Speech* 88, no. 4 (2002): 363–392.

Hariman, Robert, and John L. Lucaites. "Public Identity and Collective Memory in US Iconic Photography: The Image of Accidental Napalm." *Critical Studies in Media Communication* 20, no. 1 (2003): 35–66.

Hariman, Robert, and John L. Lucaites. *No Caption Needed: Iconic Photographs, Public Culture, and Liberal Democracy*. Chicago: The University of Chicago Press, 2007a.

Hariman, Robert, and John L. Lucaites. "The Times Square Kiss: Iconic Photography and Civic Renewal in US Public Culture." *Journal of American History* 94, no. 1 (2007b): 122–131.

Ignatieff, Michael. *A Just Measure of Pain: The Penitentiary in the Industrial Revolution, 1750–1850*. New York: Pantheon, 1978.

Maine, Henry S. *Ancient Law: Its Connection with the Early History of Society and Its Relation to Modern Ideas, 1861*. New York: Dorset, 1986.

McGee, Michael. "The Ideograph: A Link between Rhetoric and Ideology." *The Quarterly Journal of* Speech 66, no. 1 (1980): 1–16.

McKelvey, Blake. *American Prisons: A Study in American Social History Prior to 1915*. Montclair, NJ: Patterson Smith, 1968.

Meek, Allen. *Biopolitical Media: Catastrophe, Immunity, and Bare Life*. New York: Routledge, 2016.

Moore, J. M. "Is the Empire Coming Home? Liberalism, Exclusion and the Punitiveness of the British State." Paper presented at the British Criminology Conference, 2014.

Muir, Jim. "Islamic State Group: The Full Story." *BBC News*, October 17, 2017. https://www.bbc.com/news/world-middle-east-35695648.

Palu, Louie. "Image Control in the Age of Terror." In *Art as Political Witness*, edited by Kia Lindroos and Frank Möller, 57–64. Opladen: Barbara Budrich Publishers, 2017.

Pratt, John. *Punishment and Civilization: Penal Tolerance and Intolerance in Modern Society.* Thousand Oaks, CA: Sage, 2002.

Priestley, Philip. *Victorian Prison Lives: English Prison Biography, 1830–1914*. Cambridge, UK: Cambridge University Press, 1985.

Richey, Patrick G. "Unnecessary Evil: An Examination of Abu Ghraib Torture Photographs as Postcolonial Resistance Rhetoric." Doctoral dissertation, Middle Tennessee State University, 2012.

Tomlinson, Simon. "Chilling Pictures Show ISIS Militants Savagely Stoning Four Married Men to Death for 'Committing Adultery' in Iraq." *Daily Mail*, June 16, 2016. http://www.dailymail.co.uk/news/article-3645062/Chilling-pictures-ISIS-militants-savagely-stoning-four-married-men-death-committing-adultery-Iraq.html.

Wagemakers, Joas. "Invoking Zarqawi: Abu Muhammad al-Maqdisi's Jihad Deficit." *CTC Sentinel* 2, no. 6 (2009): 14-17.

Weaver, Mary Ann. "The Short, Violent Life of Abu Musab al-Zarqawi." *The Atlantic*, June 8, 2006. https://www.theatlantic.com/magazine/archive/2006/07/the-short-violent-life-of-abu-musab-al-zarqawi/304983/.

Weiss, Michael, and Hassan Hassan. *ISIS: Inside the Army of Terror.* New York: Regan Arts, 2015.

Wyke, Tom. "ISIS Release Horrific Photos of a Man Having His Hand Amputated for Theft and an 'Assad Spy' Being Crucified in the Streets of Syria." *Daily Mail*, December 19, 2014. http://www.dailymail.co.uk/news/article-2880945/ISIS-release-shocking-photos-man-having-hand-amputated-theft-Assad-spy-crucified-streets-Syria.html.

PATRICK G. RICHEY, PhD, is Director of Forensics & Associate Professor at Middle Tennessee State University. He most recently edited the International Public Debate Association textbook.

MICHAELA EDWARDS is a recent graduate of Middle Tennessee State University's College of Liberal Arts, with a focus in rhetoric and organizational communication.

Part III

Narratives of the Islamic State

9 Western Millennials Explain Why They Joined the Islamic State

Matthew Pascarella

In the year that followed its declaration of a caliphate, the Islamic State's recruitment content shifted its messaging in order to frame ISIS as a movement engaged in nonviolent, state-building activities. ISIS recruitment content shifted away from "war porn" and the violence that framed ISIS as carrying out its own brand of justice, to a framing that depicted ISIS as a community-minded, family-oriented movement, working hard each day to establish its own civic culture in newly acquired cities and villages.

As ISIS unleashed this new messaging strategy, the number of foreign fighters traveling to Iraq and Syria doubled, soaring to an estimated forty thousand, hailing from more than 104 countries.[1] Those who enlisted were participants in one of the largest global mobilizations of foreign fighters by a militant movement in recorded history. Thousands of these recruits were millennials, born and raised in Western nation-states before deciding to set off to Iraq and Syria to join the Islamic State.[2] But *why*? Why would millennials who grew up in secular Europe, the UK, Australia, Canada, or the United States leave decent lives, good families, great schools, well-earned careers and so on, in order to join a militant movement that was in direct opposition to their home countries?

This chapter analyzes the testimony of twenty Western millennials who were successfully recruited by the Islamic State and who appear in official ISIS videos. Many of these individuals explain to viewers what it was like for them to grow up in the secular West. They explain why they left behind families, good jobs, and good schools to travel to a country many of them had never been to, in order to join a movement that they argue is making history.

The Radicalization of "Radicalization"

Alex Schmid finds that the theory of radicalization began to insinuate itself into Western political discourse and policymaking following the 2004 and 2005 bombings in Spain and England.[3] However, Arun Kundnani argues the theory of radicalization did not take hold—particularly in academic and policy circles in the West—until after the execution of Osama bin Laden in 2011.[4] During this time period, Western governments began to respond to opinion polls indicating the public suddenly had renewed fears of terrorism, despite the notorious al-Qaeda leader's demise.[5] Following bin Laden's execution, the primary focus in public and policy circles on wars with "extreme Muslims" abroad began to give way to a new focus on wars with "extreme Muslims" at home in the West. Radicalization was thus brought into the mainstream political discourse by so-called terrorism experts, political leaders, and the news media. Radicalization came to act as a blanket theory, incubating all other salient explanations as to why and how Western citizens become engaged and recruited by terrorist movements in order to carry out strategic attacks. Kundnani explains, "the concept of radicalization inherited at birth a number of built-in, limiting assumptions: that those perpetrating terrorist violence are drawn from a larger pool of extremist sympathizers who share an Islamic theology that inspires their actions; that entry into this wider pool of extremists can be predicted by individual or group psychological or theological factors: and that knowledge of these factors could allow government policies that reduce the risk of terrorism."[6]

Thus, the concept of radicalization fails to include a critical self-reflection on the causative role Western governments or allies may have in the process.[7] Further, this approach fails to position individuals within the social and political circumstances in which they have come of age as citizens of Western societies. Instead, radicalization reduces the entire phenomenon in question to "individual psychological or theological journeys."[8]

An analysis of the seminal texts within terrorism studies[9] reveals the indelible imprint radicalization has had in Western political discourse and policymaking. What emerges as the central tenet in Lacquer's influential work is that a causal process is being put forth in which a "'cultural-psychological' disposition to violence is being asserted without any substantial evidence."[10] The sources of radicalization that emerge in this research are often "as diverse as they are abundant," and thus "the search for causes of radicalization on 'vulnerable' young people has produced inconclusive results."[11] In addition, the findings in the literature seem to indicate that the study of radicalization to date has been based on small samples and selective case studies; the findings that do arise are provisional and are unable to be verified or extended through comparative research.[12]

In addition, David Brannan and his coauthors find that oft-cited research within terrorism studies lacks primary sources and independent analytical frameworks, and is "characterized by an 'aligned' position dependent on a research hermeneutic of crisis management, which perpetuates the 'received view.'"[13] Corrina Mullin suggests that this deficit in the literature continues to be a trend in terrorism-related scholarship, also noting that there is a tendency to "ideologize terror," such that a double standard exists when it comes to what gets labeled legitimate or illegitimate uses of political violence in the case of Islamist movements.[14] Schmid extends these findings and argues that what has been glaringly absent from those engaged in counterterrorism scholarship is historical context, namely a reflection on the history of Western politics in relation to Muslim states.[15]

Ultimately, the use of radicalization as a conceptual framework to study terrorist recruitment has resulted in no real answers as to what the sources of radicalization may in fact be. Yet this theory continues to be used by so-called terrorism experts, journalists, and policymakers without being critically assessed through reflexive and objective empirical research.[16] Ultimately, there is a refusal within this scholarship and the political discourse it buttresses to critically engage with the fact—much less critically *assess* the fact—that the Islamic State formed in direct opposition to the West due to its military and political occupation of a Muslim state and that Westerners who join ISIS came to this decision as citizens living within the bounds of Western nation-states.

The Islamic State Is a Global Movement

Since the early days of the West's so-called global war on terror, Westerners have been leaving their home countries to travel abroad to fight on behalf of guerilla or extremist groups. In general, there has been a significant increase in Muslim foreign fighters globally over the past several decades, beginning with the conflict in Afghanistan in the 1980s.[17] Yet while much of the literature "positions Muslim fighters as an outcome of the 1980s war, it rarely asks why these fighters went to Afghanistan in the first place."[18] Through investigating recent foreign fighter movements, Thomas Hegghammer discovered that the invasions of Afghanistan and Iraq had a significant catalyzing effect, inspiring foreign fighters to travel to Muslim states that had been invaded by Western, non-Muslim states following 9/11.[19]

David Malet explains that foreign fighters are often recruited within the context of a "period effect" with nonstate rebel entities drawing in support by taking advantage of the identities and conflicts that are most salient at a particular point in time.[20] There are still significant gaps in political-science literature concerning how organizations and movements recruit foreign citizens to engage in local insurgencies and civil conflicts. Hegghammer points out that "An established term for the phenomenon does not even exist in the political science literature," and foreign fighting is a form of activism that remains "notoriously understudied."[21]

If we are to approach foreign fighting as a form of global activism, then it is worth quickly exploring the challenge global activist organizations face in attempting to become a source for change today and to provide snapshot examples of how ISIS has faced these challenges to date. Doug McAdam, Sidney

Tarrow, and Charles Tilly identify the key challenges activist movements face today, which they must overcome in order to become a force for social change.[22]

The first key challenge is to recruit core activists and sustain the organization. As discussed throughout this book, ISIS has a global network of recruiters and has attracted up to forty thousand members from more than 104 countries to fight for their cause. ISIS is able to sustain its activities by relying "on extortion and the levying of 'taxes' on local populations under its control, as well as a range of other sources, such as oil smuggling, kidnapping for ransom, looting, antiquities theft and smuggling, foreign donations, and human trafficking."[23]

McAdam and his coauthors also argue that movements must obtain attention in the mainstream media. Between August and November 2014, six Western hostages were beheaded by the Islamic State. The beheadings were captured on video and released by Western think tanks before making headlines throughout mainstream news media globally. Following the release of these videos, the Obama administration reacted with airstrikes. After that, ISIS became a fixture in Western news media. More recently, ISIS members and individuals inspired by ISIS have been engaged in carrying out attacks outside the physical caliphate, ensuring that the Islamic State remains in the headlines, even as it loses physical territory.

The third key challenge movements need to overcome is that they must mobilize beyond those who are already convinced. Frederic Todenhofer, one the few Western journalists who has managed to embed with ISIS to date, sums up their ability to mobilize individuals when describing an ISIS recruitment house: "I met French people, I met UK people, but I met also Americans. I met Americans from New Jersey. I met people from the Caribbean who had just had just passed their law exam and who preferred to fight in the Islamic State instead of being a successful lawyer. And every day more than 50 people arrived only in this recruitment center, and they have several. So, they can lose 100 men in one day and it doesn't matter."[24]

Individuals continued to travel to the caliphate until the Islamic State suffered the loss of Mosul in Iraq and Raqqa in Syria. As ISIS has lost territory, it has also suffered a loss of Western recruits. New stories are often less focused since 2017 on foreign fighters traveling to join ISIS than they are on those same fighters traveling back to the West, disillusioned with the caliphate.

Another key challenge McAdam identifies for movements today is that they must overcome social control. The Islamic State institutes its own form of social control based on their interpretations of Islam, which they frame as established ideology arising from sharia law, the Quran, and Islamic history. ISIS is also masterful at capitalizing off of the West's post-9/11 political discourse by continuously messaging the fact that Western Muslims have been politically and socially marginalized since 9/11.

The final challenge McAdam argues movements must overcome is their ability to shape public policy and state action. The Islamic State is instituting its own forms of public policy and state action through armed takeovers, instituting sharia law in newly conquered territories, and developing their own currency and economic structures. The actions ISIS has taken in Iraq and Syria and via attacks in the West have left Western governments scrambling to develop policies to counter ISIS domestically and abroad.

ISIS Produces and Transmediates Alternative News

ISIS's accomplishments as a global movement rest in the fact that it has assembled a global network of content producers, disseminators, and thought leaders who use social media to find, engage, and win over potential recruits. ISIS does this efficiently and effectively by continuously engaging in transmedia storytelling. As Henry Jenkins explains, "Transmedia storytelling represents a process where integral elements of a fiction get dispersed systematically across multiple delivery channels for the purpose of creating a unified and coordinated entertainment experience. Ideally, each medium makes its own unique contribution to the unfolding of the story."[25]

For example, the Islamic State's regularly produced magazine, *Dabiq*, will run a short story about a key battle that recently took place. The story of that battle will then seed the production of an ISIS feature-length documentary in which producers extend the story of that battle much further. Screen grabs from the documentary are then turned into graphics and memes that are then circulated across social media and messaging applications. "Fans" can then follow fighters' social accounts as the story unfolds across multiple channels. References to the online social activity around that story then end up featured in newer issues of *Dabiq*, alongside editorialized updates concerning the original story.

The intention of this transmedia cycle is to establish ISIS as the primary and most trusted source for acquiring any information related to the Islamic State. Continually evolving a story over multiple platforms keeps audiences continuously engaged and checking in for updates. ISIS practices this storytelling strategy religiously—telling story after story after story over multiple channels simultaneously. By using these storytelling strategies across multiple channels, ISIS is activating an "alternative news" paradigm.[26] When a movement frames its content as alternative news, it is engaging in discursive practices that enable the movement to create its own self-representation.[27] By producing its own alternative news via highly engaging, transmedia storytelling strategies, ISIS is able to maintain control over its narrative of who it is.

ISIS first began to shape a collective identity through the dissemination of what many have called "war porn" or other types of violent media—an identity based on the idea of Islamic State fighters as conquerors. Much of the content produced by the ISIS in the year following the declaration of their caliphate was not obsessed with violence or war—rather, much of the content tended to focuses on state-building activities. Through man-on-the-street reporting and slice-of-life vignettes, viewers were taken on tours of what life is like in the new caliphate, tours that emphasized the civic side of the Islamic State. This was not simply propaganda for propaganda's sake. This messaging matched up with what was indeed happening on the ground in 2014 as ISIS focused on restoring infrastructure in newly claimed territories. As material began to circulate more broadly online, ISIS's recruitment of foreign fighters suddenly crescendoed to an all-time high.

Testimony from Twenty Islamic State Foreign Fighters

In order to understand how Western millennials explain *why* they joined the Islamic State, it is important to use an analytical framework that can assess how a civic culture is created and communicated by a movement and its participants. The "circuit of civic culture" model put forth by Peter Dahlgren[28] is a multidimensional "door to empirical inquiry," empowering researchers to assess how a civic culture is created and sustained over time.[29] It is a model that also enables researchers to focus on the role that media and communication resources can play in facilitating the creation of civic cultures. Dahlgren's circuit is predicated on the understanding that individuals are active social agents rather than dupes being radicalized by theological content. Dahlgren's model approaches political involvement from a culturally grounded context that positions individuals' participation as meaningful actions that are based on cultural perquisites within the population under analysis. As Dahlgren points out, "this frame is thus interested in the process of becoming—how people develop *into* citizens, how they come to see themselves as members and potential participants in societal development" (emphasis added).[30] The circuit is composed of six interactive dimensions: values, affinity/trust, knowledge, practices, identities, and discussion. All of these dimensions or themes act as categories to analyze the findings of the thematic content analysis that follows.

To conduct this content analysis, a database was compiled of all media produced by the Islamic State's two main video production entities, al-Hayat and al-Furqan, during the time period of June 2013—one year before ISIS seized Mosul and Tikrit and declared the formation of a caliphate—to June 2015, one year after that declaration. Through an exploratory analysis of this database, it emerged that prior to the declaration of the caliphate, rarely did any state-building content emerge. Yet following the establishment of the caliphate, state-building content began to appear on a more consistent basis. State-building content is defined as content that propagates state-building activities, including social services, courts, infrastructure developments, safety and security, family life, etc. In this body of ISIS, state-building content was a stream of cinema verité documentaries.[31] Given the interest in studying content that has been produced to target Westerners, the database was then filtered to include only English-language documentaries produced during the aforementioned time period. From there, the sample focused only on foreign fighters who a) appeared to be of the millennial generation and b) delivered first-person testimonials directly to camera in English or with English subtitles. A population of twenty first-person foreign fighter testimonials emerged. Each testimonial was then isolated and transcribed, and the coding frame was designed.

Through deductive readings and notations of both the transcripts and video clips that composed the entire sample, an initial coding frame was designed and tested by the researcher and additional coders. The code book was then revised to include only variables that were relevant to each of Dahlgren's dimensions. Following this revision, a pilot was conducted with an additional coder. The second coder independently coded 25 percent of the total sample. Intercoder reliability was established at just about 95 percent across the entire sample.

For the purposes of this analysis, each of Dahlgren's dimensions in the circuit of civic culture act as a thematic category. The findings are then placed in the appropriate thematic category or dimension for further analysis.

Values

While Dahlgren is referring to democratic values, the unique role that values play within the circuit is that they speak to the wider yet mundane and everyday life, reflecting back the normative dispositions of how the collectivity is organized ideologically and philosophically. For example, Dahlgren describes values in the circuit of civic culture as including both "substantive values" such as equality, liberty, justice, and solidarity, and "procedural values" such as openness, reciprocity, accountability, and tolerance.[32]

Throughout the foreign fighter testimonials, fighters frame the Islamic State as an inclusive movement. Muslims from all walks of life are welcome in the newly established caliphate. Clearly, this is a reduced inclusivity that fails to be recognized as such by the fighters. Perhaps this omission of defining who is allowed in and who is not is purposefully constructed in an effort to counteract how, as Ernest Gellner[33] and others have suggested, the Islamic world is often framed as a "closed society." The findings that emerge in this area thus seem to counteract the stereotypical framing. For example, one fighter from Australia says, "You see people from all walks of life here, every single street you walk through, every single courthouse or hospital you go to, you see all different types of brothers."

Another fighter from Canada says, "This means more than just fighting, we need the engineers, we need the doctors, we need professionals, we need . . . volunteers, we need fundraising, we need everything. You know, there's a role for everybody. Every person can contribute something, to the Islamic State."

Another finding related to values is that fighters often explain that they chose to join ISIS because they value "living as a full Muslim" in a land where sharia is being established as the normative philosophy underpinning day-to-day life. The fact that the caliphate has been established shows up as the second most prevalent finding in explaining why the fighter chose to join ISIS. The third most repeated explanation that fighters state as their reason for joining the Islamic State is that they are seeking a life of meaning and that they believe self-actualization can only take place by becoming a member of ISIS and working to defend the newly established caliphate. Another major finding related to values is that the fighters consistently frame their cause as rooted in an effort to seek justice for being persecuted both within the West and within the region of Iraq and surrounding nations. This explanation is repeated by many of the fighters and seems to support the conclusion Hegghammer offers concerning the rise of Muslim foreign fighters in the past several decades as being catalyzed by foreign occupations of Muslim lands.[34]

The value of sacrifice is repeated the most among the fighters as central to their philosophy. Sacrifice by leaving the West to join ISIS tends to rank as the most widely repeated rhetorical device fighters rely on when they pose direct questions to the viewers, such as this clip from a British national: "Are you willing to sacrifice the fat job you've got, the big car you've got, and the family you have—are you willing to sacrifice this for the sake of Allah?" Other references related to sacrifice include sacrifice by working hard to maintain sharia in the new land and sacrifice by going into battle to expand the state and to defend the territories that have been taken over by ISIS. Overall, references to martyrdom rank low, while historical precedence and playing a part in a historic movement with world impact is repeated much more throughout the sample.

The notion that one can be a part of something bigger than oneself and be engaged in a historic world-changing enterprise may speak to Western millennial viewers. Some millennial viewers in the West may have come of age cultivating what June Edmunds and Brian Turner refer to as "global consciousness"—a connection across generational collectivities that is established as a result of shared traumatic media events unconstrained by national boundaries.[35] However, in this case, the viewer, the potential recruit, is being situated as what Karl Mannheim refers to as "antagonistic generational unit."[36] In other words, ISIS is playing on the fact that certain Western youth are witnessing uncensored global events and engaging with what Lilie Chouliaraki refers to as "distant suffering."[37] Yet the IS fighters take on a different and alternative perspective as to how this suffering has come about—namely that this suffering is not a result of their doing but as a result of Western foreign policy. In this case, the themes of women and children as victims of Western violence plays heavily, contributing to both the themes of seeking justice as well as the directive themes toward the viewer, implying that the viewer lacks morality by not rescuing or protecting these victims. These themes arise through statements such as "Our sisters in Fallujah day after day give birth to deformed babies." Or "the child that got beheaded for being a Muslim," or "your sisters have been violated." In other words, the fighters actively frame themselves as upholding values anchored in their perspective of what is morally imperative, given the ongoing war brought by the West into Muslim states. This may have the effect of positioning the viewers as being apathetic and indifferent to the suffering of fellow Muslims because of their continued inaction. The intention seems to be that the viewers should feel guilty for their inaction, and that the viewers' only recourse to alleviate such guilt is by getting up and joining the movement.

For example, in ISIS's English-language documentary entitled *Al Anbar Spring*,[38] young British citizens sit among other English-speaking IS fighters sharing their stories of why they chose to leave England to join ISIS. One of the young men tells viewers, "You are sitting on your couches while today Muslims are being slaughtered in every corner of the world. What will be your excuse to Allah?"[39] Another young man in the same documentary tells viewers, "The Muslims in the West number in the millions, and they are capable of inflicting mass carnage."[40] In *Iraq Risen Alive*, another fighter says, "Oh you youth of the Muslim nation, rise up to give support to your religion and let the first route be the support of your brethren on the mujahid land of the two rivers."[41]

Affinity

Dahlgren defines affinity as a sense of belonging to a group despite potential differences among its members. The concept is very similar to Benedict Andersen's "imagined community,"[42] in that ISIS foreign fighters are framing themselves as part of a movement whose members share an image of their communion. Affinity is thus a dimension in the circuit in which trust is central.[43] Dahlgren frames trust by referencing the work of Robert Putnam,[44] who differentiates between "thick" and "thin" trust. Thick trust is defined as the "general honesty and expectations of reciprocity that we accord people we don't know personally but whom we feel we can have satisfactory exchange with."[45]

Several findings emerge from foreign fighters' testimony, which suggest a sense of belonging despite differences, as well as feelings of thick trust. Within the sample, each of the fighters appears to be of the millennial generation (i.e., born between 1980 and 2000). Those from the UK feature most frequently, followed by Australia and Belgium. Other Western countries represented by foreign fighters include Canada, Finland, France, and Moldova. Roughly half of the sample consisted of native English speakers. The other half spoke a range of languages but were presented with English subtitles. This suggests the intended audience is English speakers in Western countries. Overall, these particular findings indicate that ISIS is actively targeting Western millennials for recruitment by presenting "trustworthy" Western millennials whom those viewers are likely to relate to and feel a sense of conviviality with individually, in addition to cultivating a sense of belonging to the overall collectivity.

Another finding that has emerged central to affinity is that a number of the fighters reflected on their lives before joining the caliphate. They describe, in detail, their experiences back in the Western nation where they were born. Within these reflections, having money and a family in the West before deciding to join the caliphate is referenced most often. In addition, the fighters often reference the character traits of themselves and other fighters who had left their homes to join the Islamic State. In such cases, these individuals are often framed as being normal, everyday people who only reached their potential after joining the movement and fighting on behalf of the caliphate. As an example of both of these themes, a fighter from Canada describes his journey to the Islamic State, offering this reflection to the viewer:

> Before I come here, to Syria, I had money, I had a family. I had good friends, I had colleagues. You know, I worked as a street janitor and made over two thousand dollars a month at this job. It was a very good job. And you know, even though I wasn't rich beyond wildest imaginations, I was uh, I was making it. It was good. I always had family to support me, had friends to support me, so it's not like I was some social outcast, uh, it wasn't like I was some anarchist or somebody who just wants to destroy the world and kill everybody. No, I was a very good person and uh you know mujhadin are regular people too. You know, we get married, we have families, we have lives, you know, just like any other soldier in any other army, we have lives outside of our job.[46]

In eliciting personal disclosures such as in the aforementioned example, it is likely the overall testimonial will have greater resonance with Western viewers in their situated viewing context. These disclosures are a powerful attempt to establish trust between the fighter and the viewer, and the outcome of this framing is that it likely makes the foreign fighters on screen much more relatable, as they appear to be culturally proxemic Western youth.

Further, when addressing the viewer directly, the fighters frequently use the word *brother*, suggesting this is a common practice of addressing one another in the collectivity. Andersen suggests that the promotion of national vernaculars has an essential role in the creation of an imagined national identity.[47] The use of *brother* in these cases acts to demand affinity from the viewer, as it is a direct address to them, which can be read as either a formal (i.e., Quranic reference) or an informal reference (i.e., slang), depending on how the viewer is situated. *You*, *we*, and *us* are also frequent word choices that are used by the fighters in direct addresses to the audience, as if the viewer is a member of the collectivity already.

The foreign fighters are millennials speaking in accessible languages in an attempt to engage fellow millennials situated in similar circumstances, as they were themselves back in the West, before deciding to join ISIS. This sense of commonality is extended further by the fact that more than half of the fighters are presented through close-up shots, taking up most of the frame. As Carey Jewitt and Rumiko Oyama argue, the use of close-ups tends to position the subject being filmed as if they belong or should belong to "our group."[48] In this case, it conveys a sense of close social distance in which the viewer is "brought in" close to the fighter, as if to simulate a face-to-face conversation.

Contact is established between subjects and viewers when subjects look directly at the viewer by maintaining an eyeline that is fixed to the center of the camera lens. Gunther Kress and Theo van Leeuwen call this kind of contact "demand" images, wherein the people in the picture symbolically demand something from the viewer,[49] a feature that Jewitt and Oyama refer to as "imaginary contact."[50] In filmmaking, these techniques become devices that are essential to establishing trust. Yet direct eye contact only occurs in less than half of the sample. More often, the fighters' sightline is off center, which suggests that their trustworthiness may not be read as strong as it would be if they were maintaining direct eye contact with the viewer, and as a result they may be slightly less believable despite being engaged in delivering a personal message to the viewer, particularly after establishing a close social distance through the use of close-ups.

Knowledge

Knowledge in civic cultures relates to the concept of proximity. Antonio La Pastina and Joseph Straubhaar define proximity as fluid but argue that it tends to be defined by historical and linguistic commonalities.[51] Koichi Iwabuchi extends this take on proximity, explaining that it is also often related to the ideas of desire and aspiration, as well as familiarity.[52] Mediated knowledges tend to be more readily acquired and circulated much quicker if those individuals appearing on screen share similar traits, contexts, and experiences as the viewer. When affinity becomes established between the subject and the viewer, it often establishes a closer proxemic accessibility. Consider the fact that throughout the entire sample, there is a constant disclosure of emotions and feelings that the fighters themselves are experiencing now that they are living in the newly established caliphate:

> "This is one of the best feelings I've had in my life."
> "I don't have the words to express myself about the happiness to be here."
> "I don't think there's anything better than living in the land of the Khalifa."
> "I'm thinking like I'm still dreaming. I'm feeling like I'm still dreaming. I'm thinking like I'm in a dream world. And I wake up and I'm like no, I'm in Raqqa, I'm here in Sham, allah akbir!"
> "I wish for nothing more."
> "You have to be here to understand what I'm saying."

These expressions act to simultaneously pass knowledge on to the viewer while also positioning the fighter in an open, transparent, and reflexive manner. This has the effect of reducing the proxemic distance between the accessibility to the knowledge they are sharing with the viewer and the impact that shared knowledge actually has in resonating with the viewer. In this case, the most prevalent theme was the honor the fighter felt by being a member of ISIS, followed by feelings of extreme joy and elation, and third most frequent were expressions regarding how the fighter felt better now (as a member of ISIS living in the caliphate) than they ever felt living in the West. Fighters also frequently describe vignettes from day-to-day life in the Islamic State. The fighters repeatedly assure the viewer that there is security in the caliphate, that it is a safe place to live and have a family, that infrastructure such as hospitals and schools is available, and that law and order are being enforced.

Dahlgren suggests that literacy plays a key role in the formation of civic knowledges, as citizens need to make sense of what is circulating in the public sphere. Themes that emerged related to this sense of literacy include references to individual passages in the Quran and Islamic history, as well as the procedural elements of enacting and maintaining sharia law. Much of the knowledge put forth concerns historical precedence of past attempts to establish and maintain a caliphate, comparison to other groups, the history of Western influence in the region, and the knowledge of the fighters in and of themselves as they appear on screen, documenting what they often frame as a historical transition as they work to return the region to what ISIS argues is its rightful place.

The erasure of what are considered sovereign borders (particularly related to Sykes-Picot) also appeared as a prevalent theme related to knowledge that underpins ISIS's philosophy. David Harvey argues that the state acts as "the primary site for the production of geographical knowledges necessary for the creation, maintenance and enhancement of its powers."[53] Islamic State fighters attempt to produce such knowledge in the form of critical perspectives on a history in which borders were created by foreign powers, and now ISIS is actively engaged in erasing these borders through military action. This messaging actively situates ISIS's anti-Western ideology. As one British national put it, "We don't need any democracy, we don't need communism, we don't need anything like that. All we need is sharia."

Transnational activism often appropriates counter-hegemonic discourses and action strategies as a means of constructing that movement's identity and to engage in coalition building.[54] The most prevalent findings that emerge related to knowledge tend to occur through counter-hegemonic messaging themes, the top ranking of which was that lies are being told about ISIS by the Western news media and non-ISIS-supporting Muslims. It is also important to point out that in only one case, a fighter recommends that the viewer should not listen to their family when it comes to their decision to join ISIS.

Knowledge related to Islamic history and dogma, knowledge of emotional landscapes one may encounter by joining the Islamic State, geographical knowledge, and knowledge concerning the infrastructure, resources, and ontological security available in the caliphate all act to define ISIS's baseline perspectives on the social world they argue they are creating within this newly formed state. Acquiring the aforementioned areas of knowledge enables the viewer to develop a sense of competency concerning the philosophical and ideological constructs of the Islamic State, compelling the viewer to then learn more through studying key texts that the foreign fighters often cite.

Practices and Discussion

Given the fact that these videos were produced as testimonials in which many of the fighters are shown in group settings with other fighters, sharing their stories together, it reveals that collective storytelling, in and of itself, acts as an essential and routine practice for members of ISIS. Through the practices of foreign fighters telling stories, they are engaging in problem solving, offering their solutions to the framed conflict with the West and its allies in the region, as well as explaining their interpretations of historic precedence. In addition, they offer a vision on which they have personally affixed their future as a member of the Islamic State. This situates ISIS as "being able to refer to the past without being locked in it."[55]

As previously mentioned, throughout the sample, the fighters address the viewer directly, confronting the viewer with critiques about his or her life in the West as he or she sits watching the video in the West. ISIS fighters continuously suggest that the viewer is enjoying a "life of comfort," which is typically followed up right away with critiques that the viewer is "living in sin." This tactic of direct address and critique enables the fighters to "open the door for social discomfort."[56] Of course, most of the time these critiques occur, the fighter will then immediately transition to the life of honor and sacrifice that he and his fellow fighters are enjoying, in direct juxtaposition to the material life of the viewer. Fighters, throughout the sample, position themselves as authority figures in terms of how things are talked about, what topics are discussed, and the form and style in which these practices are to transpire. Dahlgren notes that this is an important element in the civic culture model because "across time practices become traditions and experiences become collective memory."[57]

Children are present in the majority of the videos and are shown with the fighter as he engages in storytelling practices. This indicates that these practices are being passed along, not just to the viewer but also to a new generation that is coming of age in the caliphate and that will carry on such practices on into the future. Their presence is also obviously a ploy to soften the image of the fighters and to make them more accessible to the viewer, painting a picture of a safe community with smiling children at play under the protection of trustworthy adults.

Identities

The foreign fighters in this analysis hail from a wide range of nations including Canada, Chile, Finland, France, Indonesia, Moldova, Morocco, and South Africa, and they are attempting to situate their identity as a collective of transnational, "cosmopolitan" foreign fighters. The cosmopolitan is not an identity that emerges from pity or sympathy or regret for the distant other; rather, it is produced from a fundamental need "to become" a member of a global collectivity arising from, and bound by, utter realism.[58] Cosmopolitans find themselves in a world where there are issues and risks stretching beyond the borders of their nation-states, and because of such risks, it prompts them to form connections that cross borders in order to manage those risks.[59] Based on the findings in this study, it is clear that ISIS's Western millennial foreign fighters are framing themselves and their involvement with the Islamic State as a kind of "cosmopolitan pilgrimage" based on a historical trajectory of world events and a moral imperative to impact those events moving forward.

Conclusion

These findings may not offer a complete, or even a satisfactory answer to the larger question that opened this chapter: Why would millennials who grew up in secular Europe, the UK, Australia, Canada, or the United States leave decent lives, good families, great schools, well-earned careers, and so on, in order to join a militant movement that is in direct opposition to their home countries? Although the findings may not provide a complete answer, it is important to recall that these findings are based on the direct testimony of fighters, including how they answered that question verbatim themselves.

What these findings signal is that after nearly eighteen years of the West's global war on terror, movements like the Islamic State are able to form and metastasize at record-setting speeds by employing a narrative that explicitly makes the case that the war the West has waged against Muslims, both at home and abroad, has been devastating. By framing their narrative as a political movement and engaging in transmedia strategies that cultivate an alternative news paradigm, the Islamic State's recruitment content activates the unique cultural, social, and political contexts from which Western millennial Muslims came of age in the West post-9/11. ISIS and related movements are now able to capitalize off of the West's post-9/11 political discourse and its social and cultural implications, in order to establish a pathway from which the Islamic State can engage, talk to, and recruit individuals from the West to join their movement.

The tremendous difficulty for the West in attempting to counter this narrative, much less how that narrative travels, is that much of what the foreign fighters reference in these videos is indeed historically accurate. The continued intervention of the West in Muslim states, the further amplification of anti-Muslim discourse now in mainstream political discourse throughout the West, the rise of well-funded Muslim hate groups, travel bans from Muslim countries to the West, etc., are now well-established facets of the Western world in 2018. Yet these are the same characteristics that feed directly into the image of the West the Islamic State creates for its recruits to oppose. Ultimately, for the West to counter this narrative, it would require not only a monumental shift in both foreign and domestic policies concerning Muslims and Muslim states; it would also require a complete cultural, social, and political rewiring of post-9/11 Western society as well.

Notes

1. J. Siberell, "Country Reports on Terrorism 2015—Special Briefing," June 2, 2016, https://so.usmission.gov/country-reports-terrorism-2015/; Bibi van Winkel and Eva Entenmann, eds., "The Foreign Fighters Phenomenon in the European Union: Profiles, Threats & Policies," April 2016, https://icct.nl/wp-content/uploads/2016/03/ICCT-Report_Foreign-Fighters-Phenomenon-in-the-EU_1-April-2016_including-AnnexesLinks.pdf.
2. Terence McCoy, "How ISIS and Other Jihadists Persuaded Thousands of Westerners to Fight Their War of Extremism," *Washington Post*, June 17, 2014, https://www.washingtonpost.com/news/morning-mix/wp/2014/06/17/how-isis-persuaded-thousands-of-westerners-to-fight-its-war-of-extremism/?utm_term=.ecfe433dace4.
3. Alex P. Schmid, "Radicalisation, De-Radicalisation, Counter-Radicalisation: A Conceptual Discussion and Literature Review," *ICCT Research*, 2013, https://www.icct.nl/download/file/ICCT-Schmid-Radicalisation-De-Radicalisation-Counter-Radicalisation-March-2013.pdf.

4. Arun Kundnani, *The Muslims Are Coming!: Islamophobia, Extremism, and the Domestic War on Terror* (London: Verso, 2013).
5. Ibid.
6. Arun Kundnani, "Radicalisation: The Journey of a Concept," *Race & Class* 54, no. 2 (2012): 5.
7. Ibid.
8. Ibid., 4.
9. See Walter Laqueur, "Terror's New Face: The Radicalization and Escalation of Modern Terrorism," *Harvard International Review* 20, no. 4 (1998): 48-51; Marc Sageman, *Understanding Terror Networks* (Philadelphia: University of Pennsylvania, 2004); Marc Sageman, *Leaderless Jihad: Terror Networks in the Twenty-First Century* (Philadelphia: University of Pennsylvania Press, 2008); and Quintan Wiktorowicz, *Radical Islam Rising: Muslim Extremism in the West* (Oxford, UK: Oxford University Press, 2005).
10. Kundnani, "Radicalisation," 8.
11. Schmid, "Radicalisation," 4.
12. Ibid.
13. David W. Brannan, Philip Francis Esler, and N. T. A. Strindberg, "Talking to 'Terrorists': Towards an Independent Analytical Framework for the Study of Violent Substate Activism," *Studies in Conflict & Terrorism* 24 (2001): 3.
14. Corinna Mullin, "The US Discourse on Political Islam: Is Obama's a Truly Post-'War on Terror' Administration?" *Critical Studies on Terrorism* 5, no. 1 (2011): 263–281.
15. Schmid, "Radicalisation."
16. Kundnani, "Radicalisation."
17. Thomas Hegghammer, "The Rise of Muslim Foreign Fighters: Islam and the Globalization of Jihad," *International Security* 35, no. 3 (2010): 53–94.
18. Hegghammer, "The Rise of Muslim Foreign Fighters," 3.
19. Ibid.
20. David Malet, *Foreign Fighters: Transnational Identity in Civil Conflicts* (Oxford, UK: Oxford University Press, 2013).
21. Hegghammer, "The Rise of Muslim Foreign Fighters," 56.
22. Doug McAdam, Sidney Tarrow, and Charles Tilly, *Dynamics of Contention* (Cambridge: Cambridge University Press, 2001), as cited in Bart Cammaerts, "Four Approaches to Alternative Media," in *Understanding Alternative Media,* eds. Olga Bailey, Bart Cammaerts, and Nico Carpentier (Maidenhead, UK: Open University Press, 2008): 3–34.
23. Bureau of Counterterrorism and Countering Violent Extremism, *Country Reports on Terrorism 2015*, June 2, 2016, https://www.state.gov/documents/organization/258249.pdf.
24. PBSNewshour, "German Writer Spends 10 Days with the Islamic State," December 4, 2014, https://www.youtube.com/watch?v=JFNVU2TyJFo.
25. Henry Jenkins, "Transmedia 202: Further Reflections," July 31, 2011, http://henryjenkins.org/blog/2011/08/defining_transmedia_further_re.html.
26. Akil A. Awan, "Virtual Jihadist Media: Function, Legitimacy, and Radicalizing Efficacy," *European Journal of Cultural Studies* 10, no. 3 (2007): 389–408.
27. Michael Krona discusses this strategy in chapter 5 of this volume.
28. Peter Dahlgren, "Reconfiguring Civic Culture in the New Media Milieu," in *Media and the Restyling of Politics: Consumerism, Celebrity, and Cynicism*, eds. John Corder and Dick Pels (London: Sage, 2003), 151–170.

29. Nick Couldry, Hilde Stephansen, Aristea Fotopoulou, Richard MacDonald, Wilma Clark, and Luke Dickens, "Digital Citizenship? Narrative Exchange and the Changing Terms of Civic Culture," *Citizenship Studies* 18, no. 6–7 (2014): 615–629.
30. Dahlgren, "Reconfiguring Civic Culture," 153.
31. Kathleen German discusses ISIS's use of the cinema verité style of filmmaking in chapter 6 of this volume.
32. Dahlgren, "Reconfiguring Civic Culture," 156.
33. Ernest Gellner, *Encounters with Nationalism* (Oxford, UK: Blackwell, 1995).
34. Hegghammer, "The Rise of Muslim Foreign Fighters."
35. June Edmunds and Brian S. Turner, "Global Generations: Social Change in the Twentieth Century," *British Journal of Sociology* 56, no. 4 (2005): 559–577.
36. Karl Mannheim, *Essays on the Sociology of Knowledge* (London: Routledge, 1952).
37. Lilie Chouliaraki, *The Spectatorship of Suffering* (London: Sage, 2006).
38. *Al Anbar Spring*, al-Furqan, 2012.
39. Ibid.
40. Ibid.
41. *Iraq Risen Alive*, al-Furqan, 2012.
42. Benedict Anderson, *Imagined Communities: Reflections on the Origins and Spread of Nationalism*, rev. and ext. edition (London: Verso, 1991).
43. Dahlgren, "Reconfiguring Civic Culture."
44. Robert Putnam, *Bowling Alone: The Collapse and Revival of American Community* (New York: Simon & Schuster, 2000), 136 as cited in Dahlgren, "Reconfiguring Civic Culture," 146.
45. Dahlgren, "Reconfiguring Civic Culture," 147.
46. This interview was featured in a video circulated by al-Ghuraba, a media outlet that supports and circulates ISIS material.
47. Anderson, "Imagined Communities."
48. Carey Jewitt and Rumiko Oyama, "Visual Meaning: A Social Semiotic Approach," *Handbook of Visual Analysis*, eds. Theo van Leeuwen and Carey Jewitt (London: Sage, 2001): 135–156.
49. Gunther Kress and Theo van Leeuwen, *Reading Images: The Grammar of Visual Design* (London: Routledge, 1996).
50. Jewitt and Oyama, "Visual Meaning."
51. Antonio C. La Pastina and Joseph D. Straubhaar, "Multiple Proximities between Television Genres and Audiences—The Schism between Telenovelas' Global Distribution and Local Consumption," *Gazette* 67, no. 3 (2005): 271–288.
52. Koichi Iwabuchi, "Becoming 'Culturally Proximate': The A/scent of Japanese Idol Dramas in Taiwan," in *Asian Media Productions*, ed. Brian Moeran (Richmond, Surrey: Curzon, 2001), 54–74.
53. David Harvey, *Spaces of Capital: Towards a Critical Geography* (Edinburgh, UK: Edinburgh University Press, 2001), 213.
54. Bart Cammaerts, "Media and Communication Strategies of Glocalized Activists: Beyond Media-Centric Thinking," in *Reclaiming the Media: Communication Rights and Expanding Democratic Media Roles*, eds. Bart Cammaerts and Nico Carpentier (Chicago: University of Chicago Press, 2007), 265.
55. Dahlgren, "Reconfiguring Civic Culture," 158.

56. Ibid.
57. Ibid.
58. Ulrich Beck, "Cosmopolitanism as Imagined Communities of Global Risk," *American Behavioral Scientist* 55, no. 10 (2011): 1346–1361.
59. Ibid.

Bibliography

Anderson, Benedict. *Imagined Communities: Reflections on the Origin and Spread of* Nationalism, rev. and extended ed. London: Verso, 1991.

Awan, Akil A. "Virtual Jihadist Media: Function, Legitimacy, and Radicalizing Efficacy." *European Journal of Cultural Studies* 10, no. 3 (2007): 389–408.

Beck, Ulrich. "Cosmopolitanism as Imagined Communities of Global Risk." *American Behavioral Scientist* 55, no. 10 (2011): 1346–1361.

Brannan, David W., Philip Francis Esler, and N. T. A. Strindberg. "Talking to 'Terrorists': Towards an Independent Analytical Framework for the Study of Violent Substate Activism." *Studies in Conflict & Terrorism* 24 (2001): 33–34.

Bureau of Counterterrorism and Countering Violent Extremism. *Country Reports on Terrorism 2015*. June 2, 2016. https://www.state.gov/documents/organization/258249.pdf.

Cammaerts, Bart. "Media and Communication Strategies of Glocalized Activists: Beyond Media-Centric Thinking." In *Reclaiming the Media: Communication Rights and Expanding Democratic Media Roles*, edited by Bart Cammaerts and Nico Carpentier, 265–288. Chicago: University of Chicago Press, 2007.

Cammaerts, Bart. "Four Approaches to Alternative Media." In *Understanding Alternative Media*, edited by Olga Bailey, Bart Cammaerts, and Nico Carpentier, 3–34. Maidenhead, UK: Open University Press, 2008.

Chouliaraki, Lilie. *The Spectatorship of Suffering.* London: Sage, 2006.

Couldry, Nick, Hilde Stephansen, Aristea Fotopoulou, Richard MacDonald, Wilma Clark, and Luke Dickens. "Digital Citizenship? Narrative Exchange and the Changing Terms of Civic Culture." *Citizenship Studies* 18, no. 6–7 (2014): 615–629.

Dahlgren, Peter. "Reconfiguring Civic Culture in the New Media Milieu." In *Media and the Restyling of Politics: Consumerism, Celebrity, and Cynicism*, edited by John Corder and Dick Pels, 151–170. London: Sage, 2003.

Edmunds, June, and Brian S. Turner. "Global Generations: Social Change in the Twentieth Century." *British Journal of Sociology* 56, no. 4 (2005): 559–577.

Gellner, Ernest. *Encounters with Nationalism.* Oxford, UK: Blackwell, 1995.

Harvey, David. *Spaces of Capital: Towards a Critical Geography.* Edinburgh, UK: Edinburgh University Press, 2001.

Hegghammer, Thomas. "The Rise of Muslim Foreign Fighters: Islam and the Globalization of Jihad." *International Security* 35, no. 3 (2010): 53–94.

Iwabuchi, Koichi. "Becoming 'Culturally Proximate': The A/scent of Japanese Idol Dramas in Taiwan." In *Asian Media Productions*, edited by Brian Moeran, 54–74. New York: Routledge 2001.

Jewitt, Carey, and Rumiko Oyama. "Visual Meaning: A Social Semiotic Approach." In *Handbook of Visual Analysis*, edited by Theo van Leeuwen and Carey Jewitt, 135–156. London: Sage, 2001.

Kress, Gunther, and Theo van Leeuwen. *Reading Images: The Grammar of Visual Design*. London: Routledge, 1996.

Kundnani, Arun. "Radicalisation: The Journey of a Concept." *Race & Class* 54, no. 2 (2012): 3–25.

Kundnani, Arun. *The Muslims Are Coming!: Islamophobia, Extremism, and the Domestic War on Terror*. London: Verso, 2015.

La Pastina, Antonio C., and Joseph D. Straubhaar. "Multiple Proximities between Television Genres and Audiences: The Schism between Telenovelas' Global Distribution and Local Consumption." *Gazette* 67, no. 3 (2005): 271–288.

Laqueur, Walter. "Terrorism's New Face." *Harvard International Review* 20, no. 4 (1998): 168–178.

Malet, David. *Foreign Fighters: Transnational Identity in Civil Conflicts*. Oxford, UK: Oxford University Press, 2013.

Mannheim, Karl. *Essays on the Sociology of Knowledge*. London: Routledge, 1952.

McCoy, Terence. "How ISIS and Other Jihadists Persuaded Thousands of Westerners to Fight Their War of Extremism." *Washington Post*, June 17, 2014. https://www.washingtonpost.com/news/morning-mix/wp/2014/06/17/how-isis-persuaded-thousands-of-westerners-to-fight-its-war-of-extremism/?utm_term=.ecfe433dace4.

Mullin, Corinna. "The US Discourse on Political Islam: Is Obama's a Truly Post-'War on Terror' Administration?" *Critical Studies on Terrorism* 5, no. 1 (2011): 263–281.

PBSNewshour. "German Writer Spends 10 Days with the Islamic State." December 4, 2014. https://www.youtube.com/watch?v=JFNVU2TyJFo.

Sageman, Marc. *Understanding Terror Networks*. Philadelphia: University of Pennsylvania Press, 2004.

Sageman, Marc. *Leaderless Jihad: Terror Networks in the Twenty-First Century*. Philadelphia: University of Pennsylvania Press, 2008.

Schmid, Alex P. "Radicalisation, De-Radicalisation, Counter-Radicalisation: A Conceptual Discussion and Literature Review." *ICCT Research*, 2013. https://www.icct.nl/download/file/ICCT-Schmid-Radicalisation-De-Radicalisation-Counter-Radicalisation-March-2013.pdf.

Siberell, J. "Country Reports on Terrorism 2015—Special Briefing." June 2, 2016. https://so.usmission.gov/country-reports-terrorism-2015/.

van Winkel, Bibi, and Eva Entenmann, eds. *The Foreign Fighters Phenomenon in the European Union: Profiles, Threats & Policies*. April 2016. https://icct.nl/wp-content/uploads/2016/03/ICCT-Report_Foreign-Fighters-Phenomenon-in-the-EU_1-April-2016v_including-AnnexesLinks.pdf.

Wiktorowicz, Quintan. *Radical Islam Rising: Muslim Extremism in the West*. Oxford, UK: Oxford University Press, 2005.

MATTHEW PASCARELLA is an independent researcher.

10 Monstrous Performance

Mohammed Emwazi's Transformation

Arthi Chandrasekaran
Nicholas Prephan

On August 22, 2014, *The Irish Daily Mail* exposed the "sadistic brutality" of a British national accused of cutting off the head of American war journalist James Foley. A reporter and prisoner of the Islamic State, Didier Francois, noted that before the execution, Foley endured the psychological torture of mock executions at the hands of a faceless man named Jihadi John, later revealed to be Mohammed Emwazi. Emwazi was the ringleader of "his fellow British jihadi 'Beatles,' Paul and Ringo, [who] saved their most vicious beatings for Mr. Foley."[1] This villain authored and orchestrated a series of victories in the name of the Islamic State of Iraq and Syria (ISIS) through the clandestine distribution of videos depicting the violent executions of United States citizens—white cisgender men from the American heartland. This malevolence was compared by some news media outlets to the actions of a horrific slasher movie villain; in fact, *Vice News* announced at the end of 2014 that Jihadi John was recognized as their Monster of the Year.[2] The first video of Jihadi John's series, which features Foley's execution, encapsulates the push and pull between normalizing and not normalizing the monsterization of terrorists.

Jihadi John captured the Western imagination by performing a series of horrific acts while acting out his role as ISIS's executioner. He appears in seven different ISIS videos and conducted beheadings in six of them. The seventh video functioned as a ransom message to the Japanese government, demanding an exchange of money for the release of two hostages. Of his captives, five of the six victims were civilians. Three of his victims were journalists from the United States and Japan, and two were British aid workers[3]. This chapter focuses on the first video, in which Jihadi John beheads American journalist James Foley. Foley exemplifies the quintessential good guy and American hero, having served in Teach for America in addition to frequently working in the Middle East on humanitarian missions. Foley's death is significant because he was the first American citizen killed by ISIS. This video was the world's introduction to Jihadi

John, making it an ideal vantage point for understanding his construction as a monster.

Framing Jihadi John

Jihadi John was born Mohammed Emwazi in Kuwait. When he was six years old, his family immigrated to the United Kingdom. It is unclear when he became radicalized, but he claims that he suffered discrimination at the hands of British officials multiple times, both at home and abroad. MI5, a British intelligence agency, has stated that he had been connected to a group that was found to be funneling money and weapons to terrorists in Somalia.[4] Emwazi tried to move to Kuwait and start a new life there but was ultimately unsuccessful. He eventually returned to the UK, where he was equally unhappy and left to join ISIS in 2013.[5] In August 2014, the first of his beheading videos was released, with James Foley as his first victim.

Following Jihadi John's unmasking as Mohammad Emwazi by the *Washington Post* early in 2015, he was killed by a United States drone aircraft by November of the same year. Much like the monster he was portrayed as being, he died a villain's death. Jihadi John "evaporated" with a clean hit, much like a ghost leaving this world for the one beyond.[6] Emwazi's death was later confirmed by ISIS's news outlet, *Dabiq*.[7] Despite his death, Emwazi continues to be one of the most prominent faces of the ISIS terror threat. His documented actions are considered so extreme that years after his death, newspaper articles continue to cite him as an example of how far a radicalized individual will go when given the opportunity to perform.[8] To understand his transformation into a monster requires placing him within the context of an expanding discourse of monstrosity in this contemporary political and cultural moment and then further contextualizing it within the war on terror.

The transformation of Emwazi into Jihadi John is a haunting case study of a nonwhite cisgender male's rage becoming monstrous. Jihadi John is central to the media framing constructed around ISIS, not only because of his gruesome acts toward those held captive by the group but also because he was reported on as if he existed as a monster beyond our imagination that was yet able to endure in this physical reality. News outlets like *The Atlantic* and the *New York Times* condemned Emwazi's brutality, his killings were in the pages of *New York Magazine* and *Newsweek*, and what could be seen of his face became synonymous with monstrosity, as his eyes and thick brow peeked through the slit of a skull-tight black balaclava wrapping, with a knife brandished in his left hand as he stood in front of a video camera.[9]

Jihadi John's cultural moment reveals the selective attention paid to how corporeal violence against the other materializes through the evocation of "terrorist." *Terrorist* is a term that is as melodramatic as it is provocative, resulting in the creation of monsters creeping from international sites and into the heartland, as the United States negotiates its own relationship with phrases like "domestic terrorism." Terrorists are "concurrently an unfathomable, unknowable, and hysterical monstrosity" that serves to strike fear into the hearts and minds of Americans.[10]

Monsters operate in a unique rhetorical space. They are frightening deviants from whom the rest of society needs protection. They are often deployed as "agents of moralized fear in political speech."[11] The construction of a monster causes dissonance within audiences, who draw back in disgust while simultaneously leaning in to see the grotesque display. The label serves ideological ends, as it now highlights the individual categorized that way as an inhuman other. The specific monster Jihadi John enacts, classified by Jasbir Puar as "terrorist-monster," serves as a rhetorical foil to "all that is just, human, and good."[12] However, rather than having the label placed on him, Jihadi John appropriates the label himself, presenting himself in distinctly monstrous ways.

This chapter seeks to understand Jihadi John's performed monstrosity as a means of presenting a queered masculinity. Jihadi John's masculinity is queer in that it is created as consequence of the corporeality of Western militarized patriotism and its accompanying body and image. Jasbir Puar states that the construction of the terrorist relies on "failed heterosexuality . . . and a certain queer monstrosity."[13] Monstrosity serves as a queer masculinity that gives Jihadi John, as well as all of ISIS, a means of celebrating their deviations from Western norms. This chapter focuses on the intersecting literature on monstrosity and terrorism. It then examines Jihadi John as a nonnormative embodiment that is beyond human before finally exploring what the performance of monster by terrorist bodies means for ISIS recruitment and the materialization of a recurrent fear.

Terrorist as Definition and Monster

Jeremey Jeffrey Cohen's Monster Theory offers an essential critical frame for understanding the impact the monster metaphor has on ISIS-related recruitment.[14] Viewing Jihadi John through this lens helps us understand the endless potential monstrosity offers, while further clarifying Jihadi John's role in representing his organization. Monster Theory is especially helpful in locating and defining monsters and what monsters do. Monsters comprise a multitude of fragments that create the epistemological wholes temporarily assembled together in what Cohen refers to as a monstrous body.[15] Cohen presents an understanding of not only where monsters burst forth from but further situates where they reside. His ideas provide an orientation and organization for defining and understanding the animation of monstrosity. This orientation first crystalizes in his first aspect of monstrosity that makes the claim that "the monster's body is a cultural body . . . it is a construct and a projection."[16] Cohen goes on to describe the monster as the "embodiment of a certain cultural moment—a time, a feeling, or even a place."[17] Through this interpretation of the monster's body as a cultural body, Cohen explains that the monstrous body is pure culture. Monstrosity, and its performance, is negotiated in terms of upheaval and displacement, reducing the gap between itself and the created cultural moment into which it is received to be born again. Cohen's Monster Theory is helpful in situating and localizing the cultural moment that inspires the apparition of the monstrous body and furthermore constructs the primary lens to utilize when gazing on the monstrous terrorist body. Viewing the terrorist as monster by utilizing this perspective helps us better understand the ways in which the West's gaze evokes the monster into materialization. The monster exists because of a culture that summons it.

This metaphorical summoning is cast through mediated channels. Christina Spens, writer of the textbook *Shooting Hipsters: Rethinking Dissent in the Age of PR*, says there are probably more terrorist representations in media than in reality and that often this performance extends into reality when individuals challenging mainstream Western beliefs are treated as if they are villains. According to Spens, "Dehumanization is key to propaganda, whichever side is controlling its narrative arc, because it simplifies the complexities of human conflict to basic 'good' versus 'evil' ideas; a simple pantomime logic that is easily understood and consumed by the public."[18] Terrorists, and thereby monsters, are able to come into existence to aid in the simplification of conflict. The clearest way to delineate good from evil is to establish monsters and those fighting against them. Jihadi John, then, becomes a clear evil for the West to fight.

Definitions of masculinity in Western countries queer and exclude people of color, especially Muslim men. Molefi Asante, in the foreword to the book *Global Masculinities and Manhood*, articulates how "the defining characteristics of masculinity have rested in the hands of European males."[19] He states that this control over what is considered manly leads to a disempowerment of Asian males, particularly Muslim men who live in Western countries. Even if they act in accordance with Western masculine norms, they are denied access to nondeviant definitions of the label.[20] This inability to cross the border of hegemonic masculinity creates an anxiety in the mind of Muslim men in Western countries, who wonder if they will be accepted as virile and viable. Terrorists-as-monster can serve as a definable and attainable masculinity for such displaced men.

The persuasive potential of Jihadi John's monstrosity perhaps starts with his voice, drenched in a British accent, incongruous with the terrorist body that it is attached to. At the time of Jihadi John's appearance, Western members were rare within ISIS. Only fifty-three Americans are publicly known to have traveled to Syria to join ISIS, according to Seamus Hughes, the deputy director of George

Washington University's Program on Extremism in a 2017 interview with *The Atlantic*.[21] Yet the United States, according to the article, stopped more than a hundred other potential members in the process of preparing to travel or plan an attack in the name of ISIS. These Western members demonstrate that ISIS is a new culture bound to its location in Iraq, Syria, or the Levant.[22] The body of the ISIS Western recruit is not racialized so much as it is able to embody this new culture. ISIS serves as a self-selected orientation in which the marks of an individual and his or her associated individuality is obscured into monstrosity. Racial designations take a rhetorical back seat to the terrorist-monster label they present.

Monsters symbolize precarity for Casey Kelly and the uneven distribution of bodily vulnerable, class, and nationalism.[23] Precarity is the "politically induced condition in which certain populations suffer from failing social and economic networks of support and become differentially exposed to injury, violence, and death," according to Judith Butler.[24] These conditions reveal the vulnerability and desperation of a monster's actions. Precarity results in a frenzy of emotion, a rhetorical *affect*, that is routed into monstrous action.

Kelly uses precarity to explain monstrosity as concurrently a trope, an apparatus, and the symbolic return of the repressed. The radical otherness of oppressed bodies is highlighted as they negotiate periphery ideologies within a society that neither recognizes nor eradicates them. Marginalized individuals have their differences become more salient when they assert their identities that have been kept out of mainstream discourse. Monsters are "uniquely befitting the total fear that saturates the day-to-day lives of millions of Americans who find themselves antagonized by systemic, structured vulnerability: unemployment, limited upward mobility, substandard health care, crumbling infrastructure, environmental degradation, and divestment in the public good."[25]

The terrorist-monster is the resulting materialization of a fear that consumes the Western imagination. Monsters are a nebulous symbol utilized as a rhetorical device by politicians in the West, as these monsters are almost always located in some Eastern nation, resulting in constituents who are bodily safe but emotionally and mentally afraid.

Furthermore, Jasbir Puar's work on the terrorist-as-monster helps show the full potential of what a monster can do. Specifically, Puar articulates the role of terrorist in "haunting." Haunting here "signals the primacy of the past and our inheritance of the past" into our present.[26] Terrorists, like ghosts, lie in wait as they usher our futurities, theorizes Puar, and act as an approach that keeps an eye out for "shadows, ephemera, energies, ethereal forces, textures, spirit, sensations: haunting is a very particular way of knowing what has happened or is happening." The terrorist threat is, for the most part, imagined. Jihadi John poses no real harm to the average American. However, his monstrous visage fills the Western imagination, lurking behind every corner. This fear, this terror, is precisely what Jihadi John sought to accomplish.

Jihadi John's Performance

The video where Jihadi John purportedly severs the neck of James Foley takes place in the desert. The background of the scene seems to be the midday horizon, where the desert sands meet the sky, dividing the shot perfectly in half. The shot then opens on James Foley in an orange jumpsuit, reminiscent of the jumpsuits used within prisons like Abu Ghraib and Guantanamo Bay. (The history of those jumpsuits is discussed in chapter 8 of this volume.) Foley's hands are bound behind his back as his knees dig into the sandy desert hillside; the sky is strikingly clear and blue. Jihadi John is clad in all black but for his tan sand boots. He has on his left arm what seems to be a gun holster, a tobacco-colored strap that is accented by the all-black outfit. If it is a gun holster, this is not set up to be the preferred tool in this video. Jihadi John keeps his face covered at all times. By remaining faceless, he is able to tap into the nature of the monster as "difference made flesh."[27]

The face wrap gives Jihadi John an alien appearance, so very different from anything Western audiences encounter in their daily lives. It also emphasizes a visual difference between Jihadi John and the audience, as the wrap is reminiscent of the same tropes evoked in Western horror films that revolve around a faceless monster. This striking figure conjures up mental images of a slasher villain, like Michael Myers or Jason Voorhees, who also keep their faces covered. The same sort of monstrous otherness that these magical horror characters are able to embody comes out in Jihadi John's performance. He is able to tap into the same mystic quality that these immortal slashers possess in their films.

Kneeling on the foreground is the all-American war journalist James Foley, brightly lit by the desert sun early in its day. There is a short shadow drenching the sand to the left of Foley. He seems to have an almost military bearing to him, upright posture, well-cut jaw shadowed by facial hair. His hair is kept short; he squints his eyes as he speaks—concentrated on the words he is reading aloud or the harsh glare of sunlight off of the desert sands. There is limited information design. Most notable is the almost opaque gray box that contains white Arabic subtitles that translate what James Foley and Jihadi John are saying. The first words of the video are "In the name of Allah, the most gracious, the most merciful," escaping Jihadi John's lips like the prayer it is.

This invocation of Islam evokes the fantasy of Muslims in the Western imagination. It plays into the Western delusion that all Muslims are terrorists who must be rooted out and dealt with. The terrorist-monster that has been created in the minds of Americans is an image that relies heavily on this mischaracterization. Sophia Rose Arjana describes this situation, stating "Muslims are the monsters of the present, phantasms that result from an imaginary Islam that has been shaped over many centuries."[28] The use of an Islamic prayer by Jihadi John taps into this construction of the Muslim monster. He actively appropriates the framing that the West actively places on him through this prayer. This becomes part of his monstrous performance, as this simple phrase is enough to trigger the fear of the Muslim other that has been engrained in the minds of many, due to a long history of Orientalist and Islamophobic misrepresentation.

The precarity that Casey Kelly theorizes about is what empowers Jihadi John's prayer. The precarity of Jihadi John became apparent when he assumed an almost Orientalized presentation of Muslim identity that had been marginalized in the West and wielded it as a show of strength and notoriety. The prayer connects Jihadi John with his Muslim identity. After the prayer, he stated that "Obama authorized military operations against [ISIS], effectively placing America upon a slippery slope towards a new war front against Muslims." Next is footage of former United States president Barack Obama reading off his public address:

> Good evening. Today I authorized two operations in Iraq—targeted airstrikes to protect our American personnel, and a humanitarian effort to help save thousands of Iraqi civilians who are trapped on a mountain without food and water and facing almost certain death. Let me explain the actions we're taking and why.
>
> First, I said in June—as the terrorist group [ISIS] began an advance across Iraq—that the United States would be prepared to take targeted military action in Iraq if and when we determined that the situation required it. In recent days, these terrorists have continued to move across Iraq, and have neared the city of Erbil, where American diplomats and civilians serve at our consulate and American military personnel advise Iraqi forces.
>
> To stop the advance on Erbil, I've directed our military to take targeted strikes against [ISIS] terrorist convoys should they move toward the city. We intend to stay vigilant, and take action if these terrorist forces threaten our personnel or facilities anywhere in Iraq, including our consulate in Erbil and our embassy in Baghdad. We're also providing urgent assistance to Iraqi government and Kurdish forces so they can more effectively wage the fight against ISIL.

Obama, in this speech, is asserting his political position by performing Western masculinity. His call for airstrikes is portraying strength and the willingness to assist allies in the fight against ISIS. Obama is able to decouple himself from the struggle, stating that he would only attack ISIS if they go after American forces. By only authorizing airstrikes, he appears to rise above the boots-on-the-ground conflict. Obama does not want to get involved in more conflict than he needs to, according to the speech. The former president's exceptionalism is everything that Muslim men are told they can never hope to aspire to. The terrorist-monster label that haunts Muslim males in the West limits their ability to perform Western masculinity. Putting this inside of the video of an execution shows how monstrosity is able to form a new type of masculinity. The terrorist-monster does not have be rhetorically emasculated as they are in the West but can come back to the homeland in order to take back the masculinity that had been stripped from them. Jihadi John's monster image is powerfully masculine. Foley, on the other hand, is in prisoner garb and has his head shaved. His masculinity, Western masculinity, has been neutralized by the monster.

The video then cuts to a shot of bird's-eye footage of what seems to be one of these airstrikes. The footage shows what sanctioned, imperial violence is supposed to look like. The footage is bloodless, with only implied death. There are no bodies, no pain, only a sanitized version of what war is. Jihadi John and James Foley, on the other hand, are living, breathing humans. This return to the visceral nature of a beheading, in contrast to the clean erasure of an airstrike, is one of the hallmarks of monstrosity, as the monster is at its core a sexual being of the flesh.[29] There is no contemplation of the intimate nature associated with flesh during an airstrike, as it is cold and devoid of humanity. The use of a real human body serves as the antithesis to the cold, unfeeling violence of the West. ISIS and Jihadi John juxtapose their violence with that of Obama and the West, showing first the sterile killing of a mechanized airstrike and then a brutal beheading.

A monster kills its victims up close and with intimacy, becoming drenched in their blood and vitality as it rends the flesh of its victims. The previously mentioned slasher killers do not kill from afar. They got their moniker from literally slashing their victims with knives or other sharp objects. Utilizing a body, and not some far-off imagined victim such as those targeted by Obama's airstrikes, marks the beheading of James Foley as the act of a monster.

The screen after the airstrike is black, with serif text that reads "A Message to America," before cutting to the desert scene. There is a suggestion of precarity in this particular message, with ISIS presenting itself as a population that receives bodily damage through the various bombings that are carried out by United States military forces. ISIS frames themselves as precarious by showing that they are constantly under attack by America, in this case via airstrikes. The video concludes with a scripted dialogue that ends with James Foley saying, "I guess all in all, I wish I wasn't American."

In contrast, Jihadi John's body fulfills Foley's last words and wish. Jihadi John is not American; he is terrorist. Jasbir Puar describes terrorism as "the unknowable and inchoate nonwhite outside and evading the knowledge of an internal threat."[30] She goes on to explain that the hunting of terrorists "is dangerous because it consolidates the immense, unrestrained pseudo-patriotic narcissism we are nourishing." Using this definition of narcissism, we are able to examine what's at stake for those who are framed as terrorists. In becoming Jihadi John, Mohammad Emwazi had shucked any remnant of Western culture that remained in or on his body, besides that of his vocal cords. He purposely became a monstrous other, unknowable in his cruelty and inhumanity.

Within the film with James Foley, the terrorist is unmoving for almost a minute and a half as Foley reads his script. Jihadi John's head is cocked to his right, feet shoulder width apart, with his hands empty. His shoulders are broad. He shifts his weight, moving his center of gravity from his left foot to his right before repositioning and distributing his weight across both feet once more. *He knows what he's about do.* The microphone hooked up to Foley captures the sound of swallowing saliva before he continues to record the message's second part addressed to a Foley brother as he articulates the words "think about what you are doing." The camera fades to black, returning quickly to the same scene when Foley is done speaking. Where Jihadi John's hands were empty, now his right hand is resting on Foley's left shoulder, gently gesturing to this man marked by death. In his left hand is a knife. The knife looks sharp but almost too short to cut swiftly. The use of a knife again harkens back to slasher monsters in popular Western cinema. The knife materializes out of nowhere; it is not drawn from a sheath. Jihadi John again takes on a mystical quality, as he can arm himself with weapons that magically appear within his hands seemingly on demand. The gun holster remains empty, showing his disdain for Western tools of domination and war. The knife is an ancient, visceral weapon. It is a bloody, nasty, monstrous weapon, perfect for a monster to wield.

Jihadi John's appearance during this moment is demonstrative of the selective attention paid to how the United States defines terrorism. After killing Foley, Jihadi John wraps his fingers around the collar of another one of his victims at the end of the video, pulling war journalist Steven Joel Sotloff up as yet another visual aid. He says to the screen, "The life of this American citizen, Obama, depends on your next decision." When Jihadi John approaches Foley and attacks him with the knife, there is a cut away where the audience then sees unmoving flesh rising out of a sanguine puddle. Jihadi John ends the video by rhetorically haunting the audience, showing himself as a violent specter who will continue to live in their minds as a constant threat that will never be realized. Puar states that the terrorist monster is able to haunt its audience by keeping them afraid.[31] By beheading one American and threatening to kill another, Jihadi John is able to instill an abject, irrational fear in the West. Cohen reminds us that "the monster always escapes."[32] Jihadi John is able to get away with his crime and even promise more death in the future. By invoking Obama's name, he is addressing the entire West. He puts forth a challenge, knowing that the entire world is powerless to stop his killing. This assertion of monstrous dominance helps grant this video its persuasive power. Jihadi John appears to know what he did was not favorable to some of his viewers, as he gives the West a means of stopping future killings. If Obama gives in to his future demands, the executions will stop—his assumption being that the American president should want to stop future beheadings. However, the audience knows that the demands will not be met, and the rampage will continue.

Jihadi John's video begins with violence. It begins with the United States Air Force dropping a bomb. Before James Foley's death, Jihadi John was unknown in mass media. Yet, the spectacle of a self-proclaimed nation-state cutting off the head of an American journalist captured widespread media attention. The seeming impossibility of Jihadi John's act was transgressive and lawbreaking, and he acted beyond what was socially thought possible from terrorist actors.

The monster is an extreme embodiment of the transgressive, erotic, lawbreaking, or sexual extremes of the human self that must be exiled, destroyed, or repressed. The monster's deviance takes on a separate and extreme second life of practices that must to be committed or that are only acceptable to monsters. The monster's lack of moderation and performance of inhuman extremes steps over the bright line that must never be crossed for those who want to be part of a utopian construction of reality.[33] This is exactly what Jihadi John sought to do. Tapping into the extremes of the human showed just how far he had fallen and how far the West had pushed him as he fell from Western grace. The search for an alternative masculinity had led him to monstrosity, the furthest he could go from the norms of the West that he had seen as his oppressor.

When watching Foley throughout the video, the viewer will observe that he starts off with his forehead gleaming in the sun. His head is shaven, and he has visible and defined features. Lithe from capture, he kneels. He stands strongly in this video. His shoulders are squared toward the camera, and his chin is pointed forward. He is performing an address for the camera. The words come evenly, as if he has read them before, is well read, or both. When speaking theoretically on how the United States functions in the world, he is without emotion. His emotions are only communicated in the pauses of his breath as he starts speaking directly to his family in the heartland, where he left them. He becomes the opposite of a monster, especially when compared to Jihadi John. Foley's very human face stands in stark contrast to the covered visage of the inhuman monster.

With two moments of violence depicted, the decapitating of James Foley and the bombing of the ISIS claimed areas, there is a comparison and juxtaposition. The violence that is portrayed by each party seems comparable because Jihadi John seems responsible for fewer deaths than the United States. Jihadi John frames ISIS as an organization acting against the West through the utilization of terrorist war tactics as the only resource available to fight the behemoth that is America. The violence elevates ISIS, as the action puts it on the same level as the West, personified by the precarious James Foley. This vulnerability and exposure demonstrates much about cisgender politics and how this white masculine weakness is a response to the more persistent forms of precarity and those interstitial places that complicate the terms of horror as a genre and furthermore how horror operates within the Jihadi John videos. In looking and acting as he does, Jihadi

John demands a serious reaction of perhaps revulsion, shock, and the need for containment.

Monster Theory postulates that the damage wreaked by the monster is material, while the monster itself turns immaterial and vanishes only to reappear somewhere else.[34] ISIS has been able to show up in a variety of locations across the globe, sometimes even after the West considers them to have been eradicated. While they may have lost territory in Iraq and Syria, they have shown themselves in Afghanistan and the Philippines.[35] The lens of Monster Theory helps us negotiate the constant "double act" of construction and restitution that traps the monster in a cycle of becoming and becoming once more. The monster is cast out from the self and projected outward, providing a meaningful vocabulary for how we recursively see the revelation and consequence that is monstrosity. Monsters are a reading of the repressed and a dimensional tool to translate a language and metaphorical representation of the repressed.[36] Cohen communicates that a monster signifies something other than itself, that it is always a displacement, always an inhabitation of the gap between the time of upheaval that created the monster and the moment into which it is received to be born again.

Jihadi John is able to appear in this video and then disappear at the end with the promise to return. The very material damage of a beheaded journalist serves as proof that this monster exists. However, given his anonymity due to his covered face, and the near-mystic quality from the monstrosity he assumed for himself, Jihadi John is able to be everywhere and nowhere at once. He represents the greatest fear of the West: an empowered Muslim man who kills the very image of white strength. He directs a challenge to former president Obama himself, showing how he does not fear the West or reprisal for his actions. Then, he simply disappears. Only after months of investigation was it revealed that Jihadi John was Mohammed Emwazi. At first, he was a nameless monster who could come and go in the nightmares of the West as he pleased.

In further understanding the monstrous body, Robin Wood defines monsters as a traumatic substitute for what society casts out, while also functioning as a repressed element of the unconscious that returns time and time again into our collective nightmare as a measured yet ceaseless force that can neither be avoided nor eradicated.[37] The eradication of the monstrous body is considered a happy ending when it occurs, because the extermination of the object of terror signifies the restoration of original oppression that the monster was working against. The appearance of a monster signals a return of the repressed.[38] These constructions are used to disavow and normalize the overarching red herring that is the monster and how the monster is then used to distract. *Monster* is a term that is not given to those in power, because when power enacts monstrosity, it is a way of coopting the victim narrative. Rather than the terrorist being seen as victim of the West's oppression, the West becomes a victim of the terrorist-monster's attacks. As Bernadette Calafell writes in her book, "I understand that monsters are made, not born."[39]

The Critical Implications of Becoming

Above all, Cohen wants it remembered that monsters are born from us. As much as deviance and monstrosity are pushed away or hidden, they will always return. They are from a place that has yet to be reconciled. Monsters are more powerful than we realize because they are part of a self-knowledge of how we perceive the world around us. They challenge our cultural assumptions about tolerance by showing an otherwise unthinkable extreme[40] by emphasizing the dynamics of cultural creation and the politics of death. The videos demonstrate how some bodies are rendered more vulnerable to the cultural inequalities and the fabric of capitalism. Horror films produce atmospheric dimensions that are interested in the death spiral and apocalyptic masculinity that is motivated through the animation of death.

The reoccurring and regenerative nature of monstrosity is perhaps an incredible wellspring of power, especially for Jihadi John and ISIS. By adopting the monster frame, he is able to disappear and reappear at will. Every time a video of his was released, he became material again in the minds of the West. Cohen sites the "fragments" that get left behind by monsters that mark their existence. The "signifiers of monstrous passing that stand in for the monstrous body itself" are the only ways the audience knows that the monster exists.[41] Rather than "footprints" or "talismans," Jihadi John leaves behind videos. These stand in for the terrorist-monster body but make him material for all those who view this content.

The interpretation of these fragments, however, changes based on who finds them. For Western viewers, they serve as evidence of the terrorist who haunts their dreams and lurks behind every corner. Jihadi John never named himself, and his anonymity ensured that those who viewed his killings with fearful eyes would begin to see him everywhere. He could regenerate and reoccur every time they saw a Muslim. The West was already primed to view Muslims as dangerous monsters, as Sophia Arjana shows—the dangerous, imaginary Muslim that Arjana described had been lurking in their minds.[42] Now they had a far more tangible fear in their minds, embodied in the avatar of a faceless, black-garbed monster in the desert waiting for them with a knife in his hands and a prayer on his lips.

The terrorist-monster is infected by a colonial systemic holdover. Jihadi John is the site where a Muslim body is reacting, moving through and throughout the world. He asserts his rage and makes material a previously unexplored bodily terrain where the terrorist is the physical manifestation and reaction to a pervading colonial structure. By adopting the mantle of monster, Jihadi John gives in to this colonial framework but uses it as a source of power. He has reclaimed the label of monster. If the West truly wishes to view Muslims as terrorist-monsters, as Arjana claims, then Jihadi John willingly becomes exactly what the West envisions for him. He serves as an alternative, queer masculinity that is outside of Western dominion. Western countries have a history of clearly delineated lines around how he could express his masculinity. Once he utilized the persuasive potential of monster performance and rhetoric, Jihadi John was able to decide for himself what exactly being a man meant.

The purposeful adoption of the monstrous frame sets up a polysemic reading of Jihadi John's performance. The way that Jihadi John frames his actions allows for anyone who watches them to view him as a monster. Even if the viewer is sympathetic to his cause, Jihadi John is still distinctly monstrous in his performance. The polysemy, then, is not whether or not he is a monster but rather what *type* of monster he is. Edward Ingebretsen describes monsters as possessing the potential to be seen as angels.[43] The two are similar in many capacities, both instilling fear and awe in the viewer and representing an otherworldly being sent to influence humanity. Monsters show what one should not do, while angels serve the function of giving the audience something aspirational. This is how Jihadi John is able to serve as a recruitment tool for ISIS. The West views him as a monster, a demon sent to prey on their greatest fears. But for disenfranchised Muslim men in the West, he may serve as aspirational, a powerful angel who is able to defy those who kept him in thrall. Both sides view him as monstrous, but as Ingebretsen states, it's the difference between "awful" and "awe-ful," with the latter representative of the desire to become.[44]

The popularity of the ISIS videos seems to be among Muslim men, as it gives them a strength they had been otherwise denied.[45] Arjana sets forth the idea that Muslims in the West have been viewed as "terroristic villains," trapping them within the framework of monster.[46] This is how horror becomes a meaningful genre that reifies and emboldens these marginalized identities, as it is the only avenue left for them. Not only do these videos function as a rhetorical affect-inducing recruitment tool and call to action, they serve the interest of signifying the potential of generic tropes and must be examined for their roles in creating popular culture formation and materialization. Students of Stuart Hall would say that Jihadi John is more than a cultural formation and is a materialization because he is a material effect who then produced a new moment.

Jihadi John highlights one of the most difficult aspects of the war on terror to pin down. He was undefinable and intangible thanks to his monstrosity. This plays into the overarching tactic of the West to continue to fight an ill-defined war. The war on terror is largely rhetorical, with both sides existing in a nebulous space somewhere among state, hero, angel, and monster. Jihadi John is able to further this aspect of the conflict, as his actions and the fear he creates are equally rhetorical. As previously stated, the West is not in any real danger from him. He is a boogeyman, a story that keeps anxiety alive in the minds of his viewers. This is precisely what the West has done with all terrorists. By remaining undefinable and unknowable, they are able to continue to appear and reappear everywhere and nowhere at once.

To understand Jihadi John's status as a monster requires placing him in the context of an expanding discourse of monstrosity within its growing subgenre of critical cultural studies. The potential for monstrosity as a paradigm and interdisciplinary assemblage crystalizes the lens of race and performance that must be applied to terrorism and then expanded across its multiple and simultaneous incarnations of study. Jeffrey Cohen warns that "Monsters are our children."[47] Jihadi John's monstrous killing of James Foley did not happen within a vacuum. It was a response to the life Emwazi had led, the desperate search for belonging that forced him to consider becoming Jihadi John. The West needs to be able to understand its role in creating the very monsters that lurk in the darkest corners of our nightmares, especially if we seek to stop them from becoming manifest again.

Notes

1. David Williams, "Hunt for Jihadi John," *Irish Daily Mail*, August 22, 2018, http://www.pressreader.com/ireland/irish-daily-mail/20140822/281990375692198.
2. Ben Bryant, "2014 VICE News Awards: Monster of the Year—Jihadi John," *VICE*, December 29, 2014, https://news.vice.com/article/2014-vice-news-awards-monster-of-the-year-jihadi-john.
3. Dominic Casciani, "Islamic State: Profile of Mohammed Emwazi aka 'Jihadi John,'" *BBC*, November 13, 2015, http://www.bbc.com/news/uk-31641569.
4. Rachel Middleton, "Jihadi John: US Military Drone Strike 'Evaporates' British ISIS Militant Mohammed Emwazi," *International Business Times*, November 13, 2015, http://www.ibtimes.co.uk/us-military-launch-drone-strike-britons-jihadi-john-1528488.
5. Ibid.
6. Ibid.
7. Greg Miller, "Islamic State Publication Says That 'Jihadi John' Was Killed in a Drone Strike," *Washington Post*, January 19, 2016, https://www.washingtonpost.com/world/national-security/islamic-state-publication-says-that-jihadi-john-was-killed-in-drone-strike/2016/01/19/0375a2dc-bee9-11e5-9443-7074c3645405_story.html?utm_term=.ca6eeaff929c.
8. Adam Forrest, "How Four West London Men Became the ISIS 'Beatles,'" *VICE*, February 21, 2018, https://www.vice.com/en_us/article/qvezew/how-four-west-london-men-became-the-isis-beatles.
9. Patrick Sawer, "Who Is Jihadi John, and How Did Mohammed Emwazi Become the Symbol of ISIL?" *The Telegraph*, November 13, 2015, https://www.telegraph.co.uk/news/2016/03/16/who-is-jihadi-john-and-how-did-mohammed-emwazi-become-the-symbol/.
10. Jasbir Puar, *Terrorist Assemblages: Homonationalism in Queer Times* (Durham, NC: Duke University Press Books, 2007), xvii.

11. Edward Ingebretsen, *At Stake: Monsters and the Rhetoric of Public Fear* (Chicago: University of Chicago Press, 2001), 4.
12. Jasbir K. Puar, Amit Rai, "Monster, Terrorist, Fag: The War on Terrorism and the Production of Docile Patriots," *Social Text 72* 20, no. 3 (2002): 117–148.
13. Ibid.
14. Jeffrey Jerome Cohen, "Preface: In a Time of Monsters," in *Monster Theory: Reading Culture*, ed. Jeffrey Jerome Cohen (Minneapolis: University of Minnesota Press, 1996).
15. Ibid., vi.
16. Ibid., viii.
17. Ibid., xiii.
18. Christiana Spens, *Shooting Hipsters: Rethinking Dissent in the Age of PR* (London: Duncan Baird Publishers, 2016), Chapter 4 the Political Spectacle.
19. Molefi Asante, *Global Masculinities and Manhood*, ed. Ronald L. Jackson II and Murali Balaji (Champaign: University of Illinois Press, 2011), 11.
20. Ibid., 11–14.
21. Graeme Wood, "The American Climbing the Ranks of ISIS," *The Atlantic*, March 2017, https://www.theatantic.com/magazine/archive/2017/03/the-american-leader-in-the-islamic-state/510872/.
22. Ibid.
23. Casey Kelly, "It Follows: Precarity, Thanatopolitics, and the Ambient Horror Film." *Critical Studies in Media Communication* 34, no. 3 (2017): 234–249.
24. Judith Butler, *Frames of War: When Is Life Grievable?* (New York: Verso Books, 2016), 2.
25. Kelly, "It Follows," 234–249.
26. Puar, *Terrorist Assemblages*, 235.
27. Cohen, "Preface: In a Time of Monsters," vi–xiii.
28. Sophia Rose Arjana, *Muslims in the Western Imagination* (Oxford, UK: Oxford University Press, 2015), 3.
29. Edward Ingebretsen, *At Stake: Monsters and the Rhetoric of Public Fear* (Chicago: University of Chicago Press, 2001), 4.
30. Puar, *Terrorist Assemblages*, 235.
31. Ibid.
32. Cohen, "Preface: In a Time of Monsters," vi–xiii.
33. Ibid.
34. Ibid.
35. Paul Rogers, "The Islamic State Has Survived 100,000 Bombs and Is Still Very Much Alive," *news.com.au*, July 10, 2018, https://www.news.com.au/world/middle-east/islamic-state-has-survived-100000-bombs-and-missiles-and-is-still-very-much-active/news-story/0f62e90544bb8f89ef7b9706977349aa.
36. Kelly, "It Follows," 234–249.
37. Robin Wood, *Hollywood from Vietnam to Reagan . . . and Beyond: A Revised and Expanded Edition of the Classic Text* (New York: Columbia University Press, 2012), 68–70.
38. Ibid.
39. Bernadette Calafell, *Monstrosity, Performance, and Race in Contemporary Culture* (New York: Peter Lang International, 2015), 5.
40. Cohen, "Preface: In a Time of Monsters," vi–xiii.
41. Ibid.

42. Arjana, *Muslims in the Western Imagination*, 3.
43. Edward Ingebretsen, *At Stake: Monsters and the Rhetoric of Public Fear* (Chicago: University of Chicago Press, 2001), 4.
44. Ibid., 15.
45. Richard Engel, "'Jihadi John' Videos Help Drive ISIS Recruitment," *NBC News*, February 26, 2015, https://www.nbcnews.com/video/jihadi-john-videos-help-drive-isis-recruitment-405119555811?v=a.
46. Arjana, *Muslims in the Western Imagination*, 10.
47. Cohen, "Preface: In a Time of Monsters," vi–xiii.

Bibliography

Arjana, Sophia Rose. *Muslims in the Western Imagination*. Oxford, UK: Oxford University Press, 2015.

Asante, Molefi. *Global Masculinities and Manhood*, edited by Ronald L. Jackson II and Murali Balaji. Champaign: University of Illinois Press, 2011.

Bryant, Ben. "2014 VICE News Awards: Monster of the Year—Jihadi John." *VICE*, December 29, 2014. https://news.vice.com/article/2014-vice-news-awards-monster-of-the-year-jihadi-john.

Butler, Judith. *Frames of War: When Is Life Grievable?* New York: Verso Books, 2016.

Calafell, Bernadette. *Monstrosity, Performance, and Race in Contemporary Culture*. New York: Peter Lang International, 2015.

Casciani, Dominic. "Islamic State: Profile of Mohammed Emwazi aka 'Jihadi John.'" *BBC*, November 13, 2015. http://www.bbc.com/news/uk-31641569.

Cohen, Jeffrey Jerome. "Preface: In a Time of Monsters." In *Monster Theory: Reading Culture*, edited by Jeffrey Jerome Cohen. Minneapolis: University of Minnesota Press, 1996.

Engel, Richard. "'Jihadi John' Videos Help Drive ISIS Recruitment." *NBC News*, February 26, 2015. https://www.nbcnews.com/video/jihadi-john-videos-help-drive-isis-recruitment-405119555811?v=a.

Forrest, Adam. "How Four West London Men Became the ISIS 'Beatles.'" *VICE*, February 21, 2018. https://www.vice.com/en_us/article/qvezew/how-four-west-london-men-became-the-isis-beatles.

Ingebretsen, Edward. *At Stake: Monsters and the Rhetoric of Public Fear*. Chicago: University of Chicago Press, 2001.

Kelly, Casey. "It Follows: Precarity, Thanatopolitics, and the Ambient Horror Film." *Critical Studies in Media Communication* 34, no. 3 (2017): 234–249.

Middleton, Rachel. "Jihadi John: US Military Drone Strike 'Evaporates' British ISIS Militant Mohammed Emwazi." *International Business Times*, November 13, 2015. http://www.ibtimes.co.uk/us-military-launch-drone-strike-britons-jihadi-john-1528488.

Miller, Greg. "Islamic State Publication Says That 'Jihadi John' Was Killed in a Drone Strike." *Washington Post*, January 19, 2016. https://www.washingtonpost.com/world/national-security/islamic-state-publication-says-that-jihadi-john-was-killed-in-drone-strike/2016/01/19/0375a2dc-bee9-11e5-9443-7074c3645405_story.html?utm_term=.ca6eeaff929c.

Puar, Jasbir. *Terrorist Assemblages: Homonationalism in Queer Times*. Durham, NC: Duke University Press, 2007.

Puar, Jasbir, and Amit Rai. "Monster, Terrorist, Fag: The War on Terrorism and the Production of Docile Patriots." *Social Text* 3, no. 20 (2002): 117–148.
Rogers, Paul. "The Islamic State Has Survived 100,000 Bombs and Is Still Very Much Alive." *news.com.au*, July 10, 2018. https://www.news.com.au/world/middle-east/islamic-state-has-survived-100000-bombs-and-missiles-and-is-still-very-much-active/news-story/0f62e90544bb8f89ef7b9706977349aa.
Sawer, Patrick. "Who Is Jihadi John, and How Did Mohammed Emwazi Become the Symbol of ISIL?" *The Telegraph*, November 13, 2015. https://www.telegraph.co.uk/news/2016/03/16/who-is-jihadi-john-and-how-did-mohammed-emwazi-become-the-symbol/.
Spens, Christiana. *Shooting Hipsters: Rethinking Dissent in the Age of PR*. London: Duncan Baird Publishers, 2016.
Williams, David. "Hunt for Jihadi John." *Irish Daily Mail*, August 22, 2018. http://www.pressreader.com/ireland/irish-daily-mail/20140822/281990375692198.
Wood, Graeme. "The American Climbing the Ranks of ISIS." *The Atlantic*, March 2017. https://www.theatantic.com/magazine/archive/2017/03/the-american-leader-in-the-islamic-state/510872/.
Wood, Robin. *Hollywood from Vietnam to Reagan . . . and Beyond: A Revised and Expanded Edition of the Classic Text*. New York: Columbia University Press, 2012.

ARTHI CHANDRASEKARAN is a doctoral student at Wayne State University.

NICHOLAS PREPHAN received his PhD from Wayne State University in 2016.

11 Transactional Constitution

ISIS's Co-option of Western Discourse

Jacqueline Bruscella
Ryan Bisel

Legitimacy and, more importantly, *perceptions of* legitimacy, are entirely powerful in both the formation and maintenance of organizations, as well as in their dissolution and destruction. The more legitimate an organization is perceived to be, the more powerful its status becomes within its institutional field,[1] and the more readily it is able to obtain much-needed social and physical resources from stakeholders. So, how does an organization create these perceptions of legitimacy? In short, organizations model themselves after or mimic similar organizations, already perceived to be legitimate or successful.[2]

However, the dynamics involved in gaining perceptions of organizational legitimacy operate a bit differently for terrorist organizations. For such groups, the legitimacy challenge involves being perceived as a substantial competitor or threat to enemy nations and/or groups of people. Importantly, to be considered a substantial threat on an international stage means to be taken seriously by enemies, which, in turn, also means to be taken seriously by allies, current members, and potential future recruits. In that sense, legitimation attempts are an existential concern of any terrorist organization. Thus, it is no surprise that at one time or another, legitimation attempts have been at the forefront of the organizational agenda for the Islamic State of Iraq and Syria (ISIS, hereafter).

Arguably, one of the most predominant ways in which ISIS attempted to construct perceptions of organizational legitimacy was through their momentous media campaign, specifically through their use of various social media platforms and other mediated technologies. As the introduction to this volume suggests, and as subsequent chapters detail, ISIS uniquely positioned itself to provoke political, military, and social reactions to gain the attention of a global population through their use of social media platforms; for example, by taking credit for terrorist attacks, on platforms such as Twitter. However, as Jessica Stern and J. M. Berger argue, "killing civilians and destroying infrastructure are not typically a terrorist organization's *end goals*. Rather, they are a means to provoke a political reaction" (emphasis added).[3]

In this chapter, we argue that this provocation was perpetuated and reinforced through ISIS's use of mediated technologies, specifically through one of their most robust forms of external communication: the publication of their English-language propaganda magazine, *Dabiq*. Available online for anyone to download and read, this magazine bursts with page upon page of ISIS's self-described organizational "successes." According to Terrance McCoy, writing for the *Washington Post* in 2014, understanding the draw of this magazine is, and remains to be, "key to understanding the incredible recruiting successes of the Islamic State, which [was] estimated to have drawn at least 12,000 foreign fighters from 74 countries and [has] sent nations from Britain to Tunisia scrambling to stem the flow."[4] While these numbers have undoubtedly changed since the time of McCoy's argument, recent assessments of the number of recruits still suggest that defeating ISIS will require months, if not years, of work in delegitimizing and deconstruction.[5] Thus, we argue in this chapter that *Dabiq* serves as a constitutive text though which ISIS carved out a space in their stakeholder perceptions of the meaning of ISIS's organizational existence. Particularly through the online distribution of this magazine, ISIS was able to reach a global audience and present to them a set of sophisticated rhetorical images and texts to support their claims to ontological legitimacy.

Rationale

In the months following ISIS's declaration of an Islamic caliphate in the summer of 2014, the terrorist organization amassed large swaths of land, gained control over technological and natural energy resources, and claimed to have assembled numerous educational and social service programs.[6] Janine Davidson and Emerson Brooking, writing for the Council on Foreign Relations, note that at the time of their writing in 2014, ISIS controlled "a volume of resources and territory *unmatched in the history of extremist organizations*" (emphasis added).[7] Further, as Audrey Cronin argues, "holding territory has allowed [ISIS] to build a self-sustaining financial model unthinkable for most terrorist groups."[8] ISIS purported to have built administrative offices responsible for managing religious outreach and religious reinforcement, created courts and systems for punishment, and established educational programming and networks of public relations.[9] ISIS constructed offices that manage humanitarian aid, opened bakeries and grocers, and accessed and gained control over key sites of infrastructure including water and electricity. Additionally, ISIS attempted to manage large-scale industrial facilities, including dams, power plants, sewers, and power lines.[10]

However, one important resource ISIS harnessed, particularly as it relates to this volume, has been its access to, and relatively successful use of, various media platforms. In this chapter, we argue that it is ISIS's unique use and leveraging of mediated technologies that has given them the distinctive ability to spread their message of self-defined organizational "success." These messages, then, function to create and reinforce perceptions of their organizational legitimacy and existence. Importantly, together with its purported development of civil services and infrastructure, ISIS reported that it established its own department for media releases and social programing, what they call the Al Hayat Media Center. Thus, crucial to ISIS's organizational development and expansion has been not only its ability to exploit new technologies and social media platforms, but also to *report to the world* such capacities.[11] Using such resources, ISIS grew into a multifaceted, massive organizational entity, with the technological and mass media programming to show for it. In the remainder of this chapter, we discuss how ISIS's unique and sophisticated use of media to broaden the available audience of their ideological messages and self-defined organizational success was fundamental to their rapid organizational constitution and expansion.

ISIS and Media Use: A Primer

As many have already pointed out in this volume, few scholars and practitioners, military or governmental workers would disagree with the argument that ISIS developed into the organization it was and is today, due in large part to its momentous and elaborate use of online and mediated platforms (see, in particular, part II of this volume). As Stern and Berger contend, ISIS "crafted a novel formula for mixing brutal violence with illusion of stability and dignity, and it has moved the bar for recruits."[12] Again, vital to creating perceptions of ontological legitimacy and rapid expansion was ISIS's successful dissemination of their self-defined organizational success. "Through a media strategy as aggressive as its military tactics, [ISIS sought] to extend its influence around the world."[13] As an example, making use of numerous social media platforms—most infamously Twitter—ISIS was successful in "send[ing] its propaganda and messaging out to the world and [drawing] in people vulnerable to radicalization."[14]

ISIS's use of Twitter specifically is so extensive and elaborate that it has even proven to be valuable in Western counterterrorism efforts. To explain, Berger and Morgan found that ISIS's state-run Twitter accounts, as well as those operated by its ardent supporters, often contained specific details on local organizational events as they unfold.[15] Importantly, these accounts also contained early glimpses of and web-based links to media releases from Al Hayat Media Center. As Michael Weiss and Hassan Hassan contend, one phrase that may serve to characterize ISIS's use of online and social media is the following: "Don't hear about us, hear from us."[16] ISIS was uniquely successful in bombarding audiences via the media with their presence; YouTube, Facebook, Twitter, and Zello (an encrypted application for smartphones) are just several forms of technology ISIS exploited. And as a rather poignant example, two weeks prior to the fall of Mosul, ISIS produced one of its most controversial and most viewed videos, *Changing of the Swords*. Weiss and Hassan argue that it was this video that initially demonstrated ISIS's unique and unrivaled ability to "produce sleek, hour-long propaganda and recruitment films, featuring the very kind of content that Western politicians and diplomats have hoped will *dissuade* people's attraction to the group" (emphasis added).[17]

However, these videos, along with ISIS's use of other mediated technologies, have had the opposite effect on many. Weiss and Hassan quote one of ISIS's media activists, who explains, "everybody should know that we are not who they think we are. . . . We have engineers, we have doctors, we have excellent media activists. We are not *tanzim* [an organization], we are a state."[18] In other words, through their mediated messaging, ISIS convinced many that they are not only legitimate but unstoppable and indomitable. Such perceptions have actually encouraged recruitment efforts and, reflexively, also encouraged the persistence of the terrorist organization by infusing it with new membership over time.

But aside from its rampant use of videos on YouTube, Facebook, and Twitter, ISIS has made use of another, arguably more verbose, form of communication to disseminate its message: the production of an extensive and professionally composed propaganda magazine series titled *Dabiq*, referenced earlier. We contend that it is this magazine series in particular that narratively constructs ISIS's organizational identity across time, as it explains the caliphate and its place in history, presents ISIS's present military and infrastructure success, and outlines the caliphate's plans for the future. As David Denby, writing for *The New Yorker* asserts, *Dabiq* served an "up-to-the-minute digital herald of the self-proclaimed revolutionary state"; the magazine itself an "organ of ideology and struggle, a newsletter, a manual, an advice column, and a religious text."[19] Weiss and Hassan further explain how *Dabiq*'s content, as a whole, defends "ISIS's core mission and its behavior through an eschatological [i.e., end-time narrative] prism."[20] And as Denby notes, "many of the texts, citing historical precedent, assert ISIS' legitimacy."[21]

The magazine itself, then, highlights one of the many differences between ISIS and other terrorist organizations: ISIS's organizational messaging is far superior, both in terms of content and quality. Whereas *Inspire*, al-Qaeda's equivalent to *Dabiq*, served as a "how-to guide for lone-wolf Western-based terrorists," the *Dabiq* series is much "farther-reaching."[22] Specifically, as Stern and Berger argue, "by mid-2014, [ISIS's] messaging was well oiled and effective. The differentiation from al Qaeda was sharp. Despite the occasional dud, the overall storytelling and production quality of ISIS video was often incredible, the likes of which had been rarely seen in propaganda of any kind, and certainly leaps and bounds ahead of its predecessor's often sophisticated attempts."[23]

Understanding the ways in which ISIS attempts to position itself on the international stage—specifically to its English-speaking audiences—is important insofar as counterterrorism efforts are concerned. Publishing the magazine in English allows ISIS to reach out to potential recruits who may have citizenship in English-speaking countries, as well as to demonstrate their own defiance of English-speaking nations *to* those potential recruits. As will be explicated throughout the remainder of this chapter, one compelling way in which ISIS has circulated this façade of organizational "success," (thereby, we argue, positioning itself favorably to an English-speaking recruit), is through coopting Westerners' (i.e., English-speakers') descriptions and analyses of the organization. In other words, reading through the pages of *Dabiq*, it becomes clear to the audience that ISIS has been paying close attention to Western authorities' analyses of the organization. These authorities (e.g., the UN National Security Council, the Combating Terrorism Center at West Point, the secretary of defense), which have been quoted in Western media outlets, hold a certain level of credibility, at least to Westerners. Thus, ISIS's ability to coopt and exploit Western media is central to the persuasiveness of their claims, particularly in terms of appealing to their intended English-speaking readers and recruits.

As Cronin argues, ISIS *has* been successful in offering "short-term, primitive gratification,"[24] as demonstrated by the thousands of individuals migrating to Syria to join the fight, including recruits from Western Europe as well as the United States. In other words, ISIS's efforts to recruit new members and attract foreign fighters to Syria, particularly from English-speaking countries, were, at least at one point, both effective and useful for their organizational constitution efforts. As of June 2014, academic and intelligence experts estimated that over 12,000 foreign fighters have gone to Syria from at least 81 countries; about 2,500 are from Western countries (including members of the European Union, the United States, Canada, Australia, and New Zealand).[25] Richard Barrett, senior vice president of the Soufan Group—a strategic security intelligence service headquartered in New York—remarked that the continual rise in the number of foreign fighters entering Syria has remained a cause for increasing international concern. He contends, "given the potential scale of [this] problem and the limited resources available to deal with it," policies to eradicate recruitment must be based on as "full an understanding of the phenomenon as possible."[26]

This chapter is an attempt to contribute to that end: to develop a fuller understanding of ISIS's ontological status and legitimacy claims through an analysis of their propaganda magazine, *Dabiq*. To date, there have been few thorough analyses completed of this magazine series.[27] Thus, we argue that the unique case of ISIS and their constitutive texts provides us with an attractive context to begin understanding the ways in which organizational constitution unfolds through mediated messaging and communication technology.

Theoretical Framework

In this chapter, we call attention to ISIS's attempts to tout its presumed technological and communicative successes through its own mediated messaging via the *Dabiq* magazine. Similar to previous communication research investigating the constitutive force of organizational documents,[28] this research takes the *Dabiq* magazine series as an example of a constitutive text. We adopt a CCO four-flows perspective[29] as the analytic framework for this study, in an attempt to better understand ISIS's use of media messaging as well as how its own media usage becomes a central topic of its external legitimation construction attempts.

McPhee and Zaug posit that organizations are the result of four interacting communicative exchanges, or what they refer to as "flows."[30] Those flows are activity coordination, self-structuring, membership negotiation, and institutional positioning. The four flows explain how an organization (1) is linked to its members through *membership negotiation*, and (2) itself reflexively, through *self-structuring*. The flow of (3) *activity coordination* explains how an organization adapts interdependent activity to specific work situations, and the last flow, (4) *institutional positioning*, explains how the organization is linked to the outside environment. McPhee and Zaug contend that organizations are not simply communication but the result of the associations among these four constitutive flows *of* communication.[31] In this chapter, we focus on the flow of *institutional positioning* (e.g., an organization's communication to external entities), to examine *Dabiq* in an effort to highlight ISIS's communication about its organizational successes. Without question, ISIS's institutional positioning within the pages of *Dabiq* was the product of still other constitutive flows, such as activity coordination and self-structuring. For this analysis, however, we focus specifically on ISIS's institutional positioning by cataloguing how it frames its successes within the magazine series to promote an organizational image of a technologically advanced and legitimate (albeit de facto) nation-state.

In this way, analyzing ISIS's *Dabiq* series through the lens of CCO will help scholars and practitioners alike better understand the ways in which organizations like ISIS leverage their use of various technologies and the media to help constitute themselves ontologically, as well as construct and promote a specific organizational image. The fact that ISIS invested so much time, money, and resources into its media campaigns—through *Dabiq* and other outlets—to promote images of organizational legitimacy suggests that analysis of these investments is vital to understanding ISIS. Further, the ways in which we, as Westerners, *attend* to such investment is of arguably equal importance. This chapter attempts to answer the following research question: in what ways does ISIS leverage Western descriptions of its organizational success through its media campaigns, specifically those described in the pages of its propaganda magazine, *Dabiq*?

Description of Texts

In order to answer our research question, we analyzed the first set of eleven digitally produced and circulated propaganda magazines, titled *Dabiq*, published by ISIS. Subsequent issues have been distributed since the time of analysis and recently, as Kareem El Damanhoury in chapter 4 of this volume points out, ISIS has condensed the number of its publications to one monthly magazine, titled *Rumiyah*. The introductory pages of the first issue of *Dabiq* outline the purpose of the magazine as "a periodical magazine focusing on the issues of *tawhid* [unity], *manhaj* [truth-seeking], *hijrah* [migration], *jihad* [holy war], and *jama'ah* [community]," five fundamental concerns of the self-declared Islamic caliphate.[32] According to the editorial staff of the magazine, *Dabiq* "will also contain photo reports, current events, and informative articles on matters relating to the Islamic State."[33] The first issue of *Dabiq* was published on July 5, 2014, a month after the shocking fall of Mosul.[34] Subsequent issues were not published at regular intervals; the first two issues were published in July 2015 and monthly thereafter until December 2014. Then, the subsequent six issues were published in February, March, May, July, August, and November 2015. There seemed to have been a clear impetus to get the magazine out to the public, as the initial publications correspond to the official declaration of the state and its subsequent rally for territorial gains.

This particular collection of documents totals 646 pages, complete with in-depth articles, interviews, news briefs, and gruesome frontline images alongside professional-quality photographs of daily life in the state. Within the pages of *Dabiq*, the editors usually include English-language translations where phrases or concepts are left in Arabic. Gambhir suggests that because the series is, in fact, crafted in conventional, standard written English, it is likely that the magazine aims to communicate both to Arabic-speaking supporters and sympathizers in the West and worldwide, as well as to their enemies, including the United States and other Western nations.[35]

Analysis

The analytic method used in this chapter can be best described as an iterative, problem-based approach to qualitative data analysis, as advocated by Sarah Jane Tracy. An iterative, problem-based approach "alternates between emic, or emergent, readings of the data, and etic use of existing models, explanations, and theories."[36] Tracy explains, "Rather than grounding the meaning solely in the emerging data, an iterative approach encourages reflection upon the active interests, current literature, priorities, and theories the researcher brings to the data."[37] Previous work in organizational communication, recent research on terrorist and clandestine organizations as well as emerging news, reports, and books regarding ISIS and its adherents were read prior to and concurrent with analysis.

We read through the first three issues of *Dabiq* to immerse ourselves in the nature of the documents. As Tracy puts it, the goal of the data-immersion process is to "absorb and marinate in the data, jotting down reflections and hunches, but reserving judgment."[38] Here, our goal was to determine what was going on in the data.[39] A PDF version of each *Dabiq* magazine was then uploaded to NVivo, a computer program designed to aid in qualitative data management. Once all texts were uploaded to NVivo, we began primary cycle coding, or the "active process of identifying data as belonging to, or representing, some type of phenomenon"—be it a concept, belief, action, theme, cultural practice, or relationship."[40] Thus, primary-cycle coding consisted of creating first-level codes, focused on summarizing what was present in the data. As we progressed through primary-cycle coding, we returned to reread previously coded issues of *Dabiq* to reexamine and recode the content, if needed, as our understanding of the patterns within the texts evolved. Referred to as a constant comparative method of analysis, this iterative process of going back through the data is reflexive and circular and has the goal of sorting unstructured data into categories.[41] Analyzing the data in this manner allowed us to compare and sort the data applicable to each code, modify code definitions and explanations, and add new codes as we progressed through the analysis and read through new data.

The next stage of the analytic process was secondary-cycle coding, where we "critically examine[d] the codes already identified in primary codes and [began] to organize, synthesize, and categorize them into interpretive concepts."[42] Important to this phase was the identification of examples that illustrated the complexity of the data and analysis. These are the *exemplars* provided in this chapter. Finally, the concluding stages of analysis consisted of theorizing about the interrelationships among the exemplars that formed the thematic categories, which are presented in our findings. Our goal in this stage of analysis was to uncover a "sensitizing concept"[43] to bring the analysis together, providing a theoretical contribution for the overall analysis. Sensitizing concepts are defined by Clifford Christians and James Carey as "taxonomical systems that discover an integrating scheme within the data themselves" and refer to an orientation "short of formal definition, yet apropos enough to help us cultivate facts vigorously."[44]

Findings

As mentioned, ISIS is unlike any other terrorist organization the West has had to deal with to date. ISIS managed to take over a large area of land, harvest natural and energy resources, and purported to have gained financial security.

Additionally, ISIS claimed to have created social services for its members and civilian infrastructure for its recruits. As it relates to the purpose of this chapter specifically and to this volume generally, most if not all of these organizational assets are reinforced and disseminated to a global audience through ISIS's momentous media campaign and the dissemination of *Dabiq*.

The *Dabiq* magazine serves as a potent artifact through which ISIS was able to position itself in the eyes of its enemies as well as its supporters as a stable and permanent enough nation-state able to produce such professional communiqués. While much can be written in regard to how this magazine series serves to disseminate perceptions of ontological legitimacy, this chapter focuses on two particular sections within this series: (1) a section titled "In the Words of the Enemy," included in every issue, and similarly, (2) a segment supposedly authored by John Cantlie, presented first in the fourth issue and then in those thereafter.

First, inside every issue of *Dabiq*, there is a section titled "In the Words of the Enemy," wherein editors insert direct quotations from Western politicians, leaders, military strategists, and journalists. While it is unclear as to the source of these coopted texts, it may be assumed that they are obtained through simple searches of government and military debriefings, television broadcasts, and newspaper articles, among other sources. As explained in the pages that follow, this "In the Words of the Enemy" section is included in each issue of the magazine and serves primarily as a reminder to readers of the unique strength of the Islamic State and their material assets (e.g., military victories, land occupation, media campaigns, and social services). These reminders, therefore, provide credibility to their subsequent claims to legitimacy.

Second, beginning in the fourth issue, the editors include a chapter supposedly written by John Cantlie—a British war journalist who was captured in 2012, along with American James Foley. ISIS forces later executed the latter, and at the time of this writing, Cantlie still remains hostage. It has not yet been made clear whether or not these are truly Cantlie's sentiments, if he has become a victim of Stockholm syndrome, or if he has been fed these lines. Regardless, "his" (read: Western) voice is channeled through numerous exposés throughout the *Dabiq* series, as well as in other propaganda videos and social media messaging.

The remainder of this chapter calls attention to this one particular way in which the magazine series serves to position ISIS as legitimate: coopting excerpts from what can assumed to be Western media sources, which speak to ISIS's sophistication and strength. The *Dabiq* editors chose to channel extremely poignant excerpts from both Western leaders' (i.e., "In the Words of the Enemy") and Cantlie's remarks, focusing on one of two main issues: (1) recent successes of ISIS and (2) failures of the United States and the West *in response to* those successes made by ISIS. Thus, we argue that in terms of bolstering ISIS's perceptions of legitimacy based on organizational and material resources, much of the work has already been done for them, by us, through ISIS's cooptation of enemy discourse.

Reconceptualizing the "Jayvee Squad"

The first example of how ISIS has used these sections to bolster their attempts at perceived legitimacy comes from the first issue of *Dabiq*, titled "The Return of the Khilafah" (Caliphate). In this first "In the Words of the Enemy" section, the editors quote Douglas Ollivant, former director for Iraq at the US National Security Council, and Brian Fishman, former director of research for the Combating Terrorism Center at West Point. The *Dabiq* team provides several excerpts from an article the two coauthored shortly before ISIS's self-proclaimed "liberation of Mosul as well as other important cities and towns in Iraq."[45] The quotes the *Dabiq* editorial team chose to include are as follows:

> Out of the crucible of the Syrian civil war and the discontent in Iraq's Sunni regions, *something new is emerging*. The Islamic State in Iraq and Syria (ISIS) *is no longer a state in name only. It is a physical, if extra-legal, reality on the ground*. Unacknowledged by the world community, *ISIS has carved a de facto state* in the borderlands of Syria and Iraq. . . . This former Al Qaeda affiliate *holds territory, provides limited services, dispenses a form of justice (loosely defined), most definitely has an army, and flies its own flag* (emphasis added).[46]

ISIS then reminds readers of their resource-rich status by continuing to reappropriate Ollivant and Fishman's words: "This new reality *presents a challenge that rises above a mere counter-terrorism problem*. ISIS no longer exists in small cells that can be neutralized by missiles or small groups of commandos. *It is now a real, if nascent and unrecognized, state actor*—more akin in organization and power to the Taliban of the late 1990s than Al Qaeda" (emphasis added).[47]

The two conclude, noting, "The group does not have a safe haven within a state. It is a de facto state that is a safe haven."[48]

Interestingly, the *Dabiq* team provides no further commentary about these excerpts; as is the case in most of the "In the Words of the Enemy" chapters, the excerpts of enemy text are included with no additional claims or comment crafted by ISIS. Arguably, there is not much explanation needed, as the text, in the words of ISIS's enemy itself, conveys the incipient challenge the West faces when confronted with ISIS: although they were once considered by the West to be a "jayvee squad of terrorists"[49]—meaning "junior varsity" or less experienced—they are no longer a "mere counter-terrorism problem" but are now a territory-holding, service-providing, and army-training de facto nation-state.[50] (Or, at least they were before their loss of Mosul and other territory in 2017.) This is one of the major themes in the excerpts of Western text coopted into *Dabiq*—that is, ISIS is not merely a terrorist group but rather a de facto nation-state whose strength and numbers keep growing.

Additionally, the language used in Ollivant and Fishman's message here seems to communicate a clear shift in the ways the West constructed the Islamic State discursively (e.g., "new reality," "it is now," "it is no longer"). Again, this unique method of reminding audiences about the State's "successes" suggests that these successes have, in fact, been recognized and acknowledged by the West. To ISIS, we argue, the fact that enemy news and media outlets are speaking of the "real challenge" the "de facto nation-state" presents serves as reason enough for audiences to believe and trust in ISIS's message. This recognition, likewise, has resulted in a shift in the level of credibility the West affords to the Islamic State. The implication insofar as ISIS is concerned, then, is that audiences should follow suit.

Other excerpts that highlight the West's changing conceptualization of ISIS due to their organizational "successes" are included throughout the series as well. As discussed earlier, ISIS's combination of ultraviolence, a sense of civil order, and successful media messaging has been noted by Westerners to be a potentially dangerous combination. In the sixth issue's "In the Words of the Enemy" chapter, *Dabiq* editors quote former secretary of defense Chuck Hagel's synthesis of this dangerous trifecta:

> I think our capacity is different because the threats and the challenges are far more diffuse and varied. I talked about asymmetric threats. I mean the *sophistication* of ISIS—just take that for a moment. We've never seen an organization like ISIS that is *so well-organized, so well-trained, so well-funded, so strategic, so brutal, so completely ruthless*. We've never seen anything quite like that in one institution. Then they blend in ideology which will eventually lose*, we get that, and social media. *The sophistication of their social media program is something that we've never seen before*. You blend all of that together, that is an incredibly powerful new threat. So we're adjusting to this and we're trying to—we can't do it alone (emphasis added).[51]

Here, Hagel specifically addresses ISIS's sophisticated social media platforms, as well as their well-trained and ruthless army and their well-funded and strategic organizational strategies. ISIS uses Hagel's words to present itself as a new and powerful threat—one that the United States will need to adjust to. The *Dabiq* team once again underscores the fact that ISIS is different from organizations that the United States has had to deal with in the past, suggesting also that maybe the United States has not yet fully recognized the potential threat ISIS poses. Hagel's repetition of the phrase "so well" in regards to ISIS's training and funding, coupled with words such as "sophisticated" and "incredibly powerful" perpetuate this emergent image of ISIS both as an institution unlike anything the West has seen before and also as extremely advanced. In this example, ISIS uses

Hagel's words to reinforce for readers that the group is also incredibly well organized. ISIS's discursive choices here to coopt the words of the United States that take for granted its organization's existence reinforce the substance and legitimacy of their ideal organizational image.

Moreover, this particular excerpt is important in terms of understanding ISIS's response to Western discourse. For the first and only time in the series, *Dabiq* editors directly respond here to the "words of the enemy." The *Dabiq* team challenges a portion of Hagel's assertions, offset by a footnote, as denoted in the excerpt above with the asterisk. After Hagel's declaration that in the end, ISIS's ideology will lose, the *Dabiq* team writes: "Allah said, 'It is He who has sent His Messenger with guidance and the religion of truth to manifest it over all religion, even if the mushrikīn despise such' [At-Tawbah: 33]." Although Hagel is steadfast in his assessment that ISIS's ideology is inherently flawed, the *Dabiq* team evokes God's will (a trope used throughout the series) to reject and counter Hagel's claims. In this way, the *Dabiq* editors are able to reappropriate enemy voices for their own legitimation attempts, while also discounting the sections of those excerpts that do not serve their purpose.

Finally, the shift in the West's construction of ISIS is most explicitly reinforced in John Cantlie's article in issue 8 of *Dabiq*, in an article he titled "Paradigm Shift." In this excerpt, the *Dabiq* team continues to emphasize ISIS's status as a "new" yet powerful state actor, again doing so in the words of Westerners. The subheading of Cantlie's article reads: "There appears now a grudging acceptance by many Western politicians that the Islamic State is different to anything they've seen before. Their response, by necessity, has to be different too."[52] In the article that follows, Cantlie outlines several of the major material assets that ISIS has secured, emphasizing that in many ways, ISIS has developed into what Westerners would normally consider a "country" (issue 8, p. 64). Specifically, he rationalizes that ISIS "produce[s] their own currency, primary schools for the young, and [has] a functioning court system."[53] ISIS, again through channeling Cantlie's words, reminds audiences that these civic innovations are

> *Surely* hallmarks of (whisper it if you dare) a country. . . . Ah, the C-word. It's being used sporadically by the media, slowly at first, but its use is gather[ing] pace. Could the Islamic State, the Caliphate that was only announced in June, really be a country? *As uncomfortable as it may be for many in the West, there's little reason why the State shouldn't be considered a country. Countries can be born in days, in hours during a coup, or in minutes at the signing of a paper, they have been for centuries.* So there's no reason this one shouldn't have been born the way it was (emphasis added).[54]

First, this excerpt calls attention to how ISIS draws on Western discourses about whether or not to call ISIS a state. Next, this excerpt illustrates how ISIS attempts to use Cantlie's (a Westerner's) words to legitimate its "birth" by acknowledging how ISIS emerged in much the same way as other (legitimate) countries have before it. ISIS, by comparison, is no different is the claim.

Then, Cantlie goes on to explain the effects of this developing "paradigm shift." He contends that the West must begin to acknowledge that "at some stage [the West] will have to face the Islamic State as a country."[55] The article continues, "Although the West might never admit such a thing, there *are* Western politicians who are beginning to realize this fact and thus, little by little, we're seeing a changing of vernacular, a paradigm shift in how those leaders talk about the State, because if it is a country—whether recognized by anyone or not (and the Islamic State doesn't care either way)—then that changes things, dramatically."[56]

These two excerpts from Cantlie's article accomplish three simultaneous functions related to advocating for ISIS's present reality on the ground, and thus, their attempted goal of perpetuating an image of ontological legitimacy. First, Cantlie's narrative provides a powerful example of the transactional nature of ISIS's institutional positioning attempts. The Islamic State declares itself a caliphate, a label that the United States at first rejected openly. This rejection, however, is contested by ISIS through their material advances and territorial gains, resulting in their position again being discursively questioned by the United States.

Second, ISIS, through Cantlie's article, directs the reader's attention to his (and thus the West's) conclusion that ISIS is more than just a "terrorist organization" and more importantly, that there is no reason why ISIS *should not be* called a country. Significant to this point is Cantlie's statement regarding the West's hesitation to refer to ISIS as such. The importance of naming and labeling organizations must be reiterated, as the mere label of a "state" might in and of itself serve to legitimize the existence of a caliphate. Again, as numerous news articles from the past two years have indicated, this was, for a while, a point of contention among politicians, military experts, and the media. Interestingly, however, Cantlie adds that the Islamic State does not care whether or not the West refers to it as a state. Again, this calls attention their point that the very fact that this topic is contested is justification *enough* that ISIS is gaining traction. In terms of ISIS's attempts to be perceived as a legitimate threat to the West and its assets, the mere fact that this discussion is taking place there, in the West, is a step forward for ISIS.

Finally, ISIS, in using Cantlie's words, explains that conceptualizing ISIS as a state would not only result in a change in vernacular but would also affect policies aimed at defeating the group, as well as efforts aimed at influencing public perception. "You can't just conveniently write it off as merely 'a terrorist organization,'" Cantlie writes, "because [that] doesn't wash with the public."[57] To refer to ISIS as *just* a terrorist organization does not do justice to its amassing of influence and power, but, at the same time, for the West to refer to it as a nation would be equating it with what the West holds to be true of modern nation-states, thus giving ISIS some measure of symbolic legitimacy.

Western Shortcomings in Response to Paradigm Shift

Importantly, this paradigm shift comes as a result of the West's realization that traditional counterterrorism methods simply were not going to be effective at combating ISIS's advances. Thus, the compilation of examples of American admittance of potential weaknesses, difficulties, and failures in response to ISIS's advances is the second theme denoted in the *Dabiq* series. As will be explicated, the examples that follow simultaneously highlight Western (read: enemy) shortcomings while bolstering ISIS's strength—again, all through *the words of the enemy.* The following excerpts are from issue 5 of *Dabiq* and are found within an article titled, "If I Were the US President Today," written by John Cantlie.

"If I were the US President today," Cantlie begins, "I'd probably switch off my cellphone, lock the oval office doors, and go play golf instead. The war against the Islamic State just isn't going to plan at all."[58] He continues,

> The governments are like a robot that is stuck on a loop, continually performing the wrong sequence despite repeated instructions by its master to the contrary. Master to robot: *You have to find a different way of addressing the danger the mujāhidīn pose to the west.* "Cannot . . . compute . . ." Military action doesn't work, what about negotiations? "Must . . . obey . . . programming . . ." Everything you've done since 9/11 has put us in more danger, not less. "Zzzzz . . . syntax . . . error . . ." Of course, Robo-Obama doesn't listen to voices of reason and thus programs himself with the *same corrupted old data, making the same mistakes over and over again.* James Comey described the Islamic State mujāhidīn as "savages" in September (a classic example of prideful and conventionalist thinking that will progress absolutely nothing) while Nick Paton-Walsh described their tactics in CNN as "eerily sophisticated," which is a much more educated comment and closer to the truth, except Nick's just a journalist while James Comey is director of the FBI.[59]

Using John Cantlie's assessment, albeit sarcastic, ISIS presents the argument that President Obama should just give up his fight, as the West has thus far been unsuccessful in adapting to the new and incipient threat ISIS poses. As mentioned, and as Cantlie's final comments here suggest, the language used by the West (particularly that of the media and policymakers) plays an important role in how ISIS is conceptualized, and thus, how the West has been responding. For example, governmental and military leaders (represented here by James Comey's remarks) fail to use the language of a legitimate nation-state and thus fail to respond to ISIS accordingly. On the other hand, Cantlie points out how news reporters (e.g., CNN) do, in fact, highlight ISIS's sophistication and likeness to a nation-state—what he argues is a much more suitable characterization.

Although Cantlie's remarks here are very much cynical, he addresses how the United States has at least *begun* to recognize that changes must be made in order to win the fight against ISIS, a fight that the West is not currently winning. This notion is further evidenced in the following excerpts. One of the most alarming examples of this comes from issue 9, where the *Dabiq* team quotes Jonah Blank from the RAND Corporation and Gary Bernsten, a former CIA intelligence officer, from a Fox News interview.[60] The excerpt is as follows:

> "Say one group is very good at bomb making and the other group is very good at propaganda," says Jonah Blank from the US "think-tank" RAND Corporation. "If you put the right bomb in the right place for the right propaganda effect, that can be far more important than either of these things on their own."
>
> "This isn't just propaganda," said Gary Bernsten, a former CIA intelligence officer on an interview with Fox News on 9th March. "ISIS has billions of dollars. They have a network of communications for reaching out to these groups. And it shows you how deadly and effective ISIS is. They are truly the most successful Sunni terrorist group in history because they've carved out a space for a nation state, and these other groups recognize that. It shows Obama's statement that 'this isn't Islam' is a false narrative. ISIS has been brilliant at selling itself to the hundreds of millions of people out there looking for a message. What's happening now is a pooling of skills and experience that poses the greatest danger the West has seen in modern times. When you have that amount of battle-hardened mujāhidīn all cooperating and exchanging information for the first time under one flag, the potential for operations on a previously unseen level rises exponentially."[61]

Although long, this excerpt is particularly important in terms of summarizing the way ISIS positions itself within the pages of *Dabiq* and thus how it hopes to position itself to the outside world. The editors again use Western assessments, that of Bernsten and Blank, to position ISIS as "deadly," "effective," and most of all, resource rich. The Westerners evaluate the organization in terms of its successful propaganda and communication strategies, its wealth, its training, and its perpetuation and spread of a violent ideology used to frame itself as legitimate.

Importantly, though, Bernsten and Blank again point out the importance of the media's spread of ISIS's successes. Through ISIS's media campaign, they recognize ISIS has "brilliantly" convinced thousands of their legitimacy. Ironically, though, analysis of the *Dabiq* magazine shows us another way in which ISIS has positioned itself as legitimate: when the West talks about ISIS's effectiveness, those words are coopted in *Dabiq* to further legitimize those claims. In essence, we are doing the work for them, spreading this message through our own media channels.

The final example, below, comes from the eighth issue's "In the Words of the Enemy" section. The *Dabiq* editors quote "the Catholic crusader and American politician Rick Santorum."[62] Santorum's words sum up the importance of recognizing the symbolic power that material assets have in building the credibility of the Islamic State as they are propagated through mediated channels. Santorum states the following, as quoted by the *Dabiq* team:

> This is a caliphate that has been established and that means they are calling people from all over the world to come and fight this battle. As long as they hold ground and continue to expand that ground, more and more will come. The fact that we are delaying means that the Caliphate continues to exist. They are not losing ground. They are not being discredited in the eyes of the Muslim world. They will get stronger. . . . This is really important to understand. The reason the West had a thousand year war with Islam is that Islam was ever expanding. When Islam began to contract, it collapsed, and the caliphate was eliminated. Now they have established a caliphate. They are dead serious about expanding it. Unless we begin to take back that ground and make this caliphate just irrelevant in the eyes of the radical Muslim world, we are going to have a bigger and bigger problem.[63]

The inclusion of this excerpt from Rick Santorum is important for two reasons, especially in light of ISIS's military successes in various territories of Iraq and Syria. First, as previously mentioned, the Islamic State does not need to boast of its own achievements in terms of its messaging to potential recruits. As is the case here, the "words of the enemy" seems to do this for them, as noted in the lines "they are not losing ground" and "they will get stronger. This is really important to understand."[64] Santorum's insistence on emphasizing ISIS's expansion and material acquisitions contributes to this call for legitimacy.

Second, this excerpt seems to position the West as inferior, having to "catch up" to the advances of the caliphate. Plus, Santorum's tone here is urgent. The seriousness by which the Islamic State is taking its objective to create and expand its caliphate is evident; and, as Santorum warns, the caliphate is holding ground and it will continue to expand so long as the West delays.

In this way, the pages of *Dabiq* contain attempts to ontological legitimacy that are characterized by a transactional nature. Using the words of the enemy and Cantlie's remarks provide a strong basis of evidence to support their claim regarding a present context in which organizational and material accomplishments reveal ISIS's existence.

Discussion and Conclusions

The façade of success ISIS built through its sophisticated and multifaceted media campaign perpetuates its image as a nation-state (read: *legitimate* nation-state) to both potential recruits and, as we pointed out, its enemies. As Stern and Berger have argued, ISIS exploited new communicative technologies and changing social dynamics to both appeal and recruit, rather successfully, potential foreign fighters. "ISIS [is] offering something novel," Berger and Stern write, "dispensing with religious argumentation and generalized exhortation and emphasizing two seemingly disparate themes—ultraviolence and civil society. They were unexpectedly potent when combined and alternated."[65] Based on our findings here, we agree with their assessment.

We found that the transactional use of media (e.g., the cooptation of Western discourse in ISIS's propaganda) served as a key institutional positioning tactic for disseminating attempts at gaining perceptions of legitimacy. Within each issue of *Dabiq* analyzed, we found several sections of text pulled directly from Western media sources (i.e., transcripts, news broadcasts, televised accounts), coopted to serve the purpose of bolstering ISIS's claims of legitimacy. We argue that ISIS relies on the mere fact that the United States and the West (the enemy) *is even discussing* ISIS's strength, sophistication, and military might as justification enough that they exist and also constitute a legitimate threat to the West. In other words, the two sections analyzed here, the "In the Words of the Enemy" and Cantlie's articles, seem to imply that ISIS is, in fact, searching for Western media reports of Western authority's descriptions of their organization (e.g., the UN, the US secretary of state, etc.). ISIS cares what we have to say about them.

Western authorities speaking through Western media outlets do have credibility, again, especially to Westerners. ISIS's cooptation of that credibility is central to the persuasiveness of its use for the intended English-speaking audiences and potential English-speaking recruits. Arguably, constituting a threat to Western powers implies that ISIS has ontological equivalence to Western nations, a perception of "legitimacy" that could encourage potential recruits to join the terrorist organization. Put differently, the *Dabiq* editors were skillful enough to use and coopt the words of their enemies in an attempt to craft a credible and legitimate organizational image. Therefore, these findings suggest that an organization's attempts at constructing its identity can involve the cooptation of external entities' communication.

Mats Alvesson explains that an organization's identity deals with the "essence or core" of its organizational agenda, including its "coherence over time and space and its distinctiveness from other organizations or units."[66] As illustrated by the present case, the *Dabiq* team weaves the words of the West into their magazine, coopting them as their own and facilitating the construction of ISIS's organizational identity. (For example, the *Dabiq* team quotes former US secretary of defense Chuck Hagel, who comments on the "sophistication" of ISIS, noting how it is "so well-organized," "so well-trained," "so well-funded," resulting in an "incredibly powerful new threat."[67] Thus, this type of messaging helps construct ISIS's organizational identity as exactly that: an incredibly well-organized, well-trained, well-funded new organizational threat. In terms of future research, then, investigating how organizational images are constructed and shaped by external stakeholders' messaging could be interesting to explore. Investigating such processes could be particularly important for understanding identity-construction relationships in nonterrorist organizations or less extreme cases.

This work thus heeds Hamilton Bean and Ronald Buikema's charge to investigate the ways in which communication theory might help us understand the constitution and maintenance, and importantly, the deconstitution, of (hidden) terrorist organizations.[68] These findings may speak to such efforts to *de*constitute complex terrorist organizations generally and ISIS specifically. To this end, we reiterate our recommendations, published in *Communication Monographs*,[69] for understanding the ways in which strategic communication may be used to undermine terrorist organizing. First, Western leaders should include time-based qualifiers when discussing terrorist organizations' "successes," as such qualifying statements can help disrupt the sense that terrorist organizations' resources (land access, infrastructure, finances) are permanent. Again, as the findings in this present study suggest, there was only one instance in which ISIS directly inserted a response to the "In the Words of the Enemy" section, and that was when the United States made claims counter to their legitimation efforts. If the United States were to qualify its own statements regarding their assessments of ISIS and their access to and control over resources, the US response to ISIS might no longer serve ISIS's legitimatizing purposes.

We also recommend attacking ISIS's claims to legitimacy more directly, through employing tropes such as satire and sarcasm in our own (Western) discourse. The findings of this particular study further corroborate those recommendations. Through strategic diction and phrasing, for example, Western leaders could mock ISIS's attempts to frame their national infrastructure as successfully built and permanent. Phrases such as "creating crude roads to make it more efficient to subjugate innocent people" and "printing a few coins no nation would honor" could help frame ISIS's claims as weak or altogether erroneous.[70] Doing so might again help offset claims that can be used to serve ISIS's purpose of perpetuating ontological legitimacy. We do not necessarily recommend downplaying or minimizing their behaviors; rather, we suggest being mindful to *qualify* those assessments, to ensure we are not lending them undeserved credibility.

To conclude, it is clear that ISIS is a terrorist organization like no other the West has had to confront to date. The level of sophistication and depth of their media campaigns in particular have served to perpetuate a façade of organizational stability and success to potential recruits worldwide. Through an analysis of one of their most thorough and complex campaigns, the *Dabiq* series, we have found that one of the primary means of spreading this message has been through the cooptation of Western texts and claims. In other words, the editorial staff of *Dabiq* takes excerpts from Western authority figures and inserts those quotes directly into their propaganda magazine. These quotes speak to the relative strength and tenacity of this terrorist group, calling attention to their military successes and strategic plans. Importantly, however, ISIS rarely responds to those quotations directly. Instead, we argue, ISIS allows the quotations to speak for themselves. Thus, we argue that one way in which we might begin to counter this façade of legitimacy would be to no longer call attention to their successes without simultaneously calling attention to their failures, setbacks, or qualifying our assessments. Future research extending this line of theorizing is warranted to explore how terrorist organizations' use of coopted enemy discourse can be attacked symbolically as a means of undermining their organizational constitution attempts.

Notes

1. Talcott Parsons, *The Social System* (New York: The Free Press, 1951).
2. Paul J. DiMaggio and Walter W. Powell, "The Iron Cage Revisited: Institutional Isomorphism and Collective Rationality in Organizational Fields," *American Sociological Review* 48, no. 2 (1983): 147–160.
3. Jessica Stern and J. M. Berger, *ISIS: The State of Terror* (New York: Harper Collins, 2015), 142.
4. Terrence McCoy, "The Apocalyptic Magazine the Islamic State Uses to Recruit and Radicalize Foreigners," *Washington Post*, September 16, 2014, https://www.washingtonpost.com/news/morning-mix/wp/2014/09/16/the-apocalyptic-magazine-the-islamic-state-uses-to-recruit-and-radicalize-foreigners/?utm_term=.eebe4f64bca7.
5. For numbers as late as December 2017, see Paul D. Shinkman, "ISIS by the Numbers," *US News*, December 27, 2017, https://www.usnews.com/news/world/articles/2017-12-27/isis-by-the-numbers-in-2017.
6. Charles S. Caris and Samuel Reynolds, "ISIS Governance in Syria: Middle East Security Report 22," *The Institute for the Study of War*, July 2014, http://www.understandingwar.org/sites/default/files/ISIS_Governance.pdf.
7. Janine Davidson and Emerson Brooking, "ISIS Hasn't Gone Anywhere—and It's Getting Stronger," *Council on Foreign Relations*, June 24, 2014. https://www.etbrooking.com/portfolio-items/isis-hasnt-gone-anywhere-getting-stronger/
8. Audrey Kurth Cronin, "ISIS Is Not a Terrorist Group: Why Counterterrorism Won't Stop the Latest Jihadist Threat," *Foreign Affairs* 94, no. 2 (2015): n.p.
9. Caris and Reynolds, "ISIS Governance in Syria."
10. Ibid.
11. For a discussion of this, see chapter 5 of this volume, as well as Stern and Berger, *ISIS: The State of Terror*.
12. Stern and Berger, *ISIS: The State of Terror*, 197.
13. Ibid., 51.
14. J. M. Berger and Jonathon Morgan, "The ISIS Twitter Census: Defining and Describing the Population of ISIS Supporters on Twitter," The Brookings Project on US Relations with the Islamic World, no. 20 (2015): 2.
15. Berger and Morgan, "The ISIS Twitter Census."

16. Michael Weiss and Hassan Hassan, *ISIS: Inside the Army of Terror* (New York: Regan Arts, 2015), 170.

17. Ibid., 171.

18. Ibid., 173.

19. David Denby, "The Perfect Children of ISIS: Lessons from Dabiq," *The New Yorker*, November 24, 2015, https://www.newyorker.com/culture/cultural-comment/the-perfect-children-of-isis-lessons-from-dabiq.

20. Weiss and Hassan, *ISIS: Inside the Army of Terror*, 176.

21. Denby, "The Perfect Children."

22. Harleen K. Gambhir, "*Dabiq*: The Strategic Messaging of the Islamic State," *The Institute for the Study of War*, August 15, 2014, http://www.understandingwar.org/sites/default/files/Dabiq%20Backgrounder_Harleen%20Final_0.pdf.

23. Stern and Berger, *ISIS: The State of Terror*, 72.

24. Cronin, "ISIS Is Not a Terrorist Group."

25. Richard Barrett, "Foreign Fighters in Syria," *The Soufan Group*, November 2014, http://soufangroup.com/wp-content/uploads/2014/10/TSG-The-Islamic-State-Nov14.pdf.

26. Ibid., 3.

27. See chapter 4 of this volume, as well as our article, "Four Flows Theory and Materiality: ISIL's Use of Material Resources in Its Communicative Constitution," *Communication Monographs* 85, no. 3 (2018): 331–356.

28. Hamilton Bean and Ronald J. Buikema, "Deconstituting al-Qa'ida: CCO Theory and the Decline and Dissolution of Hidden Organizations," *Management Communication Quarterly* 29, no. 4 (2015): 512–538; Larry D. Browning, Ronald W. Greene, S. B. Sitkin, Kathleen M. Sutcliffe, and David Obstfeld, "Constitutive Complexity: Military Entrepreneurs and the Synthetic Character of Communication Flows," in *Building Theories of Organization: The Constitutive Role of Communication*, eds. L. L. Putnam and A. M. Nicotera. New York: Routledge (2009); Pamela Lutgen-Sandvik and Virginia McDermott, "The Constitution of Employee-Abusive Organizations: A Communication Flows Theory," *Communication Theory* 18, no. 2 (2008): 304–333.

29. Robert D. McPhee and Pamela Zaug, "The Communicative Constitution of Organizations: A Framework for Explanation," *The Electronic Journal of Communication* 10, no. 1 and 2 (2000): 21–47.

30. Ibid.

31. Ibid.

32. *Dabiq* 1 (2014): 3.

33. Ibid.

34. Cronin, "ISIS Is Not a Terrorist Group"; Gambhir, "*Dabiq*: The Strategic Messaging," 1–12.

35. Gambhir, "*Dabiq*: The Strategic Messaging," 1–12.

36. Sarah Jane Tracey, *Qualitative Research Methods: Collecting Evidence, Crafting Analysis, Communicating Impact* (Malden, MA: Wiley, 2013): 184.

37. Ibid.

38. Ibid., 188.

39. Donal Carbaugh, "Cultural Discourse Analysis: Communication Practices and Cultural Encounters," *Journal of Intercultural Communication Research* 37, no. 3 (2007): 167–182.

40. Tracey, *Qualitative Research Methods*, 189.
41. Kathy Charmaz, *Constructing Grounded Theory: A Practical Guide through Qualitative Analysis* (Thousand Oaks, CA: Sage, 2006).
42. Tracey, *Qualitative Research Methods*, 194.
43. Herbert Blumer, *Symbolic Interactionism: Perspective and Method* (Upper Saddle River, NJ: Prentice Hall, 1969).
44. Clifford G. Christians and James W. Carey, "The Logic and Aims of Qualitative Research," in *Research Methods in Mass Communication*, eds. Guido H. I. Stempel III and Bruce H. Westley (Upper Saddle River, NJ: Prentice Hall, 1989), 370.
45. *Dabiq* 1 (2014): 32.
46. Ibid.
47. Ibid.
48. Ibid.
49. Shreeya Sinha, "Obama's Evolution on ISIS," *New York Times*, June 9, 2015, http://www.nytimes.com/interactive/2015/06/09/world/middleeast/obama-isis-strategy.html?_r=0.
50. *Dabiq* 1 (2014): 32.
51. *Dabiq* 6 (2014): 57.
52. *Dabiq* 8 (2015): 64.
53. Ibid.
54. Ibid.
55. *Dabiq* 8 (2015): 66.
56. Ibid.
57. Ibid.
58. *Dabiq* 5 (2014): 36.
59. Ibid., 39.
60. *Dabiq* 9 (2015): 74.
61. Ibid., 75.
62. *Dabiq* 8 (2015): 57.
63. Ibid.
64. Ibid.
65. Stern and Berger, *ISIS: The State of Terror*, 72.
66. Mats Alvesson, *Understanding Organizational Culture* (Thousand Oaks, CA: Sage, 2002): 177.
67. *Dabiq* 6 (2014): 57.
68. Bean and Buikema, "Deconstituting al-Qa'ida."
69. Bruscella and Bisel, "Four Flows Theory and Materiality: ISIL's Use of Material Resources in Its Communicative Constitution."
70. Ibid., 17.

Bibliography

Alvesson, Mats. *Understanding Organizational Culture.* Thousand Oaks, CA: Sage, 2002.

Barrett, Richard. "Foreign Fighters in Syria." *The Soufan Group*, November 2014. http://soufangroup.com/wp-content/uploads/2014/10/TSG-The-Islamic-State-Nov14.pdf.

Bean, Hamilton, and Ronald J. Buikema. "Deconstituting al-Qa'ida: CCO Theory and the Decline and Dissolution of Hidden Organizations." *Management Communication Quarterly* 29, no. 4 (2015): 534–535.

Blumer, Herbert. *Symbolic Interactionism: Perspective and Method.* Upper Saddle River, NJ: Prentice Hall, 1969.

Browning, Larry D., Ronald W. Greene, S. B. Sitkin, Kathleen M. Sutcliffe, and David Obstfeld. "Constitutive Complexity: Military Entrepreneurs and the Synthetic Character of Communication Flows." In *Building Theories of Organization: The Constitutive Role of Communication*, edited by L. L. Putnam and A. M. Nicotera. New York: Routledge, 2009.

Bruscella, Jacqueline, and Ryan Bisel. "Four Flows Theory and Materiality: ISIL's Use of Material Resources in Its Communicative Constitution." *Communication Monographs*, 2018. doi: 10.1080/03637751.2017.1420907.

Carbaugh, Donal. "Cultural Discourse Analysis: Communication Practices and Cultural Encounters." *Journal of Intercultural Communication Research* 37, no. 3 (2007): 167–182.

Caris, Charles S., and Samuel Reynolds. "ISIS Governance in Syria: Middle East Security Report 22." *The Institute for the Study of War*, July 2014. http://www.understandingwar.org/sites/default/files/ISIS_Governance.pdf.

Christians, Clifford G., and James W. Carey. "The Logic and Aims of Qualitative Research." In *Research Methods in Mass Communication*, edited by Guido H. I. Stempel III and Bruce H. Westley. Upper Saddle River, NJ: Prentice Hall, 1989.

Cronin, Audrey Kurth. "ISIS Is Not a Terrorist Group: Why Counterterrorism Won't Stop the Latest Jihadist Threat." *Foreign Affairs* 94, no. 2 (2015).

Dabiq. "The Return of the Khalifah." Issue 1, July 5, 2014.

Dabiq. "Remaining and Expanding." Issue 5, November 21, 2014.

Dabiq. "Al Qa'idah of Waziristan: A Testimony from Within." Issue 6, December 29, 2014.

Dabiq. "Shari'ah Alone Will Rule Africa." Issue 8, March 30, 2015.

Dabiq. "They Plot and Allah Plots." Issue 9, May 21, 2015.

Davidson, Janine, and Emerson Brooking. "ISIS Hasn't Gone Anywhere—And It's Getting Stronger." *Council on Foreign Relations*, June 24, 2014. https://www.etbrooking.com/portfolio-items/isis-hasnt-gone-anywhere-getting-stronger/.

Denby, David. "The Perfect Children of ISIS: Lessons from Dabiq." *The New Yorker*, November 24, 2015. https://www.newyorker.com/culture/cultural-comment/the-perfect-children-of-isis-lessons-from-dabiq.

DiMaggio, Paul J., and Walter W. Powell. "The Iron Cage Revisited: Institutional Isomorphism and Collective Rationality in Organizational Fields." *American Sociological Review* 48, no. 2 (1983): 147–160.

Ghambhir, Harleen K. "*Dabiq*: The Strategic Messaging of the Islamic State." *The Institute for the Study of War*, August 15, 2014. http://www.understandingwar.org/sites/default/files/Dabiq%20Backgrounder_Harleen%20Final_0.pdf.

Lutgen-Sandvik, Pamela, and Virginia McDermott. "The Constitution of Employee-Abusive Organizations: A Communication Flows Theory." *Communication Theory* 18, no. 2 (2008): 304–333.

McCoy, Terrence. "The Apocalyptic Magazine the Islamic State Uses to Recruit and Radicalize Foreigners." *Washington Post*, September 16, 2014. https://www.washingtonpost.com/news/morning-mix/wp/2014/09/16/the-apocalyptic-magazine-the-islamic-state-uses-to-recruit-and-radicalize-foreigners/?utm_term=.eebe4f64bca7.

McPhee, Robert D., and Pamela Zaug. "The Communicative Constitution of Organizations: A Framework for Explanation." *The Electronic Journal of Communication* 10, no. 1 and 2 (2000): 24–47.
Parsons, Talcott. *The Social System*. New York: The Free Press, 1951.
Sinha, Shreeya. "Obama's Evolution on ISIS." *New York Times*, June 9, 2015. http://www.nytimes.com/interactive/2015/06/09/world/middleeast/obama-isis-strategy.html?_r=0.
Stern, Jessica, and J. M. Berger. *ISIS: The State of Terror.* New York: Harper Collins, 2015.
Tracey, Sarah Jane. *Qualitative Research Methods: Collecting Evidence, Crafting Analysis, Communicating Impact.* Malden, MA: Wiley, 2013.
Weiss, Michael, and Hassan Hassan. *ISIS: Inside the Army of Terror.* New York: Regan Arts, 2015.

JACQUELINE BRUSCELLA, PhD, is Assistant Professor of Organizational Communication in the Department of Communication and Media at the State University of New York, College at Oneonta.

RYAN BISEL, PhD, is Professor of Organizational Communication in the Department of Communication at the University of Oklahoma.

12 Terror Remixed

The Islamic State and the Stop the Christian Genocide Campaign

Rosemary Pennington

The word *genocide* did not exist prior to 1944 and was originally coined to describe the Nazis' attempt to wipe out Europe's Jews as well as other populations they deemed undesirable.[1] Since the end of World War II, activists have worked to frame events such as the conflict in Darfur, ethnic cleansing during the Bosnia conflict, and the forced removal of Armenians by Ottomans during World War I a genocide. The decision whether to label a violent act a genocide is about more than just labeling—it is a political act that can be used to urge the international community to step in and stop the violence.[2] Nations spar over whether the actions of their past or their present deserve the condemnation such a label brings.

The debate over what to label a genocide has been associated lately with the actions of the Islamic State, or ISIS. As discussed throughout this volume, ISIS rose to prominence in 2014 in the power vacuum created by collapsing Iraqi and Syrian governments. The apocalyptic group's purpose is to create a new caliphate, and it is using a mix of military and terroristic tactics to do so, while also utilizing various media to extend its caliphate's reach globally.[3] Philip Seib[4] has referred to such groups—whose boundaries are marked by their presence in media in lieu of physical borders—as "virtual states." They have narratively constructed a state and utilize media to circulate that narrative[5] but do not have a physical, internationally recognized state. ISIS's dream is to possess such an identity—to transform the idea of their caliphate into a physical reality. Even as they wage this physical war, they also wage a virtual one—utilizing both old and new media to spread their message and to spread fear. But what happens when the group's virtual material is taken up by non-Islamic State actors and is repurposed and remixed? Such a remixing is the focus of this chapter.

The Stop the Christian Genocide campaign is focused on the plight of Christians under ISIS and is sponsored by the Knights of Columbus and In Defense of Christians. The Knights of Columbus is a Catholic service organization that provides aid to communities around the world and is active in the defense of Catholicism; In Defense of Christians is a Christian advocacy and aid organization with a similar mission. Both are pushing for the violence experienced by Christian groups under ISIS to be called a genocide. In order to build their case for the appropriateness of this label, the groups created a media campaign: Stop the Christian Genocide. The materials produced for this campaign include interviews with ISIS victims and video of refugee camps, but they also include material produced by ISIS itself. This chapter considers this repurposing and remixing of ISIS media materials. Before engaging with the Stop the Christian Genocide campaign directly, this chapter first examines the literature on the social and political debate over defining genocide and then considers the way media messages can be repurposed and remixed as it unpacks the story the Stop the Christian Genocide Campaign tells of ISIS's actions against Christians in the Middle East.

Defining Genocide

In the aftermath of the Holocaust, when the horrors of World War II were made visible, world powers had pledged "never again"[6] and yet, time after time they find themselves debating whether or not to label an action a genocide. Defining a genocide "turns not on the numbers killed, which is always difficult to ascertain times of crisis, but on the perpetrator's intent."[7] Claudia Card argues that "social death" distinguishes genocide from other types of mass murder, in that it is not only a crime meant to destroy individuals but also to eradicate networks, relationships, and communities, pointing out that "When a group with its own cultural identity is destroyed, its survivors lose their cultural heritage and may even lose their intergenerational connections."[8] Within such an understanding, genocidal acts seek to wipe out physical populations while also wiping out the culture and history associated with those populations.

Writing in the late 1990s, Ervin Staub[9] suggested that genocide, and other types of collective violence, was widespread and that instances of such acts would continue to rise if people in power did not do more to address the root causes of such violence. Barbara Harff points out that "almost all genocides of the last half-century occurred during or in the immediate aftermath of internal wars, revolutions, and regime collapses."[10] Political upheaval, she suggests, produces environments where genocide can happen. The UN Genocide Convention does not include nonstate actors as entities that can commit genocide;[11] however, Scott Straus suggests that "If non-state actors mobilized to eliminated a population, then that campaign should be considered genocide."[12] Though the Islamic State once established footholds in the physical landscape of Iraq and Syria, its hold on those locations is tenuous at best, as seen in its loss of Iraqi and Syrian territory during 2016 and 2017. This issue of ISIS being a nonstate actor matters when one considers ideas of justice and retribution on the part of the group's victims, particularly as genocide is a crime that is typically prosecuted in international courts and tribunals.

As Straus explained in his 2005 article on the Darfur conflict, the Geneva Convention "holds that contracting parties are required to 'undertake to prevent and to punish' genocide."[13] To call something a genocide brings with it then the expectation of intervention, although intervention is not always automatic. Intervention is certainly what those who believe ISIS is attempting to wipe out Christian communities in the Middle East are calling for. They want other Christians to contribute money to relief efforts, but they also want nations, particularly the United States, to rescue the region's Christians from the terrorist actions of the Islamic State. Some of them remix ISIS media materials into their campaigns to help them make that argument.

Remixing Media

The current media ecology is one marked by interconnection and entanglement. Media scholar Mark Deuze has suggested that we live in a "liquid modern society" where "uses and appropriations of media penetrate all aspects of contemporary life"[14]; a society in which media, while ubiquitous, are often invisible. The fact that we are immersed in media makes it difficult, perhaps impossible, to escape media content. For Andrew Hoskins, this pervasiveness can make an audience feel they are watching "the world unfolding in real time,"[15] making it difficult for individuals to avoid representations of violent or traumatic acts.

In musical terms, a remix is revisioning of a piece or a song that changes or deletes elements in order to produce something new.[16] The concept of media remix emerged around the areas of youth media and fandom studies. Henry Jenkins[17] has detailed the ways fans of certain media appropriate content from their favorite books, movies, or TV shows in order to create something new but related. Remix culture also challenges conceptualizations of authorship—forcing us to consider who has the right to shape a narrative and who does not.[18] Jenkins has detailed the ways the interconnected, "liquid" experience of media allows for the quick appropriation, refashioning, and then distribution of media content.[19] Savvy media producers create content that users will spread themselves, extending the shelf life of the text while also extending its reach.[20] In the case of the Islamic State, the group has produced media events and texts featuring violence against a variety of groups, including Christians, in order to instill fear in the audience of those texts, as well as recruit individuals to their cause.[21] The group is dependent on sympathizers sharing this content in social media. But, as Simone Friis reminds us, "Videos shared on the internet are nearly impossible to control."[22] What ISIS might not have anticipated is that groups opposed to ISIS's mission would take up Islamic State materials and use them to attack ISIS itself.

The focus of this chapter is a series of sixteen videos produced by the Stop the Christian Genocide Campaign in 2015 and 2016. Several of the videos aired on television during the 2016 US presidential campaign; others were posted on the campaign's website, and all of them were accessible in a YouTube playlist.[23] In order to understand how Islamic State media was repurposed and remixed into the campaign's messaging, a textual analysis of all sixteen videos was conducted. Employing a grounded-theory methodology, I examined the videos, making note of the way certain elements were deployed, looking for commonalities in how those elements were used across the videos. I also paid close attention to how media material produced by the Islamic State was reframed and remixed by Stop the Christian Genocide to support their argument that a genocide against Christians is taking place under ISIS. What the analysis uncovered were three specific strategies for framing ISIS by Stop the Christian Genocide; the first focused on orange jumpsuits and the ISIS flag, the second on attempts by the Islamic State to erase communities, and the third highlighted the personal experiences of Christians living through ISIS violence.

The Tyrannical Jumpsuit and Flag

When visiting the Stop the Christian Genocide campaign website, the first thing one sees is a banner image (see fig. 12.1). Stretching the width of the homepage, it is a still image lifted from an ISIS video featuring ISIS fighters clad in black, standing beside a line of prisoners in orange jumpsuits. The orange jumpsuits have become a ubiquitous element in ISIS media (as discussed in chapter 8 of this volume), meant to echo the suits worn by prisoners held by the United States in the Guantanamo Bay prison.[24] (Both chapters 8 and 10 of this book describe how American journalist James Foley, whose execution by ISIS helped propel the group onto the agendas of international news outlets, was seen wearing such a jumpsuit just before his beheading by an ISIS executioner was caught on video.)

Though there is no way of knowing exactly who the orange-clad men are, their inclusion on a website devoted to raising awareness of a possible Christian genocide is at least meant to imply that these are Middle Eastern Christians who are about to be executed for their faith. Not only is it unclear who the victims of ISIS are, but the faces of the executioners themselves are also obscured by what appear to be masks or scarves covering their heads. The image was captured just prior to the execution of the prisoners; in it, ISIS becomes a faceless, looming threat meant to invoke fear, and it is fear and dread that the Stop the Christian Genocide campaign creators want to provoke in the viewer of this image. Researchers have suggested that witnessing terrorism can leave individuals

Fig. 12.1 Home page with banner of the Stop the Christian Genocide campaign.

feeling not only fear but also a sense of vulnerability,[25] while Friis notes that still images pulled from videos "do not show ISIS's motivations."[26] Both the evocation of vulnerability and the lack of context for ISIS's actions in the image—we do not know if these are Christians, if they are Western hostages, or if they are Muslims who do not practice Islam the way ISIS demands—allows the campaign creators to load the visuals with their own meaning, to remix them with other campaign materials, including the videos as well as text on the site, to try to convince individuals of the truth of their argument. Stop the Christian Genocide campaign has remixed the fear ISIS attempts to evoke in its images of executions in order to urge action against the Islamic State.

Scenes featuring orange jumpsuits also appear in several of the campaign videos (see fig. 12.2). Men are seen marching in a line along a beach; in one instance, ISIS prisoners are seen being shoved to their knees in the sand as their executioners stand behind them, their knives at the ready. Stripped from the videos is the audio that accompanied them, this audio often featuring a recitation of the supposed crimes of those about to be executed. The specific message ISIS wanted to convey with the videos has been erased, replaced with a musical backdrop that features heavy, loud drumming that seems designed to bring to mind the sound of the rapid firing of a gun. In one particularly harrowing scene, ISIS fighters, one with a gun in his hand, are seen holding a kneeling prisoner in orange over a body of some kind of water (see fig. 12.3). The man is struggling as the fighter pulls the trigger, shooting him in the head. The viewer sees another fighter holding the victim as he is shot and then throwing him into the green water below. It is the only time any of the videos show an actual execution, and it is again accompanied by the drumming music. The scene lasts two seconds and is sandwiched between the testimony of a crying woman and a crying child. Just as quickly as it appears on the screen, it is gone, and if viewers are not paying close attention, they may not even realize they have witnessed the death of the man.

Fig. 12.2 Orange jumpsuit–wearing ISIS prisoners in a campaign video.

Fig. 12.3 Still from execution video used by Stop the Christian Genocide campaign.

This remixing of the ISIS material with the crying individuals amplifies the suffering of the group's victims; however, it serves at the same time to obscure the man's death by drawing attention away from his execution and focusing instead on people we are meant to understand are ISIS survivors.

Shana Gadarian suggests that once dramatic imagery of traumatic events, such as terrorist attacks, becomes politicized it loses some of its original emotional power.[27] The message that is being framed by the visual overtakes the emotional content of the image. The Stop the Christian Genocide campaign uses images of ISIS victims to build an argument that the outside world needs to step in and stop the violence. The videos are edited in such a way that the viewer never sees more than a few seconds of ISIS prisoners in orange on the screen. And, as with the execution of the man by the water, these images are often embedded between personal narratives of witnesses to the violence, narratives that have been chosen to push the idea that what is happening in Syria and Iraq is a genocide. The Islamic State imagery has been remixed with that produced by the Stop the Christian Genocide campaign in order to push the campaign's reading of the events. The violent imagery flies by the viewer quickly, becoming almost an overwhelming kind of wallpaper for Stop the Christian Genocide's story of what is happening in the region. It is hard to find details in the onslaught of imagery. Although, in the case of the execution scene, one such detail is that in the corner of the shot stands a man who appears to be holding the black-and-white flag of ISIS.

What has become popularly labeled the Islamic State's flag features a black background with part of the shahada, the Muslim profession of faith that there is no god but God and Mohammad is his messenger, written in white Arabic script on it. Below the shahada is a white circle with text saying Mohammad is God's messenger, meant to resemble the Prophet's seal. Both the shahada and the seal are meant to lend religious and ideological legitimacy to the group. The flag was inspired by the Black Banner, a plain black flag Muhammad is said to have carried into battle; a black flag is also tied to the story of the Mahdi, a messianic Muslim figure.[28] ISIS's choice of the black banner is designed to serve as a kind of symbolic bridge between Islam's past and Islam's future. Mohammad brought the true religion to the world, and ISIS, with its goal of creating a new caliphate, will create the world anew for true believers. In Stop the Christian Genocide campaign materials, the flag is seen held by ISIS fighters, flying over ISIS gatherings, and waving from atop a tank. Images of this waving flag appear on screen against more of the gunfire-like music. The videos are edited so that each appearance of the flag is accompanied by a swell in the music—it is a visual and auditory assault on the senses of the viewer, making it difficult for the viewer to look away from the screen. Each swell punctuated with the black flag again serves to identify the threat to Christians—the Islamic State.

These images of ISIS fit within the larger cultural framework that has shaped our understanding of the group—as pundits, politicians, and journalists debate whether ISIS is really Islamic[29] or whether ISIS really has established a caliphate,[30] what has not been debated is the fact that the group is a violent threat to the Middle East as well as the larger world. Frames exist both in media and in culture.[31] They are shared and shaped through exposure and circulation. However, the way material is framed can change, and the message associated with that material can change. In the videos ISIS produces of its prisoners and its soldiers, the message the group is attempting to communicate is one of power and domination. The Stop the Christian Genocide campaign repurposes these texts, changing the message they communicate. The horrors of ISIS are still apparent in the campaign's videos; ISIS's framing of itself as soldiers of Islam as they wave their flag featuring the shahada are still visible, but the message associated with the imagery is no longer primarily what the terrorists had intended. Instead, it becomes wrapped up in Stop the Christian Genocide's narrative of the images. In the case of the images of orange jumpsuit–clad ISIS prisoners and of waving black ISIS flags, the story becomes about the danger the Islamic State poses specifically to Christians. There's an implied threat in the materials: if this could happen to these Christians, it could happen to you if you do not do your part to try to stop ISIS.

Community Erasure

The Islamic State's declaration of a new caliphate coincided with the public execution of eight men, whose bodies were hung on crosses in the square of a Syrian town.[32] It was an act meant to terrorize and terrify but also to communicate who would not be welcome in ISIS's caliphate. Genocide is not only a crime of mass murder; it is also a crime focused on wiping out the social ties, networks, and communities of the victims.[33] Perpetrators of genocide seek to not only physically destroy their victims; they are also often attempting to eradicate the culture and history of those victims. It is both physical and social community erasure. Videos produced for the Stop the Christian Genocide campaign often highlight what it sees as the physical erasure of Christian communities (see fig. 12.4). Images of smashed crosses, overturned pews, and shattered walls are juxtaposed against video of children crying, of rows of Christians crammed onto cots in a refuge, and of a priest, who claims to have been tortured and left for dead by the Islamic State, looking directly into the video camera and appealing to all Christians, to all in the West, to "help my people." One shot, pulled from an Islamic State video, appears to communicate why those people need help. It shows row upon row of what appear to be boys lying on the ground, their hands tied behind their backs. Their bodies lie still, and they appear to be dead, although the video is edited, once again, too quickly for the viewer to know for sure. The very next shot features a Christian priest crying into his hands.

Klausen reminds us that the victims of terrorism are chosen "not because they are the enemy, but because they have symbolic importance."[34] Prior to the rise of Saddam Hussein and the unrest that erupted after his toppling, Iraq was held up as an exemplar of pluralism in the Middle East.[35] ISIS's targeting of Christians, Yazidis, and other religious minorities—people with generally little

Fig. 12.4 ISIS fighter destroying a cross, featured in a campaign video.

real power—would seem to suggest the group is trying to upend the idea of Iraq as diverse. Ömür Harmansah suggests we consider videos produced by ISIS, in particular those documenting the destruction of cultural sites, as "artifacts of ideological discourse."[36] They are meant to communicate ISIS's belief that the Middle East should be refashioned into a caliphate of their design, one that has no room for ancient history or cultural and religious pluralism. However, those same media texts provide material for organizations like Stop the Christian Genocide campaign to pick up and refashion for their own purposes.

While both ISIS and Stop the Christian Genocide use the videos to highlight the group's targeting of Iraq and Syria's minority communities, the organizations attach different meanings to those texts. For the Islamic State, the videos are visual representations of the work the group is putting into the creation of their caliphate. The destruction is meant to communicate ISIS's power and to also signal to supporters that a place is being made for them in the new caliphate. Stop the Christian Genocide remixes those same materials, featuring the same scenes of destruction, into their own media to try to persuade viewers that a genocide is taking place.

Power is at the heart of the images used in the Stop the Christian Genocide videos, but the power the group is attempting to evoke is the power to intervene. Two of the videos are short, thirty-second pieces designed to be used as television ads. (The author saw one of them air during the 2016 presidential primary season.) Against yet another throbbing musical score and images of ISIS's destruction are placed photographs of several contenders from the 2016 United States presidential election (including eventual Democratic nominee Hillary Clinton), quoted as calling ISIS's violence against Christians a genocide. These are individuals, powerful individuals, who could push for intervention, whom Stop the Christian Genocide campaign seems to be purposefully framing as pro-intervention as the campaign edits their sound bites against ISIS propaganda showing the destruction of places and of people. The challenge to other politicians, and to others viewing the ads, seems to be "If these people are willing to call what's happening a genocide, why aren't you?"

It is hard to argue with the assertion that such a targeted action is taking place when the campaign's materials show evidence of churches that have been ransacked by the Islamic State and seem to show Islamic State fighters executing Christians (or members of other minority groups). Christian artifacts are also targets, as videos show an ISIS soldier sitting on what appears to be a tombstone, breaking a cross from the top; another scene features a close-up of a statue of Mary riddled with bullet holes; still another shows a building in the far-off distance being blown up, although, much as with the images showing executions, it is hard to know for sure whether the building is a church. The campaign wants its viewers to believe it is a church, and so it remixes the images of destruction with images of refugee camps and ISIS survivors produced for the campaign, erasing ISIS's original message and replacing it with the campaign's own. The campaign is working to convince the viewer that a war against not just the West, but against Christianity itself, is being waged by the Islamic State.

Referencing Samuel Huntington's clash of civilizations thesis[37] when writing about the Middle East or Islam has become something of a cliché; however, the materials produced for the Stop the Christian Genocide campaign adopt an overtly civilizationalist conflict tone. The fight against ISIS is framed as not only a fight against a group that hates anyone who does not believe as they do; it is framed as a fight against the Middle East's Christian communities. "No group is more affected than Christians," Carl Anderson, Supreme Knight of the Knights of Columbus says in one video in relation to the violence in the Middle East. Anderson's statement is reflective of news coverage of terrorism post 9/11 that framed it as a conflict between Muslims and "Christian America."[38] This framing ignores the reality that the majority of ISIS's victims are Muslim.[39] In fact, a 2011 study by the United States National Counterterrorism Center found that between 82 and 97 percent of all terrorism victims over a five-year period were actually Muslim[40]; the 2015 Global Terrorism Index shows that nine out of the ten nations experiencing the most terrorism are Muslim countries (or countries with significant Muslim populations).[41]

ISIS produces videos featuring the destruction of Muslim towns and the execution of Muslims who do not bend to their will.[42] These images do not appear in Stop the Christian Genocide campaign materials, or if they do, they are masked in such a way as to appear to be evidence of the targeting of Christians. (Outside of the personal testimony of Iraqi and Syrian Christians that appears in some of the videos, the focus of the next section of this chapter, it is hard to know if any of the prisoners or victims featured in the ISIS materials are Christian.) ISIS utilizes civilizationalist discourse in its materials as it seeks to justify its very existence; the Stop the Christian Genocide campaign remixes that discourse and pushes it forward, using it in an attempt to make viewers care about the violence in the

Middle East, to make them see that it is not simply the Christians of the Middle East who are at risk, but all of Christendom. Among the most compelling ways the campaign does this is through the inclusion of the personal testimony of ISIS victims in its videos.

The Power of Personal Testimony

Within Christianity there is power in personal testimony. Paul, the apostle credited with propelling the early Christian faith's spread across the wider Mediterranean world, leveraged his own personal story of conversion and faith as he sought to convert people to the new religion. The Stop the Christian Genocide campaign works to leverage personal testimony in a number of its campaign materials. Several videos feature individuals discussing their experiences with the Islamic State. One woman details how in Mosul, ISIS's one-time stronghold in Iraq, the group was rumored to murder any Christian they found in the city. "As soon as they hear a Christian went to Mosul," she says, "they immediately kill him." Her story is set against images, discussed earlier, of ISIS members destroying crosses and blowing up what the video suggests are Christian sites. The message is clear—if no one steps in to stop them, ISIS is going to erase Christian communities. "Genocide is an easy word," says Father Douglas al-Bazi, who was kidnapped and tortured by extremists for several days, in one of the videos, "Wake up and take action." Father al-Bazi appears in a number of the videos, recounting his experience as a victim of extremist violence, always appealing at the end for intervention of some kind. The stakes of a failure to intervene are laid out by other testimonials.

Standing in a beige courtyard, a young boy cries as he recounts the violence he has witnessed. "ISIS, they are beasts. They didn't leave us anything in this country," he says as he wipes the tears from his eyes (see fig. 12.5). His message in this moment is not aimed at the international community or politicians, the way al-Bazi's was; instead, this child's testimony is edited in such a way as to implicate the viewer in his suffering and in the suffering of his fellow Christians. He cries, a woman sitting silently in a chair cries, a grandmother cries in anger as she explains "There is no life here." All these tears are edited against the visuals, produced by ISIS, of the destruction of what appear to be Christian sites. Another video features a female voiceover explaining that Christians lived in Mosul for almost two thousand years before the Islamic State took over. "Today," she says, "not one is left." The video then moves to images of Iraqi refugees living in camps, of children being tended to by doctors, and of families waiting on food aid. The video ends with the question "If we don't help, who will?" While none of the refugees featured in the video speaks, their placement between the information about Mosul and the call for help suggests the viewer is witnessing the results of Mosul's takeover by ISIS; the very existence of refugees, their representation in

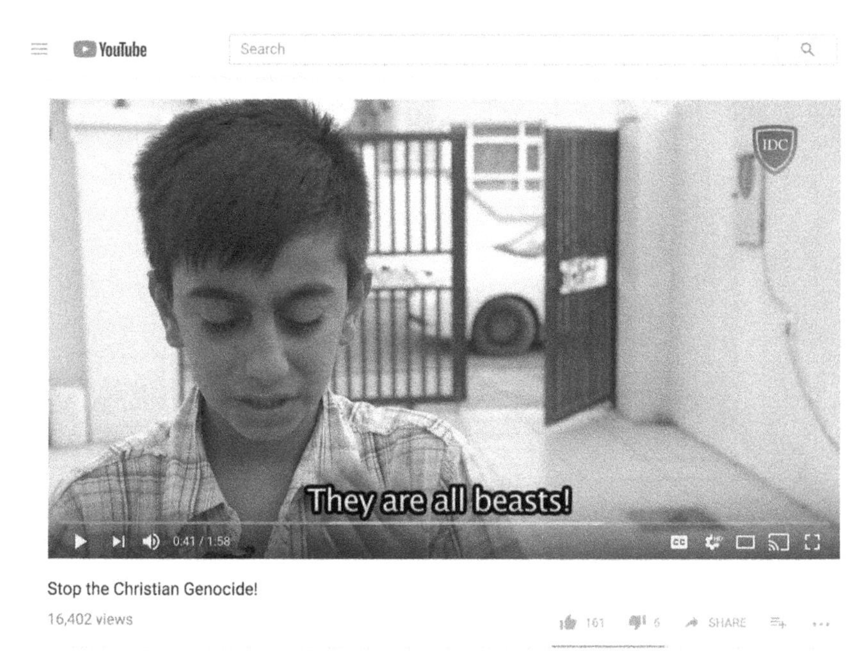

Fig. 12.5 A young boy calls ISIS fighters "beasts" in campaign video.

video and in photographs, as well as their personal testimony, serves as evidence of the Islamic State's brutality. They provide a window into the realities of living under ISIS, providing a way for the viewer to witness the suffering of the Islamic State's victims.

John Durham Peters, writing of the experience of witnessing suffering in media, suggests that "To witness an event is to be responsible in some way to it."[43] It can also create "intimacy at a distance,"[44] an intimacy that can lead to closer connection to and engagement with others,[45] as well as a feeling of compassion for those the viewer sees suffering.[46] It is those feelings of connection and compassion the Stop the Christian Genocide campaign is attempting to evoke with its use of personal testimony. The campaign wants you, the viewer, to feel responsible for what is taking place in Iraq and Syria. One of the videos ends with several ISIS victims looking directly into the camera and saying, some in very broken English, "Stop the Christian genocide." It is difficult not to feel a connection to individuals who seem to be looking directly into your eyes. "Enough is enough," Father al-Bazi says, "take action." You, the viewer, are being urged to take action. The video ends with a close-up of a hand on what appears to be a wooden beam of some kind; it is bloody, and a red cross is etched into the palm—calling to mind all the crosses that are seen to be destroyed by ISIS in their various videos (see fig. 12.6). The image with the red cross is, of course, a reference to Christ's

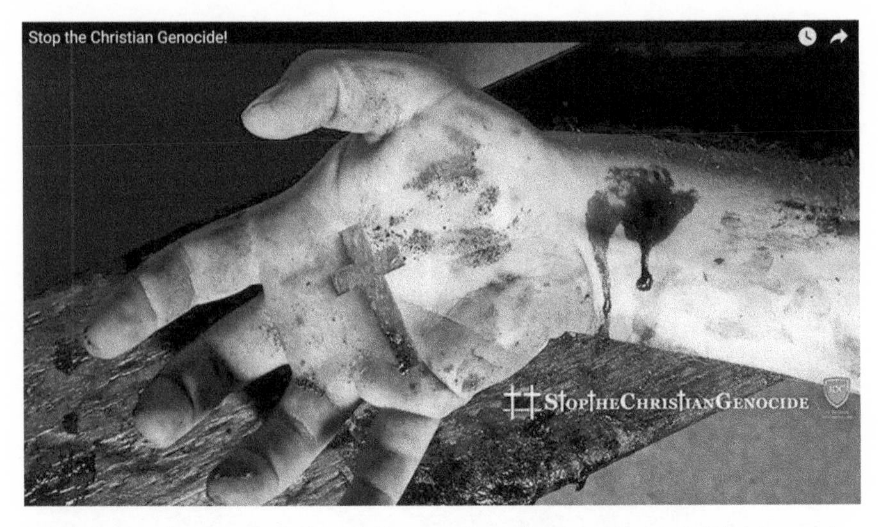

Fig. 12.6 Image that appears at the end of a campaign video, meant to remind the viewer of Jesus Christ's crucifixion.

crucifixion; to witness within the Christian faith is to not only experience something but also to publicly declare one's belief in, and love for, Christ. Christ sacrificed himself for you, the photo of the bloody hand reminds the viewer, while also seeming to ask viewers what they are willing to sacrifice in order to help their fellow Christians. Just beneath the bloody hand appears the hashtag #stopthechristiangenocide, with the pound sign and the t's designed to look like crosses, suggesting Christians can, at the very least, share the campaign's information in social media.

Though it is outside the purview of this chapter, it is worth noting that hashtags such as #stopthechristiangenocide and #BeyondGenocide are being used in social media in an attempt to frame the actions of ISIS as genocidal. Sometimes the individuals using the hashtags link to Stop the Christian Genocide campaign materials, sometimes they feature links to personal testimonies like the ones discussed above or news stories, and other times the social media posts criticize Western governments for what is seen as their inaction on the part of Iraq and Syria's Christians. The hashtags have also been used to promote marches, prayer gatherings, and petitions, but it is difficult to gauge how much of an impact, if any, they have had on the cultural framing of ISIS's actions.

Remixed Terror, Remixed Message?

The power behind the media spectacles ISIS creates is their ability to induce fear and horror in the viewer. Whether watching the destruction of ancient sites or the execution of innocent individuals, the videos and images are designed to upset and to provoke. Witnessing such events can cause individuals to feel vulnerable and to lose faith in institutions designed to protect them.[47] The Islamic State is apocalyptic in its vision and seeks to draw the wider Middle East as well as Western powers into full-blown war. As discussed throughout this book, it is a savvy producer of multimedia materials designed to communicate its ideology, instill fear in its opponents, and recruit sympathizers to its cause. ISIS is somewhat dependent on sympathizers to help spread its message; at the same time, those spreadable texts and messages can be picked up by individuals or groups opposed to the Islamic State and used to create anti-ISIS materials, as in the case of the Stop the Christian Genocide campaign. As Friis notes, "the technological innovations of the digital age have influenced not just *how* war can be shown, but also *who* can successfully produce, choose and disseminate images of war to a larger audience."[48]

Iyer et al. suggest that images "should enhance people's emotional reactions to media coverage of terrorism."[49] In the case of the videos produced by the Stop the Christian Genocide campaign, they are certainly designed to evoke an emotional response. The images of ISIS members smashing crosses and of churches gutted after ISIS fighters destroyed them are remixed in the campaign's videos, in order to provoke outrage and anger in the viewer. The eyewitness testimony of ISIS victims, including a Christian priest, is designed to shame fellow Christians, as well as those in the West who claim to care about human rights, into doing something. Emotion can influence political behavior and beliefs.[50] Stop the Christian Genocide is leveraging emotion as best it can, in order to push for more robust intervention in the conflict. The videos are designed to convince their audience that a genocide is taking place and to force the international community to act to stop the eradication of the region's Christian communities. However, Ashley Pattwell, Tyson Mitman, and Douglas Porpora argue that the utilization of violence as communication can delegitimize a political message.[51] That may be one reason why the Stop the Christian Genocide campaign dialed back its use of ISIS material over time, instead coming to rely more on imagery collected by its own producers and members. The campaign's videos began to feature first-person accounts of the Islamic State's violence, in an attempt to convince the viewer of the truth as the campaign sees it—that the Islamic State is waging a religious war against the Middle East's Christian community, one designed to wipe Christians out. On the campaign's website lives the text of a petition sent to then-US Secretary of State John Kerry, asking the United States to officially label the killing of Christians in Iraq and Syria by ISIS a genocide. To name something a genocide brings with it expectations of international intervention. It is not simply a game of definitions; it could potentially have geopolitical implications. Although the United States has not, as of this writing, declared ISIS violence against Christians or other minorities genocidal in nature, the country did partner with Iraqi forces in October 2016 to attempt to drive the Islamic State from Mosul.

Even as ISIS loses its urban strongholds, there is some suggestion that the group will begin targeting more rural parts of Iraq and Syria.[52] This means, though Mosul might find itself liberated from the Islamic State, the world may not be liberated from ISIS's violent media. Which raises the question, once again, of what happens to terrorist texts when they are repurposed by other organizations? If the Islamic State produces mediated spectacles of terror as a way to provoke the international community in hopes of kindling all-out war, and if groups like the Stop the Christian Genocide campaign then remix those same materials to try to provoke outrage in order to push Western powers into intervening in the region, have the materials truly been repurposed, or do they simply reinforce the civilizationalist frame that suggests the conflict is one of Islam versus Christianity? If those who see violence and yet do not act are somehow complicit in it, then what about those who reproduce and repurpose terrorist material for their own ends?

Journalists and media producers are now debating how and when to use material produced by terrorist and extremist groups in reporting on those groups' actions. The ethical issue that often comes up in these debates is whether journalists are doing terrorists' work for them by providing a broader audience for the spectacles terrorists produce. Advocacy groups who are working to counter the messaging of such organizations or who are working to compel individuals and governments to take up arms against them should also consider the ethics of circulating extremist-produced material. Even if the material is remixed in a way to push a different message, even if it is being used in order to gain help for the victims of extremist groups, should it be recirculated at all? Is it worth exposing the material to a broader audience than it might otherwise have had? The Stop the Christian Genocide campaign has been unsuccessful so far in getting those in power to call the Islamic State's actions against Middle Eastern Christian communities a genocide, so perhaps not.

Notes

1. Raphael Lemkin, "Genocide," *American Scholar* 15, no. 2 (1946): 227–230.
2. Scott Straus, "Darfur and the Genocide Debate," *Foreign Affairs* 84, no. 1 (2005): 123–133.
3. For a discussion of this, see chapters 2 and 5 in this volume, as well as Jad Melki and May Jabado, "Mediated Public Diplomacy of the Islamic State in Syria and Iraq: The Synergistic Use of Terrorism, Social Media, and Branding," *Media and Communication* 4, no. 2 (2016): 92–103; and Yannick Veilleux-Lepage, "Retweeting the Caliphate: The Role of Soft-Sympathizers in the Islamic State's Social Media Strategy," conference paper, 6th International Symposium on Terrorism and Transnational Crime, December 2014.
4. Philip Seib, "Public Diplomacy versus Terrorism," in *Media and Terrorism: Global Perspectives*, ed. Des Freedman and Daya Kishan Thussu (Thousand Oaks, CA: Sage, 2012), 63–76.

5. Simone Molin Friis, "'Beyond Anything We Have Ever Seen': Beheading Videos and the Visibility of Violence in the War against ISIS," *International Affairs* 91, no. 4 (2015): 725–746. See also Veilleux-Lepage, "Retweeting the Caliphate."

6. Lemkin, "Genocide."

7. Samantha Power, "Bystanders to Genocide," *The Atlantic* 288, no. 2 (2001): 84–108.

8. Claudia Card, "Genocide and Social Death," *Hypatia* 18, no. 1 (2003): 73.

9. Ervin Staub, "The Origins and Prevention of Genocide, Mass Killing, and Other Collective Violence," *Peace and Conflict: Journal of Peace Psychology* 5, no. 4 (1999): 303–336.

10. Barbara Harff, "No Lessons Learned from the Holocaust? Assessing Risks of Genocide and Political Mass Murder since 1955," *American Political Science Review* 97, no. 1 (2003): 57.

11. Ibid.

12. Scott Straus, "Contested Meanings and Conflicting Imperatives: A Conceptual Analysis of Genocide," *Journal of Genocide Research* 3, no. 3 (2001): 365.

13. Straus, "Darfur and the Genocide Debate," 129.

14. Mark Deuze, "Media Life," *Media, Culture & Society* 33, no. 1 (2011): 137.

15. Andrew Hoskins, "Temporality, Proximity, and Security: Terror in a Media-Drenched Age," *International Relations* 20, no. 4 (2006): 454.

16. Michael Knobel and Colin Lankshear, "Remix: The Art and Craft of Endless Hybridization," *Journal of Adolescent & Adult Literacy* 52, no. 1 (2008): 22–33.

17. Henry Jenkins, *Textual Poachers: Television Fans and Participatory Culture* (New York: Routledge, 1992).

18. Nicholas Diakopoulos, Kurt Luther, Yevgeniy Medynskiy, and Irfan Essa, "The Evolution of Authorship in a Remix Society," conference paper, Proceedings of the 18th Conference on Hypertext and Hypermedia, September 2007.

19. Henry Jenkins, *Convergence Culture: Where Old Media and New Media Collide* (New York: New York University Press, 2006).

20. Henry Jenkins, Sam Ford, and Joshua Green, *Spreadable Media: Creating Value and Meaning in a Network Culture* (New York: New York University Press, 2013).

21. Veilleux-Lepage, "Retweeting the Caliphate."

22. Friis, "'Beyond Anything We Have Ever Seen,'" 730.

23. This playlist was available in 2016, but since the writing of this chapter, seems to have been deleted or the videos unbundled from the list. Most of the videos examined in this chapter are still available for viewing in YouTube; they have just become more difficult to find.

24. Jytte Klausen, "Tweeting the Jihad: Social Media Networks of Western Foreign Fighters in Syria and Iraq," *Studies in Conflict & Terrorism* 38, no. 1 (2015): 1–22.

25. Aarti Iyer, Joana Webster, Matthew J. Hornsey, and Eric J. Vanman, "Understanding the Power of the Picture: The Effect of Image Content on Emotional and Political Responses to Terror," *Journal of Applied Social Psychology* 44, no. 7 (2014): 511–521.

26. Friis, "'Beyond Anything We Have Ever Seen,'" 741.

27. Shana Kushner Gadarian, "Scary Pictures: How Terrorism Imagery Affects Voter Evaluations," *Political Communication* 31, no. 2 (2014): 282–302.

28. William McCants, "How ISIS Got Its Flag," *The Atlantic*, September 22, 2015, https://www.theatlantic.com/international/archive/2015/09/isis-flag-apocalypse/406498/.

29. Graeme Wood, "What ISIS Really Wants," *The Atlantic*, March 2015, https://www.theatlantic.com/magazine/archive/2015/03/what-isis-really-wants/384980/.

30. Shadi Hamid, "What a Caliphate Really Is—And How the Islamic State Is Not One," *Washington Post*, October 28, 2016, https://www.washingtonpost.com/opinions/what-a

-caliphate-really-is--and-how-the-islamic-state-is-not-one/2016/10/28/f17dfd9a-80cb-11e6-b002-307601806392_story.html?utm_term=.7b0045b5eeb0.

31. For an introduction to the idea of framing theory generally, see Erving Goffman, *Frame Analysis: An Essay on the Organization of Experience* (Lebanon, NH: Northeastern University Press, 1974). For an introduction to framing's applications to media and communication studies, see Stephen D. Reese, "Prologue," in *Framing Public Life: Perspectives on Media and Our Understanding of the Social World*, ed. Stephen D. Reese, Oscar H. Gandy, and August E. Grant (Mahwah, NJ: Erlbaum, 2001): 7–32; and Baldwin Van Gorp, "The Constructionist Approach to Framing: Bringing Culture Back In," *Journal of Communication* 57, no. 1 (2007): 60–78.

32. Klausen, "Tweeting the Jihad."

33. Card, "Genocide and Social Death."

34. Klausen, "Tweeting the Jihad," 2.

35. Ali Mamouri, "Diversity and Religious Pluralism Are Disappearing Amid Iraq's Crisis," *The Conversation*, August 3, 2014, https://theconversation.com/diversity-and-religious-pluralism-are-disappearing-amid-iraqs-crisis-29832.

36. Ömür Harmansah, "ISIS, Heritage, and the Spectacles of Destruction in Global Media," *Near Eastern Archeology* 78, no. 3 (2015): 173.

37. Samuel Huntington, "The Clash of Civilizations?" *Foreign Affairs* 72, no. 3 (1993): 22–49.

38. Kimberly A. Powell, "Framing Islam: An Analysis of US Media Coverage of Terrorism since 9/11," *Communication Studies* 62, no. 1 (2011): 90–112.

39. Institute for Economics and Peace, "Global Terrorism Index: Measuring and Understanding the Impact of Terrorism," 2015, http://economicsandpeace.org/wp-content/uploads/2015/11/Global-Terrorism-Index-2015.pdf.

40. The National Counterterrorism Center, "Report on Terrorism," 2011, http://fas.org/irp/threat/nctc2011.pdf.

41. Institute for Economics and Peace, "Global Terrorism Index."

42. Friis, "'Beyond Anything We Have Ever Seen.'"

43. John Durham Peters, "Witnessing," *Media, Culture & Society* 23, no. 6 (2001): 708.

44. Paul Frosh, "Telling Presences: Witnessing, Mass Media, and the Imagined Lives of Strangers," *Critical Studies in Media Communication* 23, no. 4 (2006): 279.

45. Shani Orgad, *Media Representation and the Global Imagination* (Boston: Polity Press, 2012).

46. Brigitta Höijer, "The Discourse of Global Compassion: The Audience and Media Reporting of Human Suffering," *Media, Culture & Society* 26, no. 4 (2004): 513–531.

47. Carol S. Fullerton, Robert J. Ursano, Ann E. Norwood, and Harry H. Holloway, "Trauma, Terrorism, and Disaster," in *Terrorism and Disaster: Individual and Community Mental Health Interventions*, eds. Robert J. Ursano, Carol S. Fullerton, and Ann E. Norwood (New York: Cambridge University Press, 2003): 1–20.

48. Friis, "'Beyond Anything We Have Ever Seen,'" 728.

49. Iyer et al., "Understanding the Power of the Picture," 512.

50. Ibid.

51. Ashley Pattwell, Tyson Mitman, and Douglas Porpora, "Terrorism as Failed Political Communication," *International Journal of Communication* 9 (2015): 1120–1139.

52. William McCants and Craig Whiteside, "The Islamic State's Coming Rural Revival," *Brookings Markaz*, October 25, 2016, https://www.brookings.edu/blog/markaz/2016/10/25/the-islamic-states-coming-rural-revival/.

Bibliography

Card, Claudia. "Genocide and Social Death." *Hypatia* 18, no. 1 (2003): 63–79.

Deuze, Mark. "Media Life." *Media, Culture & Society* 33, no. 1 (2011): 137–148.

Diakopoulos, Nicholas, Kurt Luther, Yevgeniy Medynskiy, and Irfan Essa, "The Evolution of Authorship in a Remix Society." Paper presented at the Proceedings of the 18th Conference on Hypertext and Hypermedia, Manchester, UK, September 2007.

Gadarian, Shana Kushner. "Scary Pictures: How Terrorism Imagery Affects Voter Evaluations." *Political Communication* 31, no. 2 (2014): 282–302.

Goffman, Erving. *Frame Analysis: An Essay on the Organization of Experience*. Lebanon, NH: Northeastern University Press, 1974.

Friis, Simone Molin. "'Beyond Anything We Have Ever Seen': Beheading Videos and the Visibility of Violence in the War against ISIS." *International Affairs* 91, no. 4 (2015): 725–746.

Frosh, Paul. "Telling Presences: Witnessing, Mass Media, and the Imagined Lives of Strangers." *Critical Studies in Media Communication* 23, no. 4 (2006): 265–284.

Fullerton, Carol S., Robert J. Ursano, Ann E. Norwood, and Harry H. Holloway. "Trauma, Terrorism, and Disaster." In *Terrorism and Disaster: Individual and Community Mental Health Interventions*, edited by Robert J. Ursano, Carol S. Fullerton, and Ann E. Norwood, 1–20. New York: Cambridge University Press, 2003.

Hamid, Shadi. "What a Caliphate Really Is—And the Islamic State Is Not One." *Washington Post*, October 28, 2016. https://www.washingtonpost.com/opinions/what-a-caliphate-really-is—and-how-the-islamic-state-is-not-one/2016/10/28/f17dfd9a-80cb-11e6-b002-307601806392_story.html?utm_term=.27137313b9de.

Hamid, Shadi. "Does ISIS Really Have Nothing to Do with Islam? Islamic Apologetics Carry Serious Risks." *Washington Post*, November 18, 2015. https://www.washingtonpost.com/news/acts-of-faith/wp/2015/11/18/does-isis-really-have-nothing-to-do-with-islam-islamic-apologetics-carry-serious-risks/.

Harff, Barbara. "No Lessons Learned from the Holocaust? Assessing Risks of Genocide and Political Mass Murder since 1955." *American Political Science Review* 97, no. 1 (2003): 57–63.

Harmansah, Ömür. "ISIS, Heritage, and the Spectacles of Destruction in Global Media." *Near Eastern Archeology* 78, no. 3 (2015): 170–177.

Höijer, Brigitta. "The Discourse of Global Compassion: The Audience and Media Reporting of Human Suffering." *Media, Culture & Society* 26, no. 4 (2004): 513–531.

Hoskins, Andrew. "Temporality, Proximity, and Security: Terror in a Media-Drenched Age." *International Relations* 20, no. 4 (2006): 453–466.

Huntington, Samuel. "The Clash of Civilizations?" *Foreign Affairs* 72, no. 3 (1993): 22–49.

Institute for Economics and Peace. "Global Terrorism Index: Measuring and Understanding the Impact of Terrorism." 2015. http://economicsandpeace.org/wp-content/uploads/2015/11/Global-Terrorism-Index-2015.pdf.

Iyer, Aarti, Joana Webster, Matthew J. Hornsey, and Eric J. Vanman. "Understanding the Power of the Picture: The Effect of Image Content on Emotional and Political Responses to Terror." *Journal of Applied Social Psychology* 44, no. 7 (2014): 511–521.

Jenkins, Henry. *Textual Poachers: Television Fans and Participatory Culture*. New York: Routledge, 1992.

Jenkins, Henry. *Convergence Culture: Where Old Media and New Media Collide.* New York: New York University Press, 2006.

Jenkins, Henry, Sam Ford, and Joshua Green. *Spreadable Media: Creating Value and Meaning in a Network Culture.* New York: New York University Press, 2013.

Klausen, Jytte. "Tweeting the Jihad: Social Media Networks of Western Foreign Fighters in Syria and Iraq." *Studies in Conflict & Terrorism* 38, no. 1 (2015): 1–22.

Knobel, Michael, and Colin Lankshear. "Remix: The Art and Craft of Endless Hybridization." *Journal of Adolescent & Adult Literacy* 52, no. 1 (2008): 22–33.

Lemkin, Raphael. "Genocide." *American Scholar* 15, no. 2 (1946): 227–230.

Mamouri, Ali. "Diversity and Religious Pluralism Are Disappearing amid Iraq's Crisis." *The Conversation*, August 3, 2014. https://theconversation.com/diversity-and-religious-pluralism-are-disappearing-amid-iraqs-crisis-29832.

McCants, William. "How ISIS Got Its Flag." *The Atlantic*, September 22, 2015. http://www.theatlantic.com/international/archive/2015/09/isis-flag-apocalypse/406498/.

McCants, William, and Craig Whiteside. "The Islamic State's Coming Rural Revival." *Brookings Markaz*, October 25, 2016. https://www.brookings.edu/blog/markaz/2016/10/25/the-islamic-states-coming-rural-revival/.

Melki, Jad, and May Jabado. "Mediated Public Diplomacy of the Islamic State in Syria and Iraq: The Synergistic Use of Terrorism, Social Media, and Branding." *Media and Communication* 4, no. 2 (2016): 92–103.

National Counterterrorism Center, The. Report on Terrorism, 2011. http://fas.org/irp/threat/nctc2011.pdf.

Orgad, Shani. *Media Representation and the Global Imagination.* Malden, MA: Polity Press, 2012.

Pattwell, Ashley, Tyson Mitman, and Douglas Porpora. "Terrorism as Failed Political Communication," *International Journal of Communication* 9 (2015): 1120–1139.

Peters, John Durham. "Witnessing." *Media, Culture & Society* 23, no. 6 (2001): 707–723.

Powell, Kimberly A. "Framing Islam: An Analysis of U.S. Media Coverage of Terrorism since 9/11." *Communication Studies* 62, no. 1 (2011): 90–112.

Power, Samantha. "Bystanders to Genocide." *The Atlantic* 288, no. 2 (2001): 84–108.

Reese, Stephen D. "Prologue." In *Framing Public Life: Perspectives on Media and Our Understanding of the Social World*, edited by Stephen D. Reese, Oscar H. Gandy, and August E. Grant, 7–32. Mahwah, NJ: Erlbaum, 2001.

Seib, Philip. "Public Diplomacy versus Terrorism." In *Media and Terrorism: Global Perspectives*, edited by Des Freedman and Daya Kishan Thussu, 63–76. Thousand Oaks, CA: Sage, 2012.

Staub, Ervin. "The Origins and Prevention of Genocide, Mass Killing, and Other Collective Violence." *Peace and Conflict: Journal of Peace Psychology* 5, no. 4 (1999): 303–336.

Straus, Scott. "Contested Meanings and Conflicting Imperatives: A Conceptual Analysis of Genocide." *Journal of Genocide Research* 3, no. 3 (2001): 349–375.

Straus, Scott. "Darfur and the Genocide Debate." *Foreign Affairs* 84, no. 1 (2005): 123–133.

Van Gorp, Baldwin. "The Constructionist Approach to Framing: Bringing Culture Back In." *Journal of Communication* 57, no. 1 (2007): 60–78.

Veilleux-Lepage, Yannick. "Retweeting the Caliphate: The Role of Soft-Sympathizers in the Islamic State's Social Media Strategy." Paper presented at 6th International Symposium on Terrorism and Transnational Crime, Antalya, Turkey, December 2014.

Wood, Graeme. "What ISIS Really Wants." *The Atlantic*, March 2015. http://www.theatlantic.com/magazine/archive/2015/03/what-isis-really-wants/384980/.

ROSEMARY PENNINGTON is Assistant Professor in Miami University's Department of Media, Journalism, and Film. She is the coeditor, with Hilary Kahn, of *On Islam: Muslims and the Media*.

Epilogue

Rosemary Pennington
Michael Krona

MANCHESTER. BAGHDAD. PARIS. Tehran. Orlando. Kabul. Cities worlds apart, but cities that all share the misfortune of having been targeted by an extremist who was inspired or supported by the Islamic State. Through its use of media and its reliance on social media users to spread its message, ISIS's influence has reached a much wider audience than it may have had in a pre-social internet environment. The media ecology it has been able to develop and sustain has facilitated the creation of not only the physical caliphate but a virtual one as well. How long either will last, however, is an open question.

As of this writing, military action in Iraq has pushed the Islamic State out of its Iraqi stronghold in Mosul, and Syrian fighters backed by the United States have captured much of ISIS's Syrian territory, including its de facto capital of Raqqa. It would seem that the organization that was framed as the most pressing threat to the modern world may be on its last legs as it continues to lose territory in its physical state. Yet, as early as 2016, there were concerns that the Islamic State would regroup in more rural areas of Iraq, where it may strengthen,[1] in order to launch a guerilla war, should it be defeated.[2] The Washington Institute's Aaron Zelin was quoted by the *New York Times* as suggesting that, in defeat, ISIS will hang back and "wait out their enemies locally in order to gain time to rebuild their networks while at the same time provide inspiration to followers outside to keep fighting their enemies farther away."[3] A series of attacks in Syria in July 2018 served as a reminder that, though the Islamic State may have been pushed out of its strongholds, it has not gone away.[4]

Since ISIS's 2017 defeats in Iraq and Syria, the group has launched more frequent attacks in places like Afghanistan and Indonesia. It has also reframed its province structure, so that Iraq and Syria have become mere provinces of the large global caliphate as it begins expanding its reach outside MENA. On Twitter, scholar Charlie Winter described why this decision was more than a mere symbolic act or "rhetorical turn," writing, "#IS is now framing itself more as a global insurgency than a localised insurgency. This shift has been incrementally happening for a lonnng time, but now it's been set in stone."[5] The caliphate is no longer defined by the boundaries of the physical state it sought to create; now, ISIS's future lies in its ability to sustain the virtual caliphate it has so carefully nurtured through the development of its vast and intricate media world. Understanding how the Islamic State creates and distributes media, as well as how it uses that media to recruit and sustain supporters, has only become more urgent.

As the authors in this volume have worked to make sense of the ways the Islamic State uses media to create a sense of nation, to instill terror, and to frame particular understandings of Islam, others are looking for ways of countering ISIS's messaging, looking for ways to stop the spread of Islamic State materials, particularly online. The trouble, of course, is that once something exists on the internet, it is difficult to lock it away again. Sometimes it is taken up and uncritically reproduced by others—such as in the case of the Washington, DC-based fast-food chain that featured ISIS's video of James Foley's execution in an ad for hamburgers. (Both the chain and the company responsible for the ad's production have apologized.[6]) The content becomes, in a way, unavoidable.

In the case of the media produced by the Islamic State, it is spread by the organization's central leadership, by its various branches, by supporters, as well as by individuals who study or report on the group. ISIS is everywhere. The image of prisoners in orange jumpsuits marching under an unforgiving sun to their deaths has become ubiquitous in news stories and academic writing about the Islamic State. Documentaries and news magazines are filled with images and videos produced by ISIS and repurposed and remixed in coverage of the group. Even if the Islamic State is eventually completely dismantled, the material it produced will continue to exist and may very well continue to be circulated by those sympathetic to ISIS's mission and message, perhaps inspiring future lone-wolf attacks like those seen in Paris, Orlando, or Kabul. It's the ability of the material to continue to exist, its spreadability[7] through networks of ISIS supporters, that can make countering it so difficult. Strike one outlet down and, like the heads of a hydra, two more pop up. This has been seen with some regularity on Twitter, as there have been moves to shut down official ISIS Twitter accounts, only to have new ones appear not long after. Countering extremist messaging and extremist material is difficult and complicated, given the media environment we live in—one in which anyone can be a producer of content, anyone an audience, and anyone a purveyor, making it hard to control.

ISIS's power also lies in the stories it tells of itself. It has sold itself as the true successor of historic caliphates, promising to usher in a new Islamic golden age that will alleviate the suffering of Muslims around the world.[8] This, some experts have suggested, has been an especially appealing message for Muslims who feel marginalized or victimized where they live.[9] News reporting has covered the plight of refugees—both Muslim and non-Muslim—fleeing Syria and Iraq to escape the Islamic State's violence but has often failed to explore the lives of those Muslims left behind, thus obscuring the experiences of many Muslims who are victimized by the Islamic State because they refuse to subscribe to the group's strict and puritanical interpretation of Islam. The Islamic State's destruction of ancient sites, its attempts to erase the Middle East's history as well as the region's minority communities, has aided it in its quest to make a physical reality of the mythical narrative it attempts to weave of itself. Even if ISIS ceases to exist, the scars it has inflicted on the people, and on the landscape, will remain.

Future-Looking, but Futureless?

On the evening of June 27, 2017, Twitter was filled with images of people shining lights high up in the air as they walked together through nighttime streets. Twitter is often filled with images of gatherings and protests; what made these particular visuals so remarkable was that they came out of Mosul, the Islamic State's one-time stronghold in Iraq. One image included the caption, "This picture! This moment. I sing for love, I sing for me; I'll shout it out like a bird set free; We are Alive, we are FREE."[10] ISIS had controlled the city since June 2014, with stories coming out of Mosul chronicling water contamination and poisoning,[11] stoning and beheading by Islamic State militants,[12] and the persecution of the city's Christian population.[13] The relief that many in the city felt at the Islamic State losing ground there was palpable.

The Islamic State's conceptualization of a "true" Islam, based on its interpretation of the actions of Muhammad and his original followers, coupled with its focus on the new world it says it will usher into being, means it is trapped between past and future without a real, rhetorical sense of the present. It offers its followers a promise of a future that they may never see, while asking them to take actions that may lead to their deaths. Both 2015 and 2016 were filled with stories of young men traveling to Syria or Iraq to fight for the Islamic State, as well as with tales of young women who joined the group to become the brides of ISIS fighters. The first several months of 2017 brought with them stories of the reverse—stories of women or men who had left the group, who had traveled back to the homes they'd left behind (often in Europe), and were struggling to make sense of the lives they had lived and the lives they were left with. As the beginnings of its physical state begin to unravel, it seems that aspects of its virtual one may be unraveling as well. The organization may survive the loss of physical territory, but it cannot survive the loss of supporters and fighters.

Even if the Islamic State is not completely destroyed following military action taken against the group, with the exodus of foreign supporters and the possible killing of leader Abu Bakr al-Baghdadi,[14] what hope for a fully realized caliphate can there be if a physical state can never be recognized? Will Youmans in this book has chronicled the ways ISIS has attempted to concretize its idea of a state through the creation and regulation of passports that have no meaning. Michael Degerald, on his History X ISIS blog,[15] has written about how the Islamic State is an "incomplete state"—one that fashions the apparatus of a state but that may be unlikely or unable to achieve full statehood. Arguments have raged over whether ISIS is, in fact, Islamic, while ISIS's caliphate has been accepted as fact. A quick news search turns up headline after headline that frames the caliphate as a thing that exists, as though ISIS's declaration of the caliphate is enough to make it real. The organization certainly exists, but the caliphate, the state—incomplete or not—was given substance in part by the news media's reification of it in their reporting. This obscured the reality of the fragile nature of ISIS's existence, as well as the fact that the organization was made up of a network of actors, and perhaps overestimated the existential threat the group was purported to pose to the rest of the world, at least as a physical entity made manifest in a tangible state.

That is not to suggest that the Islamic State is not a pressing threat—as of this writing, the Islamic State has claimed responsibility for a devastating Easter 2019 attack in Sri Lanka that left more than three hundred people dead and hundreds of others injured[16]—but simply to force us to consider what may be overlooked when we focus our attention so completely on one particular group or one particular narrative of what a group is. It also asks us to question our own role in the perpetuation of the narratives and myths extremist groups spin of themselves. How culpable are we—in our roles as academics, media producers, politicians—in the perpetuation of the media worlds such groups create?

Why Study ISIS Media

The study of material produced by extremist groups—be they Islamic in nature, right-wing, or something else—helps us understand how the groups define themselves, how they use media to recruit new members, and how these groups are understood by outsiders. A number of think tanks, researchers, and activists have pointed to the rise of extremism, in all its guises, as one of the major threats the world faces today. If that is true, then it is vital that academics study the media these groups produce. In particular, it is imperative that scholars of media examine the content and narratives created and circulated by extremist groups to begin to unpack the communicative strategies employed by groups like ISIS.

This book has included a variety of approaches to the study of the media of the Islamic State—there have been rhetorical analyses, critical analyses, and historical and quantitative analyses. Extremism is a broad concept, including actors from diverse backgrounds and political contexts; our intent with this volume was to not only present the work of these scholars but also to showcase the variety of ways academics can approach the study of media produced by extremist groups. Because extremism and its twin, radicalization, are broad, complicated concepts, we feel a broad approach to their study is necessary. Obviously, a single book cannot be exhaustive, nor does this one attempt to be. Much as with the 2018 book *ISIS Beyond the Spectacle: Communication Media, Networked Publics, and Terrorism*,[17] what *The Media World of ISIS* is attempting to showcase is how different academic approaches can produce different analyses, while also asking us to consider the ways diverse perspectives can inform our own work.

Whether the Islamic State will continue to exist in the next several years is yet to be seen; however, the savvy way ISIS has utilized the affordances of both old and new media as it has sought to expand its physical and virtual caliphate is likely to serve as a model to other groups in the future of how to mobilize media. As several authors in this volume have noted, though the Islamic State is often touted as a unique threat, there are antecedents to the group—both historic and political. What has been particularly striking about ISIS in comparison with other extremist groups—including al-Qaeda, which some point to as a kind of direct precursor—is the way it has used and manipulated media. The scholars included in this volume are only a small sampling of the individuals working to make sense of the group's media strategy and messaging.

The social web, known as Web 2.0, was touted as a transformative epoch in media history, one that allowed users to become producers and allowed media content to flow freely over the internet, unreliant on traditional gatekeepers. What is gaining increasing attention is the way this web of connection, one imagined as bringing disparate peoples together, also fuels the kinds of disconnections ISIS seeks to facilitate. As ISIS has used media to bring its supporters together—physically and digitally—it has also used media to produce and to worsen fractures and fissures that exist between groups. It is not the first organization to have done this, and it surely will not be the last. While this book has been focused on the media world of ISIS, that is only one site where issues of extremism, radicalization, and violence may be examined. The Islamic State may disappear, but its media legacy will not.

Notes

1. William McCants and Craig Whiteside, "The Islamic State's Coming Rural Revival," *Brookings Markaz*, October 25, 2016, https://www.brookings.edu/blog/markaz/2016/10/25/the-islamic-states-coming-rural-revival/.

2. Margaret Coker, Eric Schmitt, and Rukmini Callimachi, "With Loss of Its Caliphate, ISIS May Return to Guerilla Roots," *New York Times*, October 17, 2017, https://www.nytimes.com/2017/10/18/world/middleeast/islamic-state-territory-attacks.html.

3. Ibid.

4. Eliza Macintosh, "Gruesome Massacre in Syria Is a Reminder That ISIS Is Far from Dead," *CNN*, July 26, 2018, https://www.cnn.com/2018/07/26/middleeast/isis-southern-syria-200-dead-intl/index.html.

5. Charlie Winter (@charliewinter), "#IS Is Now Framing Itself . . . ," Twitter, July 23, 2018, https://twitter.com/charliewinter/status/1021328114415276032.

6. Mythili Sampathkumar, "Burger Chain Apologizes for Using Images of Photojournalist Beheaded by ISIS in Latest Advert," *Independent*, July 29, 2018, https://www.independent.co.uk/news/world/americas/z-burger-james-foley-beheaded-isis-washington-dc-peter-tabibian-a8468096.html.

7. For a discussion of the concept of spreadable media, see Henry Jenkins, Sam Ford, and Joshua Green, "Spreadable Media: Creating Value and Meaning in a Networked Culture," (New York: New York University Press, 2013).

8. Shadi Hamid, "The Roots of the Islamic State's Appeal," Brookings Institute, October 31, 2014, https://www.brookings.edu/opinions/the-roots-of-the-islamic-states-appeal/.

9. Richard Maas, "Want to Help the Islamic State Recruit? Treat All Muslims as Potential Terrorists," *Washington Post-Monkey Cage blog*, November 30, 2015, https://www.washingtonpost.com/news/monkey-cage/wp/2015/11/30/want-to-help-the-islamic-state-recruit-treat-all-muslims-as-potential-terrorists/?utm_term=.e796f71a1820.

10. This image was included in a series tweeted out by the Twitter account @MosulEye, https://twitter.com/MosulEye/status/879813656271364101.

11. "Mosul Diaries: Poisoned by Water," *BBC News*, December 19, 2014, http://www.bbc.com/news/world-middle-east-29600573.

12. Fazel Hawramy and Kareem Shaheen, "Life under ISIS in Raqqa and Mosul: 'We're Living in a Giant Prison,'" *The Guardian*, December 9, 2015, https://www.theguardian.com/world/2015/dec/09/life-under-isis-raqqa-mosul-giant-prison-syria-iraq.

13. Loveday Morris and Kareem Fahim, "Iraqi Christians, Scarred by Islamic State's Cruelty, Doubt They Will Return to Mosul," *Washington Post*, October 30, 2016, https://www.washingtonpost.com/world/middle_east/iraqi-christians-scarred-by-islamic-states-cruelty-doubt-they-will-return-to-mosul/2016/10/30/64fd3dce-9a3c-11e6-b552-b1f85e484086_story.html?utm_term=.6382cf9c34fe.

14. Colin P. Clarke, "Can the Islamic State Survive if Baghdadi Is Dead?" *Foreign Policy*, June 30, 2017, https://foreignpolicy.com/2017/06/30/can-the-islamic-state-survive-if-baghdadi-is-dead/.

15. Michael Degerald, "History X ISIS," https://historyxisis.com/.

16. Jonah Shepp, "The 'Caliphate' is Defeated, but ISIS is Just Getting Started," New York Magazine: Intelligencer, April 24, 2019, http://nymag.com/intelligencer/2019/04/the-caliphate-is-defeated-but-isis-is-just-getting-started.html.

17. Mehdi Semati, Piotr M. Spuznar, and Robert Alan Brookey, eds., *ISIS Beyond the Spectacle: Communication Media, Networked Publics, and Terrorism* (London: Routledge, 2018).

Bibliography

Clarke, Colin P. "Can the Islamic State Survive if Baghdadi Is Dead?" *Foreign Policy*, June 30, 2017. https://foreignpolicy.com/2017/06/30/can-the-islamic-state-survive-if-baghdadi-is-dead/.

Coker, Margaret, Eric Schmitt, and Rukmini Callimachi. "With Loss of Its Caliphate, ISIS May Return to Guerilla Roots." *New York Times*, October 17, 2017. https://www.nytimes.com/2017/10/18/world/middleeast/islamic-state-territory-attacks.html.

Hamid, Shadi. "The Roots of the Islamic State's Appeal." Brookings Institute, October 31, 2014. https://www.brookings.edu/opinions/the-roots-of-the-islamic-states-appeal/.
Hawramy, Fazel, and Kareem Shaheen. "Life under ISIS in Raqqa and Mosul: 'We're Living in a Giant Prison.'" *The Guardian*, December 9, 2015. https://www.theguardian.com/world/2015/dec/09/life-under-isis-raqqa-mosul-giant-prison-syria-iraq.
Jenkins, Henry, Sam Ford, and Joshua Green. *Spreadable Media: Creating Value and Meaning in a Networked Culture.* New York: New York University Press, 2013.
Maas, Richard. "Want to Help the Islamic State Recruit? Treat All Muslims as Potential Terrorists." *Washington Post, Monkey Cage blog*, November 30, 2015. https://www.washingtonpost.com/news/monkey-cage/wp/2015/11/30/want-to-help-the-islamic-state-recruit-treat-all-muslims-as-potential-terrorists/?utm_term=.e796f71a1820.
Macintosh, Eliza. "Gruesome Massacre in Syria Is a Reminder That ISIS Is Far from Dead." *CNN*, July 26, 2018. https://www.cnn.com/2018/07/26/middleeast/isis-southern-syria-200-dead-intl/index.html.
McCants, William, and Craig Whiteside. "The Islamic State's Coming Rural Revival." *Brookings Markaz*, October 25, 2016. https://www.brookings.edu/blog/markaz/2016/10/25/the-islamic-states-coming-rural-revival/.
Morris, Loveday, and Kareem Fahim. "Iraqi Christians, Scarred by Islamic State's Cruelty, Doubt They Will Return to Mosul." *Washington Post*, October 30, 2016. https://www.washingtonpost.com/world/middle_east/iraqi-christians-scarred-by-islamic-states-cruelty-doubt-they-will-return-to-mosul/2016/10/30/64fd3dce-9a3c-11e6-b552-b1f85e484086_story.html?utm_term=.6382cf9c34fe.
"Mosul Diaries: Poisoned by Water." *BBC News*, December 19, 2014. http://www.bbc.com/news/world-middle-east-29600573.
Sampathkumar, Mythili. "Burger Chain Apologizes for Using Images of Photojournalist Beheaded by ISIS in Latest Advert." *Independent*, July 29, 2018. https://www.independent.co.uk/news/world/americas/z-burger-james-foley-beheaded-isis-washington-dc-peter-tabibian-a8468096.html.
Semati, Mehdi, Piotr M. Spuznar, and Robert Alan Brookey, eds. *ISIS Beyond the Spectacle: Communication Media, Networked Publics, and Terrorism.* London: Routledge, 2018.
Shepp, Jonah. "The 'Caliphate' is Defeated, but ISIS is Just Getting Started." New York Magazine: Intelligencer, April 24, 2019. http://nymag.com/intelligencer/2019/04/the-caliphate-is-defeated-but-isis-is-just-getting-started.html.
Winter, Charlie (@charliewinter). "#IS is now framing itself . . ." Twitter, July 23, 2018. https://twitter.com/charliewinter/status/1021328114415276032.

ROSEMARY PENNINGTON is Assistant Professor in Miami University's Department of Media, Journalism, and Film. She is the coeditor, with Hilary Kahn, of *On Islam: Muslims and the Media.*

MICHAEL KRONA is Assistant Professor in Media and Communication Studies and Visual Communication at Malmö University, Sweden. He works within a nationally funded research project in Sweden, exploring Salafi-jihadist information operations, with particular focus on ISIS communication practices.

Index

Lightning Source UK Ltd.
Milton Keynes UK
UKHW010935091019
351201UK00012B/134/P